The Major Charities

An independent guide

Luke FitzHerbert
Kathryn Becher

DIRECTORY OF SOCIAL CHANGE

Published by
The Directory of Social Change
24 Stephenson Way
London NW1 2DP
Tel: 020 7209 5151, fax: 020 7391 4804
e-mail: info@dsc.org.uk
from whom further copies and a full publications list are available.

The Directory of Social Change is a Registered Charity no. 800517

First published 2002 by the Directory of Social Change

ISBN 1 903991 11 0

British Library Cataloguing in Publication Data
A catalogue record for this book is available from the British
Library

Cover design by Lenn Darroux
Cover photograph courtesy of the London Marathon
Text designed by Gabriele Kern
Typeset by Tradespools Ltd, Frome
Printed and bound by Antony Rowe Ltd, Chippenham, Wiltshire

Other Directory of Social Change departments in London:
Courses and conferences tel: 020 7209 4949
Charityfair/Charity Centre tel: 020 7209 1015
Research tel: 020 7209 4880
Publicity tel: 0207391 4900

Directory of Social Change Northern Office:
Federation House, Hope Street, Liverpool L1 9BW
Courses and conferences tel: 0151 708 0117
Research tel: 0151 708 0136

Contents

Foreword and acknowledgements

Many people have helped in writing this book.

- The editorial committee:
    Lucy Swanson, Chair, Directory of Social Change
    Peter Stewart, National Consumer Council
    Debra Allcock Tyler, Chief Executive, Directory of Social Change.

- The publisher:
    Alison Baxter, Director of Publishing, Directory of Social Change.

- Other DSC colleagues and former colleagues, especially Diana Russell and Mike Eastwood.

- The following who helped us to write the 'group' entries in their particular fields:
    Valerie Barrow (Association of Charity Officers)
    Andrew Buckingham (Victim Support)
    Felicity Chadwick (Citizens Advice Bureaux)
    Allison Davey (Federation of Independent Advice Centres)
    Nicola Eastwood (Youth clubs and organisations)
    The Hospice Information Service
    Gaynor Humphreys (Community Foundation Network)
    Martin Jones (Community Transport schemes)
    Keith Kemp (Community Matters)
    Lekha Klouda (Charity Shops Association)
    Maggie Taylor (Kelly Associates)
    Richard Thompson (Age Concern England).

- The following who helped with contributions or comments on particular issues:
    Paul Breckell, Church Mission Society
    Justin Davis-Smith, Institute for Volunteering Research
    Pat Finlow, Institute of Charity Fundraising Managers
    Fiona Gordon, Lancaster Council for Voluntary Service
    Victoria Helstrip, United Society for the Propagation of the Gospel
    Bob Holman
    Suzanne Humphreys, YMCA England
    Peter Jay
    Ray Jones, Charity Commission
    John Kay
    Emma Tracey, Oxfordshire Community Foundation
    Allan Watson
    Chris Zealley, Consumers Association.

- The Charities Aid Foundation (CAF), which kindly allowed us to use data from its *Dimensions* series of publications.

- The Joseph Rowntree Foundation, which funded the research for this book.

- All those from the charities described in this book to whose helpfulness and patience we are strongly indebted.

How the entries were written

Every potentially qualifying charity was asked to send its last two annual
reports and accounts, along with any other information or materials that would
help us write a full description of its work. From this, from the charity's
website, and from any public media reporting, an entry was drafted and sent
to the charity with a request for suggested corrections or improvements. They
were also invited to contribute 50 words of their own for the box headed 'The
charity adds' at the end of each entry.

Most charities eventually responded, and to many we are most grateful for
their careful and constructive comments. Where they supplied wholly new
material, not normally available in the publicly available reports, we have
attempted to make the situation clear in the text, with phrases such as 'the
charity has added that ... '.

Our thanks go to the members of staff of the charities concerned, who dealt
patiently with our queries and requests for clarification.

It is unfortunately inevitable that there will be errors in this book, of fact and
of judgement. Every entry has been seen in draft by the charity concerned
and any concerns have been individually and carefully reviewed, but the
book, and the responsibility for it, is ours rather than theirs.

Introduction

Background

Britain's charities, large and small, are remarkable both in their numbers and in their contribution to society. Collectively, they are the envy of much of the world.

Just a handful – some hundreds out of 180,000 registered charities – are big, but it is the immense publicity generated by this group, including their mailings, advertisements and press stories, that is the main source of public information about charities generally. Because they influence so heavily our perception of charities as a whole, it is important that these few giants should be seen to be open and accountable. This book describes fewer than 200 of them, but they receive most of the money donated and account for most of the fundraising and publicity expenditures of the whole sector.

The individual entries in the book set out to describe what these charities do, and in particular to explain how the money and the time that they are given by their donors and volunteers are put to work. One aim is to help readers choose charities to which they can happily give their time or their money, but we do not attempt to do this for them. Indeed the diversity of the sector is one of its strengths, and this depends on a diversity of opinion among donors themselves about what kinds of activity or organisation they want to support.

For example, we report the levels of salaries for chief executives. One reader may use this information because they wish to support a charity where a high salary, comparable to ones in the private sector, offers the promise of strong and effective management; while another reader may feel the opposite. Are fundraising expenditures reported as high, thus maximising resources for the cause concerned, or low and thereby perhaps limiting the capacity of the charity to do good? Does the reader wish to support a fully professional service, or one delivered primarily by relatively untrained volunteers? Our aim is to enable people to make their own choices, not to make choices for them.

For this to be possible, each charity needs to have full, clear and publicly accessible information. At the end of each entry there is an assessment of how far this requirement has been met. Overall, this has been the least happy aspect of what we have described. Although there were numerous examples of excellent practice, there were also far too many charities where access even to the basic annual report and accounts was difficult, or where these documents did not explain fully or clearly how the money or time donated by its supporters had been used. In these respects, we have freely praised or criticised the available information.

When the information has been obtained, we have often been disappointed in the quality of charities' reporting of their work. Few set out clearly what they have achieved in relation to what they set out to achieve; even fewer noted their setbacks as well as their successes. The tone of the material is often promotional to a degree that stretches credibility – such perfection is not normally attainable by human enterprises. Those that appeared genuinely self-critical came across as a breath of fresh air.

What we cannot do is offer useful information about the quality of a charity's work, beyond the ways that this is expressed in publicly available information. There has been no investigative journalism. Moreover, so far as we can, we have tried to ignore our personal experiences of what it is like to deal with a particular charity, as we may have come across a particularly helpful or unhelpful individual, or just got them on a good or a bad day.

These big charities are freely and frequently criticised, in the media and in general conversation, but most of them seem to be doing a fine job. Their work is typically impressive, the salary levels of chief executives are generally modest, and fundraising costs are usually what most people would consider to be acceptable. If any aspect of a charity's work seems unsatisfactory to a particular reader, it will, we believe, also be seen by them to be the exception rather than the rule.

At the end of this Introduction there is a checklist of some basic questions which readers may want to ask themselves about a particular charity.

Collectively, the charities we examined seem to be in the rudest of health. Their revenues are growing fast, whether from individual donations and legacies or from government fees and contracts. Managerially, there is a mass of forward planning, of strategic reviews and real changes of direction to meet new circumstances; few appear to be stuck in a rut. The role of volunteers is the most weakly reported aspect of their work, but, in almost every case where it is relevant, a welcome trend towards higher levels of user or beneficiary involvement is acknowledged. All this is good news, because there is also ample evidence that the needs to be met remain far greater than the charities' capacity to meet them.

What is a 'major charity'?

Even the word 'charity' is unclear in this context. To take just the organisations registered by the Charity Commission or elsewhere under charity law would leave out some that most people would regard as charities – Amnesty, for example, is not a registered charity because it campaigns on political issues – and would include others that are not usually seen as charitable, such as the British Council or the Construction Industry Training Board. It would also exclude a number of important charities, such as some of the national museums and galleries, or Oxford and Cambridge universities, that are charities in law but are 'exempt' from registration.

We have started here from the commonsense definition of any organisation that is for public benefit, is non-profit, and is not part of government or government-controlled. Where an organisation, such as WWF (the Worldwide

Fund for Nature), has both charitable and non-charitable arms with a common management, our entry treats them as one.

What the book does not include

This book only describes those major charities that are supported largely by the public, through voluntary donations of money or time. To include those that get their resources in other ways would have produced a very different list. It would be headed by the following 16 charities, all with an income of over £100 million a year, but only seven of which (in italics) have entries in the book:

The British Council (government funded)	£430 million
The Wellcome Trust (an endowed foundation)	£311 million
The Arts Council of England (government funded)	£238 million
Nuffield Nursing Homes Trust (fee-charging)	£216 million
National Trust	£192 million
Anchor Housing Association (government funded)	£168 million
Oxfam	£168 million
Church Commissioners for England (endowed)	£152 million
British Red Cross	£150 million
Barnardo's	£136 million
Imperial Cancer Research	£114 million
The British Library (government funded)	£112 million
Construction Industry Training Board (industry funded)	£112 million
Notting Hill Housing Group (housing association)	£106 million
Mencap	£101 million
RNLI	£101 million

This book is not a guide to grant-making charities, whether for groups or for individuals. Those seeking financial support from a grant-making charitable trust should consult the directories listed at the end of this book.

What's in the book?

The book consists of this introduction; an alphabetical listing of individual entries for 165 major charities and 30 'group' entries (some of them containing further listings of individual charities); a further listing of the top 500 fundraising charities, with contact details; a geographical listing of local sources of information about local charities, such as Councils for Voluntary Service; and a subject and an alphabetical index.

Individual entries

There are individual entries for every charity we could identify that receives more than £5 million a year in 'voluntary income' – that is, from donations of every kind, from legacies and from companies or other charities.

There are also entries for all charities with voluntary income of between £2 million and £5 million a year except those appealing for support mainly from particular or local sections of society. These exceptions include:

– local hospices (which are listed separately on page 152);
– religious charities, appealing largely within a given community;
– benevolent funds for restricted occupations;
– self-help associations.

In addition there are entries for all charities that could be identified where there were large and valuable inputs from unpaid volunteers into the actual work of the charity (as opposed to its fundraising, where high levels of voluntary input are usual). The starting point was any charity with 500 or more 'highly involved', regular and trained voluntary workers.

Measuring donated income

The Charity Commission guidance (in the 'SORP', or Statement of Recommended Practice for charity accounts) on how receipts should be classified is useful but not always definitive. For this book, as in the accounts of most (though not all) of the charities described, donations – what the Charity Commission calls 'voluntary contributions' – are taken to include all monetary gifts, subscriptions and legacies from individuals, gifts from companies and grants from other charities or trusts, including the National Lottery Charities Board, or NLCB (now renamed the Community Fund), but not the other lottery grant-making bodies.

This classification relates to the Charity Commission's clear definition of 'Fundraising and publicity costs' as 'those incurred in persuading others to make voluntary contributions to the charity' (SORP).

Gifts in kind are not included as income in the data recorded for each entry, nor are goods donated for sale in charity shops, though where they are substantial they may well be referred to in the text of the entry concerned.

Group entries

Some parts of the charitable sector consist of networks of a number of legally independent charities. There are entries for 30 of these, such as the Citizens' Advice Bureaux and the Age Concern network, which are interspersed alphabetically between the entries for individual charities. The group entries are as follows (the asterisks signify that entries include further listings of member charities):

Abbeyfield movement
Age Concern movement
Arts charities*
Benevolent and occupational funds
Black and minority ethnic organisations*
Churches and religious charities*
Citizens Advice Bureaux (CABx)
Civic societies and the Civic Trust
Community associations (and Community Matters)
Community Foundation Network*

Community transport schemes
Disability advice centres and the DIAL Network
Disability charities*
Fundraising organisations
Hospices and cancer care charities*
Hospitals and their charities
Independent advice centres
Medical research charities*
Refugees and asylum seekers charities
Riding for the Disabled
Schools and charitable donations
Scouting movement
Victim Support schemes
Volunteering opportunities, and volunteer bureaux
Wildlife trusts*
Women's Institutes
Women's organisations*
YMCA England
Youth clubs and organisations
Uniformed youth movements (other than Scouts)*

Listing of further fundraising charities
The top 500 fundraising charities are listed alphabetically on pages 364–381, with their voluntary income, contact telephone number and website details, courtesy of information provided by the Charities Aid Foundation.

Sources of local information and advice
See page 383. This is a geographical listing of local Councils for Voluntary Service, Rural Community Councils and similar bodies (also see below).

Subject index
See page 397.

Alphabetical index
See page 403. This lists alphabetically the names of all individual entries, as well as any alternative names and acronyms (for example, RNLI can also be looked up under its full title of Royal National Lifeboat Institution).

Finding local charities
Some people would like to give their support to a small or local charity, perhaps in an area they do not know well. A basic reference point is the local Council for Voluntary Service (CVS) or similar body; as mentioned above, these are listed on pages 385–395. In the box below Bob Holman, who has lived and worked in council estates for 25 years, makes some suggestions on how to identify suitable organisations, especially in the more disadvantaged parts of the country.

National voluntary societies often enjoy incomes of millions of pounds and substantial reserves. They can pay enormous salaries to top staff, employ professional fundraisers and run huge advertising campaigns. Some donors may prefer to give to community projects, that is to small voluntary groups, usually in deprived areas, which are run by local residents.

The trouble is that potential givers may have difficulty finding the addresses of such groups. So here are some suggestions.

- David Robinson of Community Links has a database with details of nearly 3,000 community projects. Contact: Community Links, 105 Barking Road, Canning Town, London E16 4HQ (tel: 020 7473 2270).

- The Community Development Foundation advocates for and services a number of community projects. Contact: Community Development Foundation, 60 Highbury Grove, London, N5 2AG (tel: 020 7226 5375).

- Councils for Voluntary Services (CVSs) or similar bodies exist in many local authorities. They often publish directories of voluntary agencies which will include some community projects. Their address will be in the phone book [and their telephone numbers are listed on pages 385–395. Ed.].

- Local newspapers, especially the freebies, often give coverage of the activities of community projects.

- Councillors of disadvantaged wards are usually more knowledgeable about the community scene than MPs. But be warned: some councillors are less than enthusiastic about projects which they regard as too outspoken.

- Head teachers of schools in inner cities and peripheral council estates often cooperate with local projects. For instance, a project may use a school hall for its activities, or a school may borrow a project's minibus.

- Best of all are vicars, priests and other church ministers. Unlike most professionals, they still tend to reside in areas of gross deprivation, while their church buildings may well be where projects meet.

- Don't write to Prince Charles, Cherie Blair, Bob Geldof, Cliff Richard, government ministers, members of the House of Lords or the like. The very wealthy don't usually know much about poor people and their groups. And don't bother with chief executives of local authorities, directors of social services, chief constables, directors of education etc. They are too distant from the hard end.

The content of the entries

The statistics

Name

We have led with the name or acronym that is most widely used. If the charity you seek does not appear where expected, there may be a cross reference in the alphabetical index at the end of the book.

Total income

Even this is not simple. We have included the net rather than the gross income from shops and other trading activities, and we have not included the value of gifts 'in kind' (though these may be referred to in the text, if substantial).

Donated income

This covers every kind of donation, subscription or gift; legacies; income from fundraising events; grants from charitable trusts, companies and the Community Fund. Income from government or statutory bodies is not included.

Fundraising costs

These are the costs 'incurred in inducing others ... to make voluntary contributions', to quote the Charity Commission.

Statutory income

This means income, including all fees and grants, from all governmental sources, whether in Britain or elsewhere. This figure is not always identifiable with certainty from the accounts; we are grateful to the charities which corrected our tentative initial estimates.

Top salary

This is usually given in the accounts as a band rather than a figure.

Paid staff

This is the total number, taken from the charity's accounts. Where relevant, it may include staff employed overseas.

Volunteers

Except for membership organisations, these numbers can often only be broad approximations. The intention is to include active volunteers rather than simply donors. In some entries the charity concerned has enabled us to make a useful distinction between volunteers involved in fundraising and those concerned with the charitable activities themselves.

Aims, activities

The text was written from the information publicly available from the charity; typically the annual report and accounts (often a document using another title), the website – generally an excellent source of information – and other printed materials, usually promotional. In addition, references to the charity in the media were sometimes used. Where the available information was limited, the entry was drafted anyway and the charity invited to offer further assistance. Any such added material is usually identified as 'further information from the charity ... '.

Where a charity does not operate in all four countries of the UK, details of similar organisations elsewhere may be found at the end of this section.

Volunteers

There are a number of entries for charities which have relatively modest incomes but where there are large donations in the form of the time of volunteers rather than in money.

The input of volunteers tended to be weakly reported, so quite often considerable further information had to be sought from the charity concerned. There is often a useful section on charity websites along the lines of 'How you can help'. There is also an entry on volunteering opportunities generally on page 329.

Charity shops

About 7,000 charity shops in the UK raise over £75 million every year in general funds for their charities. Located on high streets, they provide the public face of a charity, giving information to the public, promoting the charity's name and encouraging donations. And it isn't only the large national charities that run charity shops; hundreds of smaller, more locally based charities such as hospices also run successful shops and they are often among the sector's most profitable.

An increasing number of shops are managed by paid staff, but almost all rely on volunteers to help in a variety of tasks — and many remain wholly voluntary. Over 100,000 volunteers are involved and more are always needed. 'Anyone who has a little time to spare and would like to use it to benefit a charity can be a volunteer in a charity shop — sorting goods, serving customers, pricing stock, working on the till or arranging window displays as well as making new friends, being a valued member of a team and having a laugh! Any special expertise or skill you have, such as an interest in antiques or accountancy, is also likely to be of great use.'

Features of charity shops include the following:

- Most shops are almost wholly stocked by second-hand items donated by the public, carrying only a very limited range of new items such as Christmas cards or gifts.
- A few charity shops sell only new goods related to the work of the charity, such as 'fair trade' products, or items produced by their beneficiaries.
- Almost four out of five people have donated to, and three out of five have bought something from, a charity shop.
- Charity shops promote reuse and recycling, in particular of textiles. (Around 100,000 tonnes of clothing and other textiles pass through charity shops each year; almost all of what cannot be sold enters the recycling chain or is sold for reuse as clothing overseas.)

After a boom period in the early 1990s charity shops are now facing increased competition from the discount clothing sector and other charity shops as well as difficult general retail conditions. However, they have successfully diversified their stock to include books, bric-a-brac, furniture and electrical goods, as well as developing specialist shops selling retro fashion, soft furnishings and even charity mini-department stores to help build their sales.

Local shops can be contacted through the Yellow Pages (Charity shops heading). General information can be had from the Association of Charity Shops (tel: 020 7422 8620; website: www.charityshops.org.uk).

Funding, administration

The contents naturally vary, but in general the text seeks to identify the main sources of money for the charity.

This book uses the same definition of 'free reserves' as the Community Fund (formerly the National Lottery Charities Board) – that is, net unrestricted assets less the value of tangible assets used in the work of the charity. No comment is made if the value of such reserves is neither particularly high nor alarmingly low. However, where they seem to represent more than a year's expenditure this may be noted, unless the charity concerned has unusually long-term obligations, such as the provision of long-term residential accommodation.

Most entries relate the ratio of fundraising costs to the corresponding voluntary income, expressed as so many pence for each pound raised, or as a percentage. The following wording is used as standard:

- less than 10p in the £, or 10%: very low
- from 10% to 15%: low
- from 16% to 30%; no specific comment
- from 31% to 40%: high
- more than 40%: very high

Overall, we identified slightly more charities at the low end than at the high end of the scale.

The ratios we print are often different from those given by the charities themselves. This is because we compare fundraising costs only with fundraised income and we leave out other income which is not the result of fundraising – for example, fees paid by buyers of the charity's services, or the dividends and interest on investments.

The ratio is, and must be, greatly affected by the context in which the charity concerned is operating; the figures for any one year may be wholly untypical. A charity investing for growth will have a different figure to one maintaining an established position. Ideally such issues would be described in the annual report, and then repeated in the entry here. Unfortunately this was seldom the case, and very often there was little reference by the charity to the circumstances of the expenditure.

In an attempt to provide a wider view, the one-year figure was compared with the average of the previous three years (calculated from figures kindly supplied by the Charities Aid Foundation) and any major departures have been noted.

A checklist on fundraising costs

Because the ratios can be misleading if read in isolation, we have sought to place them in the context of the charity's explanation of why or how they have been incurred. Unfortunately, many charities have nothing to say on the subject and readers will have to use their own judgement, given the issues that are particularly important to them and the kind of work that they want to support. These are some of the major factors to be considered.

● Is the fundraising costs ratio high or low?

It is not generally possible for a major charity to raise a lot of money from the public year after year without investing a substantial amount in doing so. The average for all the charities in this book is 19p in the pound, but for some this would be an impossibly low figure; for others, it could be more than they need to spend.

● Is there a high proportion of legacy income?

Charities that have succeeded in developing a regular flow of legacy income often find that this can be maintained at a relatively low cost. Other charities will have to spend more. The average for major charities that have little legacy income has been identified elsewhere as 27p in the pound.

● Are there similar charities with different cost levels?

It makes no sense to compare an overseas aid charity with a museum, but it may be reasonable to compare, say, one cancer research charity with another.

● Is the charity investing now for future growth?

A high ratio may simply mean spending now to achieve greater revenues in the future. If it does, the situation should have been explained in the annual report, but some charities are remiss in doing so. A comparison with spending levels of previous years may be an indication of what is happening.

● Does much of the money come from 'events'?

Fundraising events are often a high cost way of raising money, because the donor, besides supporting the charity, is also paying for an expensive entertainment or even holiday. Again, the position should be explained by the charity, but it may not be.

● Does it matter anyway?

If some of your money is being spent to bring in even more, do you necessarily have a problem?

The charity adds ...

Under this heading we reproduce the wording supplied by the charity itself when it was asked for any additional comment.

The information assessed

This is where we discuss the quality of the publicly available information. We are not concerned with standards of presentation, or quality of photographs or printing, but with how far the annual report and accounts, or other material available, meet the criteria suggested by the Charity Commission for complying with the duty of public accountability.

The information was systematically asesssed for each charity against this guidance (which is set out in the box on page 18).

Contact

Here we give the main address of the charity, the main telephone number, the website, and the names of the chair of trustees and the chief executive.

Some key issues

Annual reports and accounts

The main source of information for this book has been the annual report and accounts of the charities concerned. Though there have been many excellent examples to the contrary, finding (let alone reading) these documents has often been an unsatisfactory experience.

A total of 165 charities have individual entries in this book, and we asked to see the full 'Annual Reports and Accounts' of each one. No less than 51 of them either did not have a document of that name, or had one which bore the name but which turned out to be something else. The 'real' annual report and accounts, of the kind rightly required by the Charity Commission, always existed, even if in an abbreviated form, but it could have any of half a dozen other names – and could also be hard to obtain.

Given this confusion, these editors have for the moment simply assessed the total of what is available, regardless of what it is called. But we believe that every large charity should be required by the Commission to publish its annual report and accounts, under that title and meeting the excellent SORP standards (see box below), and not to offer in its place anything else that could be mistaken for being this document.

The specific problems fell into two main groups:

- Charities that had two 'Annual Reports', where the one which actually used that name was *not* the document with the required content, checked by the auditor. Instead this information was set out in a different document (which might have had one of a number of different titles). We found 25 of these.

- Charities which did not have any document called the 'Annual Report', or anything similar such as the 'Trustees' Report'. There were 26 of these. The most popular title for the document containing the required report was 'Financial Statements', but it was sometimes called 'The Accounts' or 'Chairman's Statement'.

It would be an important and welcome reform if the Charity Commission would say:

'*Every charity should have an Annual Report and Accounts, using that name, and meeting Charity Commission requirements. No other document should use that name.*'

and if it would publish on its own the information that we have extracted from different parts of the SORP and printed in the box below.

There were, happily, many excellent annual reports which did indeed meet all or almost all of these criteria. They included those from:

Age Concern England
Arthritis Care
Bible Society
Church Mission Society
Crisis
Guide Dogs for the Blind
Leonard Cheshire Foundation
Mencap
National Asthma Campaign
NSPCC
Oxfam
Royal Hospital for Neuro-disability
Salvation Army
Samaritans

The content of annual reports

The Charity Commission gives excellent if very brief guidance on the content of annual reports, but unfortunately it is presented in such an inaccessible and confused way that few trustees will have seen it.

It is to be found only in a 100-page technical accounting document, the Statement of Recommended Practice for Accounting and Reporting by Charities (the SORP) which, by the Commission's own admission 'is written in the language of accounting principles and standards and may not readily be understood by people who have little or no knowledge of accounting'.

Once extracted from their various locations, the relevant parts of the SORP say the following

Para. 3 'The purpose of ... a charity's Annual Report and Accounts is to **discharge the duty of public accountability and stewardship**. This SORP sets out recommended practice but trustees **should consider providing additional information** to give a greater insight into the charity's activities and achievements.'

Para. 4 [The Annual Report and Accounts] 'should ... enable the reader to understand the charity's **objectives, structure, activities and achievements**'.

Para. 31 'The Annual Report should explain what the charity is trying to achieve and how it is going about it. It should cover [among other things]

● An **explanation of the objects** of the charity. [It] may also include the mission statement.

● A description of **the organisational structure** of the charity and of how decisions are made.

- A **review of the activities** of the charity, in the context of its **strategy**, including significant
  **changes,
  developments
  achievements
  plans for the future.'**

Para. 100 'Material **intangible resources** not included [in the accounts] **(e.g. volunteers)** should be commented on.'

Charity accounts

Cynics sometimes suggest that a clever accountant can do wonders with a charity's figures. In this editor's experience, most charity accounts seem to be pretty reliable, having become a great deal better over the last 15 years, though there is still room for improvement.

The standards are laid down by the Charity Commission in its SORP. A particular concern is around the important figure for fundraising costs. These are unhappily called 'Fundraising and publicity costs' by the SORP, although the definition makes it clear that in fact publicity expenditure on the cause or concerns of the charity should not be included here. The heading should only cover 'costs incurred (by the charity) in inducing others to make voluntary contributions to it'. Publicity for other purposes, for example to make people aware of the danger of HIV/AIDS or to educate them about the conservation of the countryside, should not be included under this 'Publicity' heading but should be recorded as part of the costs of the charitable activities of the organisation.

Despite years of discussion on this issue, it is likely that some charities described in this book are still overstating their fundraising costs by including some general publicity costs. Where it seems obvious that this has happened, the question has been raised with the charity and its figures corrected. The Samaritans are an example of a charity in this book whose fundraising costs actually turned out to be much less than the organisation had stated. But there may well be other cases where such overstating of costs has not been picked up.

The opposite may also be happening. Publicity may be intended to achieve more than one purpose – fundraising as well as awareness raising, for example. It is then the duty of the charity to 'apportion' the costs appropriately, dividing them between the two headings. There is an obvious temptation to load the 'Charitable expenditure' heavily and the 'Fundraising' heading lightly. Auditors must see that such apportioning has been done reasonably, but the charity has the prime responsibility for this.

In the USA the way in which this distinction is to be made is prescribed by the regulations, but there is no equivalent guidance in the UK, even in the less draconian form of recommended practice rather than inflexible regulation.

What does the charity do?

It has been difficult to answer this question for charities that use phrases like 'we work with' or 'we run projects for' as the sole explanation of how millions of pounds are being spent. We have sought to identify more specific information than this, but have sometimes found reluctance to spell out how the money concerned is actually spent. The reader will see some examples of where we failed; it was not for want of trying.

The disclosure of grants

Charities often operate partly or entirely by making grants to other charities or organisations. This is particularly the case for charities raising money to be spent overseas, and it is a wholly proper method of working – indeed in some areas and kinds of work, it may be the only realistic option.

The local recipients of the grants may themselves be large organisations in local terms, perhaps the Red Cross or the Red Crescent organisation of the country concerned, or they may be modest and wholly voluntary groups, or they may be a project of a local church. If an adequate local organisation does not exist to accept the grant, the UK charity's experts may well set about encouraging people to set one up, as a necessary precondition for getting the work done (an activity probably called community development).

This all seems wholly sensible. Local people, especially working on a self-help basis, are usually the best placed to carry out such activities. The idea of an organisation based in the UK doing such things overseas with its own staff or volunteers was taken for granted in the days of missionaries, but its limitations have become evident and such practices are now restricted to a relatively small number of charities.

Nevertheless, some of these charities try hard to give the appearance of themselves being active on the ground – 'we work hand in hand with people in the poorest communities', or 'we treat thousands of sick people every year' when in fact they don't: they fund other organisations to do so.

All grants of this kind must, by law, be individually disclosed either in the accounts or in a separate document referred to in the accounts. In a number of cases there was no such disclosure; in others the documents referred to, sometimes in the smallest of print, were unobtainable without considerable persistence. Often the information was 'held' by finance departments and little known even within the organisations themselves.

The Charity Commission is remiss in permitting this situation to exist, but the charities themselves may be missing a trick too. Where full detail of the organisations supported is available, with descriptions of the work they are doing, it has usually been powerful and moving – not least in the way that it shows so much good being done for so little UK money.

Child sponsorship

Some of the most financially successful overseas aid charities described in this book raise much of their money through child sponsorship schemes. Attractive to many people, this approach to fundraising is fraught with difficulty. There is tension between the fact that many donors like to identify with the idea of helping a particular child, and the belief of almost all the charities concerned that cash payments to or for such children are an unsatisfactory way of helping them – the overall well-being of the communities in which they live is generally more important. So, often though not always, none of the money actually goes to the sponsored child or to his or her family. However the images, and sometimes the words, of the charity's promotional material can convey a different message.

There are other limitations to the sponsorship approach. It can be impracticable for helping the children in greatest need when these live in unsettled areas – sponsorship requires a settled community where contact with a named child can be sustained over time. Secondly, the costs of the process are high, although many of them may be invisible. The need to get sponsors' letters translated, and the replies written and then translated back into English, entails a daunting effort in much of the developing world (though the costs will normally be subsumed in the charity's accounts as part of its 'direct charitable expenditure').

We have tried to report fairly the way that different charities tackle this issue, and to remain aware that the personal link between the child and the sponsor can be beneficial in its own right, and in both directions, without involving any direct cash transfers – and that there are indeed situations where sponsorship payments to or for individuals may be wholly appropriate.

Children's charities and their 'projects'

A feature of some of the largest children's charities is the difficulty in establishing what they actually do, as opposed to who they do it for. Often their reports do not go much beyond something like 'We run projects' for one class of children in need or another. However, the word 'project' has no clear meaning even within the voluntary sector, let alone beyond.

Often these 'projects' are simply ongoing local services, such as a centre for parents or a playscheme or even a school. In other cases they are closer to what the word suggests: short-term interventions on some kind of pilot or developmental basis. Sometimes they are locally developed and managed activities. In other instances they are a standardised and centrally managed 'product' of the charity concerned.

Some of these charities have become what might be described as sub-contractors for social work with children, offering their services to local authority or NHS purchasing departments. The ensuing contracts or 'service agreements' are often taken on at prices that require them to be part financed by additional support from charitable funds raised from the public.

The word 'partnership' is normally used in such cases, but again the substance of its meaning may vary from an activity where the charity is the moving spirit to one where the service has been defined and offered to the best bidder by a public authority.

This whole area was one where the editors had difficulty in establishing for themselves the activities of some of the charities concernd, let alone in describing it for others.

The payment of trustees

As the Charity Commission says, 'the principle of unpaid trusteeship has been one of the defining characteristics of the charitable sector, contributing to the public confidence in charities'.

The Directory of Social Change agrees with the view of the Commission, that before considering whether to make payments to trustees or those connected with them, a charity should 'have first carefully explored whether there are any other realistic alternatives'.

In many cases it remains both legal and proper for such payments to be made, and there can be real advantages for the charity. For example, a trustee may offer the professional services of her or himself, or her or his colleagues, at preferential rates or with a more prompt service than would be easily obtained from another supplier.

Such payments do not imply any impropriety or wrongdoing, but the Directory of Social Change regrets their existence as a matter of general principle except when an imperative need is explained as such in the annual report.

Administrative costs

Levels of administrative costs are seldom a useful way of comparing one charity with another, unless among closely similar charities with common and clear definitions of what constitutes 'administration' in their field – such as housing associations, perhaps. There are three main reasons for this.

First, such costs are undefinable. In an overseas aid charity, for example, where should the line be drawn between, say, the chief executive's travel costs and those of the locally employed manager organising the training of community healthworkers? Both constitute 'administration'. In a hospice, is the work of the secretary in organising payment of the heating bill to be called administration when the time spent by the chief nurse in organising the nursing rota is not?

Secondly, what about the charities – the Samaritans are a good example – where all the charitable activity is carried out by trained volunteers, unpaid, while the financial costs are just those of the administration that makes the service happen? In such cases the ideal may be for administrative costs to be 100% of all charitable expenditure.

Finally, even where there are groups of closely similar charities, the level of public accounting required to allow meaningful comparisons to be made would be most demanding. There would have to be separate detailed and prescriptive rules for a large number of different kinds of organisations – and even then, many charities would have the characteristics of more than one such group.

However, the public interest in 'administrative costs' is soundly based. Many charities are careful, even mean, when it comes to using the money that they have been given by the public for their organisation's internal needs, while a few others may err too far in the opposite direction. People would like to know which are which. In this book, all we are able to offer as one poor token towards this is the salary of the chief executive. If this is high or low, it makes it more likely (though not certain) that salary levels may be similar throughout the organisation.

This is not to say that high salaries are bad and low salaries good. Donors may well wish to support those charities that insist on their staff being paid an attractive wage, on the grounds that this is necessary if the best service is to be delivered to the charity's beneficiaries. Others may wish to support those who accept lower salaries in return for the rewards that come from working with the charity concerned.

Fundraising costs

Many people dislike it when charities have high fundraising costs. However, it can be argued that the more spent on fundraising, the more money there will be for the cause concerned. The Institute of Charity Fundraising Managers (ICFM) suggests that: 'faced with the question "How much of the money donated to a good cause should be used to raise more funds? If it was your money would you be happy with a figure of 98%?" we should feel able to say "Yes".'

It is also possible, at the other extreme, that a charity with very low fundraising costs may be letting its beneficiaries down; if it spent more on this, more help for the beneficiaries would become available.

Despite the ICFM's view, there is an obvious possibility of high-spending charities competing expensively among themselves for money which would be given to charity anyway. It is even possible at the extreme that, with their high and overlapping costs, such organisations could actually reduce the total that would otherwise be spent on direct charitable work.

There is also an important issue of public confidence. A charity with continuing high and unexplained fundraising costs may well be able to persuade its donors to continue their support, either because of the excellence of its appeal, or because its donors remain ignorant of the charity's cost structure or because they don't mind. However, when such costs are publicised, especially in the mass media and without context, the situation may come across as a public affront – and thereby damage public confidence in charities as a whole.

For these reasons, and no doubt for others as well, there are calls for tighter regulation of how much is spent on fundraising. These editors (and the Directory of Social Change, the publisher of this book) would prefer levels of fundraising costs to remain a matter between a charity and its donors. Situations, and people, vary enormously and all need to be catered for.

There is, though, one essential qualification. The facts about these costs need to be clearly and fully set out in the annual reports and accounts and in the fundraising appeals of all charities – in an accessible and honest form. Whenever trustees decide on an unusually high level of fundraising expenditure, they should explain the reasons for their decision.

If generally done, we believe that this alone would be enough to control all but the most occasional excesses. But at present it is often not done. This book tries to take one small step towards such transparency. However, the main responsibility lies with the Charity Commission, which, in our view, has so far failed the sector in this respect. If it does not take up the challenge, we may end up in a position like that recently recommended for Scotland, or already existing in a number of other countries (such as Belgium), where a government office has to tell charities what they can and cannot do to raise the very money on which their independence from government rests.

Fundraising cost/income ratios

An excellent study, carried out by a student at the South Bank University Business School who is also himself a charity professional, reviews the existing research on fundraising costs and incomes and, in that context, examines statistically the audited accounts of no less than 873 charities with over £100,000 a year in fundraised income. These charities represent more than half of all the fundraising income of the sector. The findings, in almost every respect amplify and confirm, rather than contradict, earlier and usually smaller-scale research.

The aim of the study was to identify characteristics of charities, beyond their competence at fundraising, that influence their fundraising costs. This has been only partly achieved. A high proportion of the great variation found in these costs appears to be unrelated to the two main characteristics examined: the size of the charity and the field in which it works.

However, it does appear that overall:

● larger charities have higher fundraising cost ratios than smaller ones;

● but a small group of the very largest charities, with a high proportion of legacy income, run counter to this trend;

● the cost ratios of cultural or recreational institutions tend to be high;

● the lowest cost ratios are often found among religious charities or activities.

Key findings (when legacies are excluded) include the following:

● the average fundraising cost ratio is 27% (that is, 27p of fundraising costs for each pound donated), or, including legacies, the average is 23%;

● the median (most common) cost is 17%, showing that the average is skewed by a group of large charities with high costs;

- 22% of the charities have a ratio of more than 40%;
- 8% have a ratio of more than 60%;
- 2% spend more than they receive – in other words, their costs are over 100%.

From a paper by Paul Breckell
Finance Director, Church Mission Society
(Pub. South Bank University Business School, June 2001)

Checklist for potential donors and volunteers
What kind of work do I want to support?
The subject index on page 397 should help.

What kind of organisation do I want to support?
☐ A large or a small charity? The very largest charities have their own entries in this book. A further 300 fundraising charities are included in the list on pages 364–381.

☐ A national or local charity? Sources of information about local charities are listed on pages 385–395. See also the note on this issue by Bob Holman on page 12.

☐ A member of a national network? Some of the 'group' entries in this book, such as those for hospices or for medical research charities, include extensive listings of smaller or local charities in their field.

☐ A charity offering immediate relief to people (or animals) in need or distress, or one addressing the underlying causes of this situation? See the section on 'Aims, activities' in the individual entries.

☐ A charity that makes much use of volunteers to carry out its work? See if a charity has given the number of its 'operational' volunteers at the top of its entry. The main text should also help you to answer this question.

☐ A charity that makes much use of volunteers to carry out its fundraising? Again, the number of such volunteers may be listed at the head of the entry and there should be some information in the main text under 'Volunteers'.

☐ A charity that works directly with its beneficiaries, or one that supports and enables smaller groups to do this? This should be made clear under 'Aims, activities'.

☐ A charity with low fundraising and administration costs? See the discussion of these issues on page 16 above.

The Abbeyfield movement

Abbeyfield is the largest voluntary sector provider of very sheltered housing, with a network of more than 500 local Abbeyfield charities which provide housing and care for over 8,000 older people in about 850 separate homes. Of these, 70 are 'residential care homes' offering an even higher level of support.

Residents are usually over 75 years old and, while reasonably fit, no longer wish to live alone. In Abbeyfield, they live together in houses which usually accommodate between 8 and 12 older people. The houses are rooted in the local community, from which residents are normally drawn. It is Abbeyfield policy to give preference to local people or to those with local connections, and residents are very much part of their local community. Many will attend local clubs or churches and join in other activities locally – volunteers often provide transport.

Each local charity is responsible for its own income and expenditure. Income is mostly in the form of fees from residents or statutory residential care grants, but also often, though to a much smaller extent, from local fundraising. The charities are heavily dependent on the input of volunteers, both in the management of the homes and in local fundraising. These volunteers are estimated to number about 12,000.

The Abbeyfield Society is the umbrella and supporting organisation for the movement in England, Wales and Northern Ireland. It raises the capital sums for new developments.

Information about local Abbeyfield charities can be obtained from the Abbeyfield Society (tel: 01727 857536; website: www.abbeyfield.com).

Action for Blind People

Income	£14,326,000 (2000/01)
Donated income	£7,057,000
Fundraising costs	£5,176,000
Statutory income	£2,346,000
Top salary	£50,000–£60,000
Paid staff	
Full time	290
Part time	120
Volunteers	50

Aims, activities

Founded as the Surrey Association for the Blind and later becoming the London Association for the Blind (but not the *Royal London Society for the Blind*), the charity is over 150 years old. Its roots lie in the provision of work for blind people, moving from the making of baskets, through producing mattresses, knitting needles and military uniforms, to the present-day plastic engineering and making stationery. In 1991 the present name was adopted and the wider mission is now 'to inspire change and create opportunities to enable blind and partially sighted people to have equal voice and equal choice'.

The charity's reports describe the following four strands of activity, with their 2000/01 expenditures (and those for 1999/00 in brackets):

● Work £4.7 million (£3.8 million). The organisation provides employment and training opportunities through four Employment Development Centres and three factories. Some of the work is carried out in partnership with other organisations, including a London Community Access to Training Partnership Project – with London Development Agency funding of £472,000 from the Single Regeneration Budget.

● Housing £1.9 million (£1.6 million). A combination of independent and residential care homes are provided in six locations in the south-east of England. Bradbury Oak House in Dulwich has been completely redeveloped with input from its residents. Another unit, Swail House in Epsom, is said to have the world's first purpose-built flats for blind people.

● Leisure £1.8 million (£1 million). The charity runs three hotels which have been specially adapted for blind and partially sighted guests. These are in Devon, the Lake District and Weston-super-Mare. A fourth, in Bognor Regis, closed in 2001 to make way for a new, larger hotel with enhanced facilities and more rooms.

● Support £1.9 million (£1.6 million). The charity provides a free and impartial information and advice service. This includes a grants service which gave out £346,000 in 2000/01, a welfare rights advice service dealing with around 200 enquiries a month, and a mobile information service in the form of two vehicles that take information to local communities. The mobile service has attracted over 30,000 visitors.

The work of the charity is still concentrated in south London and the south of England, though there is another focus around Liverpool, Preston and Carlisle in the north-west.

A strategic review was carried out in 1999/00, and at the same time 'intensive planning and negotiations were underway which would have a profound effect on the charity's work and leisure activities'. There is no indication in the reports of what the conclusions or recommendations of the review may have been, perhaps because of the sensitivity of the negotiations referred to. They will probably involve an even greater degree of collaboration with other charities.

Volunteers

Volunteers work both in fundraising and in the operational services of the charity.

Funding, administration

The annual report and accounts for 2000/01 show a dramatic leap in fundraising expenditure, up to £5.5 million from £2 million in the previous year. This bold and brave decision is described in the annual report in an exemplary way, and the relevant figures are set out in some detail in the accounts.

'During the year the organisation adopted the strategic aim of refining its activities – concentrating on a defined range of services at which it could excel – and extending the reach of those activities.' A five-year programme to do this was adopted, and 'the trustees recognised that a considerable increase in income would be required ... and approved a two year programme of investment in new fundraising techniques. Two years of budgeted deficits were planned to support this investment'. In 2000/01 'the investment and initial results have been broadly as planned'.

The report continues: 'The face-to-face fundraising technique adopted has a high initial cost but is designed to generate long-term committed giving at a low continuing maintenance cost. The deficits of the first two years should be transformed into significant new income streams by 2002/3.'

Donations did rise in 2000/01 itself, though not as fast as the new expenditure. The immediate short-term consequence of this was that the ratio of fundraising costs to donated income rose to a very high 73p in the pound, or 73%, compared with the 29% of the previous year. The more significant figure will be how the ratio settles down in the next few years. The task is challenging, as the effectiveness of face-to-face fundraising is less well established for disability or welfare charities than it is for environmental or primarily campaigning organisations.

The charity adds ...
For more information about Action for Blind People's services or to find out how you can support us please call 020 7635 4800 or visit our website – www.afbp.org

The information assessed
There is a good annual report and annual review, though parts of each assume previous knowledge of the charity. The website may be the best source of information about the charity's activities.

Contact
14–16 Verney Road
London
SE16 3DZ
Tel 020 7635 4800
Website www.afbp.org
Chair Edward F Hill
Stephen Remington, Chief Executive

Action Research

Income	£4,615,000 (1999/00)
Donated income	£3,791,000
Fundraising costs	£2,309,000
Statutory income	£0
Top salary	£60,000–£70,000
Paid staff	
Full time	58
Part time	15
Volunteers	600

Aims, activities
This is a fundraising charity that makes grants for medical research with the money it collects. It is unusual in having no apparent speciality: 'With the exception of cancer, cardiovascular and HIV/AIDS research, we support a broad spectrum of research with the objective of:

● preventing disease and disability (regardless of cause or age group), and

● alleviating physical handicap.

'Our work does not focus on a single disease or condition, or even on a particular age group. We believe that we can make the most effective contribution to advances in medicine by retaining the flexibility to support only the very best research opportunities in any field.' Despite all this, the charity's activities are, by its own account in the same booklet, in fact heavily concentrated on one particular age group: 'about half our work concentrates on the period from conception to the age of 12 months'.

'Our emphasis is on clinical research or research at the clinical/basic interface ... we also support research and development of equipment and techniques to improve diagnosis, therapy and assistive technology.'

The charity funds the following two kinds of research (with their 1999/00 expenditures):

- project grants (£3.4 million) – for up to three years in support of one precisely formulated line of research;
- research fellowships (£564,000) – for training in research techniques and methodology in a subject relevant to the overall aims of the charity.

A further £802,000 was spent on 'Grants support costs' within the charity.

Volunteers

Given the nature of the charity, volunteer activity is concentrated on fundraising. There are over 320 voluntary fundraising groups across the UK. There are two scientific advisory panels whose members probably serve on a voluntary basis.

Funding, administration

The charity is mainly reliant on donations. It is notable for its very high level of fundraising costs, £2.3 million having been spent in 1999/00 to raise £3.8 million, a ratio of 61p of costs for every pound raised. This was, however, a decrease on the previous year's figure of 72p in the pound. The average for the three years to 1998 had been 54p per pound raised, and the rise has been due to

increased spending more than to decreasing income.

The annual report said only that the charity was continuing to invest in all areas of its fundraising activity and that 'it is extremely important for us to invest in long term income streams', but the charity notes that it does not have a high level of legacy income, which often comes in at a relatively low fundraising cost.

The charity adds ...

Over the last two years the charity has been investing heavily in new income streams and profile raising activity. It is agreed that the cost of fundraising is nevertheless too high and a structural review is now in hand to drive down the cost of fundraising.

The information assessed

The weak annual report and accounts have only a brief review of the charity's work. There is a short general booklet. Details of the charity's research policies can be found on the website under the charity's guidance for potential research applicants.

Contact

Vincent House, North Parade
Horsham
West Sussex
RH12 2DP
Tel 01403 210406
Website www.actionresearch.co.uk
Chair Stephen May
Simon Moore, Chief Executive

ActionAid

Income	£62,723,000 (2000)
Donated income	£44,401,000
Fundraising costs	£9,821,000
Statutory income	£9,640,000
Top salary	£70,000–£80,000
Paid staff	2,027
Volunteers	7,500

Aims, activities

This is one of the major 'child sponsorship' development agencies, with its sponsorships producing about half its total income, but the charity is reducing its dependence on this model. ActionAid works primarily in Africa (where it spent £28 million in 2000) and in Asia (£12 million), especially India. The traditional work is mainly long-term development, but when emergencies or disasters occur in these areas, as with Orissa in 1999 or Gujarat in 2000, the charity also becomes involved in emergency rehabilitation.

Overall, the charity is seeking:

● 'a voice for all' – its rights-based work;

● to strengthen the global movement against poverty;

● to influence the powerful;

● equal access to fundamental rights for everyone, especially women.

To achieve this, ActionAid is repositioning itself as more of a campaigning and advocacy organisation at national and international levels. In May 2001 a press release said: 'ActionAid today launches its new identity and logo to clarify its role as an organisation that campaigns and lobbies for the rights of people living in poverty as well as one that helps to meet immediate

needs.' This followed a decision in 1999 that the charity had to 'tackle the causes of poverty as well as its consequences ... 'The approach will shift more towards working with partners and creating alliances, which means that ActionAid will be better able to tackle constraints imposed by national and international institutions. At the same time it will connect more closely with governments at local and national levels and will encourage donors to influence attitudes, policies and practices in order to get rid of poverty.'

The annual report notes that 'some of our field staff are struggling to shift from traditional aid delivery to rights-based work', so it looks as if this issue is a live one for the charity internally as well as for those seeking to understand how it operates. However, as most of the income is given in trust for just such 'traditional work', largely in the communities in which the sponsored children live, this can only change as fast as the nature of the funding changes.

The charity was founded in 1972 by Cecil Jackson-Cole (who also founded _Help the Aged_ and _Oxfam_), originally to sponsor the education of individual children. However, as it grew it found, like other child sponsorship organisations, that it was necessary to help communities as a whole if individual children within them were to thrive, and now all the money goes to the community and none directly to the child that is being sponsored. The charity is straightforward about this as soon as you get beyond headlines such as 'Please fill in your details below and we'll send you details of a child in need of sponsorship'.

The main headings of expenditure in 2000 were:

- development £26.5 million
- emergency £6.5 million;
- support costs £9.7 million;
- influencing, education and research £5.5 million.

'ActionAid will work in a community for eight to ten years and sponsorship will usually last between three to ten years depending on the age and circumstances of the child. If the child moves from the project area, we will explain the circumstances and ask you to consider supporting another child.' The development work is carried out partly by ActionAid staff themselves, most of whom are based and employed overseas, and partly by grant-aided partner organisations. The split between the two varies greatly from country to country. In India, Ethiopia and the smaller Latin American programmes, it is primarily grant-aided partners that do the work; in Malawi and Vietnam the work is more likely to be carried out by ActionAid local staff. The grants given to partners are numerous and usually small.

In 2001, in an unusual and creditable lifting of the veil over how child sponsorship and other development charities actually organise their work, ActionAid wrote to over 1,500 child sponsors explaining that it had had to break its link with three local agencies in India that were operating some of its sponsorship supported programmes. 'The organisations were not fulfilling their contracts. They knew the standards we expect and they were not meeting them. The majority of sponsors appreciated being kept informed and have asked to transfer their donations to another project.'

The campaigning work, though accounting directly for less than 10% of the charitable expenditure, is integral to many of the local projects – establishing the right to water, for example, as well as digging a well.

These programmes operate at international, regional and national level, but the different kinds of work are interwoven. There is a good description of this in the report on work in Asia:

'The rights and dignity of poor and marginalised people were increasingly the focus of the region's work, whether addressing the causes of poverty or its acute conditions and symptoms. This resulted in a deeper engagement with the most vulnerable groups among the poor whose rights are consistently violated or denied; caste-based and other female sex workers; adolescent girls; bonded labourers; so-called "untouchable" dalits; the landless; the urban homeless; the disabled ...

'[The] work has been shifting from promoting [these people's] participation and building their capacity for project management to developing their analysis of their situations and their awareness of their legal rights and entitlements and of government policies.'

Volunteers

This is primarily a professional development agency, but with extensive voluntary input into its UK fundraising.

Funding, administration

The charity is funded primarily by donations given for child sponsorship, from the UK and through associated ActionAid charities in Italy and Greece. These accounted for £30 million in income in 2000, up from £27 million in the previous year. Other donations and legacies totalled £8.8 million, having risen even faster from £6 million. With tax relief added, the total voluntary income was £44.4 million, achieved at a fundraising cost of £9.8 million, a ratio of 22p in the pound or 22%, down from the 24% of the previous year.

During 2000 ActionAid conducted a review and restructuring of its marketing activity, at a cost of nearly £1 million. One problem for the charity is that money given for child sponsorship cannot be used for the campaigning work on which it is now placing such heavy emphasis.

The main development reported is that many sponsors were asked to change their giving to a form that can be used more generally in the country of their choice, and 9,000 sponsors have agreed to this. By 2002 it is expected that 50,000 sponsors (almost half of the total) will have agreed to give in this way. On the other hand, the attractiveness of the sponsorship model is so great that, despite the change in emphasis, this type of income nevertheless grew by 12% in the year (with new Italian donors in the lead).

The charity is unusual in that its chair, Ken Burnett, was formerly a senior member of the charity's staff, having been director of fundraising in the 1980s. He became a trustee many years later, in 1995, and chair in 1998. The trustees' report has an unusual and useful section of short biographies of each of the trustees, one of whom is, equally unusually, a development professional from one of the countries with which the charity works – Noerine Kaleeba, founder of the Uganda AIDS Support Organisation.

ActionAid was a pioneer in telephone fundraising and developed its own business, NTT, which did this kind of work, as well as face-to-face street fundraising, for other charities as well. In November 2001 ActionAid announced that it had sold NTT to another commercial company in the field.

The charity adds ...

Thanks to our generous supporters our income rose during 2000 from £49.6 million to £62.7 million. By generating less restricted funding, our new fundraising initiatives launched in 2000 allow us to work with the poorest of the poor and will become a more significant proportion of our income in future years.

The information assessed

There are both an 'Annual Report and Accounts' and a 'Trustees' Report and Accounts'. The 'Annual Report and Accounts' sent to us did not in fact include the full accounts, which were only to be found in the other document. In other respects the reports were very full, except in their account of how the charity operates.

The website is straightforward and informative.

Contact

Hamlyn House
Macdonald Road
London
N19 5PG
Tel 020 7561 7561
Website www.actionaid.org
Chair Ken Burnett
Mr Salil Shetty, Chief Executive

The Age Concern movement

There are local, independent Age Concern charities all over the UK. They work to enable older people to resolve problems themselves, providing as much or as little support as needed. They can be identified through the four national bodies:

— *Age Concern England*

— Age Concern Scotland, 0131 220 3345

— Age Concern Cymru, 029 2037 1566

— Age Concern Northern Ireland, 028 9024 5729

Locally, the Age Concerns vary widely in size and in their activities. Larger Age Concerns may work at county, city or borough level. The services they provide are dictated by local needs and resources. They may include day centres, support for the carers of older people, luncheon clubs, Meals on Wheels, drop-in centres, home visiting schemes, help with gardening, home repairs, hospital aftercare, transport, advocacy and leisure activities such as crafts, outings and, increasingly, teaching IT skills.

Smaller Age Concerns work at town and village level and usually offer a smaller range of services. All Age Concern groups provide information and advice for older people themselves and for those concerned with their welfare.

In England all Age Concerns are Members of the *Age Concern England* federation that promotes local initiatives while ensuring consistent standards of management and services. At national level, Age Concerns England, Cymru, Northern Ireland and Scotland campaign on ageing issues and provide developmental and financial support to local Age Concern groups.

Age Concern could not operate without the support of tens of thousands of volunteers. Larger Age Concerns have some paid staff, but even they depend heavily on volunteers. Many smaller groups are wholly voluntary.

Volunteers may provide all the services described above. Others help in the charity's administration, fundraise or work in shops.

The income of the Age Concern movement in the UK is estimated to be above £100 million. At national level, funding comes mainly from personal donors, corporate partners, legacies and through the provision of a number of products designed for older people – such as insurance, financial services, energy services, funeral plans and emergency alarms. The main local sources of funding are grants or contracts for services from statutory bodies such as local authorities, the sale of Age Concern products, grants from national Age Concerns, local fundraising initiatives, charitable trusts and charity shops.

Age Concern England (ACE)

Income	£29,222,000 (2000/01)
Donated income	£9,177,000
Fundraising costs	£1,935,000
Statutory income	£1,193,000
Top salary	£90,000–£100,000
Paid staff	677
Volunteers	6,000

Aims, activities

This, the working name for the National Council on Ageing, is only one, even if the largest, of the hundreds of independent Age Concern charities in the UK. For a description of the *Age Concern movement* as a whole, see the previous entry.

The country's leading charity in this field, ACE believes that later life should be fulfilling and enjoyable. 'Nationally it takes a lead role in campaigning, parliamentary work, policy analysis, research, specialist information and advice, publishing and a wide range of training.'

Locally, ACE offers support and services to the smaller Age Concern charities who are fellow members of the new Age Concern federation in England, as well as to other voluntary organisations working for the welfare of older people.

The charity also offers, on a commercial basis and through a separate Age Concern trading company, a number of services for older people – such as insurance, prepayment funeral plans, flowers sent by post and financial services. Only the net income from these appears in the figures above.

At the national level the biggest single effort has been directed towards campaigning for a rise in the basic level of the old-age pension. However, the charity is also active in seeking more generous arrangements for the payment of care services and to improve the quality of NHS services for older people.

At a local level, a major development in 2000 was the setting up of the Age Concern federation, linking over 400 English bodies using the name and offering a guarantee of consistent quality of service to those (mainly in the statutory services) who may fund Age Concern service provision.

Besides its extensive training programmes, the charity also makes grants for local work, both to pay for services such as information and advice, day care and advocacy, and also to help local Age Concerns develop their management and capacities.

In the summer of 2001, when this entry was written, Age Concern England and *Help the Aged* were considering working more closely together, even to the extent of a merger – a challenging idea as they each have strong and differing images. A preliminary consultant's report was expected by May 2001, but nothing had appeared by the end of August.

Volunteers

Volunteers work mainly with local Age Concerns, who are often almost wholly dependent on them. Age Concern England has its own volunteers at its head office in London and runs an enterprising Lottery-funded Millennium Awards Scheme which funds individuals and groups of volunteers over 50 years of age to run projects throughout the UK for the benefit of the under-25s.

Though not specifically mentioned in the annual report, the 128 charity shops also depend on the work of approximately 6,000 volunteers at a local level.

Funding, administration

In 2000/01 £6.5 million of the charity's £29.2 million income came from sales of donated goods in its shops, but these cost £6.3 million to run so the net benefit was slight. Of the remaining £22.7 million income, £7 million was earned by the commercial trading companies, and £4 million from charges for the charity's services, such as its training and publishing programmes. The government contribution of £1.2 million was mainly to support the development of volunteering in the movement.

The £9.2 million of voluntary income came from legacies (£5.3 million) and donations (£3.9 million) and was achieved at a fundraising cost of £1.9 million. This gave a cost ratio of 21p in the pound, or 21%, compared with the 26% of the previous year, mainly due to a reduced fundraising expenditure. The average for the three years to 1999 was 23%.

The charity raised some eyebrows in 2001 by developing a fundraising scheme with spread-betting company City Index. The charity saw no problem with raising money from gambling, citing the precedent of the National Lottery.

The information assessed

The excellent annual report and accounts include admirably presented financial and managerial information. The comprehensive website is exemplary in offering the annual report and accounts in full.

Contact

Astral House
1268 London Road
London
SW16 4ER
Tel 020 8765 7200
Website www.ace.org.uk
Chair Dr June Crown
Gordon Lishman, Director General

Alzheimer's Society

Income	£20,028,000 (2000/01)
Donated income	£10,545,000
Fundraising costs	£1,512,000
Statutory income	£8,702,000
Top salary	£60,000–£70,000
Paid staff	
Full time	287
Part time	707
Volunteers	5,500

Aims, activities

Alzheimer's disease and other forms of dementia affect over 700,000 people in Britain. Through its more than 250 local branches, this charity, which is strongly volunteer-orientated, provides a network of support for people with dementia, their families and carers. The society also provides comprehensive information both on the condition and on the practical and financial difficulties to which it can often lead.

All the branches provide support and information locally, but some do much more. About 50 of them purchase 'respite' care for those looking after someone with dementia. These services are typically provided by another specialist charity, such as Crossroads, or perhaps a local equivalent. Some 60 branches run day care centres and about 30 provide care in the home. These services are normally provided under contract to the relevant statutory body and probably account for about half the society's income and expenditure.

In a particularly enterprising use of Lottery money from the Millennium Commission, there is an After Dementia Awards Scheme, which gives substantial grants to support former carers while they develop new or forgotten skills and interests as they start a new stage of their lives.

The charity also funds research into dementia, to the value of £775,000 in 2000/01. This covers a remarkable programme called Quality Research in Dementia (QRD), based around a voluntary network of people with dementia and carers; it is further described under 'Volunteers' below.

In the annual review for the year, the society's president, Dr Jonathan Miller (perhaps better known as a theatrical producer), writes: 'From a Society whose initial aim was to support carers at a time when Alzheimer's disease was generally misunderstood, it has grown into an organisation with influence out of all proportion to its size ... [It] has played a leading role in every reform, every shift in attitude and every positive development that has taken place on behalf of people with dementia and their carers.'

In the same review, the chairman notes that 'in the past year, people with dementia have made an increasing contribution to the Society's work. More and more people with dementia are now speaking out on their own behalf, demanding that their voice be heard ... people with dementia are taking part in seminars, contributing to ... research ... , raising

funds and helping to run branches.' One of the elected members of the society's council has dementia, though the report notes that, inevitably, most people able to undertake such tasks are in the early stages of the disease.

Volunteers

The charity's volunteering programmes are extensive and interesting. Beyond the usual and essential fundraising, volunteers help both in running the society and its branches and in its research.

'The Alzheimer's Society is a member-led organisation with volunteers at the heart of its structure – as trustees, branch committee members, support group organisers, fundraisers and directly providing support to people with dementia and their carers.

'As a volunteer of the Society you will be provided with regular support, training if necessary, and a volunteer's handbook which gives information about your volunteer role. If you are interested ... ring the Alzheimer's Branch Helpline on **020 7306 0101**.'

On research, 'you can help us by joining the QRD Advisory Network. This is a large group of carers, people with dementia, scientists and researchers, working together to advise and help the QRD programme. Members of the network will:

● Help decide which research projects should get funding

● Monitor ongoing projects

● Advise on research strategies

● Help get the results of research into practice in local areas.

'No previous research experience is needed. What we do need is your understanding and experience, gained either as a carer or as a person with dementia. Training will be offered to all carers and people with dementia who volunteer.' For information on joining the QRD Advisory Network, ring the number below.

Funding, administration

All branches are constitutionally part of the main charity, but in practice about 60% of both the income and the expenditure is managed at branch level.

Half the combined voluntary income of branches and of the society as a whole comes from 'subscriptions, donations and fundraising' and about half from legacies. Fundraising costs of £1,512,000 in 2000/01 represented a low 14p in the pound, or 14%, of voluntary income, a slight increase on the even lower 11% or 12% of recent years.

The charity adds ...

Comprehensive information about our local services and all aspects of dementia is available from our national helpline 0845 3000 336 and our website – www.alzheimers.org.uk. The Society has over 100 publications on all aspects of dementia care and keeps a substantial library.

The information assessed

The very good annual report and annual review are excellent in most respects, but let down by a lack of information on the 'care services', described above, that account for almost half the charity's expenditures. There is a good website, especially for information about Alzheimer's disease, and exemplary materials for potential volunteers.

Contact
Gordon House
10 Greencoat Place
London
SW1P 1PH
Tel 020 7306 0606
Website www.alzheimers.org.uk
Chair Dr Nicolas Carey
Harry Cayton, Chief Executive

Amnesty International UK

Income £14,407,000 (15 months to March 2000)	
Donated income	£14,287,000
Fundraising costs	£3,516,000
Statutory income	£0
Top salary	not disclosed
Paid staff	80
Volunteers	100,000

Aims, activities

Unfortunately, campaigning for human rights is not a charitable activity under British law and Amnesty International's UK section cannot therefore be registered as a charity. However, research into human rights – as opposed to campaigning for their introduction or maintenance – does qualify, and so the UK section has established an associated Amnesty International UK Charitable Trust. The two bodies, though independent, work closely together and are described as one in this entry. However, only donations to the charitable trust can qualify for the tax incentives that are available to registered charities.

Amnesty Worldwide, of which Amnesty UK is one member, is an international human rights campaigning organisation (also based in London) with over a million members in more than 140 countries. It was founded in Britain (in 1961 by lawyer Peter Berenson) and has more than 150,000 members and supporters in the UK (and over a million worldwide). It seeks 'the release of all prisoners of conscience as long as they have not used or encouraged violence'.

A principle of the organisation is that Amnesty supporters do not become involved in cases in their own countries. The core method of campaigning is for members to flood the authorities concerned with letters and messages of protest. This example comes from the Dominican Republic: 'When the first 200 letters came, the guards gave me back my clothes. Then the next 200 letters came and the prison director came to see me. When the next pile of letters arrived, the director got in touch with his superior. The letters kept coming and coming – 3,000 of them. The President was informed. The letters still kept arriving and the President called the prison and told them to let me go.'

As well as supporting named individuals, Amnesty runs more general campaigns. Each year all Amnesty groups join up for a single campaign on one country or issue. Many groups have activities targeted specifically at the abolition of the death penalty. The rights of people needing asylum from oppression in their own countries are a big current issue.

The organisation is independent of any government, political ideology, economic interest or religion. It is to be hoped that current government investigation into the regulation of charity in Britain will lead to this most clearly charitable organisation receiving its proper legal status.

Volunteers

Amnesty's work is wholly based on the activity of its voluntary members and supporters, both individually and organised in groups (more than 330 in the UK), who write the letters and make the protests that form the core of its work. They also elect the organisation's governing body.

Funding, administration

There are about 80 paid staff in the UK who organise campaigns and publicity. The marketing department seeks new members and raises funds for both the UK section and for Amnesty International as a whole. Income in the 15 months to March 2000 was £14.4 million, an annual rate of £11.5 million.

No funds are sought or accepted from governments.

The accounts put to shame those of many of the other charities in this book in the way the different fundraising activities are analysed. Total fundraising costs were £3.5 million over 15 months, representing 25p for every pound collected. About a third of the revenue comes to the charitable trust, where it is used solely for research and educational activities.

The information assessed

Only part of Amnesty's work is charitable, so its reports are not in the usual charity format. The information available is clear and comprehensive and there is an effective website.

Contact
99–119 Rosebery Avenue
London
EC1R 4RE
Tel 020 7814 6200
Website www.amnesty.org.uk
Chair not disclosed
Kate Allen, Director

Animal Health Trust

Income	£7,934,165 (2000)
Donated income	£4,202,922
Fundraising costs	£752,438
Statutory income	£0
Top salary	£80,000–£90,000
Paid staff	
Full time	178
Part time	16
Volunteers	
Operational	12

Aims, activities

The charity exists to improve the health of animals. It does this by working to better methods of diagnosing, treating and preventing animal disease and injury, through the provision of specialist referral services and through veterinary education.

In practice, the AHT works chiefly with horses, dogs and cats. Its equine clinic in Newmarket, closely associated with the horse-racing industry, specialises in orthopaedic, cardiac and respiratory disorders, together with fitness and performance assessments. During 2000 more than 500 new cases were seen, which the charity described as 'a substantial increase' on the previous year.

The small animal clinic, focusing on cancer, eye diseases, neurological conditions and skin disease, treated over 2,000 new cases in 2000 – said to be 'a remarkable turn-around on the situation a year ago'. A new feline unit was opened during the year.

Research is concentrated on:

- inherited disease in horses, dogs and cats;
- equine respiratory disease;
- cancer, especially lymphoma in dogs and cats;
- equine orthopaedics.

The Allen Centre for Vaccine Studies, opened in spring 2001, specialises in research into infectious diseases in horses.

Volunteers

No specific mention is made of volunteer activity in either the report or the review, but information on becoming a fundraising volunteer is available through the website.

Funding, administration

Of the charity's £7.9 million income in 2000, £4.2 million came in the form of voluntary income, including £2 million in legacies. About £3.3 million was earned as fees for professional services. Fundraising costs of £752,000 represented 18p for every pound of donated income.

Reorganisation in the year 2000 led to the setting up of a small, specialist fundraising department with three core staff, whose five-year strategy is to double net fundraising income by 2005.

The information assessed

The trustees' report and annual review are good, and there is an informative website.

Contact
Lanwades Park
Kentford
Newmarket
Suffolk
CB8 7UU
Tel 08700 50 24 24
Website www.aht.org.uk
Chair EA Chandler (Executive Chairman)
Robin Pellew, Chief Executive

Anthony Nolan Bone Marrow Trust

Income	£10,007,000 (1999/00)
Top salary	£80,000–£90,000
Paid staff	
Full time	145
Part time	13
Volunteers	309,000

Aims, activities

The charity's main activity is to maintain a register of potential donors for bone marrow transplants.

Some or all leukaemia sufferers could benefit from a bone marrow transplant, if a matching donor can be found. Although carried out under general anaesthetic, the procedure is not a dangerous one for the donor. To be on the charity's register does not actually mean that such a volunteer is at all likely to be called upon: there are 300,000 potential donors on the register, and as there were 300 transplants in 1999/00 the chances of being called upon seem to be just one in a thousand.

It was hard to discover some basic facts about the charity's work. It was not clear how significant the benefits of transplants are; how many people need one each year but can't get one; how many people would have to be on the register to meet current needs; nor, as reported below, who the work is funded by.

Bone marrow matching is presumably an inherently international activity. About one third of transplants at present are cross-border, in both directions. This charity provides about 100 donors a year for people overseas.

There is also a relatively modest research-funding activity which accounts for about 10% of the charity's expenditure.

The charity was started by the Australian mother of Anthony Nolan, a boy who died of leukaemia in 1979 without a suitable donor having been found.

The number of potential donors on the register is steadily rising, from about 275,000 in 1997 to over 300,000 three years later. July 2001 saw the announcement of a new government-funded bone marrow donor awareness campaign, to which this charity responded with markedly cautious enthusiasm.

The charity was unhappy with this entry and notes that its 'annual report and accounts provide a general review of the trust's activities including fundraising, developments within the field of stem cell transplantation, and a summary of financial information. The report assumes some knowledge of the work of the trust but staff are happy to answer any queries regarding any aspect of its work, procedures or financial operations.'

As with all charities described in this book, a full set of audited accounts can be obtained, in this case by a call to the financial controller at the number below.

Volunteers

The whole nature of the charity is to persuade people voluntarily to go on to the register and to have the necessary tests so that their marrow can be accurately catalogued. The charity's fundraising seems also to be strongly volunteer-driven.

Funding, administration

The main funding for the charity is only described in the 1999/00 accounts as 'Payments in respect of bone marrow transplants and other services': £5.7 million (up from £4.8 million the previous year). Who do the payments come from?

Voluntary income of £3.6 million, mostly from donations, was achieved at a fundraising cost of £1.2 million, giving a high cost ratio of 34p in the pound, up from 24p in the previous year. This increase was caused not by a drop in income but by a 51% rise in fundraising costs. Such a marked jump would justify explanation in the annual report.

The report is largely dedicated to descriptions of fundraising events and celebrity occasions, so these probably dominate the fundraising activity – a sponsored walk, a garden at a flower show, a driving event; a literary dinner, a beer walk, a bike ride, a ball and many others.

A draft of this entry was sent to the charity, with a request for help in addressing some of the areas where information was felt to be lacking, but with limited success.

The charity adds ...

The trust manages the largest independent volunteer stem cell register in the world, recruiting and tissue typing donors from the UK population who are prepared to provide stem cells to patients suffering from leukaemia and other bone marrow deficiencies worldwide. In the last four years alone it has provided over 1200 donors for lifesaving transplants.

The information assessed

The fat and colourful, but nevertheless weak, 'Annual Report and Accounts' does not in fact include the accounts, which are in a different document. The review of the charity's financial affairs is unusually brief.

The text of the annual report assumed, in places, substantial prior knowledge of the charity's field of work. The website is the best source of information.

Contact

Royal Free Hospital
Pond Street
London
NW3 2QG
Tel 020 7284 1234
Website www.anthonynolan.org.uk
Anthony Morland, Chief Executive

Army Benevolent Fund

Income	£6,060,000 (2000/01)
Donated income	£3,698,000
Fundraising costs	£783,000
Statutory income	£155,000
Top salary	£40,000–£50,000
Paid staff	
Full time	22
Part time	18
Volunteers	
Fundraising	5,000

Aims, activities

This is the main army fundraising charity. It works in partnership with the numerous regimental and other army welfare organisations, which it supports both by giving them grants and by supplementing the financial assistance they give to individual ex-service people and their families and dependants. Grants are also made to non-service charities helping ex-service people and their families and dependants.

The charity does not respond itself to individual applications for help, but refers such enquiries to other army or ex-service welfare organisations.

The two main charitable activities – the grant support of other charities helping ex-service people in need, and the payments through them for the benefit of individual beneficiaries – attract approximately equal expenditure, with about £2 million spent on each in 2000/01. Payments in support of individuals covered 3,400 people in 2000/01, with two thirds being either annuities or individual benevolent grants. These payments are made according to a fine set of Army Benevolence Guidelines, representing the partnership between this fund and other army charities, which must go far to make up for the difficulties caused by the fragmentation of this part of the charitable sector.

Of the 90 grants in the year, all but 12 went to charities that had also been supported in the previous year. These grants can be either to help meet regular running costs, or for one-off or capital projects – with the exception of a 'new build'. Many charities receive regular grants, but must apply annually, justifying their request.

Much the largest regular beneficiary is *SSAFA Forces Help*, which received about £300,000 in each of the last two years. This is because SSAFA does 80% of the caseworking for army benevolence and the size of the grant is calculated on the basis of the numbers assisted. In 2000 a substantial grant was also given to Combat Stress.

Volunteers

Fundraising is the basic activity of the charity and for this purpose it has 49 voluntary committees throughout the UK, mostly county-based. Among other things they organise a wide range of events, well listed on the charity's website, and often supported by military bands.

Funding, administration

The central office has a modest 17 staff. As it is based in one of the more spectacularly expensive parts of London, the accommodation costs of almost £5,000 a head are high, no doubt necessarily. The charity has noted that these costs are cheap, given the location, and that the premises are cramped rather than luxurious.

The income came from the following main sources in 2000/01:

● donations and legacies £2.1 million;

● from army sources and army fundraising £1.7 million;

● investment income £1.3 million.

Though there was a surge in income in 1997/98 because of two exceptional legacies, overall receipts from donations and legacies have been dropping:

● 2000/01: £2.1 million

● 1999/00: £2.2 million

● 1998/99: £2.4 million

● 1997/98: £3.7 million

● 1996/97: £3 million

There is a fundraising team of 13, most of them part-time regional directors. These are all former army officers, most drawn from senior ranks. The cost of fundraising is not clear, as the declared figure of £783,000 includes the cost of generating income from investments – presumably payments for investment advice and management – which does not usually appear under this heading.

There was a sharp increase in fundraising costs in the previous year. The annual report properly explained that this was in order to raise more money in future from companies and from charitable trusts, and to take advantage of the opportunities offered by the new Gift Aid procedures for tax-effective donations.

The information assessed

The annual report and accounts and annual review are good. There is also a website.

Contact

41 Queens Gate
London
SW7 5HR
Tel 020 7591 2000
Website www.armybenevolentfund.com
Chair General Sir Jeremy Mackenzie
Major-General MD Regan, Controller

Art Fund

Income	£9,786,000 (2000)
Donated income	£8,501,000
Fundraising costs	£821,000
Statutory income	£0
Top salary	£84,000
Paid staff	
Full time	30
Volunteers	
Operational	10
Fundraising	540

Aims, activities

The Art Fund supports and enriches the UK's public art collections by enabling them to buy works of art of all kinds and, more recently, by increasing awareness of their value and campaigning to safeguard their welfare. 'Art has the power to transform people's lives. The Art Fund, the UK's largest independent art charity, believes that everyone should have the opportunity to experience great art at first hand. We work to achieve this by:

- enriching museums and galleries throughout the UK with works of art of all kinds

- campaigning for the widest possible public access to art

- promoting the enjoyment of art through our membership scheme.'

Since 1903 the charity has made possible the purchase of more than 400,000 works of art.

This is a membership organisation (costing £30 a year). As with other heritage and conservation charities, membership brings practical benefits as well as philanthropic satisfaction – in this case free admission to more than 200 museums, galleries and historic houses; reduced-price entry to many national exhibitions, including many of the blockbusters in London; as well as four lavish and splendid quarterly magazines and an equally fine annual review. Surprisingly, the number of members does not appear to be recorded in the annual report, but a recruitment leaflet says that there are over 100,000.

In 2000 the charity offered museums and galleries £4.4 million towards purchases of works of art. The Art Fund is usually a contributor to the amount needed, rather than its sole source, and the total value of works purchased with its help during the year was over £13 million. In all, 198 applications for help were received, of which 164 were accepted. Perhaps the most spectacular purchase was that of a Titian portrait by the Ashmolean Museum in Oxford at a cost of £2.4 million, over £250,000 of which was contributed by this charity. However, the smaller purchases were more typical, such as a fine Richard Dadd portrait for the museum of Bethlem Hospital, where Dadd was a patient for many years. Only 28% of the support by value went to the major national collections.

However, the success of the year was in a different field: the abolition of the absurd VAT regulations that penalised national museums and galleries for maintaining free entry. The fund had spearheaded the long, difficult but ultimately successful campaign to achieve this.

Volunteers

There is a network of regional volunteers, including county representatives, who carry out much of the fundraising.

Funding, administration

The Art Fund is almost wholly financed by voluntary donations and legacies. The year 2000 was atypical because of the receipt of a single legacy of over £5 million from Mrs Brenda Knapp, a life member of the Art Fund who apparently died with a pile of the fund's magazines at her bedside. The total voluntary income of £8.5 million therefore greatly exceeded the more usual £3.6 million of the previous year. This legacy also meant that the fundraising costs of £821,000 fell to 10p in the pound, or 10%, of the income generated,

compared with the 22% average for the previous three years.

The information assessed

There is an appropriately splendid annual review and an unpretentious but first-class 'Report of the Committee'. Together they give an excellent account of the charity's work. The website is a delight.

Contact

Millais House
7 Cromwell Place
London
SW7 2JN
Tel 020 7225 4800
Website www.artfund.org
Chair Sir Nicholas Goodison
David Barrie, Director

Arthritis Care

Income	£8,790,000 (2000)
Donated income	£5,547,000
Fundraising costs	£875,000
Statutory income	£871,000
Top salary	£60,000–£70,000
Paid staff	
Full time	130
Part time	142
Volunteers	7,000

Aims, activities

The charity gives an excellent summary of its work at the front of its annual report for 2000:

'Arthritis Care's mission is to empower people with arthritis to take control of their arthritis, their lives and their organisation. We are the largest UK-wide voluntary organisation working with and for people with arthritis.

'Working with people with arthritis to promote their health, well-being and independence, Arthritis Care aims to give people the chance to make their own decisions about how they want to live their lives as well as the information and support to do it as they choose.

'Quality of life can be affected when someone is diagnosed with arthritis. All too often people are told to go away and live with their arthritis. Arthritis Care aims to change that – there is so much people can do to take control once again and live a fulfilling life.

'Arthritis Care offers a range of services and support to people with arthritis at national and local levels ... we campaign for better rights, better access and better transport. [The charity] is a recognised leader in user involvement among voluntary organisations and we pride ourselves on this achievement. People with arthritis play leading roles throughout the organisation, from trustee level to members of staff and volunteers.' Since that was written, a new chair of trustees has been appointed, who has arthritis.

'Arthritis Care's network of 580 branches and groups offers people at local level the opportunity to meet others, to organise get togethers and to learn, as well as make new friends.

'One of the most exciting developments of 2000 was the success Arthritis Care and other organisations had convincing government of the benefits of user-led initiatives such as patient-led self-management programmes.' This follows from the charity's extensive development of training courses, such as its Challenging Arthritis programmes, run for people with arthritis by people with arthritis.

The charity has made striking efforts to bring young people with arthritis, of whom there are many thousands, into the centre of its thinking and activities.

The charity has both a letter and a freephone confidential helpline (**0808 800 4050** on weekday afternoons), a 24-hour information line (**0845 600 6868**) and a special helpline for young people with arthritis, their families and carers (The Source, **0808 808 2000**). There are also other services, some of them income-generating, such as four holiday hotels, and a range of information publications including a bi-monthly magazine, *Arthritis News*.

Volunteers

'None of the support we offer people with arthritis would be possible without the thousands of volunteers who:

- help run our local branches and groups
- deliver training courses
- provide telephone support
- promote Arthritis Care and its work.'

A particular success has been the charity's Millennium Awards volunteer programme, Lottery-funded. More than 300 people with personal experience of arthritis have been trained for a variety of roles on the front line of supporting people with the condition. This scheme was one of the first large-scale implementations of the notion that no one can be as well qualified to take people through the process of living with a disabling condition as someone who has been there himself or herself.

Much activity by volunteers arises within the 580 local branches.

Information on them can be obtained from the contacts below, or on the fine new website.

Funding, administration

This is a membership organisation and half the trustees, who meet six times a year, are elected regionally.

About half of the charity's income comes from donations and legacies. The total of £5.5 million from such sources in 2000 was achieved at a fundraising cost of £875,000, representing 16p for each pound given. Legacies have been a particularly important source in the last two years (£3 million and £3.8 million, respectively), but the charity's excellent report on its finances notes that these figures are well above the seven-year average on which its budgeting for legacies is sensibly based.

The charity adds ...

We are very pleased with our new website which represents Arthritis Care in the regions and nations, and are particularly pleased with our new helpline 'The Source', for which there is a link on the website. This is the first UK-wide helpline for young people with arthritis.

The information assessed

The exemplary annual report and accounts are in a different league to most of these seen while writing this book. A fine new website was set up just as this entry was going to press. It appears especially strong in having separate sections for different parts of the country.

Contact
18 Stephenson Way
London
NW1 2HD
Tel 020 7380 6500
Website www.arthritiscare.org.uk
Chair Miss Terry Oliver
William Butler, Chief Executive

Arthritis Research Campaign

Income	£20,143,000 (1999/00)
Donated income	£18,363,000
Fundraising costs	£1,791,000
Statutory income	£0
Top salary	£60,000–£70,000
Paid staff	93
Volunteers	10,000

Aims, activities

The charity supports research into arthritis mainly through its grant support for independently reviewed research programmes conducted by other organisations. In 1999/00, £15 million was spent on this. About 15% of the research expenditure goes to the support of the charity's own Kennedy Institute of Rheumatology. A further 5% or so is spent on education about arthritis, both in the form of leaflets for patients (2 million in 1998/99) and as information for medical professionals, for whom a special website is maintained.

The charity supports both basic research, seeking long-term understanding of the basic processes involved in arthritis, and clinical research, looking for practical improvements in patient care.

Formerly the Arthritis and Rheumatism Council, the charity has been reorganising itself in recent years. It now has many new trustees and a new chief executive.

Volunteers

The charity has more than 650 local voluntary fundraising groups or individuals and 28 charity shops. Perhaps as important to the charity is the input, all unpaid, of the 70 or so specialist doctors and scientists who make up the charity's various expert committees.

Funding, administration

As with many medical research charities, donated income comes mainly in the form of legacies (£14 million in 1999/00), but in many cases these are the result of the publicity created by other fundraising activities. These activities are split roughly equally between local branch operations and those organised centrally.

For the last three years fundraising expenditure has run at the already low level of 10–11p for every pound raised, but the charity has noted its determination to reduce this ratio even further.

The charity adds ...

We are keen to maintain our wide spread of basic scientific and clinical research, while at the same time launching new initiatives such as funding research into complementary therapies and encouraging health professionals such as nurses, physiotherapists and podiatrists to play an extended role in rheumatology through introducing new grant categories.

The information assessed

There is a fine, comprehensive website, including full and excellent annual reports and accounts for the last three years.

Contact

Copeman House, St Mary's Court
St Mary's Gate
Chesterfield
Derbyshire
S41 7TD
Tel 01246 558033
Website www.arc.org.uk
Chair Professor R D Sturrock
Fergus Logan, Chief Executive

Arts charities

Most (though not all) arts organisations are charities. They generally seek donations from the public and often rely heavily, or even exclusively, on the work of volunteers.

Some of the largest arts charities have their own entries in this book, such as the *National Gallery*, the *Tate* and the *Royal Opera House*, Covent Garden.

Many readers of this book will already be aware of the main organisations, both national and local, in their particular fields of interest, but they may be interested in finding out more about the mass of smaller groups that exist throughout the country. The easiest source of information should be the regional arts councils (or the Arts Councils of England, Scotland, Northern Ireland and Wales). Their details are as follows:

The Arts Council of England; tel: 020 7333 0100

   East England Arts; tel: 01223 454400

   East Midlands Arts; tel: 01509 218292

   London Arts; tel: 020 7608 6100

   North West Arts; tel: 0161 834 6644

   Northern Arts; tel: 0191 255 8500

   South East Arts; tel: 01892 507200

   South West Arts; tel: 01392 218188

   Southern Arts; tel: 01962 855099

   West Midlands Arts; tel: 0121 631 3121

   Yorkshire Arts; tel: 01924 455555

The Arts Council of Northern Ireland; tel: 028 9038 5200

The Arts Council of Wales; tel: 029 2037 6500

The Scottish Arts Council; tel: 0131 226 6051

A good source of information about voluntary/participatory organisations is the fast-growing Voluntary Arts Network (tel: 029 2039 5395).

Association for International Cancer Research

Income	£11,719,165 (1999/00)
Donated income	£11,199,000
Fundraising costs	£5,639,000
Statutory income	£0
Top salary	£37,000
Paid staff	
Full time	12

Aims, activities

AICR, a grant-making rather than an operational charity, supports research into the causes, prevention and treatment of cancer. It also funds scientific conferences and symposia.

'The association is unique in its approach to funding [cancer research]. We have set no priorities, impose no restrictions on areas of cancer to be funded, and set no boundaries, scientific, geographical or political, in accepting applications for funding. Applications are rigorously vetted – refereed by two independent scientists – and assessed in committee by our independent Scientific Advisory Committee. The committee ... grades them in order of merit and the association will then award grants in that order of merit, as far as the available funds allow.'

Despite this appealingly unrestricted and open-minded approach, 75% of funding nevertheless goes to research in the UK, because that is still where most of the applications come from.

The charity moved to Scotland in 1996 and re-registered with the appropriate Scottish authorities. It says that in 2000 it discovered the Charity Commission was stating on its website that it had ceased to exist. *(Probably a reference to the usual 'removed from the register' wording Ed.)*

'It came to light after a woman left a legacy to us. The executors of her will were told by the commission that we had ceased to exist and would have to find someone else to give the money to.' And then a person in Glasgow reported the charity to the city's Trading Standards Office after he was told by the commission that it did not exist. The charity reports that the commission has refused to amend its website to reflect the true position.

Volunteers

Volunteers, other than trustees, do not play a large part in the work of this charity.

Funding, administration

AICR is almost wholly funded by voluntary income, of which (unusually for a cancer charity) legacies form only a small part. Its finances are notable for their very high fundraising costs: 50p in the pound in 1999/00, 59p in the pound in the previous year and an average of 37p in the pound in the three years to 1998. Though the costs then were already unusually high, there has since been a very rapid further increase in fundraising expenditure, from £2 million in 1996/97 to £5.6 million in 1999/00. This was largely due to investment in the recruitment of regular donors to supplement the charity's traditional reliance on Prize Draw sweeps promoted by direct mail. Though income has also grown, it has done so at a slower rate.

The charity is relaxed about its fundraising costs, which are discussed in admirable detail: 'Any company returning a 55% profit margin would be deemed outstandingly successful in the business world.'

Also unusual is the relatively modest salary of the chief executive (perhaps indicating modest salaries generally).

The charity adds ...

Fundraising costs are entirely taken up by our Direct Mail and Donor Recruitment Programmes. We do not suffer from the costs incurred in running shops or mail order catalogues, which can incur costs of up to 80% – but are usually shown as separate from fundraising costs. This is why we are 'relaxed' about our costs, when all fundraising activities are taken into consideration (e.g. shops, mail order). AICR stands comparison with any comparable charity.

The information assessed

There is a good, clear annual report and accounts, with unusually comprehensive reporting of the charity's fundraising. There is an informative website.

Contact

Madras House
St Andrews
Fife
KY16 9EH
Tel 01334 477910
Website www.aicr.org.uk
Chair John Matthews
Derek Napier, Chief Executive

Barnardo's
Childcare

Income	£100,366,000 (1999/00)
Donated income	£40,397,000
Fundraising costs	£10,961,000
Statutory income	£51,863,000
Top salary	£80,000–£90,000
Paid staff	
Full time	2,601
Part time	2,817
Volunteers	15,000

Aims, activities

It was not easy to write a description of the work of this important social work charity from its annual report or annual review, or from the other literature sent in response to general enquiries, or from the website, because of the very general language used, even when the information runs to some length. Barnardo's states: 'We run more than 300 projects ... working with children and their families in their homes, communities and schools' (the charity is at pains to point out that it no longer runs children's homes and has not done so for many years).

Further enquiry established that these 'projects' mostly involve the provision of long-term local services for children and their parents, and are usually run for (or in partnership with) statutory services. 'The majority of the ... services are in partnership with one area or another of the statutory services – social services, education, health, police, probation, housing etc.' The word 'project', with its implication of short-term interventions, therefore seems inappropriate.

Funding for some services is divided equally between the charity and the agency involved; 'others are, for example, 60% statutory, 40%

Barnardo's or the other way round ... In some cases buildings are provided by the statutory service, in others the buildings are wholly owned by Barnardo's. It would depend on what had been negotiated.' The majority of the users are referred by the statutory partner, which then pays Barnardo's 'for our services'. The issue of supplementing statutorily funded services with the proceeds of fundraising is a difficult one, unless there is a clear statutory obligation for the service to be provided (when Barnardo's would expect to be paid the full amount).

Though not described in the annual reports, the annual review or the other information supplied, a follow-up telephone enquiry produced an excellent leaflet listing the charity's services under each of the six main headings given below. The accounts for 1999/00 use different but related headings for the year's expenditure (shown in brackets), from which it can be seen that family support accounts in financial terms for almost half of all the charity's activity.

- A family that can cope (£39 million)
- parenting courses
- fostering and adoption services
- care for disabled children
- family support services
- A stake in society (£13 million)
- schemes for young people to build their own homes
- support to young people leaving care
- vocational training for young people
- Opportunities to learn (£13 million)
- schooling for teenage mothers
- after-school schemes

- support to enable children with special needs to attend their local school
- A sense of belonging in the community (£9 million)
- community projects for disabled and disadvantaged children
- practical help for local communities
- advice to refugee children
- Protection from harm (£5 million)
- child protection services
- campaigning against child prostitution
- support groups for women and children who have suffered from domestic violence
- Emotional, physical and mental health (expenditure not apparent)
- health education
- counselling
- advice on substance abuse

In 2001 the charity came in for some press criticism over an unusually hard-hitting advertising campaign (needed, according to its chief executive, to raise the profile of the charity's work). However, the complaints were rejected by the Advertising Standards Authority and apparently by the public which, according to recent commercial research, generally accepts the need for such advertising.

Though the fact seems not to be referred to in the most recent annual review or annual report for 2000, this is a charity 'whose inspiration and values derive from the Christian faith and two thirds of whose trustees must be Christians'.

Volunteers

The website, in August 2001, referred to 250,000 volunteers, but this includes house-to-house collectors and lottery ticket sellers. A survey in 2000, carried out to determine the number of 'active volunteers', arrived at the total of 15,000 – itself an impressive figure. There is an excellent leaflet, 'Volunteering with Barnardo's', and the various volunteering possibilities are well set out on the website (under 'Get involved/volunteering/what you could do').

Funding, administration

Half of the charity's income, or £52 million in 1999/00, comes from statutory authorities as 'fees and grants for children's services'. Most of it comes from social services departments in England or their equivalents in the other parts of the UK.

The level of statutory income rose very fast in the year, by £7 million or 16%, though without arousing comment in the annual report.

About 40% of the money (£40 million) was from legacies and donations, achieved at a fundraising cost of £11 million, giving a cost ratio of 27%, or 27p for each pound donated or bequeathed. This figure, unchanged from the previous year, is very slightly above the charity's average of 26% for the three years before that.

The sources of voluntary income were categorised as follows (with 1998/99 figures in brackets):

- legacies £21 million (£21 million);
- donations and gifts from the public £17.2 million (£16.8 million);
- donations from companies and trusts £2.2 million (£2 million).

A remarkable £17.9 million was received from the sale of donated goods in the charity's shops, but as the cost of running them was £16.7 million the balance for the charity was a more modest £1.2 million.

The free reserves of £79 million are well above the £25 million Barnardo's reasonably regards as needed to guard against the possibility of a sudden drop in its voluntarily donated income. The charity is therefore deliberately spending above its income, both to sustain existing commitments and to establish new provision on an as-yet unfunded basis. It expects to have exhausted this surplus within four years, by when it is planned that the gap will have been filled by 'the generation of additional income and cost reductions'.

The information assessed
The generally good annual report and accounts and annual review are patchy in their coverage of finances and fundraising. The website has excellent information for both donors and volunteers.

Contact
Tanners Lane, Barkingside
Ilford
Essex
IG6 1QG
Tel 020 8550 8822
Website www.barnardos.org.uk
Chair Reverend David Gamble
Roger Singleton, Chief Executive

BBC Children in Need Appeal

Income	£21,486,000 (1999/00)
Donated income	£19,354,000
Fundraising costs	£233,000
Statutory income	£0
Top salary	£50,000–£60,000
Paid staff	
Full time	27
Part time	4

Aims, activities
No doubt already known to many readers, this charity raises money through its annual appeal on BBC television and supporting events, and gives out the money in grants to organisations working with children. It is the BBC's corporate charity and this support enables it to raise money in an exceptionally cost-effective way.

The 1999/00 annual review categorises the grants as follows:

● for children experiencing poverty, deprivation or homelessness £8.7 million;

● for children suffering from illness, abuse or neglect £4.9 million;

● for children with mental or physical disabilities £4.5 million;

● for children with behavioural and psychological disorders £0.7 million.

Grants are targeted at areas of greatest need and money is allocated regionally so that no areas miss out. Most of the grants are small: half of them by number are for less than £5,000, and half of all the money goes in grants of less than £25,000.

Most of the organisations benefiting are too small for inclusion in this book – some of them far too small, such as the Mawbey Brough Toy Library (which received £250). Other are bigger, but still below this book's limits, such as the Post Adoption Centre (£70,000). An exceptional £550,000 was given to the Family Welfare Association for onward distribution through a hardship fund to help children and families in immediate financial distress.

During the year it cost the charity £1.4 million to allocate and distribute all its almost 2,000 grants. This money came entirely from the interest earned on the balances awaiting distribution.

Volunteers

There is the most extensive voluntary fundraising imaginable associated with the once-a-year appeal. The grantmaking is effected with the advice of eight voluntary regional committees (and one national one).

Funding, administration

Almost all the costs of raising the money are met by the BBC, with just £232,000 of the charity's money spent on fundraising – an extremely low 1% of its voluntary income. The appeal, which is effectively ongoing, has been raising more money in each of the recent years it has run, having started with just £1 million in 1980 when it was first set up.

The appeal offers donors an exceptionally low cost way of having their money allocated thoughtfully to the children in the UK who need it most.

The information assessed

The excellent annual reports and accounts are confusingly named. The 'Annual Report' has only summarised accounts and is not the audited report and financial statements. There is a cheerful and informative website, courtesy of the BBC.

Contact

PO Box 76
London
W3 6FS
Tel 020 8576 7788
Website www.bbc.co.uk/cin
Chair Roger Jones
Martina Milburn, Director

Benevolent and occupational funds

There are several thousand benevolent and occupational funds helping individuals in need (normally without requiring that they have previously given to the charity concerned).

Between them they help people from almost every walk of life. Many are specific to particular occupations or industries. Some help people with particular medical conditions. Some help those from certain backgrounds or of a common faith. Others help only those born or living in specific parishes. Still others determine who they help by age, gender or condition – 'Elderly ladies living alone on a low income, domiciled in the British Isles', 'Charity for relief in need of residents of the old borough of ... ' or 'People from Scotland who now live within a radius of 35 miles of Charing Cross and who are in need', for example.

Most of these charities provide advice, counselling and financial grants. Some also offer sheltered housing, residential accommodation, nursing homes, and day and domiciliary services.

Benevolent funds rely heavily on volunteers to identify and visit their applicants and beneficiaries. Occupational funds are based on the strong bonds which develop in a shared working environment. Such ties may survive long after retirement. There are many funds that provide sheltered housing and care homes for people who worked in a particular industry in the past.

Some of these charities are funded primarily from past endowments, but most tend not to be active fundraisers. However, their efforts are usually concentrated in the occupational or area or the particular community concerned. For this reason, only those raising more than £5 million a year in new voluntary income have their own entries in this book (instead of the usual £2 million minimum).

Information about these charities generally can be had from the Association of Charity Officers; tel: 01707 651777.

BESO (British Executive Service Overseas)

Providing professional expertise to developing countries

Income	£2,110,000 (2000/01)
Donated income	£436,000
Fundraising costs	£90,504
Statutory income	£1,517,000
Top salary	£50,000–£60,000
Paid staff	
Full time	38
Part time	15
Volunteers	3,500

Aims, activities

The charity's purpose is to offer professional expertise to private, public and voluntary organisations, in less developed countries and emerging economies which cannot afford commercial consultants, in the hope of strengthening their local economies and societies.

BESO sends about 600 volunteers overseas each year from those on its register of over 3,500 experts. Assignments generally last between two weeks and four months. Typically BESO organises and pays for travel and insurance costs, while the client provides accommodation and pays for local expenses. There is no official upper or lower age limit, but many BESO volunteers are retired or nearing retirement age.

The areas of expertise covered are wide; at the time of writing this entry, immediate requests for help included the following:

- an expert in EU fish slaughter regulations to go to Bosnia;
- an effluent treatment expert (especially in textiles) to go to Ecuador;
- a commodity exchange expert to go to Romania;

- an expert in insurance regulation to go to Bolivia;
- a liquor manufacture expert to go to Ukraine;
- a fashion designer to go to India;
- a paint chemist to go to China;
- a urologist to go to Ukraine;
- an expert in Parkinson's disease to go to Mongolia.

Volunteers

All BESO projects are staffed exclusively by volunteers.

Funding, administration

The charity is funded mainly by a government grant from the Department for International Development, and by international aid agencies. However, BESO is active in raising further resources for itself (at a cost of 21p in the pound) and has been particularly successful in getting help 'in kind', such as its £75,000 worth of office space from HSBC and £46,000 worth of travel from national airlines. DHL provided £20,000 worth of postage and courier services in 1999/00.

The charity adds ...

BESO draws Volunteers from Service Clubs such as Rotary, Lions and Soroptimists, as well as seconding qualified employees from businesses. Increasingly BESO works in partnership with international agencies, business schools or local governments on projects which have a sectoral or regional focus, to increase the benefits to countries from assignments.

The information assessed

The charity has excellent accounts and annual review (called 'Global Partnerships'), as well as a good website and newsletter.

Contact

164 Vauxhall Bridge Road
London
SW1V 2RB
Tel 020 7630 0644
Website www.beso.org
Chair Baroness Chalker
Gael Ramsey, Chief Executive

Bible Society
(formerly the British and Foreign Bible Society)

Income	£10,503,000 (2000)
Donated income	£6,333,000
Fundraising costs	£1,354,000
Statutory income	£0
Top salary	£50,000–£60,000
Paid staff	
Full time	80
Part time	18

Aims, activities

This is the UK member of a global alliance of 130 different Bible Societies, 'making the voice of the Bible heard everywhere'. Originally concerned almost wholly with the simple distribution of copies of the Bible, the society is now working to find new ways to make the Bible heard in a world where it has virtually disappeared from many people's daily lives, 'particularly in the West'. As an example of this, the society's main millennium project was the promotion in the UK of an animated film, *The Miracle Maker* (see below).

William Wilberforce – campaigner for 'the suppression of the Slave Trade and the reformation of Manners' ('making goodness fashionable') – was, along with other members of the Clapham Sect, instrumental in founding the Bible Society in 1804. The society is, and always has been, 'resolved to work across every denomination in making the Bible available and heard'. It has a number of clergy(men) as its vice-presidents, but its chair and trustees are all lay people.

The charity works in the UK, but its main activity is the funding, through grants, of programmes of the worldwide Bible Society movement.

In the UK, £1.6 million was spent in 2000. The main activity was the promotion of *The Miracle Maker* film, which played to about half a million viewers in 400 cinemas. A video of the film was a Christmas best-seller. Other trading activity centres on the production of Bibles, including the Contemporary English Version published in association with HarperCollins.

There is impressive detail in the charity's materials on 'how we might recover the significance of the Bible as Scripture in contemporary society, rather than treating it only as an historical text to be scrutinised critically'.

Overseas, the charity contributed £3 million to the work of the United Bible Societies worldwide. It also made grants worth £174,000 to individual projects that the main international programme was unable to include within its budgets. The largest of these were both in Africa:

● £50,000 for emergency Bible work in Mozambique following the floods there;

● £42,000 for Faith Comes by Hearing in Kenya.

The charity also gave £77,000 to other partner agencies for particular projects. The largest of these grants went to:

– Hosanna (USA) £33,000

– Korean Bible Society £14,000

– Hungarian Bible Society (£14,000)

Volunteers

The website provides excellent coverage of the role of volunteers, though there are fewer details in the annual report. There are 20 voluntary local representatives supporting no less than 400 action groups around the UK, as well as 50 recognised voluntary speakers on the work of the charity.

Funding, administration

The society is funded primarily by individual and local church donations (providing 40% of total income in 2000) and legacies (20%), supplemented by sales revenue (28%) and interest and dividends on investments (11%). The donations and legacies were achieved at a fundraising cost of £1.4 million, representing 21p in the pound, a reduction from the 23p in the pound averaged in the previous three years.

Much of the charity's reserves are in the form of restricted endowment funds. Funds are being released from the remaining unrestricted investments of £5 million until the society reaches its target of holding reserves equal to six months of forecast costs. In accordance with this, the charity's accounts showed an overall deficit of £361,000 for 2000.

The annual review notes that 'the Society maintains a prudent and ethical investment policy, which has proved very successful over a number of years'. This is an example which happily more charities are now following.

The charity adds ...

Are you someone who is passionate about making the Bible heard? Are you someone who wants to see lives changed and the Bible at the heart of everyday life? Be a part of our global alliance of supporters, churches and Bible Societies, working to make the Bible heard around the world.

The information assessed

The annual report and accounts are excellent, except for their limited coverage of the role of volunteers. There is also a 'Word in Action' newsletter, and a particularly smart and effective website.

Contact

Stonehill Green
Westlea
Swindon
SN5 7DG
Tel 01793 418100
Website www.biblesociety.org.uk
Chair Dr Clive Dilloway
Neil Crosbie, Executive Director

Black and minority ethnic organisations

The term 'black and minority ethnic' (BME for short) describes a wide range of organisations. It is a label which should be treated with care because while it is intended to be inclusive, it can, on occasion, obscure the diversity within.

Organisations usually represent minority ethnic groups, but these can be white as well as black; of different national origins, faiths and languages; or indeed sometimes minorities within minorities. The ethnic landscape in the UK does not stand still, but constantly develops and changes.

Obviously BME organisations are more numerous in cities and towns, but networks and organisations have also formed in rural areas. Many BME organisations are providing services that are culturally specific to their ethnic group in the fields of general welfare, housing, health and education.

In common with all other not-for-profit and non-governmental organisations, BME organisations rely heavily on the use of volunteers both as trustees and in order to deliver their services. Their clients cover all ages and many have been in existence for ten years or more, developing a valuable pool of knowledge and skill. Their funds are raised from a range of sources but, like many charities, they find it hard to cover their day-to-day running costs.

The routes of access to individual groups are various – but umbrella organisations have now developed, such as QED in Bradford, the Progress Trust in Manchester, CEMVO (Council of Ethnic Minority Voluntary Sector Organisations) in London, and the Chinese Information and Advice Centre in London. Other useful sources of information are directories that are updated annually, such as the *Voluntary Agencies Directory* (produced by the National Council for Voluntary Organisations), or the directories produced by the minority umbrella organisations, local Councils for Voluntary Service, churches and libraries.

Useful addresses include:

Blackliners
Unit 46/47 Eurolink Business Centre, 49 Effra Road, London SW2 1BZ
Tel: 020 7738 7468
Website: www.blackliners.org

Cancer Black Care
16 Dalston Lane, London E8 3AZ
Tel: 020 7249 1097
Website: www.cancerblackcare.org

Chinese Information and Advice Centre
53 New Oxford Street, London WC1A 1BL
Tel: 020 7692 3471
Website: www.ciac.co.uk

Confederation of Indian Organisations
5 Westminster Bridge Road, London SE1 7XW
Tel: 020 7928 9889
Website: www.cio.org.uk

Council for Ethnic Minority Voluntary Organisations
Boardman House, 64 Broadway, London E15 1NG
Tel: 020 7377 8484
Website: www.emf-cemvo.co.uk

National Council for Voluntary Organisations
Regent's Wharf, 8 All Saints Street, London N19 1LL
Tel: 020 7713 6161
Helpline: 0800 2798 798
Website: www.ncvo-vol.org.uk

Progress Trust
3rd Floor, Barclay House, 35 Whitworth Street, Manchester M1 5NG
Tel: 0161 906 0020
Website: www.progresstrust.com

QED (Quest for Economic Development Limited)
West Bowling Centre, Clipstone Street, Bradford BD5 8EA
Tel: 01274 735551
Website: www.qed-uk.org

Sickle Cell Society
54 Station Road, London NW10 4AU
Tel: 020 8961 7795/4006
Website: www.sicklecellsociety.org

Blue Cross

The welfare of companion animals, mainly in England

Income	£13,717,000 (2000)
Donated income	£13,122,000
Fundraising costs	£2,108,000
Statutory income	£0
Top salary	£60,000–£70,000
Paid staff	291
Volunteers	102

Aims, activities

Formerly Our Dumb Friends League, the purpose of the charity is to foster the bond of friendship between animals and people. When founded in the nineteenth century, the problems faced by the many working horses in London were of particular concern. More recently there has been greater emphasis on meeting the needs of the growing numbers of household pets.

The charity runs:

- 11 animal adoption centres, which re-homed 7,200 animals in the year 2000. The charity says that the proportion of unsuccessful placements has fallen 'drastically' in the last 10 years, thanks to its groundbreaking animal behaviour programme;

- 2 equine centres that care for 68 horses and monitor the welfare of 300 out on loan;

- 4 animal hospitals that carried out 52,000 treatments in the year 2000.

The Animal Hospitals (based at Victoria, Merton and Hammersmith in London, and at Grimsby) work only with the pets of those without the means to pay ordinary veterinary charges, although a donation to the Blue Cross is requested. There is an affiliated Blue Cross charity in Ireland that operates ten mobile clinics in the Dublin area.

One recent project has been the rebuilding of the charity's flagship, the Victoria Animal Hospital in central London – the first hospital of its kind when first opened in 1906. The charity also spends a considerable amount each year on its programme to educate the public, for example through its Take Your Dog to Work Day, designed to reduce the number of animals regularly suffering from hours of loneliness and related behavioural problems.

The Blue Cross is as much a people charity as it is an animal charity. This dual commitment is powerfully illustrated by the continuing success of the Pet Bereavement Support Service, which is run in association with the Society for Companion Animal Studies (SCAS). For an editor new to this issue it was initially unclear whether the reference was to the needs of owners who had lost their pets, or of pets who had lost their owners, or of pets bereaved of their mates, or indeed of all three. Further reading showed that the problem in this instance is one of bereaved owners, rather than bereaved pets. The service ensures that owners who suffer the loss of a pet do not face this alone, and in 2000 over 1,600 people contacted the service's telephone befrienders for support.

There is a broad delivery across the field of animal welfare. The Blue Cross is similar to the *People's Dispensary for Sick Animals* in offering free veterinary treatment at its four animal hospitals to people on low incomes, but is different in the other services that are described above.

Volunteers

The charity's work appears, from the annual report and review, to be carried out by its paid staff – apart from its Pet Bereavement programme, for which it has 102 trained volunteers. There are references to the part played by volunteers in the charity's fundraising, and the website advertises a range of fundraising opportunities.

Funding, administration

The charity is almost wholly dependent on donations and legacies. These totalled £13.1 million in the year 2000. compared with an average of £9 million in the three years to 1999. Fundraising costs of £2.1 million represented a cost ratio of 16p in the pound, or 16%, a figure which has been roughly steady for some years.

In December 2000 reserves stood at a high £15 million, but the charity had approved capital expenditure plans to account for £7 million.

The charity adds ...

When animals suffer the distress of being given up, the last thing they need is to be rejected again. Volunteers and staff at our centres work to ensure every animal has a happy and rewarding stay with the Blue Cross, whilst finding a loving home to last a lifetime.

The information assessed

There is a good annual report and accounts and annual review, and a recently improved website.

Contact

Shilton Road
Burford
Oxfordshire
OX18 4PF
Tel 01993 822651
Website www.bluecross.org.uk
Chair Mrs D A Sinclair
John Rutter, Chief Executive

Book Aid International

Literacy and education overseas

Income	£1,380,000 (2000)
Donated income	£893,000
Fundraising costs	£142,000
Statutory income	£638,000
Top salary	£40,000–£50,000
Paid staff	
Full time	26
Part time	7
Volunteers	
Operational	18
Fundraising	2

Aims, activities

Book Aid International provides over 750,000 books every year to support literacy, education and publishing in more than 60 countries, most of them in Africa. The charity also has active programmes promoting the development of local publishing in the countries where it works. Though Book Aid's cash income would not, on its own, justify an entry in this book, the charity qualifies for a place because of the value of the books donated to it each year.

Most of the books go to one of the following kinds of organisation:

● public libraries;

- schools and colleges;
- disadvantaged groups, such as women, children, refugees.

More than half the books are donated by publishers. Most of the rest come from a variety of community and company sources, and from individuals. Most are new. The charity makes great efforts to match the books it supplies with the specific requests from its numerous partner organisations overseas.

An increasing emphasis is now being put on helping the development of local publishing infrastructure, not least because of the need for books in appropriate local languages. This is done both by providing information and training resources to publishers and booksellers, and by the direct purchase by Book Aid International of the locally published books most needed by libraries, schools and other organisations in the area.

Volunteers

Apart from the volunteers who work in the office and warehouse in south London, the charity relies on volunteers to collect donated books. Besides obvious needs, such as those for up-to-date reference and supplementary school books, books in a broad range of subjects are needed, catering for readers from nursery to tertiary levels. Any potential book donors should ring the number below to establish the suitability or scale of what they might be able to offer.

Funding, administration

Unusually and impressively, the charity relies heavily on gifts in kind to reduce the costs of its service. More than £3 million worth of books were donated in 2000 (valued at what they would otherwise have cost the charity),while transport of books to the

value of £129,000 was given, as were further discounts of £113,000 on books purchased from publishers.

However, money is still needed. In 2000, £0.9 million was donated by a combination of individuals, companies and charitable trusts, making a total value of donations of £5 million, achieved at a fundraising cost of just £142,000 – which gives a cost ratio of 16% (16p in the pound) in cash terms, but only 3% when the value of donations in kind is taken into account.

The charity adds ...

As the official charity for World Book Day we are playing an increasingly important role in raising awareness of development issues in schools across the UK. Please visit our website for more information or contact us direct for a schools information pack.

The information assessed

The charity has an excellent annual report and accounts. There is also a fine annual review and an exceptionally comprehensive website (which includes the full accounts).

Contact

39–41 Coldharbour Lane
London
SE5 9NR
Tel 020 7733 3577
Website www.bookaid.org
Chair Tim Rix
Sara Harrity, Director

Breakthrough Breast Cancer

Medical research

Income	£5,207,000 (2000/01)
Donated income	£4,101,000
Fundraising costs	£1,096,000
Statutory income	£0
Top salary	£60,000–£70,000
Paid staff	
Full time	43
Part time	4
Volunteers	4,100
Operational	50

Aims, activities

This young, growing and, in its own words, highly ambitious charity fights breast cancer both through the promotion and funding of medical research and through spreading awareness of the condition and what can be done to alleviate it among professionals and the public.

The founding aim of the charity in 1991 was to establish a dedicated breast cancer research centre. This was achieved in 1999 with the setting up of the Breakthrough Toby Robins Breast Cancer Research Centre at the *Institute of Cancer Research* (ICR) in London.

A major aim of the charity is to keep breast cancer on the political and public agendas. In this sense it is a campaigning charity.

There were three main charitable activities in 1999/00.

First, a final £3.6 million was contributed to the costs of building, under a lease finance scheme, the new Breast Cancer Research Centre. It is not clear whether the charity will contribute to ongoing costs in future years.

Secondly, now that funding of the centre is complete the charity has committed itself to 'a major programme of research'. During the year £3.1 million was spent on this, up from less than £1 million in the previous year. Though phrases such as 'our research interests continue to broaden, with recruitment on track to set up laboratories' and 'the successful team of supporters, volunteers, researchers and staff' may give a different impression, the charity is probably a funder of research rather than a research organisation itself. It employs just seven staff on 'Education and research', and the accounts refer to outstanding research grant commitments.

Most of the money in this category went to pay for research carried out at the Breast Cancer Research Centre, presumably by ICR staff, and also in Glasgow to where the Research Centre's first director has moved.

The research programme is no doubt under the direction of the scientific advisory committee, two of whose four members are noted in the accounts to be associated with the ICR. The 1998/99 annual report stated that grants were subject to independent peer review.

Thirdly, the charity spent £494,000 under the heading of education. This seems to be conducted primarily at professional level, aimed at achieving a higher priority for the charity's concerns within the NHS and medical research communities. More generally, 'our prevalence and credibility as a campaigning charity mean that we are frequently asked to comment on breast cancer issues and policy, and are rapidly becoming the "voice" of those concerned about breast cancer'. An example of this work was the Kiss Goodbye to Breast Cancer campaign. 'Supported by celebrities, MPs and the general public', a petition with 670,000 signatures was delivered to Downing Street, asking the government to support pound for pound the amount spent by charities on medical research.

Volunteers

There is a reference in the annual review to 'our network of local groups that help us to spread our message at local level', and to the fact that six new such groups were formed in 1999/00. The groups' main activity is probably fundraising, but they also help to spread awareness of breast cancer issues, for example by providing speakers to schools and on other opportunities.

Volunteers also help the charity's staff with their day-to-day workload, in all departments.

These groups are 'linked' to the main charity, but it is not clear whether they are actually part of this charity and so whether or not their accounts are consolidated with it.

Funding, administration

Donations, well analysed in the accounts, make up about 80% of the total income of the charity, and have been growing fast. Indeed the charity has committed itself to doubling its income over five years. Legacies are a relatively minor source of income, in marked contrast to the situation in many of the older, larger cancer charities.

The voluntary income was achieved in 2000/01 at a fundraising cost of £1.1 million, giving a cost ratio of 27p for each pound donated, a figure up from 24p in the previous year and the average 19p in the pound for the three years to 1999.

The fundraising is notably energetic and high-profile, with a substantial income from events for which the charity is well known, such as the 'Walk the Walk' Moonwalk in May 2000 which raised more than £600,000.

However, the charity is seeking to reduce its reliance on high-profile events and is investing in fundraising from companies and in developing its donor base of long-term committed supporters. In the former field, the charity's tie-in with the Avon cosmetics company through Avon's Crusade Against Breast Cancer has been seen as one of the most successful of the new breed of 'cause-related marketing' programmes.

The accounts note that one of the trustees works for a firm of solicitors that was paid £8,000 for its services to the charity during the year 1999/00 and £2,500 in 2000/01. There is a discussion of the issue of payments to trustees in the Introduction to this book (page 22).

The charity adds ...

Our research centre is now full with talented and enthusiastic scientists and technicians – the aim we have been working to for ten years. This milestone and the communication of its importance will help inspire on both the fundraising and awareness fronts.

The information assessed

The good annual report and accounts and annual review must be read together, as the former assumes knowledge of the purposes and activities of the charity. What appeared to be an excellent website was difficult for this editor to read (on two different screens and occasions) because of the very light colour of the text. This entry, apart from the financial and numerical data, was written from the 1999/00 annual report and review.

Contact
Kingsway House, 6th Floor
103 Kingsway
London
WC2B 6QX
Tel 020 7405 5111
Website www.breakthrough.org.uk
Chair Peter Keemer
Ms Delyth Morgan, Chief Executive

British Council of Shaare Zedek
Health in Israel

Income	£3,584,000 (1999)
Donated income	£3,511,000
Fundraising costs	£230,000
Statutory income	£0
Top salary	not disclosed
Paid staff	
Full time	3
Part time	1
Volunteers	
Operational	50

Aims, activities
The charity raises money to support the work of the Shaare Zedek Hospital and Medical Centre in Jerusalem, which seeks to treat all in need in that city, regardless of religious or financial status. A recent copy of the charity's newsletter notes that 6 of the hospital's 400 doctors are Palestinian. The hospital receives no government funding, but is supported by fundraising groups in many countries where there is a substantial Jewish population.

Originally founded almost 100 years ago, the first building was put up,

under Turkish rule, with both political and continuing financial support from the then Kaiserine German government – support which continued until 1933.

Much of the fundraising is for a specific purpose within the hospital. The UK council takes particular responsibility for the hospital's libraries.

With a relatively modest mailing list of less than 110,000 supporters, the charity raised £3.5 million in donations in 1999, its most successful year ever – up from £2.2 million in the previous year. The figure was boosted by one gift of more than £1 million. Legacies provided a further £600,000.

Recording this successful year's activity, the annual report for 1999 notes that the charity was fortunate that, in the current state of feeling towards Israel, its fundraising had a specific focus.

There are committees of the charity in Brighton, Gibraltar and Glasgow.

Volunteers
The charity acts as a conduit for volunteers going to work in the hospital. There are 500 volunteers in all, 50 of them from Britain.

Funding, administration
The charity's income comes from 'donations and legacies, solicited through mail-shots, functions and events, lectures, direct approaches and special appeals'. Though these sources are not itemised in the accounts, there is an interesting review of the activities in the annual report. In an unusual service, a solicitor supporter offers to draw up wills, free of charge, for anyone

considering a legacy to this charity as part of their dispositions.

Fundraising costs in 1999 were very low at £230,000 or just 7% of the value of donations received. This figure has been typical for the charity, although costs had risen temporarily in the previous year to 14%. The costs are broken down in the accounts in an exemplary way. Wages and on-costs, including consultancy fees paid to the former director, Angela Margolis, accounted for about two thirds of the total, with advertising and publicity totalling £17,000 and the cost of fundraising events being just £7,000.

Unusually, it is not possible to identify the names of the charity's trustees with certainty from the annual report. The accounts note that a company of which one of the trustees is a partner received £4,000 for accounting and management services. There is a discussion of the issue of payments to trustees in the Introduction to this book (page 22).

The charity adds ...

The British Council [of Shaare Zedek], founded over 60 years ago, is proud to be associated with this very special place of healing in Jerusalem which provides a haven of peace and co-operation in an area of conflict.

The information assessed

There is a succinct but good annual report and accounts, a lively magazine (*Heartbeat*), and a magnificent website for the hospital.

Contact
766 Finchley Road
London
NW11 7TH
Tel 020 8201 8933
Website www.szmc.org.il
Chair Margaret Gioia Rotham and Margot Lew
Rhoda Goodman, Executive Director

British Heart Foundation
Mainly medical research

Income	£70,147,000 (2000/01)
Donated income	£54,725,000
Fundraising costs	£11,436,000
Statutory income	£0
Top salary	£110,000–£120,000
Paid staff	1,375
Volunteers	
Fundraising	10,000

Aims, activities

The aim of this very large and still fast-growing charity is to reduce the incidence of heart disease. It does so mainly through medical research programmes, but it also has a big programme of public education as well as substantial spending on the care and rehabilitation of those with heart disease.

Expenditures in 2000/01 were as follows:

- research (including the new Cardiovascular Initiative) £53 million;

- education £9.5 million;

- care and rehabilitation £5 million.

The research programmes consist mainly of:

- support for 29 professors of cardiovascular science;
- grants for individual research projects;
- scholarships for young researchers.

The charity is currently promoting its new, major Cardiovascular Initiative, a capital programme to refurbish older laboratories, build new research centres and provide equipment for hospitals and universities.

The extensive education programme provides information for both professionals and the public. In spring 2001 the excellent website was receiving 46,000 visits a month.

Care and rehabilitation services are led by funding for 45 BHF nurses, who spend most of their time in the community, visiting patients and supporting their follow-up care from the health service. These are employed by the NHS but funded initially by the charity.

There is a major programme for the distribution of defibrillators and for training professionals, such as the police and rural GPs, in how to use them. In addition, the charity's Heartstart UK programme has more than 700 affiliated community schemes to train members of the public in emergency life support, and there are 245 school training schemes. In all 125,000 people a year are trained by over 5,500 instructors.

Volunteers

There is good coverage in the annual review of the fundraising carried out by volunteers, organised in more than 400 branches of the charity and helping to run more than 420 shops. There is a very wide range of fundraising and sponsored events, of which the best known is the annual London to Brighton Bike Ride (raising £2.3 million in 2000/01).

Over 6,000 volunteers work in the shops, which collect and sell donated goods.

Relatively little information is given on the part played by volunteers in the other work of the charity, beyond that of the 100 or more voluntary trustees and committee members. There is a reference to 3,500 Heartstart scheme instructors, some or all of whom may be volunteers.

Funding, administration

Though there is limited information on how the work of the charity is organised, the financial information is admirably well presented. BHF is primarily funded by donations and legacies, but also has a large investment income. These investments were worth a majestic £216 million in March 2001. Almost £80 million of this huge amount has been put aside to pay in advance for the whole life of the professorships funded by the charity. There seems no particular reason why these should not be funded in the normal way from the charity's income, plus a suitable contingency reserve, thereby freeing most of this reserved money for immediate charitable use. However, the charity notes that these professors and their departments are the main plank of its research programme and it is seeking to protect them against possible future inflation.

For ongoing funding, 1999/00 was a most successful year, fuelled by a 21% increase in legacies. Voluntary income in 2000/01 saw a more modest 7% growth, to £55 million.

Fundraising in 2000/01 cost £11.4 million, down 4% from the previous year and representing 21p for every pound donated (down from 24p). The large chain of shops had what the charity found a difficult year. They remained unusually successful, generating no less than £6.2 million net income, but this was less than the £7.5 million contributed in the year before.

The charity adds ...

2001 is the British Heart Foundation's 40th anniversary year and we are delighted to report that we know about half of everything there is to know about heart disease. However, we still have a long way to go in the fight against the UK's largest killer.

The information assessed

The annual review and annual report and accounts are good (the accounts particularly well presented), and both are downloadable from the website.

Contact

14 Fitzhardinge Street
London
W1H 6DH
Tel 020 7935 0185
Website www.bhf.org.uk
Chair Professor Sir D Keith Peters
Major-General Leslie Busk, Director General

British Red Cross

Income	£124,081,000 (2000)
Donated income	£41,236,000
Fundraising costs	£11,146,000
Statutory income	£9,900,000
Top salary	£100,000–£110,000
Paid staff	
Full time	1,890
Part time	1,353
Volunteers	53,000

Aims, activities

As an organisation that has been changing and developing in recent years, it is helpful that the charity has a particularly clear vision and mission. The vision, of being 'the certain sign of hope in crisis', is to be achieved by being 'the leading provider of emergency help to people in most need, anywhere in the world'. As part of the International Red Cross and Red Crescent Movement, this charity is bound by that movement's principles, including neutrality, independence and voluntary service.

The charitable activities are divided roughly equally between the provision of services in the UK (£55 million in 2000) and international work (£62 million). The UK work is described first, as in addition to the expenditure of money it includes millions of hours of time put in by unpaid volunteers.

UK services
These are mostly organised through the charity's 68 branches. They include:

- Emergency response – supporting the statutory services in time of emergency; in 2000, for example, 28 branches were involved in helping the victims of floods.

- Support for refugees and asylum seekers – the charity ensures that essentials such as clothing are available for refugees arriving at Dover. In London there is a Refugee Unit with 3 paid staff and 84 volunteers. Around the country there is an orientation service where trained volunteers work for up to four weeks to help newly arrived refugees organise basic requirements, such as medical treatment and schools for their children.

- Youth and schools work – there are a variety of programmes, including giving respite to young people caring for others, befriending schemes for young people in difficulty, and Count Me In groups for disabled Red Cross Youth members.

- Retail – there are currently over 450 Red Cross shops across the UK, which maintain a high street presence for the charity and generate vital funds to support UK and international work.

- First aid courses – these are offered at all levels.

- Fire victim support service – offered in conjunction with local fire brigades.

- Medical loans – of equipment such as wheelchairs and walking frames to cover emergencies.

- Transport and escort – helping people make essential journeys, such as to attend a hospital appointment or a funeral.

- Tracing and message services – this is part of an international Red Cross service to help reunite separated families.

- Skin camouflage – a service provided by 200 trained volunteers to assist people with a disfigurement such as scarring or vitiligo.

- Therapeutic care sessions – about 2,500 volunteers offer simple massage and hand care sessions to people under stress or in pain, such as those awaiting hospital treatment.

The accounts note that the British Red Cross received £6 million in fees for 'Day, residential and other care services', activities not covered by the headings above. The charity is a substantial provider of residential care for older people and, to a lesser extent, for those with severe disabilities, and there are day care services for people in the same categories. This work, which developed in individual local Red Cross branches before their recent unification into a single body, is generally funded by the relevant local authorities or other statutory services. The services are reducing, but still deserved a place in the annual report and review.

International services

These are mostly delivered by the local Red Cross or Red Crescent organisations in the areas concerned. In 2000, £60 million was transferred to the International Committee of the Red Cross (which works in conflict zones) and the International Federation of the Red Cross and Red Crescent Societies (which helps after natural as opposed to man-made disasters); or was assigned directly to sister Red Cross/Red Crescent organisations around the world to support projects in fields such as disaster preparedness and response, development and health.

The coverage in the charity's annual report of how this money is used is thin, consisting simply of a list of the amounts sent to different areas or countries. The leading recipient areas were:

- former Yugoslavia £5.5 million;
- Iraq £3 million;
- South-east Asia £2.1 million;
- Afghanistan £2 million;
- former Soviet Union £1.6 million;
- Mozambique £1.5 million;
- Angola £1 million;
- Ethiopia £1 million;
- Sri Lanka £1 million.

It is not clear from the British Red Cross whether the money is for particular purposes or is a 'block grant' to help the local Red Cross or Red Crescent organisation carry out its work. A look at the information on the Afghanistan Red Crescent on the website of the International Red Cross (www.ifrc.org), the country by country process recommended to this editor by the British Red Cross, did not answer this question (although it produced a remarkably complete and thoughtful review of the situation of that presently unhappy country).

In addition to making grants the British Red Cross sends experts (called delegates) on specific missions. The 2000 annual review lists, for example, 37 missions where health experts helped establish community health programmes, 6 that were staffed by disaster preparedness experts and 20 that brought logistical expertise.

The British Red Cross has long-term partnerships with nine sister Red Cross/Red Crescent organisations (in Sierra Leone, Nigeria, Ethiopia, Uganda, Mozambique, Bangladesh, Russia, Turkmenistan and Bulgaria). Information on the work carried out is available on the British Red Cross website.

In the summer and autumn of 2001 the charity was coming under sustained attack, widely reported in the media, from Emma Nicholson MP who maintained that over £50 million collected by Jeffery Archer for work with Kurds in Iraq had not been properly accounted for, and called for a police investigation. The Red Cross stated that nothing like this sum had ever been collected in the UK and that Archer's figure was a total of a number of other appeals around the world.

The publicity surrounding the dispute was damaging both to this charity and to the reputation of charities generally, despite an independent review finding that there had been no misappropriation of any money collected by the British Red Cross.

In this editor's view the charity was almost wholly in the right and Miss Nicholson's actions were seriously misjudged; but the Red Cross allowed Archer to make his claims and did not put the record straight at the time – no doubt because of the embarrassment it would have caused and the damage it might have done to the prospects of further help for the Kurds concerned. If this was the case, it was an unfortunate and expensive mistake, even if an understandable one.

As this book went to press in December 2001, a programme of consolidation in the UK activities was announced. All loss making activities – other than those directly combating crises – were to be closed, including the residential services referred to above, and about 20% of the charity's large property holdings were to be sold. Besides some county and regional offices, this would include up to 40 of the charity's shops.

Volunteers

'People who are vulnerable often lack the essentials of life, like close family or friends, access to public transport and financial resources. So when these people face a sudden crisis, there is frequently nowhere they can turn for help. That's where British Red Cross volunteers enter the picture.

'Our volunteers work in local communities, helping people make journeys, providing First Aid, lending equipment such as wheelchairs and giving emergency care at home – all caring for people in crisis.

'Each year, more than 80,000 people volunteer, either providing these services, working in our charity shops, or helping to support fundraising events. We rely on volunteers in all areas of our work, and there are opportunities for everyone, whatever age, background or experience.'

The Red Cross is a recognised leader in the training and support offered to its volunteers, often leading to the possibility of gaining National Vocational Qualifications (NVQs).

At the end of 2001 the charity's relatively new director, Nicholas Young, noted his desire to reverse a decline in the number of volunteer fundraisers. There were still more than 50,000, but he believed that unnecessary bureaucracy had alienated potential recruits. He also wanted to recruit younger volunteers , and volunteers from minority ethnic groups.

Funding, administration

In the 1990s the Red Cross underwent tremendous organisational change. Previously the branches had been largely autonomous bodies and a great variety of practices and activities had developed. They have now all been brought into the one unified organisation.

Much the largest single category of income in 2000 comprised grants for overseas work, provided by the Department for International Development (£44.5 million). The next biggest sources of funding were donations (£27.7 million) and legacies (£13.5 million). Together, these sources gave a voluntary income total of £41.2 million. This was sharply down (in respect of both donations and legacies) from the previous year's quite exceptional figure of £58 million, although it was slightly up on the total of £40.1 million for the year before that.

Fundraising costs of £11.1 million, slightly down from the previous year, represented 27p for each pound raised, or 27%, against the 20% of the previous year and 23% for 1998.

The charity adds ...

The British Red Cross cares for vulnerable people in the UK, in times of short-term crisis, and overseas, following an armed conflict or natural disaster. In the UK, we also have a special responsibility to promote International Humanitarian Law, which covers the ethical issues surrounding wars and situations of violence.

The information assessed

The generally excellent annual report and accounts and annual review are backed by a fine website and a range of further literature, although a couple of weaker areas are noted in the text above.

Contact

9 Grosvenor Crescent
London
SW1X 7EH
Tel 020 7235 5454
Website www.redcross.org.uk
Chair Professor John McClure
Sir Nicholas Young, Chief Executive

BTCV

(formerly the British Trust for Conservation Volunteers)

Income	£13,753,000 (2000/01)
Donated income	£3,404,000
Fundraising costs	£575,000
Statutory income	£6,404,000
Top salary	£60,000–£70,000
Paid staff	735
Volunteers	130,000

Aims, activities

BTCV is one of the UK's largest conservation organisations. The charity was set up in 1959 with the aim of 'developing volunteering as a means to achieve an environmental goal'. A bigger picture has emerged where conservation volunteering has become a focus for the achievement of wider social goals – tackling social exclusion and encouraging personal development and lifelong learning.

The charity promotes local conservation schemes involving volunteers of all ages and abilities (though a high proportion of them are young) from within the communities concerned. An increasing number come to the work via government schemes for people who have low employability or may be otherwise at risk of social exclusion. BTCV provides training to enable people to gain vocational qualifications which can improve their employability, more than 25,000 people during 2000/01.

BTCV has no land itself, so most of its projects are run with the cooperation of local landowners (such as local authorities and schools) and community groups. Volunteers throughout the UK can take part in organised activities in urban and rural environments during the week and at weekends. These include maintaining footpaths, building bridges, creating recycling schemes, rebuilding dry stone walls, planting trees and developing community gardens.

The charity also provides conservation holidays, offers advice and consultancy to its local partners, and sells a wide range of handbooks, plants and equipment. It has an extensive Supporters' Club with branches in many parts of the country.

Other activities in 2001 included:

- BTCV Green Gym projects, giving people the chance to improve their fitness by taking part in energetic conservation activities;

- the launch of the Lottery-funded People's Places Award Scheme to give grants to 1,000 socially excluded communities in England to develop and improve local green spaces;

- the conclusion of the Millennium Tree Campaign In Northern Ireland, after more than 1.5 million trees had been planted.

In 2000/01 the charity organised 333,000 work days for its volunteers.

BTCV also runs a major training and organisational development programme for environmental charities in Central and Eastern Europe, and is a leader in the new global Conservation Volunteers Alliance.

BTCV is an example of one kind of charity, which the present government is encouraging, that offers individuals 'the opportunity to become knowledgeable, active and responsible citizens who effect positive environmental change while improving both themselves and their community'. BTCV continues to benefit from a range of new funding programmes designed to reduce social exclusion, and as a result is now growing even faster than in its previous history.

Volunteers

All the charity's work is based on the activities of volunteers, with its own staff providing the management and training required.

Funding, administration

The charity's funding comes largely from statutory sources. Its overall programmes are funded both by central government (providing £3 million in 2000/01) and by local and other statutory authorities (£3.3 million), as well as by companies and charitable trusts (£3 million), and by donations and membership subscriptions (£3.3 million). Individual conservation projects were supported from a variety of sources to the value of £2.7 million.

There has been a rapid increase of staff to run the new programmes described above. The charity has 150 offices across the UK.

The charity adds ...

BTCV is a vibrant organisation that offers opportunities for everyone, regardless of age or experience, to take part in hands-on practical conservation activities in urban and rural areas, and learn how to transform their environment in the UK and, through the holiday programme, across the world.

The information assessed

There are an excellent annual report and accounts and annual review, as well as a clear and specific strategic plan for 2001–04. There is also a fine tri-annual magazine, *Conserver*, and a good website and supporting literature.

Contact

36 St Mary's Street
Wallingford
Oxfordshire
OX10 0EU
Tel 01491 821600
Website www.btcv.org
Chair Sue Hilder
Tom Flood, Chief Executive

CAFOD

Catholic Agency for Overseas Development

Income	£26,647,000 (2000/01)
Donated income	£20,642,000
Fundraising costs	£2,183,000
Statutory income	£2,795,000
Top salary	£50,000–£60,000
Paid staff	152
Volunteers	2,000

Aims, activities

CAFOD is the English and Welsh arm of Caritas, a worldwide network of Catholic relief and development organisations (website: www.caritas.org). CAFOD funds over 1,000 programmes worldwide, working through the relief and development structures of the Catholic church at national, regional and local level. The process is one of grantmaking, and applications are first scrutinised by CAFOD staff and then submitted to regional or specialist committees. Approval of grants for more than £100,000 is reserved to the CAFOD board. The list of such grants long required by the Charity Commission is not available, so it is impossible to identify the specific organisations that receive the grants.

Programmes include:

- education and skills training;
- healthcare;
- safe water;
- agricultural and small business development;
- emergency help in wars and disasters;
- analysis of the causes of under-development;
- campaigns on behalf of the world's poor;
- education in the UK to raise awareness of the causes of third world poverty and to promote change.

'CAFOD is a partnership organisation. We don't just give money to poor communities and walk away, or just support projects in emergencies. We work hand in hand with local people to help them to respond to their own real needs.' As CAFOD only has 150 staff, most of them in the UK, this is presumably the metaphorical hand holding of a benevolent but generally distant funder.

About 1,000 projects are supported at any one time, making the average annual grant about £30,000. As many projects doubtless need long-term support, the total cost per project will be much larger. The overseas expenditure is categorised as follows in the 2000/01 report:

- Africa £8.9 million (£5.4 million development, £3.5 million emergency);
- Latin America £3.8 million (£3.1 million development, £0.7 million emergency);
- Asia £3.1 million (£1.4 million development, £1.7 million emergency);

- East Europe £2.5 million (£0.6 million development, £1.9 million emergency).

At an individual country level the largest programmes were in Mozambique, Democratic Republic of Congo (Zaire), Guinea and Sudan.

CAFOD also runs an educational programme in the UK, aimed at creating a greater awareness here of the causes of world poverty and injustice. It has an impressive and extensive range of thoughtful reports and publications on development issues.

HIV/AIDS is a major field of work for this as for other development agencies. A Catholic agency, CAFOD sees condoms in this context as primarily a means of preventing disease, rather than as contraceptive devices. In 2000 CAFOD was welcoming an increased willingness by African leaders to confront the AIDS issue in public.

Volunteers

Volunteers work for CAFOD:

- in parishes as 'Parish Contacts' and 'Challenge 2000 Contacts';
- in schools, helping children and young people understand the complex issues surrounding CAFOD's work;
- in campaign work, raising important issues such as debt and fair trade, and moving them up the political agenda;
- as media contacts, ensuring that local events and international issues get an airing through regional press and radio stations.

There is also a limited number of volunteering opportunities in the Brixton, London office.

Funding, administration

The accounts for the 18 months to March 2001 include admirably detailed information about the charity's income. The main sources of voluntary income were, at annual rates:

- collections in Catholic parishes £5.8 million;
- individual donations £7.1 million;
- other organisations (trusts, religious communities, schools, companies) £3 million;
- legacies £2.9 million.

The charity reported an exceptionally successful year in fundraising terms in 1999 (the most recent year for which a narrative report was available when this entry was written):

'In 1999 more donations than ever before were received from CAFOD individual supporters, parishes, schools and Catholic organisations. Thanks to this incredible support from the Catholic community, overall voluntary income went up by 47 per cent – from £13.58 million to £20 million. Development income increased by 11 per cent from £11 million to £12.2 million, and emergency by 204 per cent from £2.6 million to £7.8 million.'

Almost every parish in England and Wales supported a Fast Day collection and over a third signed up to 'Challenge 2000', a scheme which enables parishes to support specific types of work each year. Overall, parish income rose by 54 per cent, with an increase of 13 per cent for development work and 172 per cent for emergencies. Many parishes gave their support to CAFOD's Millennium Gift Aid initiative, while legacy income grew by 11%.

'New fundraising programmes with schools led to an increase in their donations for development by 18 per cent, while donations from schools for emergencies rose by a 249 per cent.'

The total voluntary income of £31 million over 18 months was achieved at a fundraising cost of £3.3 million, giving a cost ratio of a low 11p in the pound, or 11%. This was up from the exceptionally low 8% of the previous year, when there had been a higher proportion of money for emergency appeals.

The information assessed

The annual report and accounts for 2001 cover an 18-month period. The figures at the top of this entry have been annualised pro rata, to make comparisons easier.

Contact

Romero Close
Stockwell Road
London
SW9 9TW
Tel 020 7733 7900
Website www.cafod.org.uk
Chair Right Reverend John Rawsthorne
Julian Filochowski, Director

Cambridge University

As with *Oxford University*, this university as a whole is a fundraising charity, and so are each of its colleges. They are exempt from registration at the Charity Commission but their accounts are readily made available to the public in two convenient volumes. In this case help with their interpretation was also willingly offered. Those for the year 1999/00 have been examined and this established that the university was, collectively, one of the largest recipients of public donations and legacies in the country (and larger than Oxford in that year).

The accounts are, by law, presented according to unusual rules, and individual colleges have their own choice of headings even within these rules. The figures below are a total of all the covenants, subscriptions, donations, development trust receipts, bequests, gifts, legacies and benefactions that could be found. Where it was not obvious whether the money was in fact a charitable gift, we have tried to check whether or not it should be included. Examples were King's College's income from 'Images, Idolatry and Iconoclasm' – as it turned out, from an exhibition of that title – and the dubious-sounding income that colleges have from property at rack rent. These were easy to exclude, but 'other income' was less so.

Much of the fundraising is conducted through periodic appeals, so the list below may be greatly influenced by whether or not a particular college had an appeal running in the year in question. However, the total should represent a reasonable annual average.

Cambridge University	£34,760,000
Colleges of the university:	
Magdalene College	£4,602,544
King's College	£3,574,273
Clare College	£2,312,614
Trinity Hall	£1,884,884
Churchill College	£1,784,479
Gonville & Caius College	£1,507,158
Newnham College	£1,467,604
Downing College	£1,255,732
Corpus Christi College	£971,775
Pembroke College	£962,765
St John's College	£752,698
New Hall	£567,359
St Catherine's College	£513,059
Fitzwilliam College	£491,955

Cavendish College	£462,660
Christ's College	£440,781
Queen's College	£392,941
Sidney Sussex College	£363,629
Girton College	£335,217
Trinity College	£250,293
Robinson College	£190,934
Wolfson College	£189,346
Emmanuel College	£142,778
Hughes Hall	£59,015
Darwin College	£39,087
Selwyn College	£38,132
Peterhouse College	£16,085
St Edmund's College	£13,254
Clare Hall	£10,001
Colleges total	*£25,593,052*
Grand total	**£60,353,052**

In 2001 a total of 151 young people from around the world began the new academic year at Cambridge as a result of one of the largest donations to a UK charity of recent times: $210 million from the Bill & Melinda Gates Foundation. The scheme will run in perpetuity and enable gifted graduate students to come to study at Cambridge from every country in the world outside the UK. For Cambridge, the benefaction is the largest single sum that the University has ever received.

The accounts of the individual colleges at Cambridge and Oxford universities are not just difficult to understand; they also omit, as present law permits, details of their capital funds. It is not therefore possible to get the usual overall view of the finances of these organisations. In this they are different from other charities exempt from registration with the Charity Commission (for example, the *National Gallery*) which generally have full and excellent annual reports and accounts. In November 2001 it was reported that this anomalous position was being examined by the review of charity law then being undertaken by the Cabinet Office.

Camphill Village Trust

Communities for adults, some with special needs

Income	£16,890,000 (2000/01)
Donated income	£5,212,000
Fundraising costs	£812,000
Statutory income	£6,751,000
Top salary	not disclosed
Paid staff	
Full time	60
Part time	59
Volunteers	
Operational	362

Aims, activities

There are 11 Camphill communities across the UK offering a home, work and the other necessities for a decent life to over 500 people with social or learning disabilities, including enabling people to move on to independent living if they wish, and regardless of disability or religious or racial background. In Camphill's most unusual feature, the communities are also homes to about the same number of other residents without disabilities, 'who see this kind of work not as a job in the usual sense, but as a way of life'.

In this sense the communities are 'staffed' by 222 co-workers and 116 helpers, all unpaid. These volunteers live as part of the community concerned on exactly the same basis as other residents; they are categorised by the Inland Revenue as 'carrying out a vocation' rather than as employees. Though there are 30 office and management staff, and 83 people in maintenance and similar posts, Camphill, which is based on Christian ideals as articulated by Robert Steiner (a philosopher who believed in each person's 'spiritual uniqueness ... regardless of disability or religious or racial background'), is probably the most 'voluntary' of all the voluntary organisations described in this book.

The communities share three guiding principles:

- an active cultural life that will enable all members to realise their potential;

- a community life in which the recognition of the special qualities of each individual forms the basis of daily life;

- an economic life in which there is a separation of work and money, and people's financial needs are met on an individual basis irrespective of the work done.

Each community also has its own character and special features. These include woodland and forestry work at Botton Village in North Yorkshire; organic beef and its butchery at Larchfield in Cleveland; very close involvement with the surrounding community in St Albans; and the garden and orchard team at Oaklands Park in Gloucestershire. Two of the communities are slightly different: Delrow in Watford is a college and rehabilitation centre and Taurus Crafts in Lydney, Gloucestershire is a centre for vocational training and work experience. However, both are also full Camphill communities in themselves.

Volunteers

Apart from the co-workers living in the communities, each also has a local management committee whose members come not just from Camphill but also from the wider community. There are further 'friends' groups that, besides other forms of voluntary help, also raise money for the community concerned.

Funding, administration

The largest single source of income for the communities is statutory money – £6.8 million in 2000/01, mainly fees from local authorities and social security, and from Supported Employment grants (there was also £421,000 in privately paid fees). A surplus of more than £400,000 was generated from sales of £2 million of workshop and other products, with a slightly smaller surplus arising from farm and land production.

Income in 2000/01 included £3.1 million in donations and an exceptional £1.9 million from legacies. Total voluntary income of £5.2 million was achieved at a fundraising cost of £812,000, giving a cost ratio of 16p in the pound, or 16%, down from the 22% of the previous year when there had been a rather low legacy income.

The information assessed

The good annual report and accounts and annual review would be better still with an overview of the group as a whole. There is an excellent introductory booklet.

Contact

19 South Road
Stourbridge
West Midlands
DY8 3YA
Tel 01384 372122
Chair Anthony Brown
Mrs Eva Heathcock, Honorary Secretary

Cancer Research Campaign

Income	£80,585,000 (1999/00)
Donated income	£67,423,000
Fundraising costs	£12,500,000
Statutory income	£0
Top salary	£90,000–£100,000
Paid staff	874
Volunteers	13,000

Aims, activities

This is a very large but relatively straightforward charity. It raises money from the public and then distributes it in research grants to universities and hospital research institutes for a range of long- and short-term programmes. It is the leading funder of such work in the UK. It is in the process of merging with the *Imperial Cancer Research Campaign*. Imperial Cancer has said that the reason for the proposed merger is the increasing cost of investing in new technologies and in world-class scientists: 'Single organisations may not always be able to fund this type of science by themselves.' This ties in with an interesting remark in CRC's 2000 annual review, in the context of progress in decoding the human genome, that 'for the first time in many years the bottleneck [in cancer research] is not technology but money'.

CRC, founded in 1923, seeks to understand cancer's causes, find ways to prevent it, develop new treatments – and then make sure that the best new treatments reach patients in the clinic in the UK and all over the world. It supports a comprehensive programme of research in institutes, hospitals, universities and medical schools throughout Britain and Northern Ireland. 'We are the European leaders in anti-cancer drug development and our extensive and effective programme of research ensures that new treatments reach patients as quickly as possible.

'The Cancer Research Campaign is determined to improve treatment for cancer patients. Over a quarter of the ... budget goes on research into the early detection of cancer, improving treatment and introducing new therapies into the clinic.'

The campaign has, in partnership with the NHS, established a number of Academic Medical Oncology Units and Clinical Trials Units around the UK. The campaign pioneered the establishment of this type of unit where clinical and laboratory research come together to provide patients with the best possible care. The doctors and staff working in these units both provide treatment and are also involved in research which will lead to new and better treatments in the future.

The charity also has extensive information services, for both professionals and the public.

In 2001 the government announced that it was to set up a National Cancer Research Institute, of which the newly merged charity will be a founder member.

Volunteers

The main roles for the 13,000 volunteers lie in the various fundraising activities and in the charity's shops. A volunteer development manager has been recruited to help develop the relationship between staff members and volunteer supporters.

CRC can also offer non-paid work placement opportunities for students and young people. These provide an opportunity to gain first-hand experience of the workplace. It also enables the campaign to raise awareness of the importance of its work among the young.

Funding, administration

The charity's income is led by legacies. These totalled £47 million in 1999/00, up from £40 million in the previous year. Donations, at £20 million, were unchanged, but collectively this was the most successful year ever for fundraising. The total voluntary income was achieved at a fundraising cost of £12.5 million, giving a cost ratio of 19p in the pound, slightly down from the 20p of the previous year but still a little higher than the 17p average for the three years to 1999.

The information assessed

The excellent annual report and accounts and annual review are backed by a website with fine information on cancer, but, as noted above, weaker on the charity itself.

Contact

Cambridge House
6–10 Cambridge Terrace
London
NW1 4JL
Tel 020 7224 1333
Website www.crc.org.uk
Chair F E Worsley
Professor Gordon McVie, Director General

Cancer Research UK

Aims, activities

This is the new charity resulting from the merger of the *Cancer Research Campaign* and the *Imperial Cancer Research Fund* (both of which have their own entries in this book) and was due to come into formal existence from February 2000.

The new organisation is expected to spend £130 million a year on cancer research. Both the chair, former health minister Helene Hayman, and the Chief Executive Andrew Miller are new appointments

Contact

PO Box 123, Lincoln's Inn Fields
London
WC2A 3PX
Tel 020 7269 3669
Chair Helene Hayman
Professor Andrew Miller, Chief Executive

Care International UK

Overseas development

Income	£36,071,000 (2000/01)
Donated income	£4,559,000
Fundraising costs	£1,484,000
Statutory income	£31,391,000
Top salary	£60,000–£70,000
Paid staff	
Full time	53
Part time	5
Volunteers	3

Aims, activities

'Care International is one of the world's largest independent relief and development organisations. Non-political and non-sectarian, it operates in over 60 countries in Asia, Africa, Latin America, the Middle East and Europe.' Each of the international offices, such as that of Care International UK, 'is a charity or non-profit making organisation in its own right, contributing to and helping manage over 500 projects around the world'. Care International UK concentrates on work in the cities of the developing world, especially in Asia, Africa and Latin America, and on emergency response.

The charity seeks to be 'the partner of choice' within a worldwide movement dedicated to ending poverty. The partnerships are primarily those with institutional funders, such as the Department for International Development, and support of this kind has been increasing. At a local level, the charity transfers most of the money to be spent to local Care offices, but it continues to be responsible to the original donors for the use of that money.

The organisation was first formed in the USA in 1946 as the Co-operative for American Remittances to Europe, sending food aid and basic supplies in the form of 'Care packages'. In the 1950s and 1960s the focus shifted from Europe to the problems of the developing world. 'Its staff is truly international. Out of more than 10,000 employees, over 9,000 are nationals of the countries in which we work.' It is one of the largest overseas development charities in the UK that is (judging from the information available) wholly secular.

Since 1985 Care International UK has been an independent, autonomous, registered British charity, which runs its own projects and leads some of the work of Care International, including the Care Urban Advocacy Strategy. The charity has a particular interest in trying to improve living conditions and expand economic opportunities in poor communities in the cities of the developing world. 'Urban projects aim to deliver essential services and to support civil society by building the organisational capacity of communities, non-governmental organisations and municipalities.' One specific method noted is the management of a grant-making programme in Lusaka, Zambia, where neighbourhood organisations are invited to apply for grants to make improvements to local services.

From its beginning the charity has developed expertise in directing emergency supplies quickly and efficiently to vulnerable people and this remains an important area of work. The year 2000/01 was notable for the need for major disaster relief work following three earthquakes, in El Salvador, Peru and then Gujarat in India.

The expenditure figures in the 2000/01 accounts for the main geographical areas of activity show, among other things, an unusual emphasis on work in Eastern Europe:

- Asia/CIS £11.3 million;
- Southern Africa £7.2 million;
- East Africa £4.6 million;
- Eastern Europe £4.4 million.

The charity has only about 50 permanent staff; most of the actual charitable activities are carried out by or through local staff employed by Care International local offices. The accounts show that the work is divided more or less equally between emergency relief and longer-term development projects.

Volunteers

This seems to be primarily a professionally staffed organisation, at least in the UK, though the charity has had input from permanent and temporary volunteers.

Funding, administration

The charity in the UK has been growing very rapidly in financial terms. In 1996/97 its income was £20 million, so the £36 million received in 2000/01 represents a growth of 80% in four years.

Most funding is from government, with over 80% of income in 2000/01 coming from statutory sources, primarily the Department for International Development (£20 million) and the European Union.

Direct donations from individuals play a modest part in the overall finances, accounting for £4 million (over £1 million of it in 2000/01 collected from the public by the appeals of the Disasters Emergency Committee). The total figure for donations of £4.5 million, given above, also includes grants from trusts and the Lottery's Community Fund, but excludes £2 million worth of gifts 'in kind' from institutions.

This voluntary income was raised at a cost of £1.5 million, representing a ratio of 33p in the pound, but only 23p in the pound if gifts in kind are taken into account. There were administration costs of £629,000. These have been rising, from £584,000 and £456,000 in the two previous years.

The charity adds ...

2000/2001 has seen the introduction of Care International's new Vision and Mission, and of a new logo, replacing the square 'Care package' with a friendly 'circle of hands', to reflect the change in approach from delivering emergency relief supplies to working with a range of partners to end poverty.

The information assessed

There are good annual report and accounts and separate annual review. There is a good website too.

Contact

10–13 Rushworth Street
London
SE1 0RB
Tel 020 7934 9334
Website www.careinternational.org.uk
Chair Ian McIsaac
William Day, Chief Executive

Cats Protection League

Income	£16,670,000 (2000)
Donated income	£15,509,000
Fundraising costs	£2,628,000
Statutory income	£0
Top salary	£70,000–£80,000
Paid staff	218
Volunteers	8,000

Aims, activities

This charity rescues stray cats and kittens, rehabilitates and re-homes them where possible, has them neutered if they are not needed for breeding, and generally encourages their good care by the public.

Most of the work is carried out by the nearly 250 branches of the charity. In

addition there are 29 purpose-built cat shelters. The league also provides vouchers to enable owners in financial need to have their cats neutered by participating veterinary surgeons, and, where it can, neuters feral cat colonies at its own expense, 'provided arrangements can be made for their continuing welfare' – an activity that sounds dauntingly difficult in almost all its aspects.

Members receive a journal, *The Cat*, while younger members receive their own magazine, naturally called *The Kitten*.

In 2000 the charity helped more than 168,000 cats and kittens, of which over 59,000 were successfully re-homed and 120,000 neutered. It spent £8.6 million on rescue and re-homing in the directly managed shelters and in the branches. A further £1.8 million was distributed in neutering vouchers and £0.6 million on information and education.

This description of the work of a local branch comes from the website of the Callington, Cornwall branch:

'The Callington Branch is run purely by a small group of volunteers working to rescue and rehome stray and abandoned cats and kittens in South East Cornwall – in the Looe, Liskeard, Callington, Gunnislake and Saltash areas. All the CP cats are looked after by dedicated fosterers in CP pens; we do not have a shelter.

'We take in and rehome stray, abandoned and unwanted cats and kittens, which are cared for by our group of volunteer fosterers who have specially built cat pens in their back gardens. Unfortunately, there are always more cats needing our help than we have facilities to take in, so we have to operate a waiting list system.

'If you live in the Callington Branch area and would like to adopt a cat from us, or if you need to put a cat on our waiting list, then contact us.'

Volunteers

The branches of the charity, where most of its activities take place, are wholly voluntary. 'Without a doubt the lifeblood of Cats Protection is our army of unpaid volunteers, who between them carry out 90% of our rescue work. A survey in 1994 showed that there are an estimated 5,000 unpaid volunteers within our Branches. They spend over 6 million hours annually caring for cats and handle over 77,000 telephone calls from the public a month – all without receiving a penny as payment. Our 13 Shelters each have a small team of paid staff and our Headquarters in Horsham employs a small number of administrative staff to keep the charity running. An extraordinary workforce with a common cause – a passion for cats!'

Funding, administration

The main sources of the charity's income in 2000 were as follows:

- legacies £9.7 million (up from £8.3 million in 1999);
- subscriptions and donations £3.8 million (up from £3.3 million);
- voluntary fundraising £2 million (unchanged).

The total voluntary income of £15.5 million was achieved at a fundraising cost of £2.6 million, giving a cost ratio of 17p in the pound, up from the low 14p in the pound of the previous year and from the 12p average of the three years to 1998. The increase was due to fundraising expenditure increasing even faster than income, having more than

doubled from the £1.2 million average in those three years. However, income has also risen and the full benefits of this increased investment may not yet have arrived.

The information assessed

The excellent annual report and accounts and annual review are backed by an admirable website (and many local branches have their own sites).

Contact

17 Kings Road
Horsham
West Sussex
RH13 5PN
Tel 01403 221900
Website www.cats.org.uk
Chair Miss L J Reeves
Derek Conway, Chief Executive

Centrepoint
Help for young homeless people, mainly in London

Income	£10,799,000 (2000/01)
Donated income	£3,381,000
Fundraising costs	£659,000
Statutory income	£4,972,000
Top salary	£60,000–£70,000
Paid staff	225

Aims, activities

The work of the charity in the UK is described well in its annual report for 2000/01:

'Centrepoint works to ensure that no young person is at risk because they do not have a safe place in which to stay.

'The charity provides a variety of accommodation

- night shelters, for emergency short stay accommodation
- medium stay supportive hostel schemes
- more independent long stay flats and bed sits

'Increasingly, we are looking to combine the provision of accommodation with access to training and skills development opportunities for young people, and where possible help them find work or further education opportunities.

'Centrepoint also seeks to act as an advocate on behalf of the young people it seeks to serve and to that end carries out a range of research projects into the causes of homelessness and provides information to influence and inform government policy.

'Our strategy for the next five years is to become a holistic service provider for poor and disadvantaged young people, because we know from what our young people tell us that just providing a bed, a roof, for the night isn't sufficient.

'A great deal of our work – especially that with the government – focuses on the prevention of homelessness. But while there are still young people becoming homeless, we have to make sure there is the support they need to get back on their feet for good.'

The charity has doubled in size in the five years up to 2001. In that year the energetic director during this period, Victor Adebowale (now Lord Adebowale) moved on to Turning Point, a major charity in the field of alcohol and drug abuse.

Centrepoint began working with homeless young people in London 30 years ago but, after requests for information and advice from local authorities and voluntary agencies, it now has offices across the country, from Cumbria to Devon and from Brighton to Durham. The aim of the work is to develop strategies to enable local agencies to work together to provide housing and support for disadvantaged young people. Examples in 2001 included studies of the youth homelessness situation in Worcestershire and Yorkshire.

Volunteers

The work of the charity appears to carried out on a wholly professional basis.

Funding, administration

Statutory grants, fees and contracts account for about three quarters of the charity's income, almost all of it to be spent only on particular specified services.

Partly because of this, 'the trustees agreed to invest significant sums in fundraising activity in 2000/01, as ... the charity needed to build a larger core of unrestricted income'. So far this has been strikingly successful, with voluntary income of £3.4 million showing a rise of 35% over the previous year, while fundraising costs, at £659,000, still only represent 19p in the pound.

The charity has set a medium-term target of having reserves equal to two months' operating costs. At the end of the year they stood at the equivalent of nine days of such costs.

The charity adds ...

Centrepoint launched a major campaign in October 2001 entitled 'Who Wants to Be ... ?' spearheaded by one of the charity's ambassadors, Chris Tarrant. For further details, log on to www.centrepointchallenge.org.uk

The information assessed

There are an excellent annual report and accounts and annual review, a good website, and a mass of other materials.

Contact

Neil House
7 Whitechapel Road
London
E1 1DU
Tel 020 7426 5300
Website www.centrepoint.org.uk
Chair Brian Pomeroy
Anthony Lawton, Chief Executive

Charities Aid Foundation (CAF)

Providing services to charitable donors and to other charities

Income	£222,867,000 (2000/01, but see below)
Donated income	£199,919,000
Fundraising costs	£1,833,000
Statutory income	£0
Top salary	£90,000–£100,000
Paid staff	727

Aims, activities

The Charities Aid Foundation (CAF), itself a charity, is primarily a provider of services to donors and other charities. The spectacular income figure given above mostly represents the funds of donors deposited with CAF before being passed on to the recipient charities of the donors' choice.

The main services for donors include the flexible Charity Account and, for those able to give larger amounts, the Charitable Trust. These enable donors to support a variety of charities of their choice, in a tax-effective way, with a single tax reclaim each year.

● The Charity Account. Taxpayers can make a single donation into such an account and CAF will reclaim the basic rate of tax and add it to the balance. The donor can then use their personalised CharityCard to make separate donations to the charities of their choice.

There are around 70,000 Charity Account holders, donating £61 million each year to a huge variety of charities. This figure includes £14.5 million in tax reclaimed by CAF.

● CAF Charitable Trust. Major donors can set up these personal trusts, where CAF will manage the investments involved and make onward payments to charity, in accordance with the wishes of the trust-holder or policy of the trust. This avoids the need to establish a free-standing charitable trust, while giving the donor the same freedom of action.

In all, 239 new Charitable Trusts were opened in 2000/01, bringing their total to £163 million.

Both Charity Account and Charitable Trust clients can make use of these services in taking advantage of the new and strikingly generous tax reliefs available for those donating shares to the charity of their choice.

CAF also runs the country's largest payroll giving scheme – Give As You Earn. Through this scheme, employees can make tax-free donations direct from their pay, to the charities of their choice. Give As You Earn donations, boosted by a 10% bonus from government, rose by 35% between 1999/00 and 2000/01 to £37 million a year.

Many charities also use CAF's investment funds, its CafCash banking services, and its range of administration services. CAF also offers a legacy account service and can enable people to lend money for charitable purposes. Generally, CAF should be an early port of call for anyone considering making the financial support of charities a significant part of their lives.

CAF is a modest grantmaker in its own right, using the surpluses earned from its financial services to award grants, usually to help small charities to develop their financial resources. It also provides funding for the National Council of Voluntary Organisations, the original parent of this charity, which receives a small 'royalty' from many of CAF's services.

On a wider scale, CAF has become a major force in arguing the case for tax reliefs for charities and other beneficial developments for the UK voluntary sector generally. Overseas it is active in helping the development of the voluntary sector in areas such as Eastern Europe, Africa and India.

The information assessed

The annual report and accounts, supporting literature and website are all excellent. The charity also hosts a number of websites, including Charitynet and All About Giving.

Contact

Kings Hill
West Malling
Kent
ME19 4TA
Tel 01732 520000
Website www.CAFonline.org
Chair Sir Brian Jenkins
Michael Brophy, Chief Executive

ChildLine

Telephone helpline for children in distress

Income	£6,973,000 (1999/00)
Donated income	£5,705,000
Fundraising costs	£1,959,000
Statutory income	£988,000
Top salary	£50,000–£60,000
Paid staff	208
Volunteers	950

Aims, activities

This relatively new charity has shown that there is an astonishing level of need among distressed children for someone to talk to – a need which the charity is only partly able to meet.

ChildLine is the volunteer-based, UK-wide, 24-hour telephone helpline for children in danger – **0800 1111**. In 1999/00, 3,500 calls a day were taken. A further 11,500 calls each day went unanswered because the charity did not have the funds to answer them. A total of 129,000 children contacted the charity for the first time, bringing to over a million the number helped since ChildLine was set up in 1986.

The main reasons that children call are:

- they have been physically or sexually abused – or both (19%);

- they are being bullied (18%);
- their families have serious problems, such as domestic violence or parents divorcing (15%);
- they are worried about other children being ill-treated (9%).

Calls are confidential, but if a counsellor believes that a child's life is in present danger, every effort is made to get immediate help to them. During the year, this situation arose for over 1,600 children.

The calls are taken by more than 900 trained volunteer counsellors, most of them at the charity's call centre in London but increasingly, and especially during the busy after-school hours, at the growing network of regional centres – where a local voice may be reassuring.

A further 50,000 calls a year are dealt with at switchboard level, and not included in the figures above. Calls are free; otherwise details would be liable to appear on family telephone bills. The spread of mobile phones is striking; about a third of calls are now made in this way. In a sad irony, the big jump in such calls came immediately after Christmas.

The helpline is now supplemented by a programme to develop help for children in their schools, often through their own peer-to-peer self-help schemes.

To be able to respond to all calls from distressed children, the charity's income would need to roughly treble.

Volunteers

Recruiting and training volunteer counsellors is a major activity for the charity, with the process excellently described in the 1999/00 annual review. The charity estimates the value of their actual counselling time at over £800,000.

There are also local Friends of ChildLine groups, which raised over £360,000 during the year.

Funding, administration

In 1999/00 overall income was up by 18% for the year. The annual review says that 90% of the charity's income is from the general public, charitable trusts and business. By the standard assumptions used in this book, donations, including legacies, made up £5.7 million or 80% of the total income of £7 million.

Fundraising costs associated with these donations came to £2 million, up by 8% from the previous year and giving a high cost ratio of 35p in the pound, or 35% (down from 36% in the previous year). However, the reported costs appear to include those of raising 'public awareness', which would cover the necessary charitable expenditure of publicising the services to and for children. These would not normally be regarded as fundraising expenditures, and so the cost ratio reported here may look higher than it really is in comparison with other charities in this book.

The charity pays telephone companies for the calls it receives, but its London premises, to an estimated value of £95,000 a year, are provided free by BT. The accounts do not break down the charitable expenditure into the costs of running the service (such as finding, training, housing and equipping the volunteer counsellors), those of publicising the service so that children know where to ring, and those of paying for the telephone calls.

The charity adds ...

Under new Chief Executive Carole Easton, ChildLine is soon to open its 10th counselling centre in Birmingham – ChildLine West Midlands, made possible by Barclays plc. In October 2001 ChildLine celebrates its 15th birthday and has now helped more than 1,157,000 children and young people.

The information assessed

The excellent annual review and report and accounts are moving as well as informative and comprehensive. There is a clear, simple and lively website, as well as extensive and high-quality supporting materials.

Contact

Studd Street
London
N1 0QW
Tel 020 7239 1000
Website www.childline.org.uk
Chair Esther Rantzen
Carole Easton, Chief Executive

Children with Leukaemia

Income	£4,694,000 (2000)
Donated income	£4,610,000
Fundraising costs	£1,786,000
Statutory income	£0
Top salary	£25,000
Paid staff	
Full time	5
Part time	2

Aims, activities

This charity was set up in 1988 in memory of Paul O'Gorman who died of leukaemia in 1987, and his sister Jean, who died of breast cancer in the same year. The O'Gorman family is still closely involved with the charity, which has set up and maintains Paul O'Gorman Childhood Leukaemia Centres at six English hospitals. Each concentrates on its own particular aspect of research and treatment, such as graft engineering at the Royal Free in London or chemotherapy in Newcastle.

A new Paul O'Gorman building houses the Bristol Royal Hospital for Children.

The charity is 'dedicating increased resources to our welfare services for leukaemic children and their families', which includes a Recuperation Centre in Sussex, and the purchase of a Parent's Accommodation Building at the Royal Free Hospital in London (completed in 2001).

The organisation is described in its literature as 'the national charity dedicated to the research and treatment of childhood leukaemia and to the welfare of leukaemic children'. Some of its activities, though, overlap with those of other charities which have their own entries in this book.

Volunteers

Much of the charity's fundraising is in the form of direct mail campaigns and events, which are organised with the help of volunteers.

Funding, administration

No paid staff are identified in the annual report, as the charity is managed directly by the trustees (who include Mr and Mrs O'Gorman) and volunteers (who do not receive any payment).

The charity is funded almost entirely from donations and appeals, which totalled £4.5 million in 2000. Many of them are connected to celebrities or events, such as the Chris Tarrant Christmas Appeal (raising £1.9 million) and the Paul O'Gorman Banquet and Ball (£306,000).

Fundraising costs of £1.8 million, much of which was for the charity's direct mail programme, represented a high 39p for each pound donated, but this was a reduction from the 44p in the pound of the previous year, thanks to an increased level of donations.

The information assessed

The generally adequate annual report and accounts are strong on the activities of the charity, but weak on how it is organised and managed. There is a straightforward website.

Contact

51 Great Ormond Street
London
WC1N 3JQ
Tel 020 7404 0808
Website www.leukaemia.org
Chair Eddie O'Gorman
not disclosed

Children's Aid Direct

Overseas development

Income	£11,240,000 (1999/00)
Donated income	£2,391,000
Fundraising costs	£994,000
Statutory income	£8,110,000
Top salary	£50,000–£60,000
Paid staff	
Full time	575
Part time	9
Volunteers	
Operational	12
Fundraising	38

Aims, activities

This relatively new charity works to improve the lives of children and their parents who are affected by conflict, disaster or poverty. Born in 1990 out of the need to respond to conflicts in the Balkans, Children's Aid Direct works with children and their communities to help support them as they move from crisis to recovery. 'Needs for food, shelter, healthcare, education, and advice are identified and support is planned and evaluated to ensure that it is appropriate and cost-effective.'

The charity has recently given up the activity for which it was perhaps best known: the collection and distribution of gifts in kind, most recently for Kosovo. The decision was taken partly because of the unsustainably high costs of managing and delivering such programmes, and partly because 'the call for donated aid has itself dramatically reduced as our programmes have moved on from emergency work to community rehabilitation'.

In 2001 the main areas of work were:

● Kosovo, Albanian and Macedonia;

● Tajikistan and Azerbaijan;

● North Korea;

● Burundi;

● Liberia and Sierra Leone.

As an example, in Burundi the charity is supporting 10 health centres and 11 supplementary feeding centres, training health staff, distributing livestock, training women in agriculture, and tracing the families of hundreds of children who have been separated from their families. On a smaller scale, in September 2001 the charity launched a modest appeal in the Reading area of Berkshire to raise £25,000 to feed starving children in the drought-stricken Khatlon area of Tajikistan. The charity's own local nutritional team will buy food in the region and screen the children so that those in greatest need will receive some supplements to their diet.

The charity is perhaps 'the professionals' development charity'; it notes that one reason it may be able to work in North Korea is 'our policy of a low profile outside the country'. Unlike many development agencies, it seems, with its nearly 500 locally employed staff, to be much more of an operational agency than a maker of grants to other organisations.

Volunteers

This is a professional agency, relying on volunteers primarily for its fundraising, especially for the organisation of its spectacular programme of outdoor sponsored events.

Funding, administration

The charity's main funding comes from governments. This accounted for £8.1 million of the total £11.2 million cash income in 1999/00, led by £4.2 million from the European Union, £1.6 million from the UN and £0.5 million each from the US government and from the UK's Department for International Development.

The voluntary income of £2.4 million was down from £2.6 million in the previous year. It was achieved at a fundraising cost of £994,000, a cost ratio of a very high 42p in the pound. The fundraising is centred on a programme of sponsored 'adventure' events, mostly involving mountain climbing – in a variety of areas, from Snowdonia to the Skeleton Coast of Namibia. This kind of fundraising is often relatively expensive, as the donors are effectively paying for an exciting holiday as well as giving a gift to the charity.

Children's Aid Direct had a difficult financial year in 1999/00. The problems are set out in the annual

report in an exemplary way. Active steps have been taken to reduce cost levels. In addition to the ending of the donated goods programme referred to above, the warehouse was closed, the office moved to Reading, and UK-based staff were reduced by 7%. This outcome was disappointing, as the previous annual report had noted high expectations for the charity's new fundraising team.

The information assessed

The excellent annual report and accounts and annual review are backed by a website with good information about the charity and its work – and a most attractive section for potential sponsored mountain climbers and those going on other expeditions.

Contact

Crown House
6–8 Crown Street
Reading
Berks
RG1 2SE
Tel 0118 958 4000
Website www.cad.org.uk
Chair Sir Martin Edwards
Nick Thompson, Executive Director

Children's Society
Child welfare in England

Income	£27,951,000 (1999/00)
Donated income	£18,624,000
Fundraising costs	£9,201,000
Statutory income	£7,609,000
Top salary	£60,001–£70,000 (2)
Paid staff	
Full time	736
Part time	615
Volunteers	2,600

Aims, activities

This is one of the major children's charities, originating within and still maintaining close connections to the Church of England (and, until recently, the Church in Wales). It recently attempted a bold expansion, as part of its 'journey from being a social welfare organisation to being a social justice organisation', but in November 2001 had to announce that it was closing 26 of its projects in England and all 13 of its operations in Wales.

The press release at that time concentrated on the withdrawal from Wales, even though the cutbacks in England seemed to be much bigger. Perhaps as a result of this presentation, substantial protests appeared to be developing in Wales in December 2001 as this book went to press, with further damaging publicity for the charity. In particular, a Welsh Assembly task force was saidd to be being assembled to support a rescue package for the work in Wales. The new organisation would ask for several million pounds of the charity's remaining reserves to be handed over for the purpose.

The charity did not like being described as a child welfare organisation in this book, and its publicity material emphasises that it concentrates on tackling the root causes of the problems faced by many children. However more than 90% of charitable expenditure in 1999/2000 was on direct work with children in around 120 'projects' (now being reduced to 80) that address the results of child poverty at least as much as they tackle its root causes. This editor, therefore, has decided to stick with the 'welfare' description as the best overall term for the society's work for the time being.

The charity's five chosen priority areas in the year were:

- 'Safe on the Streets', mainly helping runaways;
- 'Feeding Matters', dealing with nutrition (programme now ended);
- 'Youth Justice';
- 'Children in Communities', working in very disadvantaged areas;
- 'Right to Education', with an emphasis on exclusion from school.

A further five programmes have since been added:

- Housing, to enable children and young people to have a home;
- Safer communities;
- Poverty, to help regenerate poor areas;
- Children looked after (in the care of local authorities);
- A good and healthy start, to ensure that services for young children are child-centred and integrated.

The information in the report and review lacks detail on the nature of the 'projects' that make up most of the charity's activities in these fields, talking rather about generalities such as 'work with children in primary schools' or 'specialist teams to help black and Asian child runaways in Yorkshire'. The word 'projects' is probably used some of the time (as with other children's charities described in this book) simply to mean ongoing welfare services. Their funding varies, with some delivered under statutory contract, some supported wholly from the voluntary income of the charity, and some having mixed funding. It would be interesting to know the policies and practices used in deciding how far, if at all, voluntary donations should be used to support statutorily funded services.

Campaigning activity, so prominent in the annual review for 1999/00, accounted for just 5% of expenditure, though it is of course based on the experience of the welfare work on the ground.

This is one of a group of big national children's charities whose activities have appeared to overlap. The Children's Society is attempting to re-focus itself as a primarily 'social justice' organisation. It is hard for an outside observer to see how far this process has got, especially given the very wide agenda set out above, but there have been important identifiable successes, such as the new attention being paid to runaway children and to the victims of child prostitution – both issues on which this charity has taken a lead.

Volunteers

This is a professionally staffed organisation, with volunteers mostly involved in fundraising. The website refers to the welcome possibility of volunteer support, but does not offer any means of following this up (though there is a series of links for those seeking paid jobs). However, a new corporate policy on volunteering is promised, in which supporters will participate in campaigning activities.

Funding, administration

The work of the charity has deliberately been expanded very rapidly in recent years, with increased expenditures on both charitable activities and on fundraising, though the process was said to be complete by winter 2001. In 1999/00 expenditure on charitable work rose by £2 million, or 7%. This, with increased fundraising costs, reduced the charity's assets from £51 million to £43 million during the year, a 16% fall. The intention was that, with the new investment, the charity should be in surplus by March 2003, compared with the £11 million deficit of 1999/00 – if achieved, this expansion would have been a remarkable achievement.

However, in November 2001, as this book was going to print, the omens looked threatening. The charity now anticipates finishing the financial year with a £4 million deficit, following deficits over the last four years of £24 million in total, and it has but £13 million left in free reserves. 'The decision to make savings in England and withdraw from Wales was necessary on financial grounds.'

Around two thirds of the charity's revenues have come as donations or legacies, with statutory fees or grants accounting for about 28%, and investments for around 6%. Until recently, fundraising costs, averaged over three years, stood at the high level of 33p for each pound donated. In 1999/00 there was a dramatic further increase in fundraising expenditure, from £5 million in the previous year to £9 million. As the results of this investment had not yet been realised, the ratio of costs to relevant revenues rose to a very high 49p in the pound. The expectation that the ratio would decline as the benefits of the investment came through in the next two or three years seems to have been over-optimistic.

This almost adventurous attempt at growth was impressive, especially as the largest charities are often quite staid in their development, but unfortunately it looks as if it has failed – and it does seem that incautious new spending decisions were taken before the corresponding new revenues were in place.

The charity adds ...

The Society has taken steps to ensure its financial sustainability and to build a robust organisation able to tackle the injustices faced by thousands of children in England. Through its practice, research and campaigns, it aims to bring the voices of marginalised children to challenge policy and practice at the highest level.

The information assessed

The charity's annual report and accounts and annual review are both good. There is also a corporate plan, an impressive website and extensive supporting materials.

Contact

Edward Rudolf House
Margery Street
London
WC1X 0JL
Tel 020 7841 4400
Website www.the-childrens-society.org.uk
Chair Lady Elizabeth Toulson
Ian Sparks, Chief Executive

Children's Trust

Services for children with exceptional needs, mainly in the Surrey area

Income	£9,459,000 (2000/01)
Donated income	£2,469,000
Fundraising costs	£456,000
Statutory income	£6,794,000
Top salary	£60,000–£70,000
Paid staff	
Full time	195
Part time	167
Volunteers	
Operational	253
Fundraising	24

Aims, activities

The charity 'offers appropriate care, treatment, rehabilitation and education to children with exceptional needs and profound disabilities' and gives support to their families. Based on the site of the former Tadworth Court children's hospital, once owned by Great Ormond Street children's hospital, the charity is to some extent a local organisation for the Surrey and south London area, but offers rehabilitation to children with acquired brain injuries from across the UK and sometimes abroad.

There are four main services:

● expert residential and home-based nursing care;

● intensive rehabilitation and therapy for children with acquired brain injuries;

● residential education for children with profound and multiple disabilities;

● long- and short-term residential care.

Believing that 'home is best' wherever possible, much residential care – in newly built houses (a major recent undertaking) – is short-term in order to meet immediate needs or to offer respite to families. However, there are also some long-term resident children. At any one time there are typically about 70 children living at Tadworth.

The original building on the site is a beautiful though little known seventeenth-century country house, held by the charity for the benefit of the public.

Volunteers

Around 250 volunteers help with the care of the children, especially with things like outings and trips.

Volunteers also help with fundraising, administration and charity shops.

Funding, administration

Much of the charity's income comes in the form of fees from the statutory health and education authorities for the services provided, but it relies on donations both to sustain the quality of the services it offers and to replace and rebuild the premises it inherited from the former hospital.

Up until 1999 the fundraising was called 'The Hand of Hope' appeal, a name that was also unfortunately used in 2001 by an unconnected fundraising scam. The charity raised £2.5 million in donations and legacies in 2000/01, against £2.3 million in the previous year. At £456,000, fundraising costs represented 18p in the pound.

The charity adds ...

For as long as there are children with exceptional needs, children with profound disabilities or affected by degenerative and disabling conditions, The Children's Trust will strive to meet their needs for care, treatment, rehabilitation and education in partnership with their families and funding authorities.

The information assessed

The annual review and separate but sparse annual report and accounts (2000/01) are of average quality, weak in review and analysis of the year. There is a good website about the charity's activities.

Contact
Tadworth Court
Tadworth
Surrey
KT20 5RU
Tel 01737 365000
Website www.thechildrenstrust.org.uk
Chair Sir Brian Hill
Andrew Ross, Chief Executive

Christian Aid
Overseas development

Income	£53,143,000 (2000/01)
Donated income	£37,164,000
Fundraising costs	£7,119,000
Statutory income	£13,634,000
Top salary	£30,000, plus accommodation
Paid staff	476
Volunteers	310,000

Aims, activities

'Supported and sustained by the churches, driven by the Gospel, ... Christian Aid's purpose is to expose the scandal of poverty, contribute to its eradication and be prophetic in challenging the systems, structures and processes that work against ... the poor or marginalised.'

Christian Aid mainly funds local organisations, rather than carrying out its own activities in the developing world. Unlike some other charities described in this book, it presents this sensible and usual way of working without overuse of euphemisms such as 'partnership' to refer to its grantmaking: 'The majority of Christian Aid's work is carried out by making grants to partner organisations.' Indeed, its literature gives full and often moving recognition to the organisations it supports. The grants are usually made on a three-year basis.

As with some other overseas development organisations described in this book, 'there has been a shift ... beyond just identifying good projects and partners ... to a more programmatic approach [incorporating] our commitment to advocacy, lobbying and campaigning ... We are striving to build a movement of people to bring about change.'

The work supported is divided into three categories (with 2000/01 expenditures):

- development (£22.1 million);
- emergencies (£10.5 million);
- advocacy, campaigning and education (£0.9 million).

This expenditure is divided regionally as follows:

- Africa (£13.3 million);
- Asia (£7.7 million);
- Latin America/Caribbean (£5.4 million);
- Middle East/Eastern Europe (£5.5 million);
- global (£1 million);
- UK and Ireland (£0.7 million).

In all, Christian Aid funded over 500 organisations in the countries where it works, giving an average of £60,000. Skimming through the 100-page listing suggests that most grants in 2000/01 may be for amounts of between £15,000 and £30,000 (though these may, of course, have been payments towards multi-year programmes), while there are at least a few much larger awards. An example was the £160,000 for 'Gram Vikas, for permanent housing support and assistance to fishing communities in Ganjam and Gajapati (Orissa, India)'.

The effectiveness of the charity's work must depend mainly on how it selects, and then monitors and evaluates, the projects to be supported. The grants list suggests that while many of these projects emanate from Christian organisations, these still form a small proportion of the total – both by value and by number (to judge by an informal analysis of the grants in Zambia, Zimbabwe and Croatia).

The relatively modest campaigning expenditure is put to vigorous use. As an example, a report in 2001, 'How the Proposed Global Fund for HIV/AIDS is Not Needed and May Prove Counter-productive', made the case in most forceful terms that this much-hyped new initiative from the leaders of the developed world would actually be a diversion from the desperate need to support existing grassroots programmes and initiatives – rather than setting up another unnecessary global superstructure.

Volunteers

The information for volunteers is splendid. As an example, and perhaps as a model for other charities, in autumn 2001 the section on the website for the east Midlands included the following (and even then much of the detail about each post has been deleted):

'The Midlands East Team would welcome interest from potential volunteers to assist them with the following tasks:

- Youth Work Volunteer – to research church youth groups and school Christian Unions, designing and delivering Christian Aid 'sessions' and encouraging these groups to stay in touch with Christian Aid ... Commitment is for 3–10 hours per month, including preparation, Sunday evening meetings and follow-up work, for one to two years.

- Fair trade Bed and Breakfast Volunteer – to research local B&Bs, hotels or cafes and make contact to find out whether they stock/serve fair trade products.

- Fundraising Scheme Promoter – to promote fundraising schemes to groups and individuals through the post, over the phone or, ideally, in person.

- Fundraising Events Organiser – to conceive, organise and deliver fundraising events, e.g. sponsored events, concerts.

- Overseas Visitor Host – to host an overseas visitor in your home, providing meals where necessary. All expenses will be reimbursed.

- Overseas Visitor Driver – to offer lifts around the county or further for occasional overseas visitors.

- Display Volunteer – to collect, transport, set up, staff, dismantle and return displays.

- Mailing Volunteer – to help mail a locally produced newsletter and other resources.

- Resource Production Volunteer – to design and make or assemble multiple copies of visual aids and games etc. for educational work.

- Emergency Promoter – to put up posters, distribute collecting tins, organise collections and send out press releases, in the event of an emergency appeal.

- Events Steward – to be available at Christian Aid events to give practical information and help.

- Campaign Organiser – for Christian Aid's Trade for Life campaign, studying the campaigns literature, giving talks, engaging with churches and schools, hosting meetings and building a campaigns network.

- Annual Stock Take Volunteer – to assist one of the local offices in their annual stock take and enter the details on a pre-printed form.'

Funding, administration

The charity is largely funded by voluntary donations and legacies, although it does receive grants from government agencies (£13.6 million in 2000/01). The principal headings under voluntary income for the year were:

- Christian Aid week £11.8 million;
- general donations £6.5 million;
- legacies £6.5 million;
- committed giving £4.9 million;
- special emergency appeals £3.9 million;
- Disaster Emergency Committee appeals £2.4 million.

The £37 million in voluntary income was achieved at a fundraising cost of £7.1 million, which represented 19p for each pound donated, up from 15p in the previous year but close to the 17p average for the three years to 1999.

The charity adds ...

We are rooted in our support constituency in the UK and Ireland, working with and through 600 partners and strategic alliances to build a worldwide movement for justice. We are making a difference at a local, national and international level empowering people to be agents of change and build a more inclusive world community where the poor and marginalised can have their basic needs satisfied.

The information assessed

There is a colourful annual review and a report and financial statements. Together they give excellent coverage of the charity's work. The website is first-class.

Contact

PO Box 100
London
SE1 7RT
Tel 020 7620 4444
Website www.christian-aid.org
Chair Right Reverend John Gladwin
Dr Daleep Mukarji, Director

Christian Children's Fund of Great Britain

Aims, activities

As this book was being written, the charity was merging with the European Children's Trust to form a new charity, *EveryChild*.

Christie Hospital Charitable Fund

Cancer prevention, treatment and research; Manchester

Income	£17,262,000 (1999/00)
Donated income	£15,876,000
Fundraising costs	£612,000
Statutory income	£0
Top salary	nil
Paid staff	
Full time	13
Part time	1
Volunteers	
Operational	200
Fundraising	2,000

Aims, activities

This fund is the charitable arm of the Christie NHS hospital in Manchester and its associated Paterson Institute for Cancer Research. They comprise the UK's largest single-site cancer centre, seeing more than 10,000 new patients a year. Long a significant fundraiser, the charity's figures are exceptionally high at present because the hospital is in the process of (successfully) completing a £25 million one-off Christie's Against Cancer centenary appeal. Also, as explained under 'Funding' below, some of the voluntary income in the total above has already appeared under a different heading in this book.

The £25 million will be used for 11 specific improvements to the services and facilities at the hospital and at the Paterson Institute. The institute is almost entirely dependent on charitable funds.

The centenary appeal was launched in 1997 and achieved its target in June 2001, following five gifts of more than £1 million. These came in the form of two legacies, together with £1 million each from the Garfield Weston Foundation, Airtours (the north-west based holiday company) and the charity *Children with Leukaemia*. The Airtours contribution is interesting. The company had been collecting unwanted coins and running fundraising events for three years, and had collected £545,000. Then the chairman of the company, and his wife, personally made up the total to £1 million.

A large part of the regular funding of research at the Paterson Institute comes from yet another charity, the *Cancer Research Campaign*, which contributed £6.5 million in 1999/00 (a sum included in the total of donations given above).

Volunteers

The hospital, not itself a charity, benefits from over 200 voluntary helpers, while the fundraising appeal has been largely volunteer-based.

Funding, administration

The fundraising costs in 1999/00 of £612,000 represent just 4p in the pound, or 4%, of donations, but if the transfer from the Cancer Research Campaign – which had incurred its own fundraising costs in raising the money – is taken out, the figure rises to a still very low 7%.

The charity adds ...

We have tremendously loyal support from our patients and their families and friends over a very wide area. As this has been a specialist cancer Hospital for more than 100 years, everyone in the North West knows someone who has been helped by Christie's.

The information assessed

There is a good annual report and accounts and an informative website.

Contact

Christie Hospital
Withington Hospital
Manchester
M20 4BX
Tel 0161 446 3988
Website www.christies.org.uk
Chair A Sandford
Joanna Wallace, Chief Executive

Church Army
Christian and social welfare

Income	£6,109,000 (2000/01)
Donated income	£2,917,000
Fundraising costs	£694,000
Statutory income	£1,679,000
Top salary	£35,000–£40,000
Paid staff	
Full time	234
Part time	20
Volunteers	25

Aims, activities

This is 'a society of evangelists within the Anglican communion, which exists to enable people to come to living faith in Jesus Christ'. In addition to its purely evangelical activities, the charity is an important provider of services for older and homeless people as well as for others in need.

Its 2000/01 expenditure was classified under the following main headings:

- homeless people £1.7 million – a range of services, some of them residential;
- evangelism, 'church planting' and evangelist training £2 million;
- older people £1.1 million – chiefly residential care, which is a reducing activity;

• children and young people £0.8 million – principally through the work of individual army evangelists working with partner church organisations.

The balance of work in terms of the army's evangelists is different, with most of them working on evangelical activities or with young people, and relatively few with older or homeless people.

Funding, administration

The army has been suffering from falling revenues, with total income reducing from £7.1 million to £6.1 million in 2000/01, mainly because of a partial withdrawal from providing residential care for older people. Of the total, £1.6 million came from donations and £1.3 from legacies, while £1.7 million was from fees or statutory grants, and £0.8 million was from investment income.

In the previous year the charity noted that its investments were being looked upon as an important resource for the future, with £9 million in unrestricted assets held as the society's reserves and a further £3.7 million held for investment purposes. It observed that this was being done despite the fact that 'Some people take the view that Christian organisations should not hold onto a large investment portfolio. They think that the money should be used and not invested, and that current giving should finance current work.' This view does not apply only to Christian organisations but to all charities, and is part of the law of the land. Unless they were given in the first place as endowment funds, a charity is required to put all its assets, beyond those needed as a prudent reserve, to charitable use. It cannot

simply use them as a permanent source of future income.

In 2000/01 'donations have increased by 9% compared to the previous year but remain at a level significantly below the level achieved in the mid 1990s'. The total voluntary income of £2.9 million was achieved at a fundraising cost of £0.7 million, giving a cost ratio of 24p in the pound.

The information assessed

The annual report and accounts and annual review are generally excellent, being particularly strong on the charity's finances, and there is a good website.

Contact

Independents Road
Blackheath
London
SE3 9LG
Tel 020 8318 1226
Website www.churcharmy.org.uk
Chair Miss Jane Simpson
Captain Philip Johanson, Chief Secretary

Church Mission Society

Income	£8,239,000 (2000/01)
Donated income	£5,906,000
Fundraising costs	£574,000
Statutory income	£0
Top salary	Less than £50,000
Paid staff	
Full time	98
Part time	10
Volunteers	
Operational	250

Aims, activities

'CMS is a voluntary association of people rooted in the Anglican

Communion who are united in obedience to Christ's command to fulfil his Great Commission. They strive to share the love of God with people of all races and to gather them into the fellowship of Christ's Church.

'Founded in 1799, CMS has attracted upwards of nine thousand men and women to serve as mission partners during its 200-year history. Today there are about 150 mission partners in 26 countries in Africa, Asia, Europe and the Middle East. A budget of £5.75 million a year is needed to maintain and expand this work.'

The society merged with the smaller Mid-Africa Ministry (MAM) during 2001, and the figures in this entry consolidate the accounts of both charities. The scheduled completion date for the integration of MAM was 1 February 2002.

CMS's main priorities, or 'core commitments', are:

'● Evangelism

- Supporting pioneering evangelistic work

- Helping to establish and support churches in places where there are few or no Christians

- Equipping local church leaders for mission

● Transformation of community

- Working for justice, peace and reconciliation

- Encouraging holistic initiatives in community development and health care

- Supporting Christian ministry by and among the displaced and marginalised

● Building relationships with those of other faiths and none

- Developing sensitive ways of sharing our faith

- Working with those of other faiths to build a just society

- Engaging in mission amongst secular, materialistic communities'

Surprisingly, there is little indication in the otherwise comprehensive annual report of the geographical distribution of the society's work, other than that there are activities in Europe, the Middle East, Africa and Asia, but not, apparently, in the Americas or Australia.

Based on the core commitments, the missionary work is categorised as follows (with 2000/01 expenditures):

● mission personnel: supporting and sending out people in mission, short and long term (£3.2 million);

● mission grants: seed money and ongoing grant support for key projects and ministries (£1.6 million);

● mission training and experience: investing in future Christian leaders (£1.7 million);

● mission promotion and church education: building awareness in Britain (£1 million).

The charity owns and runs Crowther Hall, its resource centre and training college in Selly Oak, Birmingham.

There is much ecumenical activity. In May 2001 the society reported that 'Anglican-Orthodox relations took a huge step forward last week when the Church Mission Society (CMS) was invited to send Mission Partners to Russia to teach mission. This was only one of a number of significant results of a consultation, sponsored by CMS, held over five days in Moscow at the invitation of the Russian Orthodox Church.'

Nor is the activity all one-way. *The Times* reported in 2000: 'Formed 200 years ago to convert "the heathens" overseas, the charity is now increasingly turning its attention to the heathens on its own doorstep. It has 20 missionaries currently at work in Britain, and the number is steadily rising.' These missionaries come from other countries seeking to re-Christianise Britain, and are not necessarily Anglicans. The first Roman Catholic priest was recruited (from the Czech Republic) in 2000, while 'mission partners', as the society calls them, were expected from Orthodox churches in Ukraine in 2001.

Volunteers

The financial arrangements for those working for the charity are not spelled out, but it would be surprising if there were not a substantial 'voluntary' element to much of the work. Other aspects are well covered on the website.

Funding, administration

Since the early 1980s the charity has received a regular source of support in the 'Leech Benefactions', which contribute over £800,000 a year to its work. Otherwise it has to depend almost entirely on donations and legacies (plus a substantial 'other' category, amounting to £1,120,000 in 2000/01, which is not explained in the accounts but probably includes fees for its training programmes).

Donations of £4.1 million and legacies of £1.8 million were at comparable levels to the previous four years, except for the particularly successful 1999/00. During this period

fundraising costs have risen steadily, from £229,000 to £574,000 in 2000/01, when the cost ratio was nevertheless still a low 10p in the pound.

The charity's free reserves of £9.5 million are high, above its target of reserves equal to ten months' expenditure, and so CMS is planning to spend above its income each year to bring the level down.

The charity adds ...

CMS works hand in hand with Christians in over 50 countries – among those at the margins of society; through long term partnerships and pioneering initiatives; to transform lives and communities; sharing God's good news with those of other faiths and those with none.

The information assessed

The excellent and detailed annual report and accounts include a useful table showing the financial progress of the charity over the last five years. There is an excellent website, with good information for volunteers interested in taking part in the society's work and a selection of straightforward but informative and moving letters from missionaries overseas. (Note that it is not at www.cms.org, which covers a different mission society.)

Contact

Partnership House
157 Waterloo Road
London
SE1 8UU
Tel 020 7928 8681
Website www.cms-uk.org
Chair Right Reverend David Urquhart
Reverend Tim Dakin, General Secretary

Churches and religious charities

Charities with a religious basis or affiliation make up a very large and vigorously prosperous part of the charitable sector. Contrary to some stereotypes, many of them are relatively new or have only recently grown from a very small size. Those that we have identified with an annual donations level of £2 million a year or more are listed below.

There are many more charities that are or were inspired by a religious faith, but which, on the information we have, we have not thought of as religious charities – the *Camphill Village Trust* might be a good example of many in this book – and the distinction is imprecise. The decision about which charities should be classified as 'religious' is necessarily subjective, and these editors apologise to any organisations that feel wrongly described. The income figures in this entry come from a variety of sources and are not necessarily strictly comparable with each other.

Besides the charities associated with every religion, each church is also charitable in itself, usually as an 'exempt' charity which does not have to register with the Charity Commission, though the legal forms can be diverse. The churches are major recipients of voluntary donations of time as well as of money. The level of such voluntary activity seems unquantifiable.

The level of annual cash donations for some major churches is estimated as follows (probably excluding legacies in most cases):

- Church of England £417 million (1998);
- Methodist churches £120 million (2000/01);
- Church of Scotland £87 million (2000);
- Roman Catholic church £50 million–£100 million (estimated; see below);
- Church of Jesus Christ of Latter-day Saints £34 million.

The Church of England's financial and charitable arrangements are strikingly complex. Each bishop appears to be himself a charity, as a 'corporation sole'; so is his diocesan board of finance; and so also is each parish in his diocese. Within a parish there may be any number of separate charities, both new and old (as sometimes recorded in the lists of benefactions hung on church walls). There is also a range of appeal bodies, for church and cathedral restoration and the like, which may be seen as 'heritage' as much as 'religious' causes.

The Methodists produce a succinct but admirably clear note on 'Methodism and money'. For 2000/01 this records that 52% of the £120 million income is spent locally on buildings, pastoral and evangelical work, and on voluntary contributions to connected charities such as the Methodist Fund for World Mission. Another 40% is spent on the costs of ministry, such as stipends and housing, and is also, therefore, returned to local churches. The remaining 8% is used to run all the other activities of the church, including all its district and central activities. However, *Methodist Homes for the Aged* is a separate charity.

The donations to the 27 Roman Catholic dioceses do not seem to have been totalled up. The largest, the archdiocese of Liverpool, had a donated income of over £13 million in 1998/99, but Nottingham was probably more typical in receiving something over £3.5 million.

The Quakers receive over £2 million a year at their central office, but perhaps as much again may be collected and spent locally.

No collective figures are available for Jewish synagogues, Islamic mosques or Sikh or Hindu temples. The big United Synagogue in London had donations of over £3 million in 1998/99.

The connected Christian charities vary from those of a mainly evangelical character (such as, say, the *Church Mission Society*) to others that despite their Christian or denominational basis appeal to supporters across the whole community (the *Salvation Army* is a good example, though it is itself a church in its own right). There are still more, such as *Barnardo's*, *Oxfam* and *NCH (Action for Children)*, whose Christian origins and connections may not even be apparent to many supporters. Some of the major Jewish charities have strong religious associations, but others can be wholly secular.

This book normally has individual entries for all charities receiving donations of more than £2 million a year. However, in the case of church charities, whose work is likely to be of most interest to their own members or adherents, the numbers are so great that full entries have had to be confined to those with donations of more than £5 million, or with donations of over £2 million and whose work extends largely beyond the religious base of the charity.

This editor is uncomfortable with the current 'faith-based' terminology, as a shared faith often seems not to be the strongest bond bringing together the supporters of these charities – at least to judge by how many of them choose to present themselves. A shared approach to altruistic good works seems to be the more usual basis of their appeal. The following 'religiously connected' charities with levels of donations above £2 million have been identified (those in italics have their own entries in this book). They are listed by the size of their voluntary income; contact telephone numbers and websites are also included. This list may well be incomplete; if so, these publishers would welcome further information.

The Salvation Army £73,154,000; 020 7367 4500; www.salvationarmy.org.uk

Christian Aid £37,164,000; 020 7620 4444; www.christian-aid.org.uk

Tearfund £28,464,000; 020 8977 9144; www.tearfund.org.uk

CAFOD £20,642,000; 020 7733 7900; www.cafod.org.uk

Bible Society £6,333,000; 01793 418100; www.biblesociety.org.uk

Church Mission Society £5,906,000; 020 7928 8681; www.cms-uk.org

Leprosy Mission International £5,767,000; 01733 370505; www.leprosymission.org

Sisters of Charity £5,566,000; 020 8995 1963

The Society of Jesus Trust (The Jesuits) £4,920,000; 020 7629 2352; www.jesuit.co.uk

Methodist Homes for the Aged £4,376,000; 01332 296200; www.methodisthomes.org.uk

Baptist Missionary Society £4,249,000; 01235 517700; www.bms.org.uk

OMF International (Overseas Missionary Fellowship) £4,238,000; 01732 887299; www.omf.org.uk

Christian Vision £4,000,000; 0121 522 6087; www.christian-vision.org

United Christian Broadcasters £3,910,000; 01782 642000; www.ucb.co.uk

Baptist Union £3,591,000; 01235 517700; www.baptist.org.uk

Echoes of Service £3,483,000; 01225 310893; www.echoes.org.uk

Pontifical Mission Societies £3,404,000; 020 7821 9755; www.missionsocieties.org.uk

Scripture Union £3,090,000; 01908 856000; www.scripture.org.uk

HCPT The Pilgrimage Trust £3,044,000; 01737 353311; www.hcpt.org.uk

Wycliffe Bible Translators £3,044,000; 01494 682279; www.wycliffe.org.uk

Church Army £2,917,000; 020 8318 1226; www.churcharmy.org.uk

United Society for the Propagation of the Gospel £2,910,000; 020 7928 8681; www.uspg.org.uk

Scottish Catholic International Aid Fund £2,870,000; 0141 354 5555; www.sciaf.org.uk

The Scripture Gift Mission £2,684,000; 0207 7380 6500; www.asgm.org

FEBA (Far East Broadcasting Association) £2,650,000; 01903 237281; www.feba.org.uk

Gideons International £2,578,000; 01455 554241; www.gideons.org.uk

Christian Action Research and Education Trust £2,543,000; 020 7233 0455; www.care.org.uk

London City Mission £2,377,000; 020 7047 7585; www.lcm.org.uk

Bible Lands Society £2,361,000; 01494 897950; www.biblelands.co.uk

Tenovus £2,345,000; 029 2062 1433; www.tenovus.org.uk

Church of Latter-day Saints – Welfare £2,250,000; 0121 712 1248; www.lds.org.uk

Universities and Colleges Christian Fellowship £2,105,000; 0116 255 1700; www.uccf.org.uk

Mission Aviation Fellowship (MAF) £2,000,000; 01303 850950; www.maf-uk.org

Citizens Advice Bureaux

The network of Citizens Advice Bureaux (CABx) is is one of the largest recipients of support from the public in the charitable sector, but most of this is given by volunteers in time rather than cash. The bureaux deal with more than 3,500 new enquiries every hour of every working day: over 6 million enquiries a year. There are nearly 360,000 visitors a year to the adviceguide.org.uk website launched in 1999.

The CABx were instituted at the start of the Second World War, with government funding for the necessary administration and organisation without which volunteers cannot operate effectively. In 1950 all central government support was withdrawn and the movement struggled to maintain services with solely charitable funding. Government support restarted in 1957 when the Rent Act caused a huge leap in enquiries; today local government provides 59% of the total cash resources for the bureaux, with much of the staff time still given free by volunteers. The remaining funds are raised from the community legal service, health authorities, Community Fund, charitable trusts, companies, Single Regeneration Budget and individuals. In 1975 the Department of Trade and Industry began funding the National Association of Citizens Advice Bureaux (NACAB) on behalf of all government departments, to provide professional support to bureaux.

Each CAB is an independent local charity and must raise its own funding, normally led by support from the local authority concerned. However, non-local authority funding represents 41% of total income; as a result coverage is uneven and few bureaux can rely on a continuing stable future. Areas without CAB coverage in the summer of 2001 included cities as big as Leicester.

There are about 540 CABx, operating from 2,000 locations. Each has a voluntary local trustee board and a salaried manager. The actual giving of advice is divided between trained volunteers and a smaller number of professional staff. In many CAB offices the advice is given wholly voluntarily, though the back-up for complex issues may come from a CAB professional, perhaps from NACAB's Specialist Support Unit based in Wolverhampton. Most CABx have their own specialists in money and debt advice, benefits and employment matters.

There are nearly 12,000 trained voluntary advisers as well as over 6,500 voluntary committee members and 3,000 volunteers in other roles. In all, 82% of the people working in the CAB service are volunteers – 21,581 people in total. Around 6% are from black and ethnic minority groups and 8% have a disability. Training and working as an adviser can be an effective way of moving into paid work; 37% of volunteer advisers who leave their CAB do so to go on to paid employment.

The central organisation, NACAB, provides a massive information and training base for the movement. It is also an important influence on government legislation and practice, with its unparalleled experience of on-the-ground problems.

The main categories of problem brought to CABx, with numbers of enquiries in 2000/01, concern:

- legal 4.8 million;
- benefits 1.7 million;
- consumer 1.2 million;
- employment 630,000;
- housing 600,000.

There is some tension in the network between the increasing pressure of the central standard setting body, NACAB, to reach ever higher standards of professionalism and formalism, and the voluntary ethos from which the movement derives. The attraction of the latter is that it enables a simple and relatively low-cost service to be made available in a way that is more accessible and extensive than is the case with many statutory information services. On the other hand, the main funders of the network are local authorities, where a different, professional ethos may prevail and where the avoidance of the possibility of error may limit the overall usefulness of the service.

Full information about the CAB network is available from the National Association of Citizens Advice Bureaux, or NACAB (tel: 020 7833 2181; website: www.nacab.org.uk) – this covers England, Wales and Northern Ireland. For Scotland, contact Citizens Advice Scotland (tel: 0131 667 0156; website: www.cas.org.uk)

Local bureaux are listed in all telephone directories, and on the websites above.

Civic societies and the Civic Trust

There are almost 900 local civic societies in the UK that are affiliated to the Civic Trust, though each remains an independent charity in its own right. They have between them 330,000 individual members, a number little changed for some years. The movement exists to improve the quality of urban living and in particular the quality of the urban environment.

The Civic Trust itself has four main activities:

- Campaigning at a national level. The society works for improved policies and practices concerning the urban environment, especially at present for the implementation of the recommendations of the Richard Rogers Urban Task Force. More specifically, the trust has been fighting against unsightly advertising in streets and especially in telephone kiosks.

- The Civic Trust Regeneration Unit. This well-established and expert unit, which accounted for about half the charitable expenditure in 2000/01, pioneers, promotes and develops specific regeneration programmes and projects. Among other things it is at present preparing community-based regeneration programmes for nine small towns in the south-west, including Devizes, Helston and Bridport.

- Running the well-known annual Civic Trust Awards; the similar Green Flag awards for parks and open spaces; the increasingly popular Heritage Open Days, when the public can visit buildings and places not usually open to them; and the Civic Champions awards, funded by the Millennium Commission, which have enabled volunteer activists to receive training.

- Support for local civic societies. The trust appointed its first regional officer in 2000, in south-west England.

The local societies are varied. Some are large, with substantial assets, especially where they run successful revolving schemes for the restoration of buildings at risk. Many are very small. Almost all are wholly voluntary.

Collectively, the movement appears in recent years to have seen a slowing in its earlier dynamic growth, as other environmentally active groups have come to the fore, as it is seen by some as mainly concerned with local planning decisions and the preservation of individual buildings. The trust, with a new director, is now seeking to identify and publicise a group of 'Pathfinder Societies' that are successfully demonstrating wider ambitions, so that it can enter a new period of increasing influence locally as well as nationally.

The Civic Trust covers the whole of the UK, but there are also regional groupings including those for Wales and Scotland. Contact details:

- The Civic Trust, tel: 020 7930 0914; www.civictrust.org.uk

- The Civic Trust for Wales, tel: 029 2048 4606; www.civictrust.org.uk

- The Scottish Civic Trust, tel: 0141 221 1466; www.scotnet.co.uk\sct

CLIC (Cancer and Leukaemia in Childhood)

Mainly in the south of England, Wales and Scotland

Income	£5,192,000 (2000)
Donated income	£3,731,000
Fundraising costs	£929,000
Statutory income	£0
Top salary	£50,000–£60,000
Paid staff	74
Volunteers	600

Aims, activities

The charity helps children with cancer and leukaemia and their families. Its field is one where there has been great medical progress – in the 25 years of CLIC's existence, survival rates for all childhood cancers have improved from 30% to 70%.

The main activities (with their 2000 expenditures) are:

- The support of specialist home-care nurses and other staff within the NHS (£930,000). It is not clear on what basis these are funded, though it may be similar to that of *Macmillan Cancer Relief* nurses where the charity pays for the first three years of their training and employment. There are 41 such nurses, with six new posts being funded in 2000. The charity also funds a number of specialist doctors, five play specialists and an art therapist, and supports the training of other clinical staff.

- 'Homes from Home' accommodation near hospitals where children are treated (£235,000). There are seven of these homes, all in either Scotland or the south of England.

- Care Grants, to help with the extra costs of having a very sick child (£94,000). These are distributed through a number of specialist social workers.

- Research projects (£193,000). There are CLIC research laboratories at Bristol University, including a specialist interest in one particular cancer that affects children, Wilms' tumour.

There is also a TOPS (Teenage Oncology Patient Support) network for teenagers with cancer or leukaemia, as well as two seaside holiday flats for short-notice family respite breaks. In addition, the charity supports building projects such as a CLIC ward in the new Bristol Children's Hospital.

The charity has grown from a local initiative in Bristol. Though it now operates throughout the country, coverage is uneven.

Volunteers

There are 20 branches, which no doubt combine mutual support with fundraising, and a funder network of support groups. There are probably a number of shops, to judge by the 40 staff they employ, and these may well also have volunteer assistance.

Funding, administration

The charity, which is growing fast, is funded mainly by donations from individuals. Legacies play a smaller part than is the case with some of the cancer-related charities working with adults.

In 2000 this income totalled £3.7 million, achieved at a fundraising cost of £0.9 million, a ratio of 25%, or 25p in the pound. In the previous year the ratio had been much lower, at 19%, and the change reflects a greatly increased fundraising investment, up by 88% over the previous year. This was happily reflected in a 25% increase in donated income (and there may well be more to come), but a change in expenditure on this scale deserved some comment in the annual report. In the three years to 1998 the charity had spent a low average of 15p in the pound on fundraising.

CLIC has a substantial number of shops selling donated goods to the value of over £1 million a year and contributing a net income of £216,000 in the year 2000. These shops account for 40 of the 74 employed staff noted above. There are 18 fundraisers, ten staff managing or delivering the charity's services, and six people involved in the management and administration of the charity itself.

The information assessed

The adequate annual report and accounts and annual review are supported by a colourful website that includes a useful staff list.

Contact

Abbey Wood
Bristol
BS34 7JU
Tel 0117 311 2600
Website www.clic.uk.com
Chair Brigadier Hugh Pye
David Allis, Chief Executive

Comic Relief

Income	£21,207,000 (average for 1998–2001)
Donated income	£15,935,000
Fundraising costs	£1,243,000
Statutory income	£0
Top salary	£50,000–£60,000
Paid staff	52
Volunteers	100

Aims, activities

Comic Relief is committed to helping end poverty and social injustice both in the UK and in the poorest countries in the world – mostly in Africa so far. It was launched in 1985 from a refugee camp in Safawa, Sudan. Since then, over £220 million has been raised, primarily through Red Nose Days.

The charity operates by:

- raising money from the general public by actively involving them in events and projects that are innovative and fun;
- informing, educating, raising awareness and promoting social change;
- making grants to a wide range of carefully selected charities;
- ensuring that Red Nose Day fundraising costs are covered by sponsorship.

'We're committed to supporting long-term projects, helping people to help themselves. It's about giving people a leg up, not a hand out. We also aim to tackle the root causes of poverty by raising awareness around some of the key issues, such as unfair terms of trade and debt relief.

'Comic Relief was set up by comedians and uses comedy and laughter to get serious messages across, as well as making sure that everyone can have some fun at the same time.'

Red Nose Day is a UK-wide fundraising event organised by Comic Relief every two years which culminates in a night of comedy and of moving documentary films. It is the biggest TV fundraising event in the UK calendar. On Red Nose Day everyone in England, Scotland, Wales and Northern Ireland is encouraged to cast inhibitions aside, put on a red nose, and do something a little bit silly to raise money – celebrities included.

There have been eight Red Nose Days, all broadcast on BBC1, and the amounts raised are both remarkable and, over the last four such days, growing fast:

- 1988, £15.8 million;
- 1989, £26.9 million;
- 1991, £20.3 million;
- 1993, £18 million;
- 1995, £22 million;
- 1997, £27.1 million;
- 1999, £35 million;
- 2001, £49 million.

This is a grant-making charity. About £20 million a year is given out, two thirds to organisations in Africa and one third in the UK. Recently Comic Relief has also been funding work beyond Africa, with money raised by the charity in countries outside the UK, and supporting projects from Afghanistan and Mongolia to Guatemala and Lebanon.

The annual review and the annual report and accounts contain virtually no information about the grants, beyond the following single sentence covering all the charitable activities: 'we funded 485 projects across the UK and Africa'. With perseverance, it is possible to obtain a separate and most helpful booklet which lists and describes all the grants (on both a programme and geographical basis) in the UK, and (geographically only) in Africa (this information is not on the website).

No totals are given, so it is not easy to see to which programmes or areas most of the money is given. A characteristic of the Africa grants is

the substantial proportion that go to other UK charities, such as *Oxfam* and *Christian Aid*.

The intentions of the grant programmes are well thought through and admirably set out, but only in the 'Application Guidelines' (on the website under 'Apply for a grant'), which is not an obvious source of information for people interested in how their money is being used. The programmes are all focused on trying to help the people who are poorest or most disadvantaged.

In Africa there are six main programmes:

- people affected by conflict;
- women and girls;
- people living in towns and cities;
- disabled people;
- pastoralists;
- people affected by HIV/AIDS.

In the UK there are four programmes:

- fighting for justice;
- supporting young people;
- services in the domestic violence and refugee sectors;
- supporting communities.

These general categories are supported by extensive and detailed guidance on what the charity is seeking to fund.

Volunteers

Besides the trustees, there are six voluntary grant or advisory committees. Red Nose Day clearly involves huge numbers of people, wholly voluntarily, in its remarkable jamboree.

Funding, administration

Though Red Nose Day is the main source of funds, this is not how Comic

Relief started and it still organises other, smaller-scale events.

The charity's income is rising; the 2001 Red Nose Day raised no less than £49 million, reflected in the four-year average for total income printed above. The main event is run every second year, and the rest of the figures in this entry are the average for the two-year period reported in the 1999/00 accounts.

It would be interesting to know the nature of the arrangement with the BBC, on which the whole viability of the charity's work seems to depend. This is not referred to in the annual reports, which should cover all material matters.

The grants programme, whose average value in the last two years was £17 million, was implemented at an administrative cost of less than £1 million, or 5%. This is a low figure, given the number of grants being made and the size of the area covered.

The charity makes a point of saying that all the costs of Red Nose Day are covered by sponsorship, so that every pound given by the public can be used for charitable purposes. Though no doubt this is the case it is not demonstrated in the accounts, which might be sensible given the weight that is put on the claim. The accounts do show fundraising expenditure of an average £1.5 million a year, and 'donations and corporate support' averaging £417,000.

The information assessed

The annual review and annual report and accounts are weak. The report notes that the 'usual stuff ... measuring what we did against what we said we would do' and so on is quite right and proper, but then wonders who would read it, and so offers mostly moving anecdote in its place. This editor would have read such 'stuff', and sees it as not only right and proper but legally required and necessary to justify public confidence.

The best place to find out about the charitable activities, or at least those that are intended, is in the excellent grant application guidelines, also available on the website. There is a mass of promotional literature.

Contact

5th Floor, 89 Albert Embankment
London
SE1 7TP
Tel 020 7820 5555
Website www.comicrelief.org.uk
Chair Peter Bennett Jones
Kevin Cahill, Chief Executive

Community associations, and Community Matters

Almost every community has at least one organisation that could be loosely called a multi-purpose 'community association', though the term is not necessarily a guide to what a particular local organisation may be called – actual names vary widely, from a church hall committee to a welfare association, or just an individually named local charity.

Such community associations may have a variety of roles as:

- centres for mutual support and aid;
- service providers for local people;
- initiators of projects to meet local need;
- builders of partnerships with other local organisations;
- engaging people to become active in their communities;
- operating community buildings.

Most of these organisations are wholly voluntary and few have any substantial fundraising expenditures, yet they are visibly active in raising money for themselves and for connected good causes throughout the country.

They can usually be identified through the local Council for Voluntary Service (see list on page 385) or through Community Matters, which is the national federation for community associations and similar organisations (tel: 020 7226 0189; website: www.communitymatters.org.uk). In 2001 Community Matters' members included over 850 community associations and similar multi-purpose community organisations, together with around 30 local federations of community organisations.

The Community Foundation Network

This is the national association of the fast-growing body of independent community foundations. These are local charities which raise money for planned programmes of local grantmaking. They have been remarkably successful in tapping local sources of large donations: 'A lot of people are giving much, much more than they have before,' says Gaynor Humphries, director of the national organisation. One particularly attractive option for donors, it has been discovered, is the possibility of setting up a fund in their own name which will be managed, according to their general wishes, by the local community foundation.

Most of the foundations are seeking to build up large capital endowments and to use the revenues from these for their ongoing grant programmes. However, in practice they usually also accept money for immediate use, acting thereby as the skilled intermediaries making sure that donors' funds are put to the best possible use.

Across all foundations in the financial year 2000/01, the total figure for long-term endowment was approaching £90 million, while the total figure for grants was approximately £21 million. Some of these funds may be from statutory sources; for example the Community Foundation for Northern Ireland runs significant government funding programmes.

In 2000 it was announced that the network would also be the distributor of no less than £70 million of government money through its new Children's Fund.

There are now community foundations covering most of the UK. A listing of those that are already active follows, showing the total income received for the financial year 2000/01, and the telephone number and website (where available). Up-to-date addresses and details are available from the Association of Community Foundations on its excellent website (www.communityfoundations.org.uk) or by telephoning 020 7422 8611.

Berkshire Community Foundation £487,254; tel: 01189 303021; www.berkscommtrust.org.uk

Birmingham Foundation £700,388; tel: 0121 326 6886; www.bhamfoundation.co.uk

Cleveland Community Foundation £895,526; tel: 01642 314200

Community Foundation in Wales £173,691; tel: 029 2052 0250; www.communityfoundationwales.freeserve.co.uk

Community Foundation for Calderdale £690,000; tel: 01422 349700; www.ccfound.co.uk

Community Foundation for Greater Manchester £1,399,329; tel: 0161 214 0940; www.communityfoundation.co.uk

Community Foundation for Northern Ireland (NIVT) £300,000; tel: 028 9024 5927; www.nivt.org

Community Foundation for South Yorkshire £1,719,652; tel: 0114 273 1765; www.sycf.org

Community Foundation serving Tyne & Wear and Northumberland £5,764,763; tel: 0191 222 0945; www.northeast-online.co.uk/TWF

County Durham Foundation £660,529; tel: 0191 383 0055; www.countydurhamfoundation.org.uk

Craven Trust £40,000; tel: 01756 793333; www.craventrust.org

Cumbria Community Foundation £914,189; tel: 01900 825760; www.cumbriafoundation.org

Dacorum Community Trust £19,431; tel: 01442 231396; www.dctrust.org.uk

Derbyshire Community Foundation £285,532; tel: 01332 592050; www.derbyshirecommunityfoundation.co.uk

Devon Community Foundation £165,614; tel: 01392 252252; www.cosmic.org.uk/devoncf

Essex Community Foundation £853,010; tel: 01245 355947; www.beehive.thisisessex.co.uk

Fermanagh Trust £120,000; tel: 028 6632 0210

Gloucestershire Community Foundation £61,197; tel: 01452 522006; www.beehive.thisisgloucestershire.co.uk

Greater Bristol Foundation £1,262,000; tel: 0117 989 7700; www.gbf.org.uk

Heart of England Community Foundation £334,933; tel: 024 7688 4386; www.heartofenglandcf.co.uk

Hertfordshire Community Foundation £660,000; tel: 01707 251351; www.hertscf.org.uk

Isle of Dogs Community Foundation £1,032,079; tel: 020 7345 4444; www.idcf.org

Milton Keynes Community Foundation £597,000; tel: 01908 690276; www.mkcommunityfoundation.co.uk

Oxfordshire Community Foundation £650,000; tel: 01865 798666; www.oxfordshire.org

Royal Docks Trust (London) £127,571; tel: 02322 226336; www.royaldockstrust.org

St Katharine & Shadwell Trust £358,703; tel: 020 7782 6962

Scottish Community Foundation £770,000; tel: 0131 225 9804; www.scottishcommfound.org.uk

Stevenage Community Trust £102,038; tel: 01438 773368

Telford and Wrekin Community Trust £21,879; tel: 01952 201858

Wiltshire and Swindon Community Foundation £655,183; tel: 01380 729284; www.moneyshop.co.uk/charity/wiltshire.htm

An example: the Oxfordshire Community Foundation
'The Oxfordshire Community Foundation was set up in 1995 by a group of individuals from a variety of backgrounds throughout the county. They recognised that the charitable intent of many of the successful families and companies in Oxfordshire was not always translated into action and they were keen to increase the amount of charitable funding available to local community organisations.

'Our main aim is to help companies, families or individuals to set up new charitable funds to help groups working with disadvantaged people in their own community. We offer a professional and experienced service to those who wish to concentrate their philanthropy on their community. We can also provide a flexible service, reflecting the donor's own funding preferences.

'Since the public launch of the Foundation in 1997, we have made over £300,000 worth of grants to more than 250 local groups, representing the entire range of community activity present in Oxfordshire. We have funded toys for pre-school playgroups, ramps for wheelchair access, computer software for use by people with special needs, basic skills training for homeless people. The average size of grant made is around £700, illustrating that there are activities where a little bit of funding can make a big difference.

'Reverend Chris Knight, the chairman of the Willy Freund Youth Centre on the Bretch Hill Estate in Banbury, had this to say about a grant of £1,500 to start up the Youth Centre in 1998:

' "Through this grant from the Oxfordshire Community Foundation, we were able to establish the Youth Centre in one of the most deprived estates in the county. But, crucially, this grant gave us breathing space, to show the local community that the project was important and worth supporting and for us to draw up a plan to continue to fund this valuable project. After the first year, we have totally achieved our aims and have built strong links with residents, young and old. The Oxfordshire Community Foundation have been our lifeline." '

Community Transport schemes

Community Transport is the name given to a wide range of community-based transport services run by organisations in the voluntary sector. Almost all of these organisations make extensive use of volunteers as drivers, passenger assistants, office staff and management committee members.

The main types of community transport project are:

- Dial a ride – providing door-to-door services using minibuses or 'people-carriers' for older or disabled people unable to use public transport. Volunteers are frequently used as drivers or passenger assistants.

- Community car schemes – another form of door-to-door service but here the volunteer usually uses his or her own vehicle to take people to a variety of destinations. This form of project relies completely on volunteers (expenses can be claimed for costs such as petrol).

- Group transport services – here minibuses are hired out to local community organisations and charities. Many of these local groups do not have their own driver, so the community transport group often has its own pool of volunteers to help support the service.

- Community buses – a form of timetabled bus service most commonly used in remote rural areas where there is no commercial bus service. There are about 100 buses operating in England and Scotland. At the moment, the law requires such schemes to use voluntary drivers only, so these projects are constantly on the lookout for new volunteers.

- Furniture recycling – redistributing no-longer-wanted domestic furniture and appliances to families or individuals in need. This is often used to help refugees or people who have lost homes or possessions in a fire, for example.

- Safe transport schemes – for those who are reluctant to use public transport, especially at night, because of concerns about their personal safety. Such schemes might be aimed exclusively at women (but not all of these require female drivers only), young people, older people or people from ethnic minority groups, or they might be more general.

- Travel to work schemes – often located in areas of high unemployment where poor transport links make accessing job or training opportunities very difficult.

Where volunteers are employed as drivers, training is usually given, particularly using the nationally recognised MiDAS scheme for minibus drivers in the voluntary sector. At the time of writing, the Community Transport Association (CTA), which runs MiDAS, was planning to introduce a parallel course for passenger assistants in 2002. The CTA in fact runs many courses aimed at staff and volunteers working in community transport; most community transport projects attempt (finance permitting) to give their volunteers access to appropriate training.

Community Transport projects tend to have a firm base in their local community and recruit their management committees from people involved with their member groups or from other interested individuals. People with specific skills such as fundraising, bookkeeping and marketing are especially sought after.

For further information, including contact details for your local community transport project, contact the Community Transport Association (tel: 0161 366 6685; website: www.ctaa.org).

Crisis

Income	£5,476,000 (1999/00)
Donated income	£4,863,000
Fundraising costs	£1,220,000
Statutory income	£423,000
Top salary	£40,000–£50,000
Paid staff	60
Volunteers	2,500

Aims, activities

Crisis's mission is to end mass street homelessness in the UK. The sector (Crisis, other agencies and the government) has largely achieved this, with the estimated number of rough sleepers falling from 1,850 in 1998 to 700 'on any one night' in England today. However, rough sleeping is only the tip of the iceberg, as there are 400,000 single homeless people in bed and breakfasts and other temporary accommodation. The charity seeks to help these people more and more.

In the summer of 2001 Crisis was in discussion with *Shelter* about a possible merger.

The annual review 2001 gives the following excellent listing of the charity's activities:

- ReachOut – Crisis workers go out on to the streets and visit hostels to identify homeless people with mental health problems and help them access the services they need at their own pace, with 1,300 people helped between July 2000 and June 2001.

- SmartMove – 35 of these schemes enable homeless and vulnerable people to obtain comprehensive advice and decent private accommodation, involving about 5,055 people in the year.

- FareShare – Crisis runs one scheme, and has franchised six others, to collect surplus high-quality fresh food and redistribute it to hostels and day centres, contributing to over 20,000 meals a week.

- Rolling Shelter – a temporary short-stay emergency service, funded by the government.

- WinterWatch – a national network of 18 projects for winter shelters and support services, which helped 1,535 people between December 2000 and March 2001.

- Open Christmas – 800 people came to the London shelters, which were run by 2,500 volunteers, for companionship and support.

- Mobile Health Unit – involving trained volunteer nurses and first-aiders in an ambulance around London, with 504 clients seen in 37 outings.

- Befriending – a pilot volunteer project in London to help former rough sleepers settle in their accommodation.

- Health Action at Crisis – a research and development programme.

- New Solutions – a research programme.

Crisis also works with Shelter on Millennium +, a three-year joint initiative which greatly extends the success of resettlement work from Crisis's WinterWatch schemes.

Focusing outside London, the new Home Straight programme has teams across the country, with each area chosen for its high number of rough sleepers. A project worker has been assigned to every resident at a WinterWatch shelter and in these designated areas to get people the support they need to start to rebuild their lives.

Volunteers

'Crisis began over 30 years ago as a volunteer-led organisation. Volunteers still play a crucial role whether by working face-to-face with homeless people or providing essential administrative support or rattling tins to collect much-needed funds. We believe that volunteering should be a mutually beneficial experience.'

A range of volunteering opportunities is described and offered on the website. The charity estimates the value of its volunteers' time at more than £0.7 million a year.

Funding, administration

The charity is funded mainly by donations and legacies, which totalled £4.9 million in 1999/00. This was achieved at a fundraising cost of £1.2 million, giving a cost ratio of 25p in the pound. Crisis is particularly successful in obtaining support from companies, raising £0.9 million from this source, compared with £0.8 million from the much larger charitable trust sector.

Income was higher than in the previous year, but only slightly, and the annual report is honest and unusually self-critical in finding this disappointing in relation to the charity's expectations. It 'has been a tough financial year', and the charity had to reduce its spending plans. The growth of donations from individuals has slowed: 'Perhaps we are finally seeing the donor fatigue syndrome that appears to have affected other charities in recent years.'

The full and frank discussion of the financial situation, one which many charities would have glossed over as wholly acceptable, sets an example of good practice for the sector.

The charity adds ...

We have been developing a new range of services, some of which have already been successfully piloted and are awaiting a national roll-out. The aim is to continue helping rough sleepers but also to support those who move off the streets enabling them to integrate back into society.

The information assessed

The annual report and accounts is excellent, though unpretentious, and much of it could be a model for many other charities described in this book. There is a fine, lively website, and very good supporting literature.

Contact

Warwick House
25–27 Buckingham Palace Road
London
SW1W 0PP
Tel 0870 011 3335
Website www.crisis.org.uk
Chair David Edmonds
Ms Shaks Ghosh, Chief executive

CSV (Community Service Volunteers)

Income	£26,025,000 (1999/00)
Donated income	£2,553,000
Fundraising costs	£1,020,000
Statutory income	£12,828,000
Top salary	£80,000–£90,000
Paid staff	721
Volunteers	
Operational	100,000

Aims, activities

CSV is dedicated to giving everyone the chance to take an active part in their community through volunteering, training, education and the media. It enables people to undertake a variety of volunteer work and training in local projects. In 2000 over 100,000 people volunteered through the charity, which has an impressive 'non-rejection policy'. No one, no matter how disadvantaged, is turned away.

In practice there are a number of separate programmes, most operating pretty independently of each other and with their own promotional or explanatory literature (contact details are best accessed through the website). They are as follows (with 1999/00 expenditures in brackets):

- CSV Volunteering Partners (£5.4 million). This is probably the programme described elsewhere as Volunteer Action in the Community. National Network CSV volunteers are young people aged from 16 to 35 who volunteer away from home for 4–12 months in a network of about 700 community projects nationwide. They get a weekly allowance, accommodation and food, and supervision. The work is usually in social care settings, for example helping people with disabilities in their daily lives.

Local Action CSV volunteers enable and encourage vulnerable people from disadvantaged backgrounds to become volunteers locally, again usually in social care settings. There are nearly 800 such schemes, and over 2,000 people a year volunteer through them.

- CSV Media (£4.1 million). This programme works with broadcasters and voluntary and statutory organisations to produce over 350 campaigns a year on a wide range of health and social issues. (One example in 2000 was a feature on Manchester's Piccadilly Radio on the dangers of carbon monoxide poisoning.) CSV Media trains over

750 people a year. 'We target our training ... at those traditionally disadvantaged in these areas. CSV Media also works with local people to produce community newsletters, RSLs [Restricted Service Licences for radio broadcasts], videos and websites.'

- CSV Training and Enterprise (£3.9 million). 'We meet the special training needs of 3,500 young people and adults at 28 local centres nation wide ... training people who are most disadvantaged in the labour market.' This is concentrated on helping unemployed young people and long-term unemployed adults get back to work.

- CSV Education for Citizenship (£0.9 million). There are 21,000 volunteers in 2,600 schools, colleges and universities. Other literature says: 'Each year CSV enables 45,000 young people to learn and develop in and beyond the classroom by participating in activities that enrich local communities.' Schemes include Peer Support [perhaps the same as CSV Learning Together], in which older school pupils or undergraduates support the learning of younger pupils; the Council for Citizenship and Learning in the Community, in which CSV works with colleges and universities to create opportunities for students to meet community needs; Barclays New Futures Awards, in which £1 million is used to support the community activities of schools; and the promotion of, and training in, the teaching of citizenship.

- CSV Environment (£0.9 million). This involves people with little or no environmental experience in improving areas where they live and

work. 'We tackle social exclusion and encourage active citizenship by providing opportunities for people of all ages and backgrounds to volunteer.'

- CSV RSVP (£0.8 million). This is the Retired and Senior Volunteer programme, and is a growing organisation of older and retired people with a network of groups and projects, helping, for example, in schools, doctors' surgeries, museums, day centres, woodlands, gardens and much more.

- CSV Innovations (£0.5 million). These are pilot programmes, currently covering Employee Volunteering; Allies, involving mature volunteer befrienders who act as role models, mentors and friends for young people in the care system; and GO, which offers short hours volunteering opportunities at weekends for busy people.

- CSV Other Projects (£0.8 million).

Volunteers

'Volunteering is at the heart of CSV's activities and last year over 100,000 people volunteered through us. There are volunteer opportunities for everyone.'

Funding, administration

The programmes are largely funded by government, both central and European (£15.1 million) and local (£2 million), by earnings or payments for expenses (£6.1 million), and by voluntary income in the form of donations from trusts, foundations, companies and others (£2.6 million). This last was achieved at a fundraising cost of £1 million, a ratio of a high 40p in the pound, but a reduction from the 43p of the previous year. These figures, of course, take no account of the huge value of freely donated charitable work that is generated by the expenditures of the charity.

The information assessed

There are two annual reports: one under that name consisting mainly of six examples of the work of the charity, plus summary accounts; and the 'Report of the Council', attached to the audited accounts. Neither on its own, nor both together, constitutes more than a weak review of the work and progress of the charity as a whole.

The website has good information about the separate programmes, each of which has its own excellent literature.

Contact

237 Pentonville Road
London
N1 9NJ
Tel 020 7278 6601
Website www.csv.org.uk
Chair John Pulford
Elizabeth Hoodless, Director

Cystic Fibrosis Trust

Income	£5,734,000 (2000/01)
Donated income	£5,052,000
Fundraising costs	£1,177,000
Statutory income	£20,000
Top salary	£60,000–£70,000
Paid staff	
Full time	46
Part time	7
Volunteers	330

Aims, activities

Cystic fibrosis is a lung defect caused by a faulty gene. Of the 7,500 sufferers from the condition, 6,000 are aged 25 or less. At present no cure has been found, but recent advances in the science of genetics make such a discovery far more likely. The society, dedicated mainly to research into the condition, is currently trying to raise £15 million over five years to take advantage of these new discoveries.

' "Gene therapy for Cystic Fibrosis continues to make steady progress towards becoming a realistic therapeutic option for the disease." These are the words of an editorial from a recent edition of The Lancet. Steady progress is all very well, but for families coping with Cystic Fibrosis, every day counts. To speed things up, we approached the top researchers in this field. They told us that given an additional £15 million over five years, they would commit to making gene therapy a clinical reality ... It is therefore likely that Cystic Fibrosis will be one of the first major diseases to be treatable by gene therapy: the faulty gene would be repaired or replaced with a healthy copy.'

Meanwhile the charity continues to research into the better control of the symptoms of the disease, and of the associated conditions they cause. It is also concerned with the quality of clinical care for patients, funding specialist staff in more than 40 cystic fibrosis centres. A characteristic of the list of research grants is the relatively large number of comparatively modest awards. The total £3.2 million spent was distributed between almost 70 different programmes.

In May 2001, after a long campaign by the charity, the government agreed that all children should be screened for cystic fibrosis shortly after birth.

In addition to research, there is a family support network, which includes advice and welfare grants.

Volunteers

There are 70 trained voluntary support workers throughout the country. The trust also has an interesting new advocacy project, funded with a £0.6 million grant from the Lottery's Community Fund, through which young adults, who have cystic fibrosis themselves, represent patients in their area (mostly children) to the NHS professionals in charge of the relevant services.

Funding, administration

The charity is almost wholly dependent on voluntary fundraising, with donations generated locally or regionally contributing £2.2 million or almost half of the total in 2000/01. Legacies accounted for £658,000 and company support for an impressive £400,000. Fundraising costs of £1.2 million represented 23p in the pound, or 23%, of voluntary income, similar to the figure for the preceding year but somewhat higher than the 20% average for the three years to 1999.

The decision to seek to raise an additional £3 million a year is ambitious; 'we will have to tap new sources of revenue'. Though the sources intended were not yet clear, the annual report for 2000/01 noted with satisfaction the successful introduction of fundraising through direct mail.

The information assessed

The charity has both a trustees' report, with the accounts, and an annual report. Together they give a good view of the charity's work. There is a good website.

Contact
11 London Road
Bromley
Kent
BR1 1BY
Tel 020 8464 7211
Website www.cftrust.org.uk
Chair Duncan Bluck
Mrs Rosie Barnes, Chief Executive

Diabetes UK
(formerly The British Diabetic Association)

Income	£16,255,000 (2000)
Donated income	£13,091,000
Fundraising costs	£1,811,000
Statutory income	£0
Top salary	£60,000–£70,000
Paid staff	
Full time	29
Part time	145
Volunteers	10,000

Aims, activities

The charity exists both to improve the lives of people with diabetes and to work towards a future without diabetes.

It was difficult to determine the specific activities of the charity from the information available. There are examples, but the work is not classified or categorised beyond three general headings, and these headings differ in the two places where they are to be found.

The charity's annual report for 2000/01 notes its three core areas of work as:

● campaigning;

● information;

● research.

The accounts for 2000 show expenditure as:

● social care £7.1 million;

● research £5.5 million;

● support costs £1.9 million.

The description in the 2000/01 annual review headed 'Caring' describes a number of information services. There is a telephone 'Careline' which handled more than 47,000 enquiries (tel: 020 7636 6112; e-mail: careline@diabetes.org.uk). A number of care-related publications and audiotapes were produced, and events were organised to allow young people and their families to learn more about managing diabetes. Nevertheless, this list seems unlikely to account for the full £7 million apparently expended under this heading, and there may well be a range of other care services and activities. Indeed, in one limited field, the annual review for the previous year refers to no less than '43 projects focused on helping people with diabetes in black and other minority ethnic communities'.

The 450 local groups offer the chance for people with diabetes to share their experiences. Some or all of them may offer more specific caring services, or they may be mainly fundraising entities. The 2000/01 annual review says that 'we have transferred some resources from central office to be administered locally', perhaps by these groups. Otherwise there is little reference to the work of this apparently extensive local network.

The 'How we can help' section of the website offers two specific services: these are low-cost insurance and other financial planning services, delivered through a partnership with the Heath Lambert insurance brokerage.

The charity does not carry out research itself, but is a funder of research by others. There was exciting progress to report in 2001. A technique has been developed in Canada to implant insulin-producing 'islet' cells into people with Type 1 diabetes and this charity has set up the Diabetes UK Islet Transplantation Consortium to replicate and refine the procedure. It potentially offers some people with diabetes a much less disruptive way of tackling the disease than the current need for regular injections of insulin. This research project, and other similar ones being set up around the world, may be the most important development in the treatment of diabetes for a long time.

Campaigning in 2000/01 was led by the 'Missing Million' campaign, centred on the fact that there are probably a million people in the UK who have diabetes and don't know it. There were also campaigns centred on the limitations of commercial driving licences for people with diabetes, and consultation about the forthcoming Diabetes National Framework for the NHS.

The 2000/01 annual review refers to a new campaigning programme as part of 'the relaunch of the organisation'. This is probably a reference to the change of name in 1999, and to a 'new management structure' and the fact that 'we are looking at changes in the way we operate'. There is a welcome emphasis on regionalisation and on local outreach, but details of what this means in practice are still to come.

Volunteers

There are over 450 voluntary groups which 'are at the frontline in supporting people living with diabetes, raising awareness of diabetes as an issue, and promoting the organisation – to name just a few activities. Groups also contribute around £500,000 towards the £4.5 million spent annually by Diabetes UK on research into diabetes and related issues.'

Groups undertake a range of core activities, including fundraising, campaigning, support, self-help and information provision. However, each group is different and decides which activities or range of activities to undertake (though none offer medical advice).

Funding, administration

This is a membership organisation, with over 190,000 members. There are 30 trustees, some of them elected by the membership, some representing different sections of the charity. This would generally be regarded as an uncomfortably large number for an active governing body, but the governance structure of the organisation is currently under review.

The head office is in Westminster, London, and there are national offices in Wales, Scotland and Northern Ireland, as well as regional offices in the north-west, in Darlington in the north-east and in the west Midlands. There are 174 paid staff. The 'new management structure' is not described.

Legacies were the biggest source of funding in 2000 (£6.2 million), followed by donations (£5 million) and subscriptions (£1.5 million). The charity has an income of over £1 million from its publications, but it is not clear whether this is before or after deduction of the costs involved. Its trading activities, led by two lotteries, contributed a net £1 million.

The voluntary income was achieved at a fundraising cost of £1.8 million, or a low 14p in the pound. This income should rise further in coming years, because during the year fundraising expenditure rose by 16% 'as we invested in future income streams', which makes the low costs ratio even more impressive.

The information assessed

The weak annual report and accounts and annual review did not allow a satisfactory description of the charity to be drafted, as they were especially lacking in description of how the charity is organised (though they were admirable from the point of view of readability). The website seems excellent about diabetes and connected issues, but is also weak on the organisation itself.

Contact

10 Queen Anne Street
London
W1M 0BD
Tel 020 7323 1531
Website www.diabetes.org.uk
Chair Sir M Hirst
Paul Streets, Chief Executive

Disability advice centres and the DIAL Network

DIAL UK is the national organisation for the DIAL Network – 140 disability advice centres run by and for people with disabilities, normally on a voluntary basis.

DIALs are local services offering free, independent information and advice on any aspect of disability. They provide telephone information and drop-in advice centres and many can arrange home visits for less mobile clients. DIALs are independent organisations with their own management committees, staff and volunteers; the majority of those involved are people with disabilities themselves. DIAL services are designed especially for disabled people, but they are open to anyone with a need to know about disability and they are used by carers as well as health professionals and social workers. Volunteers can expect support and training, and out of pocket expenses may be paid.

DIAL UK coordinates the network and provides members with a range of specialist support, including:

● information on paper and on the 'Tracks' computer database;

● training for advice workers and managers;

● telephone support with rights and management queries.

To find out more about opportunities for volunteering, or for advice, contact a local DIAL. They can be identified locally or through DIAL UK (tel: 01302 310123; website: www.dialuk.org.uk).

See also the entry for *Disability charities*.

Disability charities

Many people are interested in supporting charities which deal with particular illnesses and conditions, perhaps because they have affected their family or friends. There are many thousands of such charities, but the following partial list of some of them might be useful (those organisations which have their own entries in this book are shown in italics). The telephone numbers refer to the head office for each charity; where there is also a helpline number this is shown in bold; website addresses are given where possible.

Perhaps the best general source of information is the directory produced by Contact a Family (tel: 020 7383 3555; website: www.cafamily.org.uk). Those interested in scientific and medical research on particular conditions should refer to the entry for *Medical research charities*; or for more general advice concerning life with a disability, the infomation on *Disability advice centres and the DIAL Network* should be helpful.

Allergies: Action Against Allergy; tel: 020 8892 2711

Alzheimer's: *Alzheimer's Society*; tel: 020 7306 0606, **0845 300 0336**; www.alzheimers.org.uk

Anxiety disorders: National Phobics Society; tel: 0870 770 0456

Arthritis: *Arthritis Care*; tel: 020 7380 6555, **0808 800 4050**; www.arthritiscare.org.uk

Asthma: *National Asthma Campaign*; tel: 020 7226 2260, **0845 701 0203**; www.asthma.org.uk

Autism: *The National Autistic Society*; tel: 020 7833 2299, **0870 600 8585**; www.nas.org.uk

Brain tumours: Brain Tumour Foundation; tel: 020 8336 2020

Brittle bone diseases: Brittle Bone Society; tel: 01382 204446, **0800 028 2459**; www.brittlebone.org

Cancer: Cancerbacup; tel: 020 7696 9003, **0808 800 1234**; www.cancerbacup.org.uk

Cerebral palsy: *Scope*; tel: 020 7619 7100, **0808 800 3333**; www.scope.org.uk

Coeliac disease: Coeliac Society: tel: 01494 437278; www.coeliac.co.uk

Cot death: Foundation for the Study of Infant Deaths; tel: 020 7222 8001, **020 7233 2090**; www.sids.org.uk/

Cystic fibrosis: Cystic Fibrosis Trust; tel: 020 8464 7211; www.cftrust.org.uk

Deafness: *Royal National Institute for Deaf People*; tel: 0808 808 123, textphone: 0808 808 9000; www.rnid.org.uk

Diabetes: *Diabetes UK*; tel: 020 7323 1531; www.diabetes.org.uk

Down's syndrome: Down's Syndrome Association; tel: 020 8682 4001; www.downs-syndrome.org.uk

Dyslexia: The British Dyslexia Association; tel: 0118 966 8271/2

Eating disorders: The Eating Disorders Association; tel: 01603 621414

Eczema: National Eczema Society; tel: 020 7281 3553, **0870 241 3604**; www.eczema.org

Epilepsy: The National Society for Epilepsy; tel: 01494 601300, **01494 601400**; www.epilepsynse.org.uk

Haemophilia: Haemophilia Society; tel: 020 7380 0600, **0800 018 6068**; www.haemophilia.org.uk

Heart defects: *British Heart Foundation*; tel: 020 7935 0185; www.bhf.org.uk

HIV infections & AIDS: *Terrence Higgins Trust*; tel: 020 7831 0330, **020 7242 1010**; www.tht.org.uk

Kidney disease: National Kidney Federation; tel: 01909 487795, **0845 601 0209**; www.kidney.org.uk

Learning disability: *Mencap*; tel: 020 7454 0454; www.mencap.org.uk

Leukaemia and allied blood disorders: Leukaemia Care Society; tel: 01905 330003, **0800 169 6680**; www.leukaemiacare.org

Liver disease: British Liver Trust; tel: 01473 276326

Lung diseases: Breathe Easy; tel: 020 7831 5831

Lupus: LUPUS UK; tel: 01708 731251

Meningitis: *National Meningitis Trust*; tel: 01453 768000, **0845 600 0800**; www.meningitis-trust.org.uk

Mental health: *Mind*; tel: 020 8519 2122; www.mind.org.uk

Metabolic diseases: CLIMB; tel: 0870 770 0326; www.climb.org.uk

Migraine: The Migraine Trust; tel: 020 7831 4818

Motor Neurone Disease: *Motor Neurone Disease Association*; tel: 01604 250505, **08457 626262**; www.mndassociation.org.uk

Multiple Sclerosis: *Multiple Sclerosis Society*; tel: 020 8438 0701, **020 7361 8000**; www.mssociety.org.uk

Muscular Dystrophy and allied disorders: *Muscular Dystrophy Campaign*; tel: 020 7720 8055, **020 7819 1801/1816**; www.muscular-dystrophy.org

Osteoporosis: *The National Osteoporosis Society*; tel: 01761 471771, **01761 472721**; www.nos.org.uk

Parkinson's disease: *Parkinson's Disease Society*; tel: 020 7931 8080, **0808 800 0303** www.parkinsons.org.uk

Pituitary disorders: The Pituitary Foundation; tel: 0117 927 3355

Sickle Cell Anaemia: The Sickle Cell Society; tel: 020 8961 7795, **0808 800 0303**; www.sicklecellsociety.org

Speech and language impairment: AFASIC; tel: 020 7490 9410; www.afasic.org.uk

Spinal injuries: Spinal Injuries Association; tel: 020 8444 2121; www.spinal.co.uk

Stroke: *The Stroke Association*; tel: 020 7566 0300; www.stroke.org.uk

Thyroid disorders: British Thyroid Foundation; tel: 0113 392 4600

Visual impairment: *Royal National Institute for the Blind*; tel: 020 7388 1266, **0845 766 9999**; www.rnib.org.uk

Dogs Home Battersea

Income	£10,375,000 (2000)
Donated income	£8,304,000
Fundraising costs	£477,000
Statutory income	£188,000
Top salary	£60,000–£70,000
Paid staff	220
Volunteers	50

Aims, activities

The charity, to this editor's surprise, turned out to be a cats' home too. It takes in lost or stray dogs and cats, 'rehabilitates' them if necessary and, wherever possible, finds them a new home. Famously, 'no dog or cat suitable for rehoming is ever put to sleep'. The charity operates at three locations: Battersea, London; Old Windsor, Berkshire; and Brands Hatch, Kent.

Set up in 1860, by 1896 the charity was taking in over 40,000 dogs a year, nearly four times the present 12,000 or so. The Dogs Act reduced the flow in 1906 to about 23,000. During the First World War the home took in soldiers' pets as their owners went to war – this is the first mention of cats. During the Second World War, among other things the home supplied dogs to be parachuted into minefields. In 1995 a specialist rehabilitation unit was introduced.

In 2000 about half the 12,000 dogs and 4,000 cats arriving at the homes were given to the charity. Most of the other cats were strays; of the dogs most came via the police or the local authorities. Half the dogs and three quarters of the cats were re-homed. Over a quarter of the dogs were reclaimed (though few cats), and 461 dogs had to be put to sleep.

Volunteers

The main reference to volunteers in the annual report is to the team of volunteer dog walkers, who both went on 7,000 walks but also put in 1,000 hours of on-site socialising with dogs and cats. The website's enticing suggestion of '101 ways to help' led to only five suggestions, mostly to do with fundraising.

Funding, administration

The charity is funded primarily by legacies, which made up over three quarters of its income in 2000 and 69% in the previous year. Donations of £421,000 accounted for just 4% of total income. The charity also earns substantial amounts from sales and claims fees, and from the police and local authorities who pay it to take in dogs from them.

The voluntary income of £8.3 million was achieved at a fundraising cost of just £477,000, giving a very low ratio of 6p in the pound.

The charity has free reserves of over £30 million, equal to more than four years' expenditure, and showed a surplus of £2 million for the year (compared with a surplus of £5 million the year before), no doubt helped by its massive TV exposure. The charity has plans for substantial building expansion at both Battersea and Old Windsor, though the London project has been much delayed by problems in taking over two acres of land from the former British Rail.

The information assessed

The good annual report and accounts are presented in a nostalgically old-fashioned form. There is a clear, straightforward website.

Contact

4 Battersea Park Road
London
SW8 4AA
Tel 020 7622 3626
Website www.dogshome.org
Chair The Earl of Buchan
Duncan Green, Director General

Donkey Sanctuary

Income	£11,629,000 (2000/01)
Donated income	£10,867,000
Fundraising costs	£688,000
Statutory income	£0
Top salary	£60,000–£70,000
Paid staff	
Full time	232
Part time	47
Volunteers	
Operational	37
Fundraising	900

Aims, activities

Now aiming to prevent the suffering of donkeys and mules worldwide, the charity was originally set up in 1969 to offer a sanctuary to donkeys in the UK. It has 11 farms in Britain and Ireland, though its original base in Devon appears to be much the largest, with about 500 mostly elderly donkeys in residence. Since 1969 over 8,000 donkeys have been taken into care and more than 1,500 have been fostered out to individual homes.

Donkeys are given a home for life, but they are not bred and stallions are normally castrated. The Devon centre is open to the public and has become a significant tourist attraction. There is no charge for admission, but 'visitors are generous' with donations, so the closure to visitors in 2001 due to foot and mouth disease was a cost rather than a saving.

One aspect of the charity's operations is the production of its own hay; impressively, over 3,000 tons in 2000/01, worth nearly £200,000.

The charity has a large network of Welfare Officers (both full/part time and voluntary), and spends considerable energies in improving public awareness of the needs of donkeys. The sanctuary employs five of its own veterinary officers and is a centre of expertise on the care of the donkey.

In October 2000 the charity merged with the International Donkey Protection Trust and it now has projects in Kenya, Ethiopia, Mexico, Europe and India.

Volunteers

The majority of volunteers are fundraisers and/or voluntary speakers and are essential in raising awareness and funds for the charity. Unfortunately, the charity is unable to use volunteer workers at the donkey farms, because it likes to maintain a constant group of carers for the donkeys, who often need specialist care.

The sanctuary is in constant need of help to raise funds to continue with its work for the donkeys. When the opportunity arises for an Area Welfare Officer, volunteers are considered.

As a connected charity, the Elisabeth Svendsen Trust for Children and Donkeys brings donkeys into the lives of children with special needs and disabilities. Volunteers local to the three centres provide valued help.

Funding, administration

The charity's founder and moving spirit, Elisabeth Svendsen, is not a trustee but is the salaried chief executive. The trustee body is unusual in not having a named chair.

Funding comes overwhelmingly from legacies. These made up £9.1 million or 85% of the charity's £10.9 million voluntary income in 2000/01. This was achieved at a fundraising cost of £688,000, giving a cost ratio of a very low 6p in the pound. The charity has a mailing list of over 170,000 ('guarded carefully'!) and a quarter of a million pounds each year is spent on postage – the biggest single fundraising cost.

The charity adds ...

To us, donkeys come first, second and third. We are now working worldwide for donkeys, and have a mammoth task. We are so very grateful to everyone who supports our work and helps us to help so many donkeys in distress.

The information assessed

The good annual report and accounts and annual review are backed by an informative website and a range of literature.

Contact

Sidmouth
Devon
EX10 0NU
Tel 01395 578222
Website www.thedonkeysanctuary.org.uk
Dr Elisabeth Svendsen, Chief Executive

Duke of Edinburgh's Award

Developing youth initiative

Income	£6,444,000 (2000/01)
Donated income	£4,093,000
Fundraising costs	£933,000
Statutory income	£338,000
Top salary	£70,001–£80,000
Paid staff	92
Volunteers	55,500

Aims, activities

The charity offers a Scheme of Awards for young people in the UK and internationally, to develop character and promote 'good citizenship'. The programme is open to any young person between the ages of 14 and 25, and is intended to challenge the individual, not to introduce competition between participants.

There are three awards aimed at different age groups – Bronze (for those over 14), Silver (over 15s), and Gold (over 16s) – which are usually promoted by 'schools, youth clubs, open Award centres and local voluntary groups'. Qualification depends upon the completion of four sections (service, expeditions, physical recreation and skills) which are each monitored by an expert advisory body. Over 100,000 young people enter for an award each year.

Expansion of the scheme is a major goal, both geographically and within new areas of society, such as in the prison service.

The scheme is run by more than 400 'operating authorities', mainly local authorities but also voluntary organisations, independent schools and industry and business. These delegate the day to day running of the programme to over 10,000 operating groups. This structure is supported by 480 paid staff, usually employed by the operating authorities, who perform a variety of roles, from processing the awards and general administration, to award development and promotion (for example within schools).

There are 11 regional offices, with full time staff, who coordinate and regulate the 434 local operating authorities.

Volunteers

The award is largely organised and supported by an estimated 70,000 volunteers, 55,000 of whom run and support local operating groups. Their responsibilities vary from working directly with award groups, to advising the regional and national committees.

Funding, administration

Voluntary income for 2000/01 was almost £4.1 million, down from £4.3 million in the previous year. It represented about two thirds of the total income. Fundraising costs were £933,000, giving a cost ratio of 23p in the pound.

Most of the money was spent on regional operational support – £3.8 million.

The charity has built up free reserves of £11.1 million, equal to 19 months' expenditure. This has been done deliberately to 'assure the viability of the charity in the longer term'.

The charity adds ...

The year to March 2001 showed a pleasing increase of over 6% in new entrants. Significant headway has also been made in enhancing the Award's 'reach' to young people of all backgrounds and abilities. New operational and marketing initiatives aim to build on the achievements of the past 45 years.

The information assessed

The annual report and the trustees' report and accounts are excellent. There is a good website.

Contact

Gulliver House
Madeira Walk
Windsor
SL4 1EU
Tel 01753 727430
Website www.theaward.org
Chair Sir Tom Farmer
Vice-Admiral Michael Gretton, Director

Elizabeth Finn Trust

(formerly the Distressed Gentlefolks Aid Association)

Income	£16,670,000 (2000/01)
Top salary	£70,000 £80,000
Paid staff	380
Volunteers	750

Aims, activities

Founded by Elizabeth Finn in 1897 as the Distressed Gentlefolk's Aid Association, and previously widely known as the DGAA, the charity has now taken on the name of its founder.

The trust's goal is to help British and Irish people who come from a professional or similar background, and their immediate families. The two main activities (with their 2000/01 expenditures) are:

- Running 13 residential and nursing homes, with over 550 residents (£14.7 million). All but one are in the midlands or the south of England. Fees are paid partly by residents and partly by the relevant local authority.

- Providing financial support and assistance (£2.5 million). Support is always at a level that will not affect statutory benefits, and over 1,700 people were helped in this way, or simply by receiving advice and support.

The charity is presently considering the introduction of a domiciliary care service for people suffering from dementia.

Volunteers

'Meeting the needs of everyone in the Elizabcth Finn Trust "family" requires the hard work of some 1,600 people. Of these, 750 are volunteers ... who serve on a variety of committees and maintain contact with our beneficiaries all over the world.'

Funding, administration

The charity is funded primarily by fees from or for patients and residents, totalling £11.6 million in 2000/01. Voluntary income was £3.6 million, about 90% of it in the form of legacies. It was achieved at a fundraising cost of £745,000, a ratio of 21p in the pound.

The accounts do not distinguish between income from the fees paid by individuals and those that come from social service departments, which makes it difficult to get an overall view of the charity's finances.

The information assessed

The charity has an annual report as well as a report of the board of trustees, both of them nicely presented. Together they give a good view of the charity's work. The website was 'under construction' in October 2001.

Contact

1 Derry Street
London
W8 5HY
Tel 020 7396 6700
Website www.elizabethfinntrust.org.uk
Chair Billy Carbutt
Jonathan Welfare, Chief Executive

English National Opera

Income	£26,367,000 (1999/00)
Donated income	£2,028,000
Fundraising costs	£448,000
Statutory income	£13,996,000
Top salary	£100,000–£110,000
Paid staff	547
Volunteers	10

Aims, activities

The singular characteristic of English National Opera is that its performances are sung in English, usually requiring translation of the libretto concerned. It is based at the Coliseum Theatre in London, which it owns (and where it now intends to stay). ENO operates on a repertory basis, with a permanent company of about 200 singers and musicians, seeking to offer top quality opera at accessible prices. In the year 1999/00 there were 175 performances to audiences of 318,000 people, representing 77% of capacity. The theatre is also used for performances by visiting opera and ballet companies.

The company does not normally tour or perform outside London.

ENO has substantial educational and outreach activities, called the Baylis programme, but there is no information about this work in the annual report. The website says that it 'runs a wide range of projects with individuals and groups of all ages, aiming to encourage access to English National Opera's productions, artists and resources'.

Volunteers

There is a 'Friends of ENO' scheme for supporters of the organisation.

Funding, administration

The main source of income for the charity is its grant from the Arts Council, a government-funded body. In 1999/00 this grant was for £12 million. Another £7.2 million came from the sale of tickets and £1 million from the proceeds of other companies using the Coliseum. Voluntary income totalled £2 million. This was divided roughly equally between support and sponsorship from companies, and donations and legacies from individuals. Fundraising costs of £448,000 represented 22p in the pound of this income.

The charity is being helped to pay off past debts by further support from the Arts Council lottery funds, to a level of £1.3 million in the year. It is also seeking additional funds from this source for the rebuilding and development of its theatre. If agreed, these will require matching funds to be raised from other sources.

The information assessed

The adequate but brief annual report and accounts are backed by a simple website.

Contact

The London Coliseum
St Martin's Lane
London
WC2N 4ES
Tel 020 7836 0111
Website www.eno.org.uk
Chair John Baker
Nicholas Payne, General Director

European Children's Trust

Aims, activities

As this book was being written, the charity was merging with the Christian Children's Fund of Great Britain to form a new charity, *EveryChild*.

EveryChild

Child welfare overseas

Income	See below
Top salary	£50,000–£60,000
Paid staff	
Full time	46
Part time	13
Volunteers	10

Aims, activities

As this book was being written, this new charity was being formed from a merger of the former European Children's Trust and the Christian Children's Fund of Great Britain. The new charity will be taking on all the programmes of the two individual organisations and so will be working in 18 countries in the following areas:

● South America (3 countries);

● East Africa (3);

● India and South-east Asia (3);

● Eastern Europe and the former Soviet Union (9).

The new charity is non-denominational. 'Our focus is on practical projects ... that enable communities ... to fight poverty and to bring about long-term, sustainable and locally owned change for children.'

The European Children's Trust worked in Eastern Europe and the former Soviet Union, promoting improved social services and care for children. It developed from the Romanian Orphanages Trust and represented one of the few surviving links with the surge of new charities that sprang up after 1989 to help orphaned and abandoned children in Romania. Its projects, which will continue, were primarily concerned with preventing abandonment and with providing alternatives to the institutionalisation of children. The charity used its experience to advise national and regional governments on how best to move away from the old-style institutional care that used to be standard in the region.

In 1999 a critic of the charity persuaded a television programme to make a damaging attack on it that was, in this editor's view at the time, largely unfounded.

The Christian Children's Fund was the fairly recent offshoot of the much bigger US charity of that name, which has an income of about $120 million a year, more than half of it deriving from child sponsorship – an approach of which it was a pioneer over 60 years ago. Its projects, involving community development (particularly health and education), are run in all four of the geographical areas listed above.

This charity had grown rapidly and had an income of £5 million in 1999/00, over £3.5 million of it from child sponsorship contributions.

Volunteers

It was too early for information to be available about the volunteer policies of the new charity. But they certainly welcome volunteers – contact Jill Forster or Heather Stephenson for details.

Funding, administration

The income and fundraising costs of the two charities in the most recent year for which accounts are available were as follows:

European Children's Trust

Total income	£4.3 million
Voluntary income	£4.2 million
Fundraising costs	£1.4 million

Christian Children's Fund of GB

Total income	£4.7 million
Voluntary income	£4.1 million
Fundraising costs	£0.3 million

The fundraising costs of the European Children's Trust were a high 34p for each pound raised. This, though, was a sharp improvement on the 51p in the pound of the previous year, due to both a rise in the value of donations and a modest fall in fundraising costs.

The Christian Children's Fund of GB had been growing in recent years, with income rising from £3.5 million in 1995 to £4.7 million in 1999. Most of this came from child sponsorship. Fundraising costs of £330,000 in 1999 were a very low 8% of the voluntary income received. The charity, a little unusually in its field, did not receive support from statutory sources such as the Department for International Development. However, such support will now be sought by EveryChild.

The charity adds ...

Merger offers us a great opportunity to share expertise and bring increased benefit to disadvantaged children around the world as effectively as possible.

The information assessed

There were at the time of writing no new materials available from this charity. The website is probably the best source of up-to-date information.

Contact

4 Bath Place
Rivington Street
London
EC2A 3DR
Tel 020 7729 8191
Website www.everychild.org.uk
Chair John Gerry
Robert Pritchett, Chief Executive

Fairbridge

Young people in England, Wales and Scotland

Income	£4,871,000 (1999/00)
Donated income	£2,898,000
Fundraising costs	£643,000
Statutory income	£1,753,000
Top salary	£40,000–£50,000
Paid staff	168
Volunteers	35

Aims, activities

The charity helps disadvantaged young people living in inner cities. It has 12 centres where those aged between 14 and 25, identified as being in need of support, are offered the chance to voluntarily attend a programme to enable them to develop the personal and social skills they need. Each centre has a team of 12–20 staff.

The young people concerned include those excluded from school, in trouble with the police or removed to local authority care, among many other circumstances. They are identified by the charity's 19 outreach workers, who work mainly with thousands of other organisations where young people's need of the Fairbridge programme may become apparent, but they also make particular efforts to find those who have fallen through all the gaps and are not known to any other agency.

After an initial induction course there is a range of other courses or activities and the programme continues for as long as necessary. In 1999/00 some 75% of those on the induction course went on to further Fairbridge activities, a high retention rate. Each young person has the long-term support of a personal mentor.

In 1999/00 over 3,000 young people benefited from these programmes, an increase of 20% on the previous year. The 12 centres are in Edinburgh, Glasgow, Newcastle upon Tyne, Teesside, Manchester, Liverpool, Birmingham, Cardiff, Bristol, London, Chatham and Southampton.

One aspect of the charity's work is the opportunity for young people to live and work on its fine sail training ship, *Spirit of Fairbridge*, itself built by unemployed shipwrights on the Mersey.

Volunteers

This is a primarily professionally staffed charity, though there are a few volunteers working with the 12 local teams.

Funding, administration

The charity's funding is diverse, but dominated by voluntary donations, including legacies. This voluntary income made up £2.9 million of the total £4.9 million in 1999/00 and was achieved at a fundraising cost of £643,000, giving a cost ratio of 22p in the pound – an average maintained for four years, during which the charity's voluntary income has increased by about 50%.

Another £1.8 million was received from a disconcerting array of no less than 35 separate statutory sources. Each of these has to be separately negotiated, which seems an unnecessarily complicated way of distributing public money.

The charity adds ...

Working with young people, aged 14–25, in 12 of the most disadvantaged areas in the country, we aim to do nothing less than change the way they think about themselves.

Through a combination of long-term personal support and practical learning experiences, Fairbridge give young people an opportunity to overcome the odds and prove to themselves and others what they are capable of achieving.

The information assessed

The excellent annual report and accounts and annual review are backed by first-class fact sheets and a good magazine, *Challenger*. The website is simple and clear.

Contact

207 Waterloo Road
London
SE1 8XD
Tel 020 7928 1704
Website www.fairbridge.org.uk
Chair Antony Beevor
Nigel Haynes, Director

Friends of the Earth UK

Environmental campaigning; England, Wales and Northern Ireland

Income	£5,859,000 (1999/00)
Donated income	£5,330,000
Fundraising costs	£302,000
Statutory income	£114,000
Top salary	see below
Paid staff	121

Aims, activities

Friends of the Earth is an international network, probably the world's largest in the environmental field. This entry covers the two central organisations of Friends of the Earth in England, Wales and Northern Ireland (to whom the figures above apply) and also to the many local FoE groups in the country (there is a separate Friends of the Earth Scotland; tel: 0131 554 9977).

The activities of Friends of the Earth are not necessarily charitable according to archaic British charity law. FoE Trust Ltd, a registered charity, carries out those activities, mainly educational in the broadest sense, that do qualify. The environmental campaigning is conducted by the non-charitable (though equally non-profit-making) FoE Ltd. This entry covers both bodies together, but readers should note that only donations to the trust can benefit from the tax benefits available to registered charities. The organisation is at pains to ensure that money given to the charity is only used for appropriately charitable educational or research activities, even when some of these are carried out for it by the non-charitable body.

In Britain the two national organisations, which share offices and staff, are supported by over 200 local FoE groups. These, though authorised by the central organisation to use the FoE name and logo, are legally independent bodies. They also do not qualify to be recognised as charities.

There are three key activities:

- campaigning – pressuring government and business to adopt policies and practices which ensure environmental protection, conservation and the sustainable use of natural resources;

- citizen action – activating people and communities locally and nationally to reduce their impact on the environment, and to push government, industry and financial institutions to adopt the environmental agenda;

- research and communication – providing reliable, accessible and provocative information and ideas about environmental problems and their solution.

In addition to the many local campaigns of the individual groups, the organisation has seven main campaigning areas on a national or international scale:

- Real food: FoE campaigns against toxic residues from pesticides and against the introduction of genetically modified (GM) foods, working especially through pressure on the major supermarket groups.

- Climate change: this is mainly an international campaign, with different FoEs working together, but there is also extensive work at home, such as the now successful campaign that led that to the Warm

Homes and Energy Conservation Act. This should lead to efficiency improvements in more than 6 million homes.

- Safer chemicals: FoE campaigns against the use of untested chemicals in household products; over 300 of these have been identified.

- Living world: based on a bill drafted by FoE, the Countryside and Rights of Way Act 2000 gives legal protection for the first time to over 40,000 local wildlife sites.

- Corporate alert: this campaign demonstrates links between big UK financial companies and destruction of the living world. For example, Norwich Union's high exposure to unethical investments led to the company adopting a new ethical engagement strategy.

- Waste and recycling: this is mainly concerned with improving UK practice.

- Trade and social justice: this is a campaign against the harmful aspects of globalisation, especially in agriculture.

Though each local group is independent, they are supported by the main organisation, which, for example, spent £0.5 million in 1999/00 on supporter recruitment for the movement as a whole.

Volunteers

Much of the voluntary activity is carried out by the 200 or so local FoE groups, although there are also substantial numbers of volunteers in the main organisations. There are no figures for the numbers of people involved in these groups, which are not normally charitable in law, or for their cumulative income, but in each case these will be in addition to the figures given above.

Funding, administration

FoE is almost wholly funded by donations from individuals. No breakdown is given for the £3.7 million of supporters' contributions to the non-charitable FoE Ltd in 1999/00, but £258,000 of the £1.3 million given to the charitable FoE Trust was in the form of legacies – so perhaps the stereotype of the environmentally active citizen as primarily youthful needs some adjustment.

Fundraising costs of £302,000 represented a very low 6p for each pound donated, but a further £500,000 was spent on the recruitment of supporters, many of whom will have become subscription paying members as well as supporters of the campaigns. Even including this amount, the total costs would still be a low 15p in the pound.

The £114,000 of statutory funding came from the London Boroughs Grants scheme, for a London-wide environmental information and enquiries project.

The charity operated with reserves equal to a modest two months' of operating costs.

The accounts of the Friends of the Earth Trust show that no member of staff received a salary of as much as £40,000. There are no comparable figures for Friends of the Earth Ltd, but the accounts note that the chairman, Sam Clarke, received just over £5,000 in recompense for the time given to the organisation.

The charity adds ...

Friends of the Earth provides a free Information Service, which responds to over 30,000 enquiries per year. We provide a

range of resources including publications, many of which are free, and more briefings, reports and press releases on our website at www.foe.co.uk. Contact by email: info@foe.co.uk or by freephone: 0808 800 1111.

The information assessed

The annual report and accounts and annual review are adequate. More information on the input of volunteers and on the work of local FoE groups would be welcome. The accounts for the non-charitable FoE Ltd are in the same general format as is required of charities, but the level of the higher salaries is not noted.

There is an adequate website and good supporting materials.

Contact
26–28 Underwood Street
London
N1 7JQ
Tel 020 7490 1555
Website www.foe.co.uk
Chair Sam Clarke
Charles Secrett, Director

Friends of the Hebrew University of Jerusalem

Income	£4,736,826 (1999/00)
Donated income	£3,903,780
Fundraising costs	£445,258
Statutory income	£0
Top salary	£50,000–£59,999 (2)
Paid staff	10

Aims, activities

The charity's object is to promote in the UK and Ireland the academic and research interests and development of the Hebrew University of Jerusalem.

FHU states that its priorities are to achieve this 'by supporting students and providing financial assistance to improve the infrastructure and research facilities of the University; to encourage academic exchange; and recruit students for the various courses for overseas students offered by the University'.

FHU places school and university students on courses at the Hebrew University of Jerusalem that range from six weeks to a year. The charity does not say how many students were placed on courses in 1999/00, but the figure for the previous year was over 100.

The charity is also playing 'a major role' in the university's worldwide campaign, launched in 1997, to raise US$1,000 million over five years.

Volunteers

Volunteers are involved in raising money and gifts in kind. There are 18 'Friends' Groups', some of which are regional (one each in Ireland, Scotland and Wales, for example), while others are London-based interest groups (such as an archaeological group and a legal group).

Funding, administration

Of the £4.7 million total income in 1999/00, £3.9 million was in the form of donations – including £843,000 in legacies. This compared with donations of £3.8 million in 1998/99, including £285,000 in legacies.

The steep rise in legacy income followed a successful 'Legacy Tour' to Israel in 1998/99, which resulted in several pledges being made to FHU; this exercise was repeated in 2000/01, with participants pledging a minimum legacy of £10,000.

Fundraising costs of £445,000 in 1999/00 meant that the charity spent a low 11p for every pound it raised in donations and gifts. This figure was little different from the previous year's 13p in the fundraised pound.

The information assessed

The charity's financial report adequately describes FHU's objects and financial position, but gives little detail on its structure or activities. A newsletter covers special events and awards. There is no website for general access.

Contact

126 Albert Street
London
NW1 7NE
Tel 020 7691 1500
Chair Michael J Gee
Andrea Mail, Executive Director

Fundraising organisations

Some charities, and many organisations that are not charities, raise money not for their own activities but to be passed on as grants to other charities or causes.

A few of these charities are big enough to have their own entries in this book, such as *BBC Children in Need*, the *Variety Club of Great Britain* and *Comic Relief*. There are many smaller local equivalents, such as the appeal charities set up by some local TV or radio stations, or the mayor's appeal funds in many local authorities.

However, much local fundraising is carried out by organisations that are not themselves charities – often social groups such as Rotary clubs or Freemasons' lodges.

Sometimes local groups of these kinds organise their fundraising through associated charities that they have set up for the purpose. This practice is likely to spread as more donors come to expect their gifts to benefit from the Gift Aid tax concession, which is only available to registered charities.

There are no figures for the total amounts of money collected in these ways, though they must be considerable. An attraction is that almost all the activity is carried out voluntarily, involving negligible fundraising costs.

Such groups need to be distinguished from commercial or non-profit fundraising organisations that are raising money under contract to a charity. This is particularly common with telephone fundraising and the recently developed face-to-face fundraising in the street. In these cases the fundraiser is required by law to explain to donors the organisation they represent and the method of remuneration for the fundraiser.

Great Ormond Street Hospital Children's Charity

Income	£22,015,000 (1999/00)
Donated income	£12,595,000
Fundraising costs	£2,879,000
Statutory income	£0
Top salary	£50,000–£60,000

Aims, activities

Great Ormond Street is one of Britain's specialist children's NHS hospitals. As a teaching hospital, its charitable funds were never incorporated into the NHS but remained in the hands of the hospital's 'special trustees'. These now operate primarily under the name of this charity.

Some years ago, the charity's Wishing Well appeal paid for the rebuilding of about one third of the hospital, including the high-dependency wards and the operating theatres. About half the wards are still in the 1930s-built Southwood Building.

The NHS pays the day-to-day running costs of the hospital. The charitable funds are used to enable the rapid acquisition of the most up-to-date equipment, for much-needed family support services, and for research at the associated Institute of Child Health.

A major example of the charity's recent work has been the conversion of two houses next to the hospital into accommodation for the families of children who are having treatment in the hospital.

Volunteers

The hospital's volunteering activity is organised directly rather than through this charity, whose fundraising opportunities are well set out on the website. For more information contact the Volunteer Bureau on 020 7405 9200.

Funding, administration

The sources of the voluntary income are listed, without totals but with examples, as follows:

- corporate partners – an initiative by the Ford car company raised over £100,000;

- donor appeals – the Christmas appeal alone 'raised a net income of £635,000';

- grants from charitable trusts – one majestic gift of £750,000 was received from the Somers Charitable Trust;

- events – these raised a net £235,000;

- schools fundraising – this contributed a net £164,000.

The hospital is gearing up for a new expansion of its fundraising to support another stage of its physical redevelopment.

The charity adds ...

Great Ormond Street helps over 100,000 children every year, often with the most complex or difficult problems. In our 150th year we are looking forward, to provide better care than ever before. Public generosity allows us to support our families, research new cures, or develop new services.

The information assessed

The annual report of the hospital as a whole is excellent, and there are good accounts for this charity. There is also good fundraising literature and a fundraising website.

Contact
40–41 Queen Square
London
WC1N 3AJ
Tel 020 7916 5678
Website www.gosh.org
Chair Andrew Fane
Nigel Clark, Chief Executive

Greenpeace
Environmental campaigning

Income	£5,438,000 (2000)
Donated income	£5,402,000
Fundraising costs	£2,141,000
Statutory income	£0
Top salary	not disclosed
Volunteers	
Operational	2,000

Aims, activities

Greenpeace is dedicated to the protection and enhancement of the environment, using non-violent direct action – on the Quaker-originated basis of 'bearing witness'. It is an international organisation with '2.9 million supporters in 158 countries; 29 national and three multinational offices worldwide. We are based everywhere from Buenos Aires to Moscow, from Tunis to Tokyo. The International office is based in Amsterdam, from where Greenpeace's campaigns are co-ordinated and the fleet of campaign vessels are managed.

'In the UK, Greenpeace is divided into two parts. Greenpeace Limited undertakes campaigning work ranging from promoting solutions, to direct actions, political lobbying and scientific research.' The group has 169,000 supporters. The campaigning work is not all charitable in law, but the organisation's scientific research and educational projects are charitable and are carried out by Greenpeace Environmental Trust, a registered charity. The two organisations have a common management.

This book uses the word 'charity' in the popular rather than the legal sense, and so this entry covers both of these legally separate bodies. It was not possible to get from Greenpeace the accounts for the limited company, but a publication entitled 'Annual Review 2000 Greenpeace' has summary figures that probably apply to the two UK bodies together, so the figures above are taken from this (and are also discussed under 'Funding' below).

Greenpeace uses direct action, such as the successful recent efforts to destroy trial crops of genetically modified (GM) maize, and this can be controversial. 'Greenpeace acts to defend nature. Our use of direct action is legitimate. First, we are always non-violent. Second, we act in defence of a clear moral principle, not economic self-interest. Third, we act to prevent real and irreversible environmental threats, such as genetic pollution.'

In the autumn of 2001 there were seven main Greenpeace campaigns around the world, focusing on:

- protecting the Amazon forests;
- preventing damaging oil development, especially in Alaska;
- promoting renewable energy;
- stopping the use of hazardous chemicals;
- ending commercial whaling;
- confronting the nuclear energy operators;
- direct action against GM foods.

In 2000 the most publicised event for Greenpeace in the UK was the trial, and acquittal, of a group of supporters (including the then director, Peter Melchett) accused of damaging a trial field of GM maize. However, successful efforts to change the practices of major companies, which received less publicity, may be of equal long-term importance. For example, there is a major and successful campaign to stop the use of HFC gases being used to replace the equally damaging CFCs in refrigeration, when there are safe alternatives. The British government has now accepted this as one of its environmental aims, and companies as large as Coca-Cola have been forced to go HFC-free.

Volunteers

There are over 2,000 active supporters, with about 50 'area networkers' around the country as the key contacts. Full information about how to contact them is on the website.

Funding, administration

The governance of the various organisations that make up Greenpeace is unclear. No information was easily available on how the charity takes its decisions or manages its affairs.

The main expenditure figures in the 'Annual Review 2000' are as follows:

- campaign expenses £3,533,000;
- campaign information £460,000;
- other salaries, administration and office costs £514,000;
- subscriptions and donations, direct expenses £717,000;*
- recruiting new supporters, net expenses £517,000;*

- fundraising, research and other marketing costs £507,000.*

These totals are not in the standard charity format where there is a single total for fundraising costs. Of the figures above, those asterisked have been taken as covering fundraising. They suggest that Greenpeace spent £2.1 million to raise £5.4 million in voluntary income, a high cost ratio of 40p in the pound. It is unfortunate that full accounts were not made available so that a more certain figure could have been arrived at.

Greenpeace has been one of the pioneers of face-to-face recruitment, where in-the-street requests are made for regular direct-debit donations. In 2001 Cathy Anderson, Greenpeace's fundraising director, said she thought this market might have reached saturation level, noting that while face-to-face recruitment suits Greenpeace's 'cheeky' image it might not be appropriate to all charities. Even Greenpeace found a high lapse rate of 30% in the first year, but it was still the organisation's most cost-effective fundraising tool.

The information assessed

The accounts for the Greenpeace Charitable Trust and the annual review for Greenpeace 2000 were seen, Together, they were a weak source of information for anyone seeking to understand how Greenpeace is organised and funded. The website, excellent in other respects, was also thin in these areas. Since Greenpeace as a whole is not a charity in law it is not under the same legal obligations to provide such information as most other organisations in this book, but its supporters are being asked to take quite a lot on trust. It may be felt that the charity's achievements justify this.

Contact
Canonbury Villas
London
N1 2PN
Tel 020 7865 8100
Website www.greenpeace.org.uk
Chair Robin Grove-White
Stephen Tindale, Director

Guide Dogs for the Blind

Income	£38,340,000 (2000)
Donated income	£31,853,000
Fundraising costs	£8,181,000
Statutory income	£0
Top salary	£80,000–£90,000
Paid staff	
Full time	1,035
Part time	116
Volunteers	10,000

Aims, activities
The charity is changing and developing. As the original mission of providing a guide dog to everyone who could benefit from one was successfully accomplished some years ago, the charity had been diversifying somewhat randomly – for example into running hotels for blind and partially sighted people (with their dogs) and the existence of massive reserves had led it to run down its fundraising. Under a new chief executive, Geraldine Peacock, it has now been sharply re-focused and is once again driving ahead.

The 'objects' of the charity were extended in 1998 to the wide 'provision of mobility training for blind and partially sighted people in the UK'. Though this includes the provision of guide dogs, it can also cover much else. 'Research commissioned by the association indicates that up to 200,000 people in the UK could currently benefit from outdoor mobility training. The current guide dog service reaches under 5,000 people.' The charity has therefore committed itself to develop new areas of activity to help many more people.

Administratively, the annual report for 2000 notes a 'wholesale reorganisation', in which much of the existing work is being moved from 7 large training centres, for dogs and their owners, to 32 district teams. One intention is to bring the work of providing guide dogs and matching them with their owners closer to the charity's service users. Another and perhaps less obvious reason is that the new arrangements will be 'an ideal structure for developing potential partnerships with local authorities'.

In fact this is very relevant, because the charity is extending its work in this direction. 'Over our seventy years of assisting visually impaired people to enjoy independent and fulfilling lives, we have built up considerable professional expertise in the mobility field. We have also recognised ... that there are many thousands of blind and partially sighted people who may not want or need a guide dog but who could still benefit enormously from other forms of mobility training. This may involve learning to use the long cane or being helped to make more of one's residual vision ... In the summer of 2001 we will have completed 12 pilot projects, testing out different kinds of partnerships with local authorities and blind societies ... working with a wider range of visually impaired people than was hitherto the case.

'The aim is therefore to expand what we do best, helping more people live dignified and independent lives. We will offer our mobility services at no cost to the local authority provided the statutory partner commits to continue to make available their current resources in the visual impairment field ... If the local authority wishes the association to provide other rehabilitation services (such as communication and independent living skills) we can do that too, but only under proper fee-paying contractual agreements.'

As well as this, the charity is already the largest trainer in the UK of rehabilitation workers for blind and partially sighted people, spending £3 million on this in 2000.

The charity is also active in research and in the promotion of good eye care. A total of £5 million is being spent on ophthalmic research up to 2005, 'making us by far the largest voluntary sector contributor to this important field', and in 2001 the charity was running its One Vision campaign, focusing on the dangers of prolonged use of VDU screens and of non-UV-protected sunglasses.

Another new initiative is to assist in the development of mobility-related technology and a centre is being established to test and develop existing aids and, with other organisations, to seek partnerships with technology companies to assist in the development of future mobility aids. In the accessibility field the charity also runs a Joint Mobility Unit, with the Royal National Institute for the Blind, to help industry ensure that its workplaces are accessible to blind and partially sighted people.

The charity has been seeking to transfer its non-core services to other managements that will secure their future. Two hotels have been transferred to *Action for Blind People*, while negotiations were underway in 2000 for the transfer of the charity's holiday service to the *Winged Fellowship Trust*.

Volunteers

The charity has over 350 fundraising branches, 1,000 puppy walkers and 250 brood stock holders (presumably those who look after dogs owned by the charity for breeding purposes). 'A major project to improve our recruitment, training, management and retention of volunteers is well under way.'

Funding, administration

The finances of the charity are set out and reviewed in an exemplary way in the annual report. It is funded by voluntary donations and legacies (£32 million in 2000), and by the investment income from its large reserves (£5 million). The voluntary income was broken down as follows (with figures for 1999 in brackets):

- legacies £24.8 million (£26.4 million);
- fundraising branches and other donations £6.8 million (£6.4 million).

This total was achieved at a fundraising cost of £8.1 million, giving a cost ratio of 26p in the pound, or 26%, up from the 21% of the previous year, a level also typical of the previous three years. The charity has been implementing a conscious decision to invest in fundraising to a much greater degree than in the past, when it was 'behind all its major competitors of similar size in both resources committed to fundraising and income derived from it'. It is therefore 'investing substantially in developing a new fundraising infrastructure, with a view to creating

sustainable new sources of income in the future'. Even so, the 21% ratio of recent years puts the charity little above the average for those in this book.

The figures for 2000 reflect the fact that the costs for the year included £1.3 million specifically employed in beginning to recruit and develop new long-term, loyal donors for the charity. Nevertheless, 'growth in new fundraising income has not been as fast as predicted'.

The charity has huge reserves, widely noted in press comment, and totalling £171 million at the end of 2000, which are held in various designated funds. One of these is a £30 million fund for the development of the new services described above, intended to be financed by voluntary income when up and running.

However, because of its long-term commitment to guide dog owners, the charity still intends to maintain a general fund at a level equal to two years' expenditure (£102 million). This seems excessive. The future revenues are firmly based on legacy income, which while sometimes volatile in the short term is less so over longer periods – indeed it is a form of fundraising backed by at least one element of inevitability missing for other kinds of donation. This charity might be contrasted with the even larger *Royal Society for the Protection of Birds*, which has a similar number of staff, a substantial dependency on legacy income and numerous long-term commitments to the maintenance of its reserves, but which is content with reserves equal to less than three months' expenditure.

The information assessed

The annual report and accounts are exemplary, being comprehensive without being long; they are exceptionally clearly written. There are excellent supplementary materials and a deservedly award-winning website.

Contact

Hillfields
Burghfield Common
Reading
RG7 3YG
Tel 0118 983 5555
Website www.guidedogs.org.uk
Chair B N Weatherill
Geraldine Peacock, Chief Executive

Guy's and St Thomas' Charitable Foundation

Hospital endowment

Income	£23,949,000 (2000/01)
Donated income	£4,694,000
Fundraising costs	£370,000
Statutory income	£0
Top salary	£60,000–£70,000
Paid staff	19

Aims, activities

In April 2000 this charity was formed by the amalgamation of the charitable funds of these two formerly separate hospitals.

In 1947 a few of the major teaching hospitals kept their charitable endowments, which were otherwise swept up into the general funds of the new NHS. Guy's and St Thomas' were two such hospitals and for many years had their own 'special trustees' to look after these charitable assets, and,

indeed, to seek to augment them with new money.

Now that the two hospitals have been amalgamated, the new combined charity has a magnificent endowment fund worth almost £300 million in March 2001, as well as £75 million in unrestricted general funds. Total investment income in 2000/01 was £18 million.

The purposes of the new charity are not clearly set out in its first annual report, other than to say that the trustees have the power to hold property for any purpose of the hospital trust or the health service generally, and that it seeks 'to support the delivery of the best possible services to patients and users of health services'. In practice most of the money (£45 million in 2000/01) is being spent on new buildings and environmental improvements to support the work of the hospitals.

The charity has two major current building projects. First, it has contributed £50 million towards a new building for the independent Evelina Children's Hospital on the St Thomas' site. Secondly, in 2001 it was planning a residential development on land opposite St Thomas' that would house up to 400 staff as well as a 100-place day nursery for the children of staff.

During the year the foundation also supported new equipment and technology and research. The research seems very much geared to the practical rather than the theoretical, most of the projects described being directly concerned with the better treatment of patients.

Volunteers

The volunteering activity in the hospitals is probably organised by them directly, rather than through this charity.

Funding, administration

In April 2001 some £260 million shown in the accounts as unrestricted funds were reclassified as expendable endowment funds. This is unusual, as unrestricted funds must be applied for charitable purposes and cannot be held indefinitely for the generation of investment income. This does not apply to endowment funds. The change is described in the annual review as a 'crystallisation' of the funds, a term new to this editor. No doubt there were special circumstances allowing for this apparent exception to the usual rules.

Voluntary income, which is the reason for the charity's entry in this book, totalled £4.7 million in 2000/01, arising from donations (£3.6 million) and legacies (£1.1 million). This was achieved at a fundraising cost of £370,000, giving a cost ratio of a very low 8p in the pound, or 8%.

The donations come from individuals and corporations. They are usually for a specific purpose and 'are therefore credited to the most appropriate of over 400 special purpose funds' managed by the charity. This seems an almost extravagant number.

The information assessed

The good annual report and accounts sometimes presuppose familiarity with the institutions concerned.

Contact
Guy's Hospital
St Thomas's Street
London
SE1 9RT
Tel 020 7955 4074
Chair Sir Tim Jessels
Geoffrey Shepherd, Director

Help the Aged

Income	£42,921,000 (2000/01)
Donated income	£27,235,000
Fundraising costs	£9,719,000
Statutory income	£6,519,000
Top salary	£80,000–£90,000
Paid staff	700
Volunteers	255,000

Aims, activities

'Help the Aged was set up in 1961 to respond to the needs of poor, frail and isolated older people at home and overseas. As a national organisation we campaign with and on behalf of older people, raise money to help pensioners in need and provide direct services where we have identified a gap in provision.

'There are many charities throughout the UK that help older people at a local level. Help the Aged works to bring these groups together to share information and expertise and fund their grass roots work. In this way we avoid duplication and make the best use of money and resources.'

The charity was set up by Cecil Jackson-Cole, also known as the founder of *ActionAid* and *Oxfam*.

The charity's work is divided almost equally between delivering services itself, at a cost of over £13 million and with over 700 staff in 2000/01, and by giving grants to other organisations to do so, to a value of £12 million.

The services are described as follows:

- SeniorMobility Campaign – this helps voluntary groups provide transport for older people, Meals on Wheels vehicles, mobile day centres, repair vans and door-to-door services for older people who are not in good health (for example, taking them on shopping trips and visits to day centres). Over 1,367 vehicles have been presented to groups around the country, with the charity providing either fundraising assistance, a grant or support through its bulk-buying scheme.

- Seniorlink – this is an immediate response service for people aged over 50. The equipment provided allows help to be quickly and easily summoned.

- Handyvan – this is a home security service, which aims to help older people feel more secure in their homes.

- Grants – these are made to a wide variety of projects, including day centres, lunch clubs, transport services and work carried out with, for, or for the benefit of older people who are isolated or not in good health (and/or their carers).

- SeniorLine – this is a free welfare rights advice service for older people and their carers. Trained advice workers can offer advice or information about a wide range of issues, including community/ residential care, welfare/disability benefits and housing (**0808 800 6565**, or in Northern Ireland **0808 808 7575**).

- Care Fees Advisory Service – specialist advisers provide free,

impartial financial advice, helping people find the best ways of paying for care.

- Information Point – the charity offers a wide range of information leaflets and the like, being especially strong on financial issues.

- Retirement services – there is a range of paid-for services, including insurance, specifically designed for those aged over 50.

This list leaves out what has long been one of the most important Help the Aged services, its sheltered and supported housing and associated care services. These are in the process of being transferred to another organisation as part of this charity's intention to focus its work more sharply.

The charity also operates internationally as a member of HelpAge International, a global network with over 50 member organisations of which it was a founder and is a leading member. It contributed £7 million to this in 2000/01.

In May 2001 the charity announced that it was considering a closer relationship, even a merger, with *Age Concern*. In October 2001, as this entry was written, it seemed unlikely that there would be a full merger, though no final decision had been taken. The suggestion followed a merger between Help the Aged and the much smaller Research into Ageing earlier in 2001.

Outside England, the charity can be contacted as follows:

- Help the Aged, Edinburgh: 0131 556 4666

- Help the Aged Cymru: 029 2041 5711

– Help the Aged, Belfast: 028 90
230666

Volunteers

The website has the following, in
addition to solely fundraising
activities:

'Whatever your reasons for
volunteering, Help the Aged can offer
a range of opportunities, from helping
out on an occasional basis to
volunteering several days a week.

- Help the Aged Local Committees –
  our voluntary committees are an
  important source of fundraising and
  also provide vital feedback about
  local issues and the needs of older
  people in their area.

- Help the Aged Shops – if you have
  some spare time why not help in
  one of our 373 shops across the
  UK?

- Church Friends Network – find out
  how to get involved with our
  Church Friends Network. Could you
  be the Help the Aged contact in
  your parish?

'For more information call the
Volunteering Co-ordinator on 020
7278 1114.'

The website section on volunteering
ends with an excellent cross
reference: 'To help with gardening,
shopping or visiting older people, call
the National Association of Volunteer
Bureaux on 0121 633 4555 for your
local branch.' (See also page 329.)

Funding, administration

The charity's accounts for 2000/01
show that its usable income was
dominated by £25 million in donations
and legacies. The total voluntary
income of £27.2 million was achieved
at a fundraising cost of £9.7 million,
giving a cost ratio of a high 36%, little
changed from the previous year but
higher than the 32% average for the
three years to 1999. The voluntary
income concerned has dropped a little
from that time. Fundraising
expenditure has also reduced, but
more slowly.

The accounts show £4.9 million
income for the charity's residential
care services which are now being
transferred to another organisation.

The accounts are in the new format
issued by the Charity Commission in
2000 and the income from sales in
charity shops is now shown separately
from the costs of running the shops.
This has led the annual report to note
that the shops are the charity's main
source of income (at £26.3 million). In
fact the shops cost £23.5 million to
run, so their contribution to the
charitable activities was a more
modest £2.8 million, down from the
£3.9 million net contribution of the
previous year.

The information assessed

There is a good annual report and accounts
and a first-class website.

Contact

St James' Walk
Clerkenwell Green
London
EC1R 0BE
Tel 020 7278 1114
Website www.helptheaged.org.uk
Chair John Mather
Michael Lake, Director General

Home-Start UK

Helping families under stress

Income	£2,175,000 (2000/01)
Donated income	£1,242,000
Fundraising costs	£253,360
Statutory income	£666,000
Top salary	£40,000–£45,000
Paid staff	
Full time	27
Part time	25
Volunteers	
Operational	8,004

Aims, activities

Home-Start UK is the umbrella organisation for over 300 local Home-Start schemes in which volunteers offer regular support, friendship and practical help to young families under stress in their own homes. Though financially modest, the scale of the movement's work on the ground makes it as important as many of the financially much larger child welfare charities described in this book.

Reasons why parents and families come to Home-Start include bereavement, children's behavioural problems, disability, domestic violence, ill health, isolation, poor housing, post-natal depression, poverty, relationship difficulties, single parenthood and the birth of twins or triplets.

Families accepting the offer of a Home-Start volunteer are usually, though by no means always, referred by health visitors and social workers. The scheme is based on simple home visiting. By sharing their time and friendship, volunteers offer families an opportunity to develop new relationships, ideas and skills. 'This usually leads to a renewed interest in the children, an improved response to their needs and greater confidence to avail themselves of other resources within their community.'

In the year to March 2001 the number of schemes reached 308, up 10% in the year, and the 8,000 volunteers supported 48,000 children in 21,000 families.

The schemes vary in detail, but have the following in common:

● they focus on families with at least one child under the age of five;

● each scheme has its own local multi-disciplinary management committee, ensuring close links with other voluntary and statutory agencies;

● each scheme has at least one paid organiser to run the scheme, who combines a warm personality with administrative competence;

● close attention is paid to the recruitment, matching, retraining and support of the volunteers.

The schemes are not started until secure ongoing funding has been put in place, usually from local statutory sources, and all sign up to the Home-Start ethos, training and support programmes. However, Home-Start UK (the parent body) has to find its own funding year by year to keep up the support of the local schemes while also continuing to expand and develop, not only in the UK but also now overseas, where its model of local voluntary support for families has been found to be equally applicable.

The local Home-Starts are one of the most important volunteer based support networks in the country for families and their children who are finding the going hard, and, for those who are uncomfortable with professional social work support in such an intimate area of their lives, they can be a hugely welcome alternative.

Volunteers

Volunteers of all ages and backgrounds are welcomed, provided that they have their own experience of parenting. Parents who have been visited often become volunteers themselves.

All volunteers take part in a preparatory course before being matched with families. These are often run on one day a week for ten weeks, but they also happen at evenings and weekends. The volunteers are then matched with one, two or three families and visit for as long as necessary – sometimes for a few months, but often for a year or more. Throughout, they are supported by the local scheme organiser.

'The approach varies according to the needs of each family and draws on the flexibility, good humour and imaginative skills of the volunteer. Talking with the parents, playing with the children, helping in the home or accompanying the family on outings or appointments may all be offered.'

Funding, administration

The schemes are an invaluable resource for the local health and social services, who are themselves usually unable to offer much in the way of preventive services, as their professional staff are fully stretched in meeting day-to-day crisis obligations. They therefore usually support the salary of the key local organiser who enables the voluntary activity to take place.

Home-Start UK, the umbrella organisation whose figures for 2000/01 appear above, is funded mainly by donations and grants, many of them from charitable trusts (£1.2 million); by government grants (£0.7 million); and by fees contributed by each local scheme (£0.2 million).

The voluntary income of £1.2 million was achieved at a fundraising cost of £253,000, a ratio of 20p in the pound.

The charity adds ...

A new-look website will be online before the end of 2001.

The information assessed

There are an excellent annual report and accounts and annual review, a simple but effective website, and very good supporting materials.

Contact

2 Salisbury Road
Leicester
LE1 7QR
Tel 0116 233 9955
Chair James Sainsbury
Brian Waller, Director

Hospices and cancer care charities

As well as the well-known network of local hospices, there are large national cancer care charities such as *Macmillan Cancer Relief*, *Marie Curie Cancer Care* and *Sue Ryder Care*. Once assumed to be mainly providers of residential care for the terminally ill, hospices now deliver many of their services to patients living at home – where 25% of deaths of hospice patients take place.

The best national starting point for further information about local hospices is the Hospice Information Service (tel: 020 8778 9252, or see its excellent website at www.hospiceinformation.co.uk). At an immediate local level, the practice nurse at a GP's surgery is likely to be well informed.

Local hospices may be independent charities (there are 150 of these), part of a larger charity (17), or part of the National Health Service (57). The funding relationship between charitable hospices and the NHS is complex, with costs typically being shared, but not on any nationally agreed basis.

Fundraising plays a large part in almost all cases. In general, local charities such as individual hospices have much lower fundraising costs, compared with their donated revenues, than the major national charities do, though no doubt the bigger charities, with their extensive fundraising programmes, reach donors who would not otherwise be contributing to the movement at all. Both local and national cancer charities rely heavily on volunteers for much of their fundraising. The use of volunteers to help in the delivery of services is varied, and enquiries will have to be made locally. Funds are also raised by Help the Hospices, a national charity.

Contact details follow for many local hospices, though probably not for all. They are grouped by area as listed by the Hospice Information Service.

Eastern

Basildon: St Luke's Hospice; tel: 01268 524973

Bedford: Sue Ryder Care – St John's; tel: 01767 640622

Benfleet: Little Haven Children's Hospice; tel: 01702 552200

Berkhamstead Hospice of St Francis; tel: 01442 862960

Bury St Edmunds: St Nicholas' Hospice; tel: 01284 766133

Cambridge: Arthur Rank House; tel: 01223 723110

Cambridge: East Anglia's Children's Hospices; tel: 01223 860306

Chelmsford: Farleigh (Mid Essex) Hospice; tel: 01245 358130

Colchester: St Helena Hospice; tel: 01206 845566

Harlow: St Clare Hospice; tel: 01279 413590

Ipswich: East Anglia's Children's Hospices; tel: 01473 714194

Ipswich: St Elizabeth Hospice; tel: 01473 727776

King's Lynn: Tapping House Hospice; tel: 01485 543163

Letchworth Garden House Hospice; tel: 01462 679540

Luton: Keech Cottage Children's Hospice; tel: 01582 492339

Luton: Pasque Hospice; tel: 01582 492339

Maldon: Farleigh at St Clare's Hospice; tel: 01621 857727

Norwich: East Anglia's Children's Hospices; tel: 01953 888604

Norwich: Priscilla Bacon Lodge; tel: 01603 288981

Watford: The Peace Hospice; tel: 01923 330330

Welwyn Garden City: Isabel Hospice; tel: 01707 330686

Westcliff-on-Sea: Fair Havens Hospice; tel: 01702 220350/344879

London

Abbey Wood: Greenwich & Bexley Cottage Hospice; tel: 020 8312 2244

Clapham: Trinity Hospice; tel: 020 7787 1000

Hackney: St Joseph's Hospice; tel: 020 8525 6000

Hampstead: Marie Curie Centre, Edenhall; tel: 020 7853 3400

Harrow: St Luke's Hospice (Harrow and Brent); tel: 020 8382 8000

Leytonstone: Margaret Centre; tel: 020 8535 6604

N Cheam: St Raphael's Hospice; tel: 020 8335 4575

N Finchley: North London Hospice; tel: 020 8343 8841

Northwood: Michael Sobell House; tel: 01923 844302

Orpington: South Bromley HospisCare; tel: 01689 605300

Romford: St Francis Hospice; tel: 01708 753319

Southall: Meadow House Hospice: tel:020 8967 5179/8571 4222

St John's Wood: St John's Hospice; tel: 020 7806 4040

Sydenham: St Christopher's Hospice; tel: 020 8778 9252

North West

Ashton-under-Lyne: Willow Wood Hospice; tel: 0161 330 1100

Blackburn: East Lancashire Hospice; tel: 01254 342810

Blackpool: Trinity – the Hospice in the Fylde; tel: 01253 358881

Bolton: Bolton Hospice; tel: 01204 364375

Burnley: Hospice Care for Burnley and Pendle; tel: 01282 440100

Bury: Bury Hospice; tel: 0161 725 9800

Cheadle: St Ann's Hospice; tel: 0161 437 8136

Chester: Hospice of the Good Shepherd; tel: 01244 851091

Chorley: Derian House – Children's Hospice; tel: 01257 233300

Lancaster: St John's Hospice; tel: 01524 382538

Liverpool: Macmillan Service; tel: 0151 263 2355

Liverpool: Marie Curie Centre; tel: 0151 801 1400

Liverpool: St Joseph's Hospice; tel: 0151 924 3812

Liverpool: Woodlands Day Hospice; tel: 0151 529 2299

Liverpool: Zoe's Place – Baby Hospice; tel: 0151 228 0353

Macclesfield: East Cheshire Hospice; tel: 01625 610364

Manchester: Francis House Children's Hospice; tel: 0161 434 4118

Manchester: St Ann's Hospice; tel: 0161 437 8136

Oldham: Dr Kershaw's Hospice; tel: 0161 624 2727

Ormskirk: Hettinga House – St Joseph's Hospice; tel: 01695 578713

Prescot: Willowbrook Hospice; tel: 0151 430 8736

Preston: St Catherine's Hospice; tel: 01772 629171

Rochdale: Springhill Hospice; tel: 01706 649920

Rossendale: Rossendale Hospice; tel: 01706 240083

Runcorn: Halton Haven; tel: 01928 719454

Southport: Queenscourt Hospice; tel: 01704 544645

Ulverston: St Mary's Hospice; tel: 01229 580305

Warrington: St Rocco's Hospice; tel: 01925 575780

Wigan: Wigan and Leigh Hospice; tel: 01942 525566

Winsford: St Luke's (Cheshire) Hospice; tel: 01606 551246

Wirral: St John's Hospice in Wirral; tel: 0151 334 2778

Northern and Yorkshire

Bishop Auckland: Butterwick Hospice at Bishop Auckland; tel: 01388 603003

Carlisle: Eden Valley Hospice; tel: 01228 810801

Darlington: St Teresa's Hospice; tel: 01325 254321

Durham: St Cuthbert's Hospice; tel: 0191 386 1170

Elland: Overgate Hospice; tel: 01422 379151

Harrogate: St Michael's Hospice; tel: 01423 879687

Hartlepool: Hartlepool and District Hospice; tel: 01429 282100

Hexham: Tynedale Community Hospice; tel: 01434 600388

Huddersfield: Kirkwood Hospice; tel: 01484 557900

Hull: Dove House Hospice; tel: 01482 784343

Jarrow: St Clare's Hospice; tel: 0191 451 6378

Keighley: Sue Ryder Care – Manorlands; tel: 01535 642308

Lanchester: Willow Burn Hospice; tel: 01207 214729/529224

Leeds: St Gemma's Hospice; tel: 01132 185500

Leeds: Sue Ryder Care – Wheatfields; tel: 01132 787249

Middlebrough: Teesside Hospice Care Foundation; tel: 01642 816777

Newcastle upon Tyne: Marie Curie Centre; tel: 0191 219 5560

Newcastle upon Tyne: St Oswald's Hospice; tel: 0191 285 0063

Pontefract: The Prince of Wales Hospice; tel: 01977 708868

Scarborough: St Catherine's Hospice; tel: 01723 351421

Stockton-on-Tees: Butterwick House Children's Hospice; tel: 01642 607742

Sunderland: St Benedict's Hospice; tel: 0191 569 9192

Wakefield: Wakefield Hospice; tel: 01924 213900

Wetherby: Martin House; tel: 01937 845045

York: St Leonard's Hospice; tel: 01904 708553

South East

Andover: Countess of Brecknock House; tel: 01264 835288

Ashford: Pilgrims Hospice in Ashford; tel: 01233 504100

Aylesbury: Florence Nightingale House; tel: 01296 394710

Banbury: Katharine House Hospice; tel: 01295 811866

Basingstoke: St Michael's Hospice (North Hampshire); tel: 01256 844744

Brighton: The Sussex Beacon; tel: 01273 694222

Canterbury: Pilgrims Hospice in Canterbury; tel: 01227 812612

Chichester: St Wilfrid's Hospice; tel: 01243 775302

Crawley: St Catherine's Spc Centre; tel: 01293 447333

Eastbourne: St Wilfrid's Hospice; tel: 01323 644500

Esher: Princess Alice Hospice; tel: 01372 468811

Farnham: Phyllis Tuckwell Hospice; tel: 01252 729400

Gravesend: The Lions Hospice; tel: 01474 320007

Guildford: CHASE; tel: 01483 454213

Henley on Thames: Sue Ryder Care Centre; tel: 01491 641384

High Wycombe: South Bucks Hospice; tel: 01494 537775/463198

Hove: The Martlets Hospice; tel: 01273 273400

Kettering: Cransley Hospice; tel: 01536 493041

Lewes: St Peter & St James Hospice; tel: 01444 471598

Lymington: Oakhaven Hospice; tel: 01590 670346

Maidston: Pilgrims Hospice in Thanet; tel: 01843 233920

Milton Keynes: Willen Hospice; tel: 01908 663780/663636

Newport: Earl Mountbatten Hospice; tel: 01983 529511

Northampton: Cynthia Spencer Hospice; tel: 01604 678030

Oxford: Helen House Children's Hospice; tel: 01865 728251

Oxford: Sir Michael Sobell House; tel: 01865 225860

Rochester: Wisdom Hospice; tel: 01634 830456

St Leonards on Sea: St Michael's Hospice (Hastings); tel: 01424 445177

Sittingbourne: Demelza House Children's Hospice; tel: 01795 842111

Southampton: Countess Mountbatten House; tel: 023 8047 7414

Tunbridge Wells: Hospice in the Weald; tel: 01892 820500

Waterlooville: The Rowans; tel: 023 9225 0001

Winchester: Naomi House – Children's Hospice; tel: 01962 760060/761532

Windsor: Thames Valley Hospice; tel: 01753 842121

Woking: Woking Hospice; tel: 01483 881750

Worthing: St Barnabas Hospice; tel: 01903 534030/264222

South West

Barnstaple: Children's Hospice South West; tel: 01271 321999

Barnstaple: North Devon Hospice; tel: 01271 344248

Bradford-on-Avon: Dorothy House Hospice; tel: 01225 722988

Bristol: The Jessie May Trust; tel: 01179 616840

Bristol: St Peter's Hospice; tel: 0117 915 9400

Cheltenham: Sue Ryder Care; tel: 01242 230199

Dorchester: Joseph Weld Hospice; tel: 01305 251052

Exeter: Hospiscare; tel: 01392 402555

Gloucester: Wheatstone Day Hospice; tel: 01452 371252

Hayle: St Julia's Hospice; tel: 01736 759070

Plymouth: St Luke's Hospice – Plymouth; tel: 01752 401172

Poole: Forest Holme; tel: 01202 448115

Poole: Lewis Manning House Cancer Trust; tel: 01202 708470

St Austell: Mount Edgcumbe Hospice; tel: 01726 65711

Stroud: Cotswold Care Hospice; tel: 01453 886868

Swindon: Prospect Hospice; tel: 01793 813355

Taunton: St Margaret's Somerset Hospice; tel: 01823 259394

Torquay: Rowcroft – Torbay & S Devon Hospice; tel: 01803 210800

Weston-super-Mare: Weston Hospicecare; tel: 01934 625926

Weymouth: Trimar Hospice; tel: 01305 767527

Trent

Ashby de la Zouch: Sue Ryder Care Centre; tel: 01332 694800

Barnsley: Barnsley Hospice; tel: 01226 244244

Chapel-en-le-Frith: High Peak Hospicecare; tel: 01298 815388

Chesterfield: Ashgate Hospice; tel: 01246 568801

Derby: Treetops Hospice; tel: 0115 949 1264

Doncaster: St John's Hospice; tel: 01302 796666

Grantham: GIFTS Day Hospice; tel: 01476 591010

Grimsby: St Andrew's Hospice; tel: 01472 350908

Leicester: LOROS Leicestershire and Rutland Hospice; tel: 0116 231 3771

Lincoln: St Barnabas Hospice; tel: 01522 511566

Loughborough: Rainbows Children's Hospice; tel: 01509 230800

Melton Mowbray: Dove Cottage Day Hospice; tel: 01949 860303

Newark: Beaumond House; tel: 01636 610556

Nottingham: Hayward House; tel: 0115 962 7619

Nottingham: Nottinghamshire Hospice; tel: 0115 910 1008

Retford: Bassetlaw Hospice; tel: 01777 869239

Rotherham: The Rotherham Hospice; tel: 01709 829900/837807

Scunthorpe: Lindsey Lodge Hospice; tel: 01724 270835

Sheffield: St Luke's Hospice; tel: 0114 236 9911

Sutton in Ashfield: John Eastwood Hospice; tel: 01623 622626

West Midlands

Birmingham: Acorns Birmingham; tel: 0121 248 4815

Birmingham: John Taylor Hospice; tel: 0121 255 2400

Birmingham: St Mary's Hospice; tel: 0121 472 1191

Bromsgrove: Primrose Hospice & Cancer Help Centre; tel: 01527 871051

Hereford: St Michael's Hospice; tel: 01432 851000

Kidderminster: Kemp Hospice; tel: 01562 861217

Lichfield: St Giles Hospice; tel: 01543 432031

Oswestry: Hope House; tel: 01691 671999

Shrewsbury: Shropshire and Mid Wales Hospice; tel: 01743 236565

Stafford: Katharine House Hospice; tel: 01785 254645

Stoke-on-Trent: Douglas Macmillan Hospice; tel: 01782 344300

Stourbridge: Mary Stevens Hospice; tel: 01384 443010

Stratford-upon-Avon: Shakespeare Hospice; tel: 01789 266852

Walsall: Acorns Walsall; tel:01922 422500

Walsall: Little Bloxwich Day Hospice; tel: 01922 858735

Warwick: Myton Hamlet Hospice; tel: 01926 492518

Wolverhampton: Compton Hospice; tel: 01902 758151

Worcester: St Richard's Hospice; tel: 01905 763963

Northern Ireland

Belfast: Northern Ireland Children's Hospice; tel: 028 9077 7635

Belfast: Northern Ireland Hospice; tel: 028 9078 1836

Derry: Foyle Hospice; tel: 028 7135 1010

Newry: St John's House; tel: 028 3026 7711

Scotland

Aberdeen: Roxburghe House; tel: 01224 555641

Airdrie: St Andrew's Hospice; tel: 01236 766951

Ayr: Ayrshire Hospice; tel: 01292 269200

Brechin: Macmillan Centre; tel: 01356 665014

Clydebank: St Margaret's Hospice; tel: 0141 952 1141

Cupar: Hospice Unit; tel: 01334 652901

Denny: Strathcarron Hospice; tel: 01324 826222

Dumfries: Alexandra Unit; tel: 01387 241347

Dundee: Roxburghe House; tel: 01382 423000

Dunfermline: Hospice Ward (Ward 16); tel: 01383 627016

Dunoon: Cowal Hospice; tel: 01369 707732

Edinburgh: Milestone House; tel: 0131 441 6989

Edinburgh: St Columba's Hospice; tel: 0131 551 1381

Glasgow: Prince & Princess of Wales Hospice; tel: 0141 429 5599

Greenock: Ardgowan Hospice; tel: 01475 726830

Inverness: Highland Hospice; tel: 01463 243132

Johnstone:St Vincent's Hospice; tel: 01505 705635

Kinross: Rachel House Children's Hospice; tel: 01577 865777

Kirkcaldy: Victoria Hospice; tel: 01592 648072

Orkney: Orkney Macmillan House; tel: 01856 885449

Paisley: Accord Hospice; tel: 0141 581 2000

Perth: Macmillan House; tel: 01738 639303

St Andrew's: Hospice Unit; tel: 01334 472327

Stornoway: Bethesda Hospice; tel: 01851 706222

Wales

Cardiff: George Thomas Hospice Care; tel: 029 2048 5345

Cardiff: Ty Hafan Children's Hospice; tel: 029 2053 2200

Llandudno: St David's Hospice; tel: 01492 879058

Newport: Gwent Healthcare/St David's Foundation; tel: 01633 234934

Newport: St Anne's Hospice; tel: 01633 820317

Newport: St David's Foundation Hospice Care; tel: 01633 271364

Newtown: Shropshire and Mid Wales Hospice; tel: 01686 610215

St Asaph: St Kentigern Hospice; tel: 01745 585221

Tredegar: Hospice of the Valleys/Hosbis y Cymoedd; tel: 01495 717277

Wrexham: Nightingale House Hospice; tel: 01978 316800

Channel Islands and Isle of Man

Douglas: St Bridget's Hospice; tel: 01624 626530

St Andrews: Les Bourgs Hospice; tel: 01481 51111

St Helier: Jersey Hospice Care; tel: 01534 876555

Hospitals and their charities

Hospital charities receive about £250 million a year in donations and benefit from the work of more than 60,000 active volunteers, whose total hours are the equivalent to those of over 7,000 full time paid staff.

Most hospitals are not themselves charities but, as with education, the relief of sickness is itself a charitable activity, and there is usually a League of Friends or similar charity that supports each hospital with both fundraising and the assistance of volunteers inside the hospital.

Collectively, 800 such 'Friends' Groups raise about £36 million a year and provide about 30,000 active volunteers. Each is independent, but were they to be organised as a single charity it would be among the 15 largest in the UK. For information about these charities, contact the League of Hospital and Community Friends (tel: 01206 761227; website: www.hc-friends.org.uk).

From 1947 (when the old hospital endowments were swept up into the new NHS) until 1980, only a few teaching hospitals which had 'Special Trustees' could fundraise directly, though all could receive unsolicited gifts on charitable trust. In 1947 these unsolicited gifts were expected to be just 'modest tokens of appreciation' for 'patients and staff comforts', but by the 1980s the part of such gifts that had not yet been spent had grown to £1 billion in the NHS accounts, divided into a huge number of small local ward or unit funds. Some hospitals had hundreds of these funds, but they have now been reorganised and collected together within each NHS unit.

Since 1980 every part of the NHS can fundraise directly for support of its own connected charitable trusts, as well as through its 'Friends', and can charge the fundraising costs to Exchequer funds. However, active fundraising is still dominated by the teaching hospitals, mainly in London.

Some of the 'Special Trustees' for the teaching hospitals are extremely wealthy. In 2001 *Guy's and St Thomas' Charitable Foundation* in London had charitable endowments and investments worth £375 million.

There are also independent fee-charging hospitals which are charities, such as the well-known London Clinic. Few of these seek voluntary support.

Some of the medical research charities described in this book also have close connections with particular hospitals; for example, the *Institute for Cancer Research* is almost inseparable from the Royal Marsden Hospital in London.

Many hospitals, some of them charitable rather than governmental, also recruit volunteers directly, without using an intermediary group of 'Friends', and have their own 'volunteer officers'.

Information about charitable and voluntary activity in any hospital can usually be obtained from its 'Friends' organisation. Big hospitals may have an 'appeals' or 'development' office. Readers interested in this field may also wish to see the entry for *Hospices and cancer care charities*.

Imperial Cancer Research Fund

Income	£103,713,000 (1999/00)
Donated income	£90,347,000
Fundraising costs	£23,127,000
Statutory income	£0
Top salary	£120,000–£130,000
Paid staff	2,080
Volunteers	15,000

Aims, activities

This charity carries out its own research with its own staff and often in its own institutions. This is a different way of working from that of many medical research charities described in this book, which raise money that is then allocated in grants to other medical research organisations that actually carry out the work. In particular, it is different from the practice of the big *Cancer Research Campaign*(CRC), with which this charity is merging.

ICRF employs over 1,000 doctors and scientists on projects in hospitals and research laboratories throughout the UK. There are two laboratories in London and research programmes in six London hospitals. There are five programmes in Oxford, a research unit in St James' Hospital, Leeds, and major programmes in Edinburgh and Dundee. Smaller scale activities take place in Newcastle upon Tyne, while a very large new research institute is being developed at Addenbrooke's Hospital in Cambridge.

The charity's research covers a wide range, with smoking hazards and screening technologies prominent alongside work in the more dramatic field of specific therapies. Increasing emphasis is being given to population-based research (epidemiology). However, the lay reader of the charity's reports may find most striking the repeated emphasis on smoking: 'stopping smoking is still the single most beneficial thing people can do to safeguard their health'; and 'In the UK there are over 13 million smokers – half of whom will die of smoking-related diseases if they continue.' More happily, 'the UK now leads the world in reductions in smoking-related deaths'. It also good to see that 'breast cancer deaths in young and middle-aged women fell by 30% in the 1990's'.

The reason given for the merger with CRC is the increasing cost of investing in new technologies and in world-class scientists: 'Single organisations may not always be able to fund this type of science by themselves.' This was expanded in November 2001 by the charity's director of communications, whose speech to the Charities Aid Foundation conference was reported as follows: 'The only reason to go through this painful experience is that we can achieve our overall mission better together than we can do apart.' He observed that analysis of the two charities' donor bases showed only a 10% duplication and that overlap in fundraising strengths was also minimal, as ICRF was strong in direct marketing while CRC's forte was community fundraising. But 'there are over 600 cancer charities in the UK and the evidence shows that public is sick to death with being approached by them'.

In October 2001 Sir Paul Nurse, director general of this charity, was awarded the Nobel Prize, a remarkable tribute not only to him personally but also to the standing of the UK's medical research charities.

Volunteers

There are 450 voluntary groups of 'friends' of ICRF but their contribution to the charity's income is not identified as such in the accounts. It may form all or just a part of the £14 million coming from 'Regional activities'.

Funding, administration

The voluntary income of the charity was classified as follows in the 1999/00 accounts

- legacies £46 million;
- donations £22 million;
- regional activities £14 million;
- trusts and foundations £5 million;
- corporate fundraising £3 million.

This total of £90 million was achieved at a fundraising cost of £23 million, a ratio of 26p in the pound, or 26%, and a slight increase from the 24% of the previous year. Both figures are sharply up from the average 19% of the three years to 1998. However, the increased fundraising 'spend' (up by £11 million a year since then) has led to an increase in income of £23 million.

The information assessed

The adequate annual report and accounts and annual review have no particular gaps, but are surprisingly brief. Few of the headings in the accounts are broken down in the notes, while the text of the report is short for this size of enterprise.

The website is excellent about cancer, but weak on how the charity is organised and what it does.

Contact
PO Box 123, Lincoln's Inn Fields
London
WC2A 3PX
Tel 020 7269 3669
Website www.imperialcancer.co.uk
Chair Professor R D Cohen
Sir Paul Nurse, Director General

Independent advice centres (and FIAC)

There are over 900 independent advice centres around the UK that are members of FIAC (the Federation of Independent Advice Centres). Membership is particularly strong in London, where there are nearly 300 centres.

Most FIAC members are community-based charities providing information and advice as part of a wider range of services. All offer a service that is free, independent and confidential. Active community involvement is very strong, with around 70% of staff in centres being volunteers.

FIAC members are very diverse, reflecting their 'bottom-up' origins. In almost all cases members have their roots in voluntary self-help and community action in response to specific local, regional or national needs.

Members vary considerably in terms of size, resource levels and communities served. They range from small centres serving local communities, through city-wide agencies, to major national organisations. They operate in both rural and urban settings, with over half based in the UK's 50 poorest local authority districts.

The advice provided is also varied. Many centres supply a generalist information and advice service, whether to the general public or to a particular section of the population. Others provide specialist advise services in areas such as housing rights, welfare benefits, employment law, money and debt, consumer rights, drugs and alcohol, immigration and nationality, disability, and HIV/AIDS.

The combination of strong community ties with a focus on specialised needs is what distinguishes most FIAC members from more standardised advice agencies such as *Citizens Advice Bureaux*.

Most FIAC centres receive funding support from their local authorities, supplemented by grants from the European Union, central government, regional funds, the Community Fund and other trusts and donors. A significant number hold Legal Services Commission contracts to offer what used to be called legal aid, and most are participants in the government's Community Legal Service scheme.

Most FIAC members can, therefore, be found in the Community Legal Service directory, or through its 'Just ask' website (www.justask.org.uk). They can also be found on the FIAC website (www.fiac.org.uk) or by telephoning FIAC on 020 7489 1800.

For more specific legal information, the best contact would be the Legal Centres Federation (tel: 020 7387 8570; website: www.legalcentres.org.uk), which has a network of 52 branches nationwide. Legal centres provide free legal advice and information to the most disadvantaged members of society.

Institute of Cancer Research

Income	£43,536,000 (1999/00)
Donated income	£5,433,000
Fundraising costs	£1,193,000
Statutory income	£5,200,000
Top salary	£125,000
Paid staff	804

Aims, activities

This is one of the longest established medical research charities in the UK, set up in 1909 and working in close association with the Royal Marsden cancer hospital at its sites in Chelsea and Sutton, London. The institute carries out its own extensive research programmes and also provides education and training in relevant subjects. As far back as the 1920s its scientists identified the carcinogen in tar in tobacco (though sadly it is a substance that is still being widely advertised and sold 80 years later).

About half the work of the charity is financed from competitively won grants for specific research projects and programmes, a quarter with research funding from the government funding councils, and the remainder from its own fundraising and investment income.

The biggest single funder is the *Cancer Research Campaign*, which provided £10 million of this charity's income in 1999/00. The institute also works in close cooperation with *Breakthrough Breast Cancer*, recently sharing with that charity a building development in Chelsea to house the UK's first dedicated breast cancer research centre.

This editor cannot comment on the quality of the research undertaken, but the annual review and report are able to cite unusually impressive evidence of the institute's scientific standing. The 1999/00 annual review notes two exciting new developments in its field. The first is the remarkable success of the human genome project, in whose origin institute staff played a large part. The second is the commitment of the government to a new and high-visibility NHS Cancer Plan.

The annual review also notes that 'three of the main drugs used to treat common cancers were developed by scientists in our laboratories'. The accounts show 'income from inventions' of a modest £156,000. It would be interesting to know who gained the commercial benefit from these discoveries.

Volunteers

The extensive membership lists of the institute's various committees suggest that much valuable professional time is donated to the charity.

Funding, administration

The charity earns its living primarily by competing for research grants. In 1999/00 it also received £5.4 million in legacies and donations, achieved at a fundraising cost of £1.2 million, a ratio of 22p in the pound. This figure has fluctuated considerably in recent years, probably reflecting the progress of the charity's substantial, but not continuous, capital appeals. There is no review of the fundraising activity in the annual report or review, other than a restating of figures already present in the accounts.

The accounts note that £35.6 million of the total £44.3 million of expenditure went on research activities, with £1.5 million spent on directing and administering the institute.

The information assessed
The annual report and review are good. Both are available in full on the institute's website, though with limited information on the organisation of the charity's work.

Contact
123 Old Brompton Road
London
SW7 3RP
Tel 020 7352 8133
Website www.icr.ac.uk
Chair Lord Faringdon
Dr Peter Rigby, Chief Executive

International League for the Protection of Horses

Income	£4,118,227 (1999)
Donated income	£3,112,580
Fundraising costs	£689,611
Statutory income	£0
Top salary	£70,000–£80,000
Paid staff	95

Aims, activities
The charity was founded in 1927 to prevent the ill treatment of horses exported to Europe for slaughter. It is now, it says, the world's leading international equine welfare charity, describing its principal objectives as being 'To protect horses from abuse and alleviate their suffering by educating, rehabilitating and campaigning worldwide'.

Dealing with ponies as well as horses, ILPH focuses its activities on rehabilitation and re-homing. To this end it has six recovery and rehabilitation centres around the UK (the newest one, near Blackpool, opened early in 2001) where a total of up to 300 animals can be rehabilitated at any one time. Some of these are retired working horses or racehorses; others have been rescued from ill treatment.

ILPH then aims to place suitable horses with individuals as riding or companion animals. These animals are regarded as being on permanent loan; the charity still has responsibility for them. A total of 415 horses and ponies were re-homed in this way in 1999 and there are now almost 1,700 rehabilitated animals in approved homes.

There are also 15 full-time field officers (nearly all former mounted police officers) who investigate cases of cruelty and neglect, inspect markets and ports, and check the animals on the equine loan scheme.

The ILPH's campaigns for legislation to promote equine care include its continuing opposition to the live export of horses, ponies and donkeys. It also sponsors veterinary scholarships and research projects connected with equine welfare.

Internationally, the charity runs educational and training courses in saddlery, farriery, veterinary care and nutrition in a range of countries, from Mexico to Ethiopia and from Fiji to Ukraine.

Volunteers
The charity runs a membership scheme, with members based overseas as well as in the UK. Volunteers organise and take part in a variety of fundraising activities.

Funding, administration

Total income in 1999 was £4.1 million, including £3.1 million in voluntary income. The largest part of this (£2.1 million) came from legacies – the first time the charity's income from legacies had exceeded £2 million. Voluntary income was almost exactly the same in 1998, although legacy income in that year stood at £1.7 million. Fundraising costs of £690,000 in 1999 were also little changed from the previous year (£694,000), and in both years were the equivalent of 22p for every pound donated.

A remarkable £432,000 was received in a retrospective payment of VAT, most of it representing a one-off gain, perhaps suggesting some slowness in reclaiming the charity's dues in earlier years.

Until 1998 the charity was run by two managing trustees who were paid for the job. There is a discussion of the issue of payments to trustees in the Introduction to this book (page 22). The salary now being paid to the new chief executive, not a trustee, is handsome for a charity of this size and should promise vigorous future development.

The information assessed

The (separate) annual review and financial statements are good. The website is informative and up-to-date.

Contact

Anne Colvin House
Snetterton
Norwich
Norfolk
NR16 2LR
Tel 01953 498682
Website www.ilph.org
Chair Captain G Maitland-Carew
Jonny McIrvine, Acting Chief Executive

ITDG (Intermediate Technology Development Group)

Overseas development

Income	£11,924,000 (2000/01)
Donated income	£6,485,000
Fundraising costs	£1,106,000
Statutory income	£2,359,000
Top salary	£50,000–£60,000
Paid staff	464

Aims, activities

This charity is an offshoot of the Small is Beautiful movement that grew out of Fritz Schumacher's book of that name in the 1960s. Schumacher saw 'intermediate technology as belonging between the capital-intensive advanced technologies of the West, driven by large scale production and profit, and the traditional subsistence technologies of developing countries'.

'Intermediate' or 'appropriate' technology is intended to build upon the existing skills, knowledge and cultural norms of women and men in developing countries, while increasing the efficiency and productivity of their enterprises or domestic activities.

Though perhaps best known for ingenious but simple technical developments, such as efficient cooking stoves and water pumps, ITDG views technology as 'not only meaning the hardware or technical infrastructure, but also the information, knowledge and skills which surround it, and the capacity to organise and use these'.

There are currently 79 active projects (as well as consultancy projects) across the world, centring on Peru, Sri Lanka, Bangladesh, Nepal, Zimbabwe, Sudan and Kenya. Examples in 2000 included:

- supporting the building of village roads in Sri Lanka;

- helping to organise a house-building project in Kenya;

- training Sudanese brickmakers in production and in business skills;

- developing a honey-processing centre in Zimbabwe;

- introducing information technology systems for local businesses in Peru.

The main headings for charitable expenditure in 2000/01 were as follows (with 1999/00 figures in brackets):

- food production £2.2 million (£1.7 million);

- energy £1.2 million (£1.4 million);

- food processing £1.2 million (£1.5 million);

- communications £1.1 million (£1 million);

- building materials/shelter, £1 million (£0.6 million);

- policy research £0.7 million (£0.6 million).

Volunteers

'The majority of ITDG's staff are drawn from within the countries in which we work. In this way we ensure that our programme staff are truly "close to local people" and able to work in genuine partnership with them. We therefore do not run a volunteer programme.'

Funding, administration

ITDG's income of £11.9 million in 1999/00 included £2.4 million from governments and £6.5 million from donations, legacies, NGOs, charitable trusts and so on. Another £2.2 million was attributable to the charity's subsidiary companies.

Fundraising costs for the year were reported as £1.4 million, but the charity notes that this figure includes the cost of negotiating government payments. Excluding these, costs were £1 million, representing 17p for every pound voluntarily donated.

The charity adds ...

ITDG helps people living in poverty to make their lives safer and their futures brighter. We will help people find simple, appropriate answers to their problems. Answers that will go on working, today and everyday.

The information assessed

The separate annual review and annual report and accounts are good, and there is an interesting website.

Contact
The Schumacher Centre
Bourton Hall
Bourton-on-Dunsmore
Rugby
Warwickshire
CV23 9QZ
Tel 01926 634400
Website www.itdg.org
Chair Jennifer Borden
Cowan Coventry, Chief Executive

Jewish Care
Health and social care, mainly in London and south-east England

Income	£36,213,000 (2000)
Top salary	£110,000–£120,000
Paid staff	1,205
Volunteers	2,500

Aims, activities

This is Britain's largest Jewish health and social services agency. Serving mainly London and south-east England, it was created in 1990 as the result of mergers between a number of formerly independent Jewish agencies in response to the need to avoid duplication and make the best use of the Jewish community's resources.

Jewish Care offers a comprehensive range of services and facilities to meet the needs of older people, those with learning disabilities, visual impairments or other disabilities, and those who are unemployed. The charity is in the process of developing a new support service for the families of people with alcohol or drug problems.

The charity also runs a number of community centres, as well as specialist services for Holocaust survivors.

Residential homes are by far the largest activity in terms of money expended, accounting for £22.7 million of the £34.7 million total in the year 2000.

Volunteers

'We have around 2,500 volunteers working in Jewish Care's operational services, where they interact with clients, relatives, paid staff and other volunteers as part of their work. We have several hundred other volunteers involved with fundraising activities.'

Funding, administration

The accounts show income of £18 million from maintenance fees and grants in 2000. These are mainly to cover the costs of residential care. There was £15.1 million of voluntary income, including £5.2 million in the form of legacies, achieved at a fundraising cost of just £759,000, giving an apparent costs ratio of a very low 5p in the pound.

However, and unusually, the accounts note that the income from fundraising events is shown net – that is, after the costs of the events have been deducted. It is possible therefore that both the income and the costs have been understated when compared with those of other charities described in this book.

The information assessed

The weak and very brief directors' report for 2000 was supported in November 2001 by the good but undated annual review for '1999/2000', which included a summary of the 1999 financial accounts. There is a good website.

Contact

Stuart Young House
221 Golders Green Road
London
NW11 9DQ
Tel 020 8922 2000
Website www.jewishcare.org
Chair Malcolm Dagul
Jeremy Oppenheim, Chief Executive

JNF Charitable Trust

(formerly the Jewish National Fund)

Income	£5,197,000 (1999)
Donated income	£5,170,000
Fundraising costs	£788,000
Statutory income	£0
Volunteers	15

Aims, activities

The purpose of this charity is 'the relief of poverty and other charitable activities in Israel'. It achieves this by raising money in the UK to be put to use in Israel by its partner organisation, Keren Kayemeth Leisrael.

Activities include direct fundraising, events and legacy programmes. Major events in 1999 included 'Walk for Water' and the London-Jerusalem car rally.

In 1999, £5.2 million was raised at a fundraising cost of £788,000, equivalent to 15p in the pound, or 15%. In the previous year £4.9 million was raised at a cost of £968,000 (20%).

There is no information in the annual reports about the charitable activities in Israel, other than that the charity is in dispute with its local agent, Keren Kayemeth Leisrael. A total of £53 million, sent by JNF over the years, has been used by that organisation to buy land and properties in Israel which JNF has been advised remain in its own trust. JNF should therefore receive the rents arising, said to be £398,000 (it is not clear from the accounts whether this is an annual or a cumulative figure). The directors of Keren Kayemeth Leisrael dispute this interpretation. The auditors in the UK took no view but it is noted in the accounts that, if the charity is correctly advised, its balance sheet is due for massive amendment.

A fuller explanation in the annual report of the charity's relations with its agent, and of the work carried out in Israel with its money, would be helpful.

Funding, administration

In 1999, £5.2 million was raised at a fundraising cost of £788,000, equivalent to 15p in the pound, or 15%. In the previous year £4.9 million was raised at a cost of £968,000 (20%).

The information assessed

The annual reports are exceedingly slight, with the charity's activities recorded in just five lines of text, repeated unchanged in 1999 from the previous year. The accounts are also brief.

Contact

58–70 Edgware Way
Edgware
Middlesex
MA8 8GQ
Tel 020 8421 7600
Website www.jnf.co.uk
Simon Winters, Chief Executive

John Grooms

Support for people with disabilities, chiefly in England

Income	£12,872,000 (2000/01)
Donated income	£3,956,000
Fundraising costs	£871,000
Statutory income	£6,798,000
Top salary	less than £50,000
Paid staff	414

Aims, activities

Originally established as the Flower Girls' Mission, founded in the City of London in 1866 by John Grooms, this Christian-based charity exists 'to help people with disabilities live with the maximum amount of independence'. It seeks to achieve this by:

- providing residential care services;
- training and employing people with disabilities;
- developing a specialist and innovative brain injury rehabilitation centre;
- enabling disabled people and their friends, relatives and carers to take holidays.

Residential
During 1999/00 John Grooms closed most of its estate in Edgware, which had become unsuitable for clients' current needs, and opened two new residential care homes in Hertfordshire and Middlesex. It now has nine residential and nursing homes, chiefly in London, East Anglia, Essex and south Wales. Two of these are specifically geared towards helping residents to move on to live independently in the community, although 24-hour care is available at all the homes.

A sister organisation, John Grooms Housing Association, provides accessible housing for wheelchair users and others with specialist needs, such as people with head injuries. It currently manages over 1,000 housing units. New programmes include the building of six homes in the Portsmouth area in 2000/01.

A capital appeal launched in April 1999 by both the charity and John Grooms Housing Association is intended to raise £8 million over two years. Some of this money will be put towards the costs of the two care homes opened in 1999/00 (with the rest of the costs paid for by the sale of the Edgware site). The remainder will be used to build a third residential home in Southend, as well as 176 wheelchair-accessible homes. By March 2001, £4.2 million had been either raised or pledged.

Training and employment
The charity runs a training project in Haringey, London. This project, called FAITH, provides training and work experience for people with disabilities.

Brain injury rehabilitation
The charity's Icanho Centre in Suffolk provides rehabilitation therapies for people with serious brain injuries. This centre opened in April 1998 at a cost of £1.5 million. Therapists also carry out rehabilitation programmes in clients' homes. During 1999/00, more than 90 clients were treated at the centre, including 12 who were able to return to work.

Overseas, John Grooms 'continues to develop its work in the Asia Pacific region'.

Holidays
Grooms Holidays is the largest specialist provider in the UK of

wheelchair-accessible holiday accommodation, with properties in 17 holiday destinations. A total of 20,000 disabled people and carers took a holiday with the charity in 2000/01.

Volunteers

The charity's newsletters and website describe the volunteer-based fundraising activities.

Funding, administration

In 2000/01 the charity's income was £12.9 million, up from £11.2 million the previous year. Of this, nearly £1.4 million came from legacies and £2.6 million from other donations.

The combined voluntary income was thus £4 million, achieved at a reduced fundraising cost of £871,000, an average 22p for every pound raised.

A further £6.8 million was received as 'Income from services for disabled people', probably mostly from local and health authority support of individuals in the charity's residential homes and the sheltered employment activities.

The information assessed

There are adequate, separate annual report and financial statements, supplemented by newsletters and brochures for potential clients. The website, helpfully including summarised accounts, was being updated when this entry was written.

Contact

50 Scrutton Street
London
EC2A 4XQ
Tel 020 7452 2000
Website www.johngrooms.org.uk
Chair D H Thompson
Reverend Michael Shaw, Executive Director

Jubilee Sailing Trust

Sailing for people with disabilities

Income	£2,791,000 (2000/01)
Donated income	£881,000
Fundraising costs	£163,000
Statutory income	£0
Top salary	£40,000–£50,000
Paid staff	
Full time	37
Part time	8
Volunteers	
Operational	24
Fundraising	50

Aims, activities

The charity was established in 1978 with money from the Queen's Silver Jubilee Fund. Its objectives 'are to enable physically disabled and able-bodied people to share the challenging and integrating experience of crewing a sailing ship at sea, and to provide facilities for the building of vessels for such purposes'.

To this end, the charity owns and operates two large sailing ships, the only ones in the world purpose-built to allow people with disabilities to share in the working of such vessels. Each can carry 40 crew, who sail alongside a professional crew of 10. The aim is for each voyage crew to comprise 20 able-bodied and 20 disabled people, including up to 8 wheelchair users. Each ship makes about 30 voyages a year, chiefly around the British Isles, northern France and the Canaries.

The first ship owned by the JST was the *Lord Nelson*. In 2000/01 this sailed 20,000 miles, carrying almost 700 voyagers to 33 ports overseas.

More than half of them were people with disabilities.

The second ship, *Tenacious*, was built by the charity with 1,500 volunteers working alongside professional shipwrights and was launched in February 2000 at a total cost of £15 million. Of this, £6.5 million was met by a grant from the Sport England Lottery Fund.

Some bursaries are available for those who could not otherwise afford to sail on the ships, and successful applicants under the JST Youth Leadership@Sea Scheme (for those aged 16–25) receive a partial grant towards the costs involved. Otherwise people have to raise the costs for their voyage.

Volunteers

The annual report for 2000/01 thanks the volunteer maintenance crew 'who turn out in all weathers to work on the ships', and notes that the charity's 43 voluntary branches raised £116,000 in the year (up from £98,000 in the previous year).

Funding, administration

Of the £2.1 million regular income in 2000/01 (which excludes part payment of the Sport England building grant referred to above), fees for voyages and from donations and gifts each raised about £900,000. The fundraising costs were £163,000, or 19% of the value of donations and gifts.

The charity adds ...

The JST are world leaders – no other organisation has purpose built tall ships for disabled people or promotes integration of not only physical ability but of age, gender, culture and background. The experience for crew members of living and working alongside one another builds up confidence and leads to greater understanding of mutual abilities, qualities and interests which can help to break down the barriers of ignorance so often found in society at large.

The information assessed

There are brief but adequate annual report and accounts. The website has much additional detail, including full information about the charity's ships, the programme of voyages for the year and, recently introduced, a daily update from the ships (from the *Lord Nelson* in Vigo, Spain in November 2001)

Contact

Jubilee Yard
Hazel Road
Woolston
Southampton
SO19 7GB
Tel 023 8044 9108
Website www.jst.org.uk
Chair Chris Dunning
Lindsey Neve, Director

King George's Fund for Sailors
Welfare provision for seafarers and dependants

Income	£2,875,000 (2000)
Donated income	£1,531,000
Fundraising costs	£581,000
Statutory income	£0
Top salary	£60,000 – £70,000
Paid staff	
Full time	15
Part time	4
Volunteers	550

Aims, activities

The charity is a central fundraising and grant-making resource for other institutions helping seafarers and their dependants. It raises about £1.5 million a year in donations, and receives nearly as much again in investment income. In 2000, after administrative and fundraising costs of about £900,000, £2.9 million was given in grants to around 100 institutions. This was achieved by additional spending of almost £1 million from the charity's reserves.

The main groups of beneficiaries were:

- charities giving financial support to individuals £1.4 million;
- hospitals, homes and sheltered housing £707,000;
- children's homes, schools, ships and scholarships £614,000;
- seafarers' missions, clubs, etc. £258,000.

About half the support is for charities connected with the Royal Navy, and half for charities helping other seafarers (including fisherfolk) and their dependants.

Though the charity notes that the number of ex-seafarers will reduce by half by 2010, the age and the level of need of those who remain will increase. It has therefore said that despite its existing reserves of £43 million – enough to allow for a spend of over £2 million a year for 20 years – it needs to 'continue to fundraise vigorously, constantly exploring new areas'.

An important influence on the future support for seafarers' charities may lie with the little-known but wealthy Greenwich Hospital, a charity exempt from registration whose sole trustee is the secretary of state for defence. The hospital has recently been contributing £100,000 a year towards the grantmaking of this charity.

Volunteers

The charity notes the existence of around 550 volunteers in 55 volunteer fundraising committees. These are primarily involved in organising local fundraising events. KGFS stages 30 Royal Marine Band concerts throughout the year.

Funding, administration

The annual report for 2000 says that 'the fund has for some time been conscious of the high cost of its fundraising activity'. This was a high 38p for every pound donated, although that figure was lower than in many previous years, when the ratios were 68p in the pound (1999), 44p (1998), 31p (1997) and 69p (1996). In the past, the main variable from year to year has been the volatile level of legacy income. However, although income from legacies was indeed high in 2000, there was also a substantial increase in donations from the living as well as a big reduction in fundraising costs.

Though full details are not given, the charity's local events appear to have been the most expensive part of the fundraising programme; reduction in staff time spent on this may have contributed to the improvement in costs.

The information assessed

The adequate annual report is backed by a slow-to-load website and a fundraising leaflet. The annual report presupposes an understanding of the charity's field of work – having, for example, unexplained acronyms such as VDP and RNBT.

Contact
8 Hatherley Street
London
SW1P 2YY
Tel 020 7932 0000
Website www.kgfs.org.uk
Chair Admiral Sir Brian Brown
Captain Martin Appleton, Director General

Leonard Cheshire Foundation
Services for disabled people

Income	£102,896,000 (2000/01)
Donated income	£11,974,000
Fundraising costs	£3,399,000
Statutory income	£88,549,000
Top salary	£80,000–£90,000
Paid staff	
Full time	2,370
Part time	4,696
Volunteers	4,000

Aims, activities
This is the UK's largest charity for disabled people. Still often referred to as the 'Cheshire Homes', the charity has moved on; of the 19,000 people now using Cheshire services, just over 2,000 are in residential homes. Many use the charity's day services, but even more (9,500) are supported at home through its Care At Home service. Though the charity's mission is to work with disabled people throughout the world, most of its activities are in the UK, where it is active in almost every part of the country.

Many of the services are provided under contract to the relevant local authority, or are based on the fees they pay for individual people with disabilities. These contracts can be very large. For example, in 1999 the charity agreed to provide care in their own homes to some 1,900 new clients through a contract worth about £7 million a year with Hertfordshire County Council.

Specifically, services in the UK include:

- residential homes;
- nursing homes;
- support for independent living;
- care at home;
- day services;
- drop-in centres;
- resource centres;
- respite care;
- support and training for those seeking jobs;
- acquired brain injury units;
- rehabilitation services.

The foundation has achieved a striking degree of decentralisation and of voluntary involvement in its management. Each local service, and there are 142 of them, has its own voluntary committee, with strong user involvement.

The charity also runs an enterprising Workability scheme that trains young people with disabilities in computer skills and is developing new services for people with 'acquired brain injuries' – typically the result of car accidents and the like. It operates throughout the UK, serving people with all kinds of disability, and with multiple disabilities, though people with physical disabilities make up the majority of users.

The charity caters for people with specific impairments rather than those suffering from the general frailties of old age. Residents in its homes may be of any age, though more than 80%

are between 18 and 64. Users of the home care services are typically rather older.

The Cheshire movement is also active in more than 50 other countries. In these cases each national organisation is independent and the role of this charity is to offer advice and support. In financial terms the charity spends about £1 million a year on this work, and gives grants to its overseas associates of a further £0.5 million.

The charity was started by Leonard Cheshire VC, a celebrated Second World War RAF pilot who was Britain's observer at the dropping of the atom bomb on Nagasaki. He built up and managed the organisation in a fairly personal way almost until his death in 1992 (his wife having meanwhile founded the charity *Sue Ryder Care*), relying, as the charity still does, on local voluntary management committees to run each specific service. Given the size it had reached, there was remarkably little public awareness of the work of the organisation.

Since the founder's death, the charity has been comprehensively reorganised on a basis that does not depend on a single charismatic leader. This process is now almost complete.

The foundation is a leader in the fight for better provision for people with disabilities. At present there are two main issues. The first is that the costs of personal care are met by the statutory welfare services in some areas and not in others, where up to 55% of a person's net income can be deducted to pay for this. This can obviously act as a huge deterrent to finding employment and getting the income that goes with a job. Secondly, the government, with the strong support of this and similar charities,

introduced new Care Standards in 2000 which will regulate care provision to 'more modern and appropriate standards'. However, it is far from clear that the corresponding funding will be made available. If it is not, some of the charity's services may become economically unviable.

Volunteers

The chairman, Charles Morland, writes in the 2000/01 annual report: 'If I had to identify one thing that sets Leonard Cheshire apart from public or private care providers it would be the involvement of volunteers with the charity.' This is backed up by the unusually clear role laid out for the work of trustees at all levels of the organisation, well described in the charity's excellent 'Opportunities' booklet.

Volunteers fall into the following four broad categories:

- Governance volunteers – these are responsible for governing the organisation and its constituent parts and for guarding and promoting the ethos of Leonard Cheshire. They include the trustees of the charity as well as the members of local, regional and national committees. There are about 1,000 people filling such roles.

- Support volunteers – these are usually linked to a specific local service. Examples of their roles include letter-writing and reading, driving, escorting, sharing activities and hobbies, gardening and shopping. All involve befriending service users as well as helping them. About 4,000 volunteers carry out these kinds of activities.

- Fundraising volunteers – these may be linked directly to a local service, be part of a local fundraising group or be involved in a specific event or appeal. There are about 1,000 regularly active volunteers in such roles.

- Overseas volunteers in the UK – these provide support in a Cheshire service for between 3 and 12 months, in return for bed, board and a subsistence allowance. A few dozen of these full time volunteers are involved in this enterprising scheme at any one time.

The voluntary activities are overseen by a special Central Advisory Committee, chaired by Christine Vickers, one of the charity's trustees.

Funding, administration

The charity is now managed by a reduced committee of 23 trustees, 10 of whom are the chairs of the regional committees. Each trustee has his or her specific role and responsibilities.

Funding, as set out in the 2000/01 accounts, is of two kinds. The first (and largest) is the £89 million received in fees and charges for specific services, all but a few percent of which comes from statutory sources. Most such income is tied to the individual service concerned, and is both received and spent at a local rather than national level.

Secondly, the charity received £12 million in voluntary income, most of it available to be used at the trustees' discretion. Of this, £6.5 million came in the form of legacies, £4.2 million in donations from individuals and £1.2 million in grants, mostly from charitable trusts and the then National Lottery Charities Board (now the Community Fund).

A major problem facing the charity is the gap between what it costs to run its services and the amount the various statutory services will pay for them. The charity, reluctantly, has to find the difference, either by finding economies in the services it provides, or by subsidising them from its voluntary income. It has followed both paths, the second with particular reluctance. The 1999/00 annual report noted that there had been a 'major swing' towards the achievement of self-financing by the different services and in 2001 this was said to be continuing, though at a slower rate.

However, the problem remains: 'Voluntary income should be used to ... improve existing facilities and ... develop new projects that create fresh opportunities for disabled people. This is a firm policy but unfortunately the charity still has to use a significant amount of voluntary funds to supplement the fees paid by local authorities in order to provide an acceptable level of care ... Voluntary funds were used to subsidise such operational income to the extent of £5 million for residential services and £1.6 million for other services.'

The charity has grown very large on the basis mainly of statutory funding, but without a corresponding growth in voluntary income. Its public face was modest and its fundraising spend was, for many years, below average for this kind of charity. The trustees have now decided that the charity must increase its voluntary income and it has therefore embarked on a major programme of investment in fundraising and in increasing the public awareness of its work. As a result, the proportion of voluntary income spent on this has risen from an average of 19p in the pound (or 19%) for the three years to 1999, to 28% in 2000/01. However, this figure may reduce in future as the investment (labelled the Enabled programme) should lead to a marked rise in donations in the relatively short term – and to an increase in legacies over a longer period.

The charity adds ...

Leonard Cheshire exists to enable ordinary lives. Quite simply we work with disabled people so that they have a greater independence, choice and quality of life; but we need help to do it.

The information assessed

The excellent annual reports and accounts are in general a model for a charity of this kind (though a more detailed breakdown of income and expenditure headings in the accounts would be welcome). There is an exceptionally good booklet for potential volunteers, as well as other impressive supporting literature. There is also a very good website.

Contact

30 Millbank
London
SW1P 4QD
Tel 020 7802 8200
Website www.leonard-cheshire.org
Chair Charles Morland
Bryan Dutton, Director General

LEPRA

Income	£3,842,000 (2000)
Donated income	£2,614,000
Fundraising costs	£931,627
Statutory income	£0
Top salary	£50,000–£60,000
Paid staff	473

Aims, activities

Interestingly, 'our work to seek out and treat those affected [by leprosy] is only a tiny part of what we do'.

However, this 'tiny' part leads the charity's description of its own work. 'With our trained teams of paramedics and health workers, LEPRA seeks out and treats those affected, enables them to care and provide for themselves and, through information, education and communication encourages those affected to seek early treatment and endeavours to remove the stigma attached to leprosy.'

The bulk of the activity is probably in the areas of providing advice on how people with leprosy can avoid developing further disabilities a result of their condition; and the raising of awareness and understanding of leprosy in the areas affected so that prejudice will be reduced and treatment sought at an earlier stage.

The charity appeared to work in three main ways in 2000. First, it operated its own programmes for the relief of leprosy in India, Nepal, Bangladesh, Mozambique and Brazil. There was also a reference to staff in Malawi (and the charity has an educational and awareness programme in the UK). To carry out this work there were 429 overseas employees, a big increase from the 321 of the previous year.

Secondly, the charity gave grants to other 'partner' organisations for them to carry out similar work. Thus £1.2 million was given to the closely related organisation, LEPRA India, and further grants appear to have been made for work in Madagascar as well as for independent work in India. The charity noted that it was also to support new leprosy and TB initiatives in Angola and was looking for opportunities to support work in other priority countries such as Myanmar (Burma) and Nepal.

Other recipients of grants included bodies as diverse as the London School of Hygiene and Tropical Medicine (£133,000) and the Associations Raoul Follerau in both France and Spain (£51,000 and £75,000, respectively).

Thirdly, the charity supports and carries out research into leprosy and related diseases, especially at its new state of the art Blue Peter Research Centre in Hyderabad, India. This, and other research and education projects, cost £676,000 in 2000.

Regional budgets for 2001 were as follows:

- India, Bangladesh and Nepal £2.5 million;
- South America £300,000;
- Africa £300,000.

The level of activity grew sharply in 2000, partly through an increased level of donations, partly because of an extra £200,000 received from ILEP, the international association of leprosy charities, and partly through spending from reserves, which still remain near the top end of the charity's policy that reserves should represent between 6 and 12 months' running costs.

A striking feature of the annual reports is the references to the charity's holistic approach and its willingness to work with diseases other than leprosy, such as TB, HIV/AIDS or malaria: 'LEPRA will fight allied diseases ... wherever appropriate.'

Volunteers

The only voluntary input recorded is that of the trustees, though there is a reference to the existence of a medical advisory board, whose members may well be unpaid.

Funding, administration

Most of the charity's income is from donations and legacies (£1.6 million and £819,000, respectively, in 2000).

The fundraising costs were high at £932,000, or 36p for each pound donated (36%), up from 33% the previous year. The value of donations and legacies had risen but the fundraising costs had increased even faster, from £765,000 in 1999. (In that year the charity noted that its fundraising costs represented only 21% of total expenditure. This book prefers to compare fundraising costs to fundraised income, not to total income, because the latter includes government contracts, payments for services provided and investment income, which are not the result of fundraising effort.)

There is a reference to a new project working for the prevention of the spread of HIV infection among Indian truck drivers that is funded by the UK Department for International Development.

In an interesting comment, the charity notes that all the drugs it uses to treat leprosy patients are donated by the Novartis pharmaceutical company.

The information assessed

The weak annual report presupposes considerable understanding of the charity and of the field in which it works. There was a useful four-page annual review in 1999, on which much of this entry is based, but apparently this was not repeated in 2000, when there was just a much briefer leaflet, 'The Way Ahead'. Overall, it was difficult to establish what the charity actually does, particularly how far it is an operational charity and how far a grantmaker supporting of the work of other agencies or government.

Contact
Fairfax House
Causton Road
Colchester
CO1 1RJ
Tel 01206 562286
Website www.lepra.org.uk
Chair Mrs P P Scarlett
Terry Vasey, Director

Leprosy Mission International

Income	£6,126,000 (2000)
Donated income	£5,767,000
Fundraising costs	£829,000
Statutory income	£203,000
Top salary	£40,000–£50,000
Paid staff	46

Aims, activities

'The Leprosy Mission International, which is a UK registered charity, co-ordinates income from national Leprosy Mission charities in 23 countries, three of which are within the UK, in England and Wales, Scotland and Northern Ireland.' The income and cost figures above are for amounts raised in the UK by these three charities.

Leprosy Mission International funds leprosy prevention and treatment activities. Despite some appearance otherwise in its own self-descriptions, it operates 'mostly' by giving grants to other organisations and governments. It is not, however, solely a grantmaker, as it has its own operational staff and facilities in at least some countries. It is not possible to say for sure how the work is divided between each of these two different activities.

The 2000 accounts give only the following breakdown of charitable expenditure:

- grants (South Asia £4 million; South-east Asia £1.7 million; Africa £1.7 million);
- international staff (from outside the fields above) and related expenditure £0.8 million;
- support costs £1 million.

There is a country-by-country breakdown of the grant-assisted programmes, and details, in the Leprosy Mission International accounts, of the organisations supported. 'Hospital programmes' account for 28 of the 62 organisations listed.

This is a Christian charity, but it is not clear to what extent it should be seen as a missionary organisation. Other than a reference to the Christian ethos underlying its work, the annual report and annual review describe only the charity's practical good works. Elsewhere, however, the charity has been reported to support 50 missionaries overseas, which suggests a more specifically Christian role.

In 2000 the Leprosy Mission acknowledged with gratitude the single-handed contribution of Eddie Askew, the best-selling author of 11 Christian books of meditations and prayers, the sales of which over several years have contributed some £1.75 million to the charity.

Volunteers

'The International Office is connected to their supporters through the fundraising and support raising initiatives of the 26 National Councils and Support Groups worldwide, all of whom use volunteers in a variety of activities. In the UK, details of volunteer activities can be found on the websites of the individual UK Councils, and through the supporter magazine New Day (E & W and Scotland) and In Touch (Northern Ireland).'

Funding, administration

The three national fundraising charities had a collective income of £6.1 million in 2000, of which £4.2 million was passed on to Leprosy Mission International to be put to charitable use.

Voluntary income was £5.8 million and reported fundraising costs were £829,000, giving a low cost ratio of 14p for each pound donated. However, there were further management costs of £600,000 and as the main work of these charities is to raise money it would seem reasonable to regard these also as largely fundraising costs.

The information assessed

There are separate annual reports and accounts for the three UK charities with this name, and annual reviews for one, but collectively they were no more than adequate, making it hard to get a full understanding of the charity's work. There is a straightforward website.

Contact

80 Windmill Road
Brentford
Middlesex
TW8 0QH
Tel 020 8569 7292
Website www.leprosymission.org
Chair Stewart Smith
Trevor D Durston, General Director

Leukaemia Research Fund

Income	£15,243,000 (2000/01)
Donated income	£11,153,000
Fundraising costs	£814,000
Statutory income	£0
Top salary	£50,000–£60,000
Paid staff	36

Aims, activities

One of the major cancer research charities, the fund raises money to be given out in grants for research into leukaemia and related diseases by UK institutions.

Each year about 21,500 people in the UK are diagnosed with leukaemia or one of the related cancers of the blood. The charity notes that developments in effective treatment have been slow; 'although survival for some adult leukaemia now exceeds 50%, others remain stubbornly hard to treat'. However, there is one marked and happy exception: 'Around 600 children in Britain develop leukaemia or lymphoma every year, accounting for half of all childhood cancers. Since Leukaemia Research Fund began in 1960 survival for the most common type of childhood leukaemia has risen dramatically, and now approaches 80%. Progress in adult leukaemias has been slower but is encouraging.'

The work of the charity is described better in the annual review for 2000 than in that for 2001.

A total of 30 ongoing specialist programmes are funded. 'These programmes target the big questions , interacting closely with hospital doctors and the day-to-day diagnosis and treatment of patients.' These programmes were said in the text to have received £10.1 million in 2000/01, a great leap from £5.7 million in the previous year.

The charity also supports many shorter-term project grants which 'focus on key questions, very often at the most fundamental level of our understanding ... ' These cost £6.7 million, again an increase from the £4.9 million spent in 1999/00.

The charity has recently moved into the field of funding clinical trials.

Research grants are subject to a full peer review process. In 2000/01 £6.1 million or one third of all research expenditure went to the LRF Centre for Clinical Epidemiology at the University of Leeds, 'a world leader in major lifestyle studies' that investigates these diseases. The other major beneficiary institutions were the universities of Southampton (£2 million) and Oxford (£1.9 million) and University College, London (£1.3 million). However, as applications for funding the different centres come up at different times, the charity points out that one year's figures alone may not be a good guide to where most support is going.

Volunteers

'We rely on the dedicated support of more than 200 voluntary fundraising branches.' The research is also supervised by medical and scientific advisory committees, all of whose members are unpaid.

Funding, administration

The total income shown in the accounts for 2000/01 is £19.9 million, but this could mislead because, contrary to Charity Commission recommended practice, it includes £4.6 million of capital gains, shown simply as investment income. This needs to be shown separately to distinguish it from what is normally found under this heading. The income shown above is without this transfer, to make it comparable with other entries in this book.

The voluntary contributions totalled £11.1 million (£10.5 million in 1999/00). The main headings were as follows (with 1999/00 figures in brackets):

- legacies £4.3 million (£4.2 million);
- head office £3.1 million (£3.2 million);
- voluntary branches £2.8 million (£2.6 million).

The declared fundraising cost of £814,000 was down from £894,000 in the previous year and represented a very low ratio of 7p in the pound, a level reported for some years. However, this figure may not be wholly comparable with others reported in this book as the accounts of the charity's branches have not been consolidated into the accounts of the main charity. These only shows the net amounts that the branches have sent in, after paying their own local fundraising costs. The result of this will be that both the voluntary income and the fundraising costs of the charity as a whole are understated in comparison with other charities in this book. As the branches contributed well over a quarter of the declared voluntary income, the omission of their full income and their costs could in theory be significant – especially as they are reported to run fundraising events such as fashion shows and concerts, activities where fundraising costs often represent a high proportion of the income received.

In fact the accounts of the branches are submitted to and examined by the main charity even though they are not audited or brought into the main accounts, and the charity believes that the overall level of their fundraising costs is small.

The Charity Commission requirements (the SORP) call for all accounts to be consolidated and for any exceptions to be explained. In this case the trustees simply say that the branch income has not been consolidated because 'it is not considered practical to do so'. Other apparently comparable charities, described in this book, have succeeded in overcoming the difficulties.

The theoretical danger is that, in the absence of consolidation, branches can, in a charity's name, carry out all kinds of activities without any independent audit or review.

At a national level, over £3 million has been raised over the years by hairdresser Tony Rizzo's Alternative Hair Show. It is not clear whether the show incurs costs as well as revenue, and, if so, where these appear in the accounts.

The charity adds ...

We work for people with haematological cancers, supporting high calibre research, an academic programme and provision of patient information. We place great emphasis on voluntary fundraising, reflected in overall running costs of 5.3% last year. Our volunteer Branches make huge sacrifices in time and financially to maintain this low figure.

The information assessed

The adequate annual report and annual review are let down by a failure to set out sufficiently clearly the ways in which the accounts do not follow the SORP specifications of the Charity Commission. It was hard to identify the charity's main programmes, without asking directly. The website was the best source of information.

Contact

43 Great Ormond Street
London
WC1N 3JJ
Tel 020 7405 0101
Website www.lrf.org.uk
Chair The Earl Cadogan
Douglas Osborne, Chief Executive

Lord's Taverners

Sport and recreation for young people

Income	£4,879,000 (2000)
Donated income	£4,837,000
Fundraising costs	£2,089,000
Statutory income	£0
Top salary	£60,000–£70,000
Paid staff	15
Volunteers	4,500

Aims, activities

The Lord's Taverners' website opens with an exemplary brief description of the charity and its work: 'The Lord's Taverners was founded in 1950 by a group of actors who enjoyed watching cricket from the Old Tavern at Lord's. We have now evolved into a national charity and club with an exclusive membership of over 4,000 who set out to raise money to give young people, particularly those with special needs, a sporting chance.

'Since the beginning we have been supported by HRH The Duke of Edinburgh, as our Patron and 12th Man, as well as sporting heroes, show business stars and captains of industry, all who work exceptionally hard raising money to increase the quality of lives for many disabled and disadvantaged youngsters.

'We are a national organisation with regions throughout the UK, Northern Ireland, Guernsey and Jersey, and our head office in London. The Lady members of The Lord's Taverners eventually set up themselves as The Lady Taverners in 1987, and The Young Lord's Taverners caters for the 18 to 35 age bracket.'

'Money raised benefits disadvantaged and disabled youngsters throughout the country and enables them to participate in team sports and recreational activities in the following ways:

- We are the recognised national charity for cricket and support inner city schools and various youth cricket clubs by funding all weather pitches, cricket equipment and Kwik cricket kits, as well as providing coaching and sponsoring youth competitions.
- We finance specially adapted minibuses capable of transporting up to 15 young people to recreational and sporting activities outside their home or school. Each bus is tailored to the individual requirements of the recipient organisation and costs around £30,000 each. During the year 2000 we presented our 500th bus and hope to consistently be able to fund one bus every week of the year.
- We support sport and recreation for young people with disabilities by financing specialist equipment such as pool hoists or multi-sensory play equipment.'

The annual report for 2000 notes that the charity normally allocates its grants:

- 50% for cricket;
- 40% for minibuses;
- 10% for sport for young people with disabilities.

Volunteers

The charity is primarily a voluntary fundraising organisation. It has about 3,000 members, who all contribute handsomely to be members of a star-studded and, in the charity's own word, 'exclusive' organisation.

Funding, administration

Nearly three quarters of the fundraised income comes from charitable events – when this entry was written the list was headed by a classic car rally, followed by a range of golf days, lunches, dinners and a ball. On summer Sundays the charity's celebrity cricket team raises money around the country.

The annual report for 2000 notes that 'costs attributable to fundraising' were 9p in the pound (9%). This is strange. The total income of the charity in the accounts is given as approximately £4.9 million, of which £42,000 was income from investments, leaving £4.8 million in voluntary contributions. Fundraising costs are stated as £2.1 million, which represents a very high 43p in the pound (43%). However, this is a reduction from the 45% of the previous year and the 50% average of the three years to 1998.

These costs may be the result of the form of fundraising employed. 'Events' are often a high-cost way of raising money, because the donors are being offered entertainment or other enjoyable activities for their money, and these may be at least as big an attraction as the charitable cause itself – but such attractions are expensive to provide. In recognition of this, some charities have hived off their event management into a separate trading activity.

The fundraising costs are set out in the accounts in commendable detail, but unfortunately under different headings from those used for analysing the income that resulted, so the related costs of the different activities cannot be seen.

The information assessed
The annual report and accounts are good, and there is a simple but nice website.

Contact
10 Buckingham Place
London
SW1E 6HX
Tel 020 7821 2828
Website www.lordstaverners.org
Chair Roger Smith
Mark Williams, Chief Executive

Macmillan Cancer Relief

Income	£64,801,000 (2000)
Donated income	£59,473,000
Fundraising costs	£18,777,000
Statutory income	£807,000
Top salary	£90,000–£100,000
Paid staff	430
Volunteers	30,000

Aims, activities
Macmillan Cancer Relief is primarily a fundraising and grant-making body supporting improved cancer care within the National Health Service. The charity is concerned with the care of people with cancer, rather than with research into the causes of these diseases or their prevention in the first place.

The emphasis of the work is to improve the quality of care for people with cancer who continue to live at home.

Grants to NHS units accounted for over 95% of direct charitable expenditure in 2000. They are made for two main purposes: first, to meet the employment and training costs of Macmillan post-holders, mostly nurses and doctors, in the initial years of new appointments; and secondly, for the development of buildings that are then transferred to the NHS unit concerned. The charity also has an important grants programme for the relief of individual need among people with cancer, and it runs extensive information services and education programmes both for other professionals within the NHS who may come into contact with people with cancer and for the general public.

The well known 'Macmillan' nurses and doctors are employed by a relevant part of the NHS. They continue to use the Macmillan name after the initial funding from the charity (usually for three years) has come to an end, and to benefit from the charity's ongoing training and support. The 2,000th such nurse was appointed in the year 2000; and there are about 200 Macmillan doctors, most of them GP facilitators working to raise standards of cancer care at the community level, though there are also specialist Macmillan doctors in hospital oncology (cancer) departments.

Macmillan buildings are usually centres for day treatment, most commonly chemotherapy, and are intended to give the reassurance and comfort of surroundings of greater quality and attractiveness than are usually available within mainstream NHS provision.

The NHS Cancer Plan was developed with input from this charity. It is reported to include a variety of ways in which the charity can continue to provide and develop its support for improving cancer care.

The grants to the NHS are made under nine main headings (with the value of new 2000 commitments in brackets):

- nursing programme (£14,551,000);
- medical services programme – mainly doctors (£7,679,000);
- building programme (£5,304,000);
- patient welfare (£5,022,000);
- day and in-patient care (£1,914,000);
- information support officers (£1,694,000);
- nurse education programme (£1,387,000);
- grants to associated charities (£567,000);
- other (£1,341,000).

One aim of the charity is to work towards equal quality of treatment and care for people with cancer throughout the UK. There is no information about whether the geographical distribution of Macmillan grants is part of this programme. The full list of grants is not disclosed (despite a note in the accounts saying 'Details of these grants are disclosed in a separate publication', the publication, or rather sheet of paper, referred to only 50 grants covering less than half the total expenditure) and so no geographical comparisons are possible. The grant recipients are sometimes identifiable, as in the case of the biggest recipient, Highland Acute Hospitals NHS Trust, which received £1.2 million for building works, but they may not be: the second largest named recipient, of £1.1 million, is the effectively

anonymous 'Queen Elizabeth Hospital'.

Under the leadership of its former director, Sir Nicholas Young, who recently left to become director of the *British Red Cross*, Macmillan has become an important influence on NHS policies and practice – as indeed befits its role as a substantial source of funds for cancer care. At a time when there is much discussion of the increasing role of public money in the funding of charities, Macmillan is a useful reminder that the process can also work in the opposite direction.

Volunteers

Given the nature of the charity, most of its volunteers are concerned with its fundraising, 70,000 of them occasionally, 30,000 of them regularly. There is also a reference to volunteers helping in Macmillan day care units and information centres, but there is little information on the extent of such involvement. Most of the work funded is professionally delivered, but the charity has recently merged with Cancerlink, which has a strong element of self-help and mutual support, and Macmillan intends to develop these aspects.

Funding, administration

The income of the charity is overwhelmingly derived from individuals, with only a small amount of the £65 million total coming from investment income (£2.5 million), trading income (£2.1 million net) and government (£0.8 million).

The donations are categorised in the 2000 accounts as follows, though the distinctions between some of the headings could do with further explanation:

- legacies £19.9 million;

- appeals and projects £19.5 million;
- other fundraising and donations £13.5 million;
- direct mail £6.6 million.

The total was a remarkable 24% increase on the previous year. The greatest increase was in the level of legacies, always a volatile source of income in the short term, but other donations were also substantially up. Fundraising costs increased by £1.2 million, or 19%.

The local fundraising committees are directly responsible for £7 million of the £59 million total, and their work will also have an influence on the overall level of legacies, even when these cannot be directly attributed to a particular local committee.

The costs of fundraising were £18.8 million, or a high 32p for every pound raised, but this was a reduction from the 34p of the previous year. Of this total, £7.8 million was spent on fundraising staff costs, leaving £10.3 million for other items such as advertising, event costs and mailings.

Overall the voluntary income of the charity has been rising rapidly in recent years, with high levels of fundraising investment producing corresponding increases in donations.

The information assessed

The annual report and accounts and annual review are good; weak only in their explanation of the organisational and funding relationship with the NHS, and in the fact that the recipients of the charity's grants are not clearly or fully apparent. The supporting literature is clear and succinct.

The good website is the best source of information about how the charity is organised. It includes a history of the organisation and some information about its relationship with the NHS, though some of this is on the Macmillan pages in a linked epolitix site.

Contact

Anchor House
15–19 Britten Street
London
SW3 3TZ
Tel 020 7840 7840
Website www.macmillan.org.uk
Chair Jamie Dundas
Peter Cardy, Chief Executive

Marie Curie Cancer Care

Income	£61,444,000 (2000/01)
Donated income	£46,329,000
Fundraising costs	£16,043,000
Statutory income	£12,207,000
Top salary	£80,000–£90,000
Paid staff	
Full time	1,164
Part time	4,005
Volunteers	100,000

Aims, activities

The charity cares for about 30,000 cancer patients each year. It has the following four main activities (with their 2000/01 expenditures):

- 10 Marie Curie centres (hospices) £23 million;
- the Marie Curie nursing service (home care) £10.7 million;
- research £3.5 million;
- education £2.2 million.

The hospices, with 257 in-patient beds ('the largest number of beds outside the NHS'), care for 4,000 patients a year, while twice that number attend the centres as out-patients. Almost half return home after their stay; 'the emphasis in hospice care has switched from providing long term general nursing support to much shorter stays for those patients with more complex symptoms and specialist needs'. The centres are spread around the UK, including two in Scotland (Edinburgh and Glasgow), and one each in Wales and Northern Ireland.

The nursing service works under contract to 220 health authorities in the UK. Employed by the charity, the nurses work flexible hours and care for about half of all cancer patients who die at home. There are no charges for the service.

Supporting this work, the Marie Curie Palliative Care Research and Development Unit seeks to improve care for those affected by life-threatening illnesses through the implementation of evidence-based practice. Areas currently being investigated include aromatherapy massage, constipation in cancer patients and communication skills for healthcare professionals.

Marie Curie's Education Service seeks to improve care for cancer patients by enhancing the skills and knowledge of healthcare professionals. There is a new £1 million education centre at the hospice in Edinburgh, and a new IT learning suite at the centre in Bradford.

Given its name, referring to cancer care rather than cancer research, it was a slight surprise to find that the charity also runs the Marie Curie Research Institute in Surrey. The charity notes that its research is highly specialised, and that its Cancer Research Committee includes representatives of the *Cancer Research Campaign* and of the *Imperial Cancer Research Fund*.

Volunteers

While the emphasis is on the volunteer input to the charity's extensive community fundraising, and even more to its 170 unusually successful shops (all dealing solely in donated goods), volunteers are also important to the work in the hospices. They carry out such tasks as driving day care patients to and from their homes, working on reception and helping with day care.

The charity's first 'Head of Volunteering' was appointed in 2000. Marie Curie reckons that more than 100,000 people volunteer for the charity in a year, donating the equivalent of £4.3 million worth of time.

Funding, administration

Marie Curie is funded primarily by donations and legacies, which accounted for £46 million of its £61 million income in 2000/01. This was achieved at a fundraising cost of £16 million, giving a high cost ratio of 35p in the pound, or 35%, though this was slightly down on the 37% average of the three years to 1999.

As with most cancer charities, legacies are important, accounting for £14 million income in each of the last two years. Though bequests are often referred to as a particularly unpredictable source of income, they may be less so for charities of this size.

An excellent chart in the annual review shows the rapid growth of the charity over the last ten years. By far the largest increase has been in 'community fundraising', usually meaning fundraising events (whether local or national) and local appeals. For the future the emphasis here will be on 'establishing more volunteer support groups in villages, towns and cities'. However, this growth has been accompanied by a corresponding rise in fundraising expenditures, suggesting that the marginal cost of raising money in this way may be higher than for the charity's more traditional direct mail and legacy income. The annual report notes: 'we must remember that fundraising does require investment to be successful'. However, the accounts showed that there had been a reduction in the number of fundraising staff, from 666 to 652, following an even greater reduction in the previous year.

In early 2001 the charity's fundraising organisation was reported to be in some turmoil. A planned further reduction in staff was said to open the possibility of 50 staff being made redundant, while a newly appointed fundraising director found his appointment had evaporated before he had even taken up the post.

The charity receives a relatively modest £12 million from health authorities, £8.2 million of it for its hospices and £3.8 million for its nurses. There is little information on how Marie Curie addresses the difficult issue of the relative financial responsibilities of the charity and of the NHS.

The charity adds ...

Following a number of new initiatives and some streamlining of our fundraising operations, voluntary income for the current financial year (to date) and net contribution are ahead of budget and ahead of the same period last year. Our fundraising cost ratios have also improved. All of which will help the charity's plans to deliver more care to more cancer patients and to conduct more cancer research work.

The information assessed

There is an excellent annual report and accounts and an annual review, plus fine supporting materials. There is a good website.

Contact

89 Albert Embankment
London
SE1 7TP
Tel 020 7599 7777
Website www.mariecurie.org.uk
Chair Sir Nicholas Fenn
Thomas Hughes-Hallett, Chief Executive

Medical Foundation for the Care of Victims of Torture

Income	£4,721,000 (2000)
Donated income	£4,402,000
Fundraising costs	£1,132,000
Statutory income	£236,000
Top salary	£50,000–£55,000
Paid staff	
Full time	49
Part time	48
Volunteers	
Operational	102
Fundraising	13

Aims, activities

The foundation 'exists to enable survivors of torture and organised violence to engage in a healing process to assert their own human dignity and worth'.

Just over 5,000 people were referred to the charity's specialist doctors and caseworkers in the year 2000, an appalling 52% increase from the previous year's 3,300, which itself had up till then been the highest for any year in the charity's history. The foundation provides medical care and treatment, alongside counselling, advice and practical help. It also documents injury from torture in official medico-legal reports – 822 in the year.

The terrible growth in potential clients has outstripped the charity's ability to fund the necessary services, so a waiting time for new clients has unfortunately developed. In most cases, there are no alternative sources of the kind of help that this charity provides.

The countries of origin of the greatest number of clients in 2000 were as follows (though the foundation points out that this is not necessarily the country in which the abuse took place):

- Turkey 699;
- Sri Lanka 684;
- Iran 508;
- Iraq 475;
- Kosovo 318;
- Democratic Republic of Congo (Zaire) 207;
- Afghanistan 199;
- Somalia 134;
- Algeria 129;
- Eritrea 102.

The charity produces 'country' reports based on the evidence it sees. In 2000, for example, it published an account of torture suffered by Tamil asylum applicants, suggesting that this evidence was being ignored by the Home Office. The report concluded, apparently reasonably, that the Home Office 'should accept medical evidence as sufficient proof of torture unless challenged by a medical expert of equal standing'.

The work of the charity, at the time of writing, was overshadowed by the supposed 'asylum seeker' issue. The founder and director of the charity is Helen Bamber, who started on this work in the concentration camps liberated at the end of the Second World War. She points out in the annual review for 2000 that the victims of the appalling tortures that she sees are among the people who are referred to disparagingly by the media as 'asylum seekers':

'[The] rhetoric that now surrounds refugees and asylum seekers in Britain has reached crisis point. There no longer seems to be any recognition within the phrase "asylum seeker" that these are people who may have been tortured; or suffered atrocity, or who are carrying physical injuries (not always visible); or who have quite devastating memories of carnage and loss of family members and loved ones.'

Despite continued financial growth, the charity is being overwhelmed by the even faster growth in the number of victims of torture being referred to it. It is therefore having to consider how to reorganise its services 'in an environment where providing a direct service to the majority of those referred, as we have sought to do up to now, may no longer be feasible'.

In this editor's view, the NHS, which has a responsibility for the health of everyone in the country, should step in to ensure that the kind of specialist help that the charity provides, on a voluntarily funded basis, should continue to be available to all who have the appalling misfortune to need it.

Volunteers

In 2000 the charity 'was fortunate to have the services of 115 part-time volunteers. 102 of them worked in the areas of medical, relief and casework.'

Funding, administration

The charity has 46 medical, relief and casework staff, 6 for overseas and human rights activities, 5 who work on education, training and information, 9 support staff and 5 fundraisers (all these numbers are for full-time equivalents).

The ongoing work of the charity is funded primarily by the donations of individuals (£2.3 million in 2000), and from charitable foundations (£0.6 million). Modest support from the Department for International Development related to a project in Kosovo and Macedonia, has recently come to an end.

The charity has also been running an appeal, 'Under One Roof', to enable it to move to appropriate premises. This brought in £1.2 million in the year.

Fundraising costs of £1.1 million represented 26p for each pound donated; the ratio is reducing from those of previous years.

Administrative costs, properly reported in the way called for in the Charity Commission's 'SORP' guidelines, were just £20,000 or less than half of one per cent of expenditure.

The charity adds ...

The Medical Foundation is working hard to maintain its front-line services in London while addressing the huge problems created by the Government's dispersal of asylum seekers nationwide. Training of health professionals in dispersal locations, combined with direct service provision for torture survivors in selected cities, is the immediate challenge.

The information assessed

There is an excellent annual report and accounts, with particularly good coverage of the financial position of the charity, and a powerful annual review. The first-class website includes the summary accounts.

Contact

96–98 Grafton Road
London
NW5 3EJ
Tel 020 7813 7777
Website www.torturecare.org.uk
Chair Rex Bloomstein
Helen Bamber, Chief Executive

Medical research charities

Fundraising members of the Association of Medical Research Charities (tel: 020 7269 8820) spend about £250 million a year on research. The association sets rigorous standards for its members, including the insistence on a peer review process for new research projects.

The list below shows only those medical research charities which are mainly reliant on voluntary income, were planning to spend at least £200,000 on research in 2000/01, and are members of the association. (There are many others.) Those in italics have their own entries in this book. In each case, the name of the charity is followed by the amount of money it planned to spend on research in 2000/01, and then by its telephone number.

Action on Addiction, £0.4 million; tel: 020 7793 1011

Action Research, £4.8 million; tel: 01403 210406

Alzheimer's Society, £1 million; tel: 020 7306 0606

Arthritis Research Campaign, £22 million; tel: 01246 558033

Association for International Cancer Research, £4.6 million; tel: 01334 477910

Ataxia, £0.3 million; tel: 020 7582 1444

Brain Research Trust, £2 million; tel: 020 7636 3440

Breakthrough Breast Cancer, £3 million; tel: 020 7405 5111

Breast Cancer Campaign, £1 million; tel: 020 7749 3700

British Heart Foundation, £46 million; tel: 020 7935 0185

British Lung Foundation, £1 million; tel: 020 7831 5831

British Neurological Research Trust, £0.3 million; tel: 020 8913 8555

British Retinitis Pigmentosa Society, £0.4 million; tel: 01280 860195

Cancer Research Campaign, £61 million; tel: 020 7224 1333

Chest Heart and Stroke Scotland, £0.5 million; tel: 0131 225 6963

Children Nationwide Medical Research Fund, £1.4 million; tel: 020 7724 5727

Children's Liver Disease Foundation, £0.3 million; tel: 0121 212 3839

Chronic Granulomatous Disorder Research Trust, £0.3 million; tel: 01725 517977

Cystic Fibrosis Trust, £2.4 million; tel: 020 8464 7211

Defeating Deafness (Hearing Research Trust), £0.7 million; tel: 020 7833 1733

Diabetes UK, £4.4 million; tel: 020 7323 1531

Digestive Disorders Foundation, £0.7 million; tel: 020 7486 0341

DEBRA (Dystrophic Epidermolysis Bullosa Research Trust), £0.8 million; tel: 01344 771961

East Grinstead Medical Research Trust (plastic and reconstructive surgery), £0.5 million; tel: 01342 313088

Epilepsy Research Foundation, £0.4 million; tel: 020 8995 4781

Guide Dogs for the Blind, £0.6 million; tel: 0118 983 5555

Imperial Cancer Research Fund, £57.4 million; tel: 020 7242 0200

International Spinal Research Trust, £1 million; tel: 01483 898786

Iris Fund for Prevention of Blindness, £0.7 million; tel: 020 7928 7743

Juvenile Diabetes Foundation, £0.9 million; tel: 020 7436 31112

Liver Research Trust, £0.8 million; tel: 020 7679 6510

Marie Curie Cancer Care Research Institute, £2.5 million; tel: 020 7599 7777

Meningitis Research Foundation, £1.5 million; tel: 01454 281811

Meningitis Trust, £0.4 million; tel: 01453 768000

Migraine Trust, £0.2 million; tel: 020 7831 4818

Motor Neurone Disease Association, £0.8 million; tel: 01604 250505

Multiple Sclerosis Society, £1.5 million; tel: 020 8438 0701

Muscular Dystrophy Campaign, £1.7 million; tel: 020 7720 8055

National Association for Colitis and Crohn's Disease (NACC), £0.3 million; tel: 01727 830038

National Asthma Campaign, £2 million; tel: 020 7226 2260

National Eye Research Centre, £0.5 million; tel: 0117 929 0024

National Heart Research Fund, £0.5 million; tel: 0113 234 7474

National Kidney Research Fund, £3 million; tel: 01733 704650

National Osteoporosis Society, £0.4 million; tel: 01761 471771

North West Cancer Research Fund, £1 million; tel: 0151 709 2919

Parkinson's Disease Society, £1.1 million; tel: 020 7931 8080

Primary Immunodeficiency Association, £0.2 million; tel: 020 7976 7640

RAFT (Restoration of Appearance and Function Trust), £0.8 million; tel: 01923 835815

Research into Ageing, £0.9 million; tel: 020 7843 1550

Royal National Institute for the Blind, £0.3 million; tel: 0845 766 9999

Stroke Association, £1.8 million; tel: 020 7566 0300

Tenovus (cancer), £1.8 million; tel: 029 2062 1433

Tommy's Campaign (foetal health, miscarriage, premature and stillbirth), £1.4 million; tel: 020 7620 0188

Tuberous Sclerosis Association, £0.2 million; tel: 01527 871898

Tyneside Leukaemia Research Association, £0.2 million; tel: 0191 222 7791

Ulster Cancer Foundation, £0.3 million; tel: 028 9066 3281

Wellbeing (the health of women and newborn babies), £1 million; tel: 020 7772 6400

Wessex Medical Trust (general, in Wessex), £0.6 million; tel: 023 8033 3366

William Harvey Research Foundation (cardiovascular, inflammatory and diabetic disorders), £1 million; tel: 020 7882 6120

Wishbone Trust (orthopaedics), £0.8 million; tel: 020 7869 6930

Yorkshire Cancer Research, £5 million; tel: 01423 501269

Mencap
Royal Mencap Society; England, Wales and Northern Ireland

Income	£110,022,000 (2000/01)
Donated income	£9,924,000
Fundraising costs	£2,929,000
Statutory income	£93,964,000
Top salary	£70,000–£80,000
Paid staff	4,570
Volunteers	3,800

Aims, activities

Mencap's aim is to improve the lives and opportunities of children and adults with a learning disability, as well as those of their families and carers. It is working towards a world where everyone with a learning disability has an equal right to choice, opportunity and respect, with the support that they need.

'Mencap is unusual among major charities in the proportion of its income which comes from statutory sources ... almost 80% of it for residential care and support alone' – to quote the 1999/00 annual report.

This key activity provides permanent homes for close to 3,000 people with learning disabilities. The chief executive notes with regret that many of the relevant contracts with local authorities do not pay for the full costs of the services, which therefore have to be further subsidised from the donations of the public. In an indication of the increasingly commercial nature of this part of the charity world, the report also notes that it is 'working to give our service managers greater flexibility to match price to the local marketplace'.

Mencap is also an important provider of other services for people with learning disabilities (though this accounts for only a minor part of its financial commitments) and campaigns extensively for greater attention to be paid to their concerns.

In 2001 the charity was divided into six business units:

- housing and support;
- education and employment;
- community support;
- campaigning;
- Wales;
- Northern Ireland.

The charity is at the centre of an extensive national network of independent local Mencap and other groups. There are about 400 independent but affiliated local charities; both within and outside these local Mencaps there are about 600 Gateway social clubs. Some local groups are very small, and most are wholly voluntary. However, others (such as Westminster Mencap) are large charities, employing staff and delivering services under contract just like Royal Mencap itself.

The main use of the central charity's voluntary (as opposed to statutory) income is to finance a team of over 60 district officers who support local Mencap and other groups in their area, and organise collective pressure for the improvement of services there for all people with learning disabilities.

There is no centrally available information about the collective income or staffing levels of this great local network, but Mencap estimates that its overall level of voluntary donations may be as much again as the £9 million of the parent charity.

The central charity categorised its direct charitable expenditures in 2000/01 under the following headings:

- residential services £74 million, or 72%;
- support and information £10 million, or 9%;
- education and employment £9 million, or 9%;
- leisure services £3 million, or 3%;
- support costs £7 million, or 6%.

'Support and information' includes a family adviser system. 'Education and employment' is centred on 'Mencap National College', which is in practice a network of three colleges supporting and enabling students who take courses at nearby mainstream institutions, and on the Pathway employment service which 'is supporting several thousand people in work'. 'Leisure services' covers support for the Gateway network of clubs and projects (many of which are part of the operations of independent local Mencap affiliated charities).

The charity has been comprehensively reorganised in recent years, to ensure that people with learning disabilities are closely involved in its decision making. Previously it was in practice controlled by the local societies who were its members. Now it has 15,000 individual members, each with one vote. Members of affiliated local Mencaps or Gateway clubs can become individual members for an extra £1 a year. A total of 59 district committees are being established. There is also a 50-strong national assembly, elected by a combination of the members of the society and by Mencap staff; 17 of the assembly members have learning disabilities themselves. The assembly elects seven of the ten trustees, one of whom has a mild learning disability.

A five-year plan has been published for the period 2001–06. In the main this is a list of fairly general intentions, such as 'to improve access to direct payments', but there are also some important specific targets, including:

- to get the 'Income Support Disregard' increased to at least £30 a week;
- to increase residential care places from 2,800 to over 3,000;
- to increase the number of 'Supported Living' clients from 300 to over 1,000;
- to double the number of people benefiting from the charity's information services;
- to double the number of people undertaking personal and community development programmes.

There has long been disagreement about the continued use of the Mencap name. While the decline of the 'mental handicap' terminology is generally welcomed, 'Mencap' is a name that attracts a valuable level of public recognition. The issue was considered by the directly elected assembly in 2000 and it was decided not to abandon the word. A couple of local groups took this as the occasion to give up use of the Mencap name (though not their Mencap affiliation). Then at its Annual General Meeting in November 2001 the charity decided to compromise by changing its name to Royal Mencap Society (from the previous Royal Society for Mentally Handicapped Children and Adults).

Looking at the reports, this editor felt that the residential care homes have become so big financially in relation to the rest of the charity's work that there may be a case for setting them up as a separate non-profit business, reliant on statutory funding. This would leave the main charity, with largely voluntary funding, to concentrate on support, representation and campaigning for all people with learning disabilities.

The comparable organisation in Scotland is Enable Scotland; tel. 0141 226 4541.

Volunteers

Most of the voluntary activity of the Mencap network takes place in the hundreds of local Mencap societies and Gateway clubs. There is no collective measure of the scale of this, though it must be very large. The main role of volunteers in Royal Mencap itself is as individual members. The five-year plan sets a target of raising the number of these to 25,000 by 2005.

Funding, administration

The charity's main income is in the form of payments from public bodies for services provided. In 2000/01 there were further donations of £5.2 million, up from £5 million in the previous year. Legacies, at £4.7 million, showed an increase from both of the preceding two years. The charity also runs important fundraising events and promotions, but through a separate trading company. This raised a further £3.3 million, at a cost, reasonable for this kind of fundraising, of £1.6 million. The overall fundraising costs were £2.9 million, giving a ratio of 30p for each pound given to the charity (a lower figure than the accounts would appear to suggest, because these do not follow the

Charity Commission definitions in this respect).

The five-year plan envisages raising fundraised income to higher levels. This may be difficult, given the substantial costs of achieving the existing figures.

Just six of the 4,600 staff are employed in the administration of the charity. There are 70 fundraising staff. All the rest work on the delivery of the charitable services and activities.

'Support costs' of £7 million may reflect the very high costs of negotiating and maintaining a mass of differing contractual arrangements with a diverse range of public bodies. This is unavoidable if a charity is to provide the services that are required, by people least able to secure them for themselves – but it is both unfortunate and unnecessary that the government system of allocating public funds in the welfare field should impose such costs on a charity.

The charity adds ...

Mencap has changed so much since 1946, when it was set up by a few dedicated parents who campaigned so effectively to ensure their children had a right to education and would no longer have to live in isolated long-stay hospitals. But there is still so much to do if we are to end discrimination against people with a learning disability and create a fully inclusive society. Please join us in the fight for equality.

The information assessed

The annual report, previously weak for a charity of this size, is now excellent, with an admirable 'Guide to the Accounts' that could be a model for many other charities. There is a good five-year strategic plan.

Contact

123 Golden Lane
London
EC1Y ORT
Tel 020 7454 0454
Website www.mencap.org.uk
Chair Brian Baldock
Fred Heddell, Chief Executive

Mental Health Foundation

Primarily funding medical research

Income	£3,387,000 (2000/01)
Donated income	£2,899,000
Fundraising costs	£550,000
Statutory income	£34,000
Top salary	£60,000–£70,000
Paid staff	39
Volunteers	15

Aims, activities

The charity describes itself as 'the leading UK charity working in mental health and learning disabilities' (though there are larger charities featured in this book which work in one or other of these fields). It aims to improve the support available for people with these conditions through:

- funding research;
- developing new models of service delivery;
- influencing government and service providers;
- providing information for professionals and for the general public.

Overall, the foundation is more of a research and development organisation than a provider of ongoing services.

The foundation mainly funds others to carry out its research and to provide the community services referred to in its literature, and then uses the results of these activities to positively influence policies and practices. The information services, however, are provided directly by the foundation itself.

The breakdown of expenditure for 2000/01 demonstrates this way of working:

- grants and allocations £1,676,000
- information, education and advisory services £825,000

The main activities in 2000/01 were described as follows:

- The mental health of children and young people. Grants have been made for research into, for example, the mental health of children in residential care and of street children.
- Older people and dementia. Action research has been funded to develop a new model of local inter-agency support for people newly diagnosed with dementia.
- Growing older with learning difficulties. A total of 13 research projects were funded in 2000/01.
- Anti-stigma campaign. The charity runs the annual Mental Health Action Week.
- Mental health service users. The foundation is developing user-led research work.

The largest recipients of grants were Dementia Voice at Blackberry Hill Hospital in Bristol (£65,000) and Manchester University (£46,000), but the purposes of these grants were not disclosed. While most of the large grants were to hospitals or universities, some were to mental health charities – as were a majority of the smaller grants.

Work with people with learning disabilities is carried out through the Foundation for People with Learning Disabilities, which is part of the Mental Health Foundation but which has 'developed a clear and distinct identity'.

The foundation has a separate Scottish presence, chaired by Lord Dalhousie, which can be contacted on 0141 1572 0125.

Volunteers

There is no reference to voluntary input in the foundation's printed materials, but it has previously reported having about 15 active volunteers.

Funding, administration

The foundation is primarily funded by donations from the public, grants from charitable foundations (including the Lottery-based Community Fund) and legacies. The accounts do not distinguish between the income from individuals and that from institutions (though the £658,000 received in legacies must have been from the former). There is only a very small amount of funding from government.

Income was £3.4 million in 2000/01, down from £3.6 million the previous year, mainly due to an unusually high level of legacy income in the earlier year.

Fundraising costs of £548,000 were much reduced from the exceptional £1 million invested in the previous year. This had led to an increase in grants and donations, from £1.7 million to £2 million, and was reported to have already brought in over 7,000

new, young and committed givers (approached in their own homes). These new supporters were expected to contribute an extra £400,000 in 2000/01 – as indeed happened – as well as further support in subsequent years.

The cost ratio of 19p for each pound donated was correspondingly down from the exceptional 31p of the previous year.

The information assessed

The annual report is adequate. The analysis and explanation of the charity's grants are weak. The good website, including the full accounts, was due to be replaced by a more extensive site in autumn 2001.

Contact

20–21 Cornwall Terrace
London
NW1 4QL
Tel 020 7535 7400
Website www.mentalhealth.org.uk
Chair Christopher Martin
Ruth Lesirge, Director

MHA (Methodist Homes for the Aged)

England, Scotland and Wales

Income	£27,685,000 (2000/01)
Donated income	£4,376,000
Fundraising costs	£692,000
Statutory income	£21,000,000
Top salary	£80,000–£90,000
Paid staff	
Full time	708
Part time	1,581
Volunteers	
Operational	3,000
Fundraising	2,000

Aims, activities

This energetic charity, with its roots in the Methodist church, is now operating as part of the MHA group which also includes the Methodist Housing Association, itself a charity.

The charity, which caters for people of all denominations, offers the following services:

- 32 residential homes;
- 2 nursing and dementia homes;
- 3 dementia care homes;
- 5 residential and dementia homes;
- 30 sheltered housing schemes;
- 50 community-based Live at Home schemes.

In all, these services support over 6,000 older people. The Live at Home schemes are the fastest growing part of the work and the charity is a leader in developing good practice in organising the volunteer input that lies at the heart of such schemes.

The new combined MHA group is developing further services for older people, which will focus on community-based services in disadvantaged areas. It is already spending more than £7 million a year on capital development and has impressive experience in the specialised field of dementia care.

Volunteers

The charity has over 4,700 active volunteers, whose work is excellently described in the 'Get involved' section of the website. In particular each of the 50 local Live at Home schemes has its own group of volunteers, where the work includes visiting older people, helping with lunch clubs and the like, and organising trips. There are also voluntary representatives at many Methodist churches, and others, not necessarily Methodists, who help with the charity's fundraising.

Funding, administration

As is usual with charities of this type, most of the income is in the form of fees from local authorities for the costs of individual residents. These payments totalled over £20 million in 2000/01. The charity, however, has to top up this sum with money from its own fundraised income in order to maintain its standards. The Live at Home services are largely funded from the charity's own income.

Total voluntary income amounted to £4.4 million, from legacies (£3.3 million) and donations (£1.1 million). This was raised at a fundraising cost of £692,000, representing 16p for each pound donated, or 16%. This was something of a jump from the average for the previous three years of a low 13%.

The information assessed

A good annual report and accounts for 2000/01. There is also a biennial review for 1999/

2001. The website has good materials for potential volunteers. Confusingly, there were two 'Annual Reports' for 1998/99, both nicely presented but each with a different text.

Contact

Epworth House
Stuart Street
Derby
DE1 2EQ
Tel 01332 296200
Website www.mha.org.uk
Chair Susan Howdle
Mrs Barbara Leighton, Chief Executive

Mind
England and Wales

Income	£10,573,000 (1999/00)
Donated income	£4,075,000
Fundraising costs	£1,118,000
Statutory income	£1,772,000
Top salary	£70,000–£79,999
Paid staff	283
Volunteers	1,200

Aims, activities

The Mind network consists both of this national charity and more than 200 local Mind groups. These are independent charities, with their own incomes and expenditures which do not show in the figures above.

The charity's website notes some of the background to its work:

- mental distress affects young and old, rich and poor;
- one in four people seeks help for mental health problems at some time in their lives;
- over 4,000 people take their own lives each year in the UK;

- more than 2 million prescriptions are issued every year for major tranquillisers, while minor tranquillisers account for over 19 million;
- over 250,000 people are admitted to psychiatric hospitals annually;
- only 13% of people with significant mental health problems have paid work – a lower proportion than for any other disability group.

'Mind is the leading mental health charity in England and Wales, working for a better life for everyone in mental distress. We do this by:

- campaigning for jobs and rights in the community
- providing high quality and innovative mental health services by supporting a network of more than 200 local Mind associations
- advising government, health and local authorities on good practice and service development in mental health and community care.'

The charity gives confidential information and help to tens of thousands of people through Mindinfoline (**08457 660163**) and through its website; runs a series of active campaigns at national level for better services; and makes grants. However, the biggest single activity (at least in financial terms) is supporting regional or local Mind activities. These include support for volunteering through the government's Opportunities for Volunteering scheme, and one of the excellent Lottery-funded Millennium Awards schemes for volunteers.

MindLink is a national network of mental health service survivors. Membership is free and open to anyone who has, or has had, personal experience of mental distress. The primary purpose of MindLink is to be a consultative body that ensures that users and survivors of mental health services have a direct say in shaping Mind's policies and campaigns.

Around the country there are local Mind associations (LMAs), which offer many services – including supported housing, crisis helplines, drop-in centres, counselling, befriending, advocacy, employment and training schemes – around the country. However, all associations are different and there can be no guarantee that what is available in the way of support in one area will also be there in another.

National Mind has set up a strong Local Mind Support Team to give LMAs help and guidance on key organisational matters, such as ensuring an effective structure, and on providing the highest quality mental health support services. 'The foundation for much of this work lies in the implementation of "Quality Management in Mind", a newly developed quality system which was designed specifically for the diversity of all local Mind associations.' The appointment of this new team at the end of 2000 involved the contentious closure of some of the former regional offices, but Mind has said that in fact the new initiative represents a larger as well as a stronger commitment to support for local associations.

Volunteers

Mindinfoline uses a mix of trained volunteers and salaried staff at its centre in east London, and many Mind campaigns benefit from voluntary support. There is good information on the website. However, most voluntary activity is concentrated in the local associations. Information about these is also on the website, or they can usually be contacted locally through any doctor's surgery or Community Health Council.

Equivalent organisations are:

– Scottish Association for Mental Health (tel: 0141 568 7000)

– Northern Ireland Association for Mental Health (tel: 028 9032 8474)

Funding, administration

Voluntary donations (£2.9 million) and legacies (£0.9 million) were the main sources of income in 1999/00, along with £2 million in grants, about half of them from government. The extensive chain of shops contributed £370,000 from sales of £4.2 million.

The voluntary income was achieved at a fundraising cost of £1.1 million, giving a cost ratio of 27p in the pound, which was a considerable reduction from the level of 38p in the pound in the previous year and from the average of 39p in the pound for the three years to 1999. This was thanks to a substantial reduction in fundraising expenditure, from £1.6 million in 1998/99 down to £1.1 million, which had little immediate effect on donations.

The charity notes that it is planning increased investment in fundraising over the next couple of years, and anticipates an associated growth in its income.

The annual review for 2000 contained a potentially misleading chart, 'How we spent our money', in which the £1.1 million of fundraising expenditure is not shown. This reflected a presentation in the accounts where fundraising costs (called 'Other costs of raising funds') appeared as a deduction on the income side of the accounts rather than as one of the charity's costs, and did not appear at all as part of the final 'Total resources expended'.

The charity notes that the presentation in the review for 2001 will be clearer.

The charity adds ...

For comprehensive information about mental health, job opportunities, current campaigns, sponsorship and fundraising initiatives visit our website – www.mind.org.uk. To discuss opportunities to fund or sponsor our work call 020 8215 2235.

The information assessed

The generally adequate annual report and annual review are brief and the clarity of the accounts is criticised above in one important respect. The good website was found to be the most useful source of information when writing this entry.

Contact

Granta House
15–19 Broadway
London
E15 4BQ
Tel 020 8519 2122
Website www.mind.org.uk
Chair David Peryer
Richard Brook, Chief Executive

Motor Neurone Disease Association

Income	£5,749,000 (2000/01)
Donated income	£5,285,000
Fundraising costs	£1,044,000
Statutory income	£0
Top salary	£50,000–£60,000
Paid staff	
Full time	64
Part time	10
Volunteers	1,500

Aims, activities

There are about 5,000 people in the UK living with Motor Neurone Disease (MND), a fatal condition where the motor neurones (nerves) that carry messages to the muscles die, and for which there is at present no known cure. The average time between diagnosis and death is just 14 months. Cruelly, MND removes the power to talk while leaving intellect and senses intact.

This charity seeks both to support people with the disease, and their families, and to fund research into the causes of the condition, which are as yet unknown. The need for its work was well set out in the annual review for 1999/00:

'Twenty-one years ago [when the charity was founded] people with MND received minimal care and support. Few doctors had heard of the disease, and there was virtually no research into its causes. There was scant support for carers, little understanding about the disease and no provision of specialised equipment. People with MND, their alert minds trapped in failing bodies, could not make their voices heard. Today, many people with MND receive a better standard of care and support ... and research is expanding.'

The caring work is based on seven care centres; an information service including a helpline (**08457 626262**), which was contacted by 8,000 people in 1999/00; 20 regional care advisers; over 250 volunteer visitors; an equipment loan service; and a system of grants for families in need, especially for respite from their caring responsibilities.

On the research side, the charity contributed £1.1 million to a range of research programmes, especially those at the Institute of Psychiatry at Kings College London. Remarkably, the charity has been able to fund all the grants that its Research Advisory Panel has recommended over the last five years.

In 2000, for the first time, a drug named Riluzole was found which, while not offering hope of a cure, does slow down the progress of the disease. After a massive effort by the charity, the National Institute for Clinical Excellence (NICE) has approved the drug for general use within the NHS in January 2001, ending the former lottery governing whether or not it would be prescribed.

The equivalent organisation in Scotland is the Scottish Motor Neurone Disease Association; tel: 0141 945 1077; www.scotmnd.org.uk

Volunteers

The trained association visitors are an important feature of the charity's work. The association's 85 branches, besides raising money for the charity, also offer a focus for mutual support among families affected by the disease.

Funding, administration

Almost all of the charity's income is from donations and legacies, reaching a total of £5.3 million in 2000/01, which represented a large increase of 23% from the £4.3 million of the previous year. This resulted from a big rise in 'donor and volunteer' income, a separate heading from 'donations and gifts' in the accounts, though the difference is not explained. The voluntary income was achieved at a fundraising cost of £1 million, giving a cost ratio of 20p in the pound, or 20%. This was a slight increase on the average of 17% of the previous three years, but the trustees are confident that the increased investment will generate even higher incomes in the future. A similar prediction, about income from charitable trusts that was made in the previous year, was indeed justified in the event.

The charity adds ...

Motor Neurone Disease is a devastating condition. The MND Association works to ensure people with MND and their carers receive the care and support they need, and funds research into causes, treatments and a cure for MND.

The information assessed

The annual report and accounts, when combined with the annual review, are generally excellent. The accounts are particularly clear, including an unusual and excellent section on how costs are allocated between different headings. However, the 'review' of financial activities has no content beyond what is already in the accounts. There is a colourful magazine and a useful website, with clear information for potential volunteers.

Contact
David Niven House
PO Box 246
Northampton
NN1 2PR
Tel 01604 250505
Website www.mndassociation.org
Chair Professor Paul Spencer
George Levvy, Chief Executive

Multiple Sclerosis Society

Income	£22,005,000 (1999)
Donated income	£15,462,000
Fundraising costs	£2,539,000
Statutory income	£391,000
Top salary	£80,000–£90,000
Paid staff	417
Volunteers	7,000

Aims, activities

There are about 85,000 people with multiple sclerosis (MS) in the UK. It is a neurological condition, generally found in adults, that affects the coating surrounding nerve fibres. Both the actual symptoms and their severity vary greatly from person to person. Many people with mild MS live out a normal life span. Remarkably, MS becomes more common the further one goes from the equator. It is more common in Britain than in India, and in Scotland than in England.

The society has three main roles:

- It provides support and care for people with MS through its head office, country and regional offices, 371 branches, respite centres and holiday homes.

- It works for better provision for people with MS through its public awareness campaigns and through work with the NHS and other public bodies.

- It funds research into MS.

The charity refers to the breadth of services provided, but these were not described in the literature made available to these publishers. There was a reference to 'the growing number of professional services provided by the society and its partners', including 'more specialist MS nurses' who may be NHS staff funded in whole or in part by the society. There was little information about whether the 'range of services' is organised nationally, regionally or by the voluntarily staffed branches.

The branches are described on the website as follows: 'Branches offer a range of activities, support, information and advice, and also hold fundraising events. Some hold special meetings for people who are newly diagnosed with MS and a growing number have their own resource centres.'

A major current issue for the society is the NHS's provision of beta-interferons and similar drugs for people with MS. Despite a vigorous campaign, the National Institute for Clinical Excellence (NICE) provisionally decided against this in the summer of 2001, on the grounds that the drugs did not offer sufficient benefit to justify their cost. The society disputes the analytic methods used by the committee, suggesting that the substantial costs of the drugs may have been given undue weight, and was urging its members to lobby against the decision. In November 2001 the charity still planned to appeal against NICE's verdict, despite a BBC report the previous month stating that the Department of Health was reviewing NHS prescriptions for the drugs 'positively' and had proposed 'extensive clinical trials'.

In the field of information there is a National MS Helpline (**0808 800 8000**), and a range of publications.

A big recent initiative has been the creation of a new MS National Resource Centre in north London, opened in August 2000, as 'a unique resource for everyone affected by MS'.

About 15% of the society's resources are put into research, under the direction of the charity's medical research advisory committee.

Volunteers

There are 370 local branches which are all voluntarily managed. The branches are not independent, but considerable powers have been delegated to them. They are where 'so many of our services to the MS community are delivered', and they also raise about one third of the society's income.

Funding, administration

The charity is funded mainly by legacies and donations, in roughly equal proportions, with about £7.5 million received from each in 1999. The other major source of income is 'fees', probably representing statutory payments for people attending the respite centres.

The donated income of £15.5 million was achieved at a fundraising cost of £2.5 million, representing 16p in the pound. Despite a substantial increase in fundraising costs from the previous year (reported as being up by a third, though the accounts show a 25% increase), this ratio was still lower than the average for the previous three years.

The good report by the honorary treasurer, Maureen Dickson, properly notes some concern over 'the flat trend of fundraising income over the last year', particularly the 5% drop in donated income. This report is also unusual in including welcome details of the charity's (very small) income from pharmaceutical companies, 'because there has been a lot of public interest in the relationship between health charities and the pharmaceutical industry'.

The society had £33.8 million in free reserves at the end of 1999, representing almost 18 months' expenditure. Of this, £13.5 million was designated, though not yet committed, for building the new National Resource Centre in north London. The policy of the charity is to hold a working reserve equal to six months' expenditure, plus another 7.5% of the value of investments (£1.9 million) in case of a medium-term fall in their value. This would make a total of £13.5 million against the actual £19.6 million held, so the charity is in a position to invest further in its activities.

The charity has a strongly devolved structure, with two additional national MS societies having their own management structure:

– MS Scotland (James Hope Thompson, General Secretary); tel: 0131 472 4106

– MS Society Northern Ireland (Kieran Harris, Director; tel: 028 9080 2802

The information assessed

The weak annual report and accounts and annual review include a good treasurer's report, but are thin in describing the activities of the charity. The website is perhaps the best source of information about the services of the charity. It has links to the separate websites of a number of the local branches.

Contact

372 Edgware Road
Staples Corner
London
NW2 6ND
Tel 020 8438 0700
Website www.mssociety.org.uk
Chair Sarah Phillips
Peter Cardy, Chief Executive

Muscular Dystrophy Campaign

Income	£4,493,000 (2000)
Donated income	£4,270,000
Fundraising costs	£1,390,000
Statutory income	£0
Top salary	£50,000–£60,000
Paid staff	77
Volunteers	18,000

Aims, activities

The charity's aims are to identify the causes, develop treatments and discover cures for the range of conditions known as muscular dystrophy; and to provide support for people affected by these conditions.

During 2000 the campaign made awards totalling £1.5 million to 36 research projects in the UK. In addition, it funds three Muscle Centres at hospitals and three Muscle Networks around the country; these combine clinical care with training and research. There are also around 16 field care officers who provide support, in hospitals or at home, to people with muscular dystrophy and related conditions.

The charity campaigns for improved access, home adaptations and other facilities for people with neuro-muscular conditions. Its subsidiary charity, the Joseph Patrick Memorial Trust, provides individuals with equipment such as wheelchairs, beds and computers; it spent £224,000 on this during the year.

Volunteers

The charity has a 'grassroots network of 130 branches and 140 representatives, all of which is staffed wholly by volunteers. They fundraise, build awareness of Muscular Dystrophy and offer peer support to those affected by the condition.'

Funding, administration

The charity is funded entirely by voluntary contributions. The year 2000 was a difficult one, chiefly because income from legacies fell sharply, to £1.1 million, compared with £1.8 million in 1999. Income from branches and representatives, and from events, also fell. However, new fundraising sources were developed, including a schools campaign (centring on the charity's mascot, Rupert the bear) and the Chain of Hope direct debit appeal (launched at Christmas 2000 and scheduled to run throughout 2001). Income from trusts and companies also rose strongly.

Fundraising costs in 2000, at 33p for each pound donated, or 33%, were high – up from 27% in 1999 and from 26% averaged across the three previous years. This is attributed to the unexpected drop in income, together with increased costs associated with the new fundraising campaigns, noted above. For 2001, the campaign planned to reduce its expenditure while drawing further upon its reserves to meet existing grant commitments.

There are over 70 full time staff, of whom about half are based in the London office and about half based around the UK, including in regional offices.

The charity adds ...

The Muscular Dystrophy Campaign values and relies on its volunteer base. The charity's membership is an essential mechanism for getting information to those who need it. It would like to try and reach everyone affected by muscular dystrophy in the UK. To achieve and maintain this and to find eventual cures, the Campaign is looking to increase its number of supporters including event attendees.

The information assessed

The annual report and accounts and the annual review are adequate; some extra information is given on a photocopied sheet containing an overview of the charity.

Contact

7–11 Prescott Place
London
SW4 6BS
Tel 020 7720 8055
Website www.muscular-dystrophy.org
Chair Professor M Bobrow
A M Lee, Executive Director

National Asthma Campaign

Income	£10,416,000 (1999/00)
Donated income	£9,624,000
Fundraising costs	£2,125,000
Statutory income	£49,000
Top salary	£56,000
Paid staff	83
Volunteers	100,000

Aims, activities

This fast-growing organisation is the only UK charity dedicated to conquering asthma and improving the quality of life of people with asthma today and in the future. It was formed initially in 1990 by an amalgamation of the Asthma Research Council and the Asthma Society (showing that such amalgamations are not an entirely new idea).

The charity has three core areas of work:

- research needed to conquer asthma;
- independent help and advice for everyone affected by asthma;
- campaigning for a better deal for people with asthma.

Research: nearly half the charitable expenditure, or £4 million in 1999/00, went on research. Of this, £2 million was in the form of research grants, mainly directed at the long-term search for a cure for asthma but also covering improvements in treatment and on the prevention of childhood asthma.

Interviews for the charity's own big and ongoing study, 'Needs of People with Asthma', have already shown the probability that asthma is having a significant impact on the lives of about 1.4 million people in the UK: a finding that the charity reasonably calls 'shocking'. There will be a full report on the conclusion of this research which will identify areas of unmet need for the charity to tackle in the future.

The charity also manages the NHS Research and Development Programme on Asthma Management (the only such NHS programme to be managed by a charity).

Information, advice and support: the charity produces a wide range of information materials, including a credit card sized 'personal asthma plan' and a more detailed asthma diary, which were launched in 1999/00. A comprehensive new information pack for people diagnosed with asthma was introduced in 2001; it provides information to enable people to make informed choices about their condition at the point of diagnosis.

The charity also runs the Asthma Helpline (**0845 701 0203**), staffed by trained asthma nurses, while its activity holidays and Junior Asthma Club aim to give children and young people the information and confidence they need to understand and control their asthma.

Influencing policy makers and providers: a big success has been the progress of a new Code of Practice for workplace smoking. Apparently, up to 80% of people with asthma say that other people's smoking can make their condition worse. The charity has also been working hard for improvements in asthma management in schools – where the condition is distressing for staff as well as for pupils both with and without asthma themselves.

More generally, the charity acts as an independent authority and voice on asthma, ensuring that the needs of people with the condition are considered across a wide range of issues, and are kept at the forefront of media attention.

For the future, the charity is promoting two very different developments at opposite ends of the spectrum. First, it is pushing for a national, coordinated approach to asthma throughout the NHS, to reduce inequalities in treatment and care. Secondly, it is working to increase awareness of the benefits of

self-management plans as a routine part of asthma care.

Volunteers

The charity relies on the voluntary input of its trustees and of members of its development, research and investment committees. These are mostly professional people whose time is a most valuable resource. Although there is a reference to 'our volunteers working the length and breadth of the community', the only weakness of the charity's otherwise superb reporting is the lack of any more detailed information on the role of such volunteers.

Funding, administration

The charity's financial resources, nearly all from donations and legacies, have been growing fast, doubling between 1996 and 2000. Recent figures have been as follows:

- 1999/00 £9.6 million;
- 1998/99 £7.0 million;
- 1997/98 £6.2 million;
- 1996/97 £4.7 million.

The 1999/00 report notes a particularly high and perhaps unsustainable level of legacy income, which accounted for about a third of that year's receipts. Meanwhile the charity has substantially increased its very successful spending on the face-to-face recruitment of committed donors, with fundraising costs rising to £2.1 million from the £1.5 million of the previous year. Because of the greater income this has meant only a very small increase in the fundraising cost ratio, from 21p to 22p for each pound given, and the charity notes that the high proportion of ongoing commitments being received bodes well for future revenues. This work is carried out for the charity by a commercial fundraising agency.

The annual report notes increasing difficulty with some older fundraising approaches, including sponsored events and corporate fundraising.

The charity, however, also notes that it still does not have the resources to do all that it needs to do, and must seek further growth. The fine quality of its public reporting suggests that it may be better placed than many charities to achieve this.

In September 2001 the charity was named 'Employer of the Year' for London and the south-east.

The information assessed
The charity has exemplary annual reports and accounts, supporting literature and a good website.

Contact
Providence House
Providence Place
London
N1 0NT
Tel 020 7226 2260
Website www.asthma.org.uk
Chair Professor Duncan Geddes
Donna Covey, Chief Executive

National Autistic Society

Income	£42,428,000 (2000/01)
Donated income	£3,635,000
Fundraising costs	£812,000
Statutory income	£37,701,000
Top salary	£60,000–£70,000
Paid staff	
Full time	1,264
Part time	626
Volunteers	
Operational	345
Fundraising	350

Aims, activities
Autism and the related Asperger syndrome are complex lifelong disabilities affecting people's communication with others, their imagination and their social interactions. Symptoms range from the slight to the profound, affecting, to a greater or lesser degree, over 500,000 people in the UK, or about one in 100 of the population.

Started in 1962 by a group of parents, this charity has been growing very rapidly. Its 10,100 members in March 2000 compared with 7,900 a year before, while the number of branches was up from 44 to 60 over the same period.

The work of the charity can be divided into three:

- the provision of direct services (much the largest area financially);
- training, diagnosis, information and awareness raising;
- support for individuals, families and local groups.

Direct services – the charity runs 6 schools and 18 adult residential centres caring for nearly 400 children and adults. There is a Prospects Supported Employment Scheme and a new Earlybird Programme for early intervention when there is a possible diagnosis of autism. These programmes cost £35 million in 2000/01, or 90% of the charity's total expenditure.

Training, diagnosis, information and awareness raising – in 2000/01 nearly 1,500 professionals were given in-house training; the charity's Elliott House diagnostic centre (the only comprehensive one in the country) piloted a new 'DISCO' interview schedule; over 100 organisations were registered with the society's quality assurance programme; more than 20,000 people contacted the Autism Helpline (**0870 600 8585**); and there were over 400,000 hits on the society's website. A new Education Advocacy Line was opened. About 120 MPs and peers have joined a new all-party Parliamentary Group on Autism.

Support for individuals, families and local groups – among a number of other services, the society runs workshops for members and works with numerous local groups, helping them to develop their own activities and initiatives.

Volunteers

At a local level the society is almost wholly voluntary, based on mutual self-help and support. There is a volunteer befriending service and trained volunteers staff the new education advocacy service. In 2000/01 some 280 volunteers supported over 1,120 individuals through the society's parent-to-parent and befriending schemes.

Funding, administration

Financially, the society's work is dominated by the extremely expensive, though obviously important, direct school and residential provision for a relatively small number of severely affected individuals. This work is funded by fee income from statutory bodies, mainly local education authorities and the NHS, which is intended to cover fully the ongoing costs of the services. The intention is that charitably donated resources should be used solely to establish new services or to extend existing ones.

There was a sharp financial setback in 1999/00, when costs grew faster than income (even though the latter increased as well) and the society had a deficit (its first) of about £1.5 million. Despite concern at the time, there was a prompt recovery in 2000/01, under new management arrangements, with the charity comfortably back in surplus. This was achieved both by a reduction in costs of over £1 million, and by a surge in income for the schools and residential services.

The relatively small income from donations and legacies, invaluable because it is generally 'free' money, also increased, rising by 13% to £3.6 million, and was achieved at a reduced fundraising cost of 22p in the pound.

More generally, this editor feels that in charities such as this there may be an argument for separating the ongoing and very costly statutorily funded services from the main organisation. Such services represent but one part of the charity's role, and not necessarily one that is more important than the others, yet their disproportionate financial scale may unbalance the charity.

The information assessed

The annual report and accounts and annual review are excellent. So is the website, which is now linked to a general 'autism connect' portal. The charity also has good supporting literature.

Contact

393 City Road
London
EC1V 1NG
Tel 020 7833 2299
Website www.nas.org.uk
Chair Bob Noble
Vernon Beauchamp, Chief Executive

National Canine Defence League

Income	£20,222,000 (2000)
Donated income	£17,522,000
Fundraising costs	£4,139,000
Statutory income	£0
Top salary	£40,000–£50,000 (2)
Paid staff	350
Volunteers	50

Aims, activities

The aim of the charity is to see that 'all dogs can enjoy a happy life, free from the threat of unnecessary destruction'. There are three main programmes. The original and still the chief task is that of finding new homes for lost or abandoned dogs, called re-homing, and the charity spent £8.6 million on this in the year 2000. In 1999 the new Give a Dog a Life campaign also introduced, initially in north-east England, but now also in the north-west of England, south Wales and Northern Ireland, the microchipping and neutering programmes, at a cost of £2.4 million.

The principal areas of work are as follows:

- Re-homing – the charity runs 16 re-homing centres and these found homes for over 8,000 dogs in 2000, 10% more than in the previous year (all of these dogs were microchipped and neutered).

- Microchipping – this means fitting an electronic tag so that lost or stray dogs can be identified. A total of 10,000 dogs had these insertions in the year 2000, in addition to those that were re-homed by the society. Middlesbrough, one of the local authorities in the pilot north-east area, noted a 40% drop in strays and 48% fall in dogs destroyed. If these kind of figures become general, the charity will have achieved a great success.

- Neutering – a MORI survey for the society reports that there are more than 120,000 stray dogs in Britain, and the charity seeks to make it unacceptable for a dog to have an 'unwanted' litter. The neutering programme addresses this issue, with almost 12,000 dogs so treated in the year 2000. The charity generally subsidises the cost to the owners, with more generous arrangements for those on means-tested benefits.

The society is also active in education and the raising of public awareness, spending £1.5 million on this in the year 2000 and 'fielding more than 500,000 telephone and website enquiries'.

Volunteers

From its reports, the charity appears to be mainly a professionally staffed organisation, but in a response to an earlier survey it noted that it was supported by about 50 active volunteers (probably its dog walkers). The charity is apparently a membership organisation, but the annual report/review does not say how many members – as opposed to donors – there are, just mentioning 'over 500,000 members and supporters'.

Funding, administration

The income of the charity is derived mainly from donations and legacies, generally in roughly equal proportions, though in 1999 a massive single legacy of more than £7 million temporarily changed the pattern. The two sources totalled £17.5 million in 2000, raised at a fundraising cost of £4.1 million, or 24p in the pound.

Fundraising expenditure in 2000 was a third up on the £3.1 million spent in the previous year. This increase was so great that it is surprising that it was not mentioned in the trustees' report.

However, both these years represented improved cost-effectiveness over the previous three years, when the charity spent an average of 29p in the pound on its fundraising.

The reserves of the charity seem unusually high, even after taking existing commitments into account, but the situation was hard to disentangle as the trustees' report says that 'Unrestricted Funds stood at £435,000', while the balance sheet shows that 'Unrestricted Funds' included investments worth £24.5 million.

The trustees are probably confused by the fact that they have already 'designated' their intentions with regard to using some of the reserves. These remain, however, 'unrestricted' in law and are at the disposal of the trustees for any purpose within the powers of the charity.

The charity adds ...

The NCDL never destroys a healthy dog. To keep this promise, we are reliant upon the generosity of the UK's dog lovers. Please call us to find out how you can help, or visit our website.

The information assessed

The charity has adequate annual report and accounts and annual review. The annual review 2000, with summarised figures, covers 1999. There is also a cheerful doggy website.

Contact

17 Wakley Street
London
EC1V 7RQ
Tel 020 7837 0006
Website www.ncdl.org.uk
Chair P J M Prain
Mrs Clarissa Baldwin, Chief Executive

National Deaf Children's Society

Income	£3,894,000 (1999/00)
Donated income	£3,605,000
Fundraising costs	£993,000
Statutory income	£0
Top salary	£50,000–£60,000
Paid staff	71

Aims, activities

The NDCS provides advice, information and technology services to deaf children and their families (defining 'deaf' as the full range of hearing loss). It also campaigns on issues concerning these families. One of its campaigns has been for all newborn babies to be screened for hearing loss, as a quarter of all deaf children are currently undiagnosed at the age of three years. This campaign bore fruit when the government announced a pilot programme for universal screening early in 2001.

The charity has nine regional officers for England, plus a development officer and family support workers for each of Northern Ireland, Wales and Scotland. These individuals work with local representatives to offer support and advice to families with deaf children, often within the home or in schools.

NDCS also runs a telephone helpline (**020 7250 0123**) providing information and confidential advice, which is part funded by the Community Fund (formerly the National Lottery Charities Board).

One of the charity's aims is to provide deaf children with access to existing and new technologies that may improve their quality of life. Families are kept informed about what equipment is available through:

- the Listening Bus roadshow, which visits schools, deaf clubs and health clinics around the country;

- annual technology exhibitions held in Wolverhampton, Scotland and Northern Ireland;

- the NDCS Blue Peter Lend-An-Aid Library, from where radio aids and other equipment can be borrowed for up to three months.

Children's equipment grants are also available to help families purchase items such as teletext televisions and personal computers.

In 1999 the charity launched the Jack Ashley Millennium Awards (named for the former MP and disability campaigner) with a grant of £1.7 million from the Millennium Commission. At £2,000-£15,000 each, these awards are aimed at enabling deaf people aged 14–25 to undertake a variety of personal and community projects. It was intended to make more than 300 such grants by 2002. The first eight awards were made during 1999/00; they went to individuals embarking on projects that ranged from coral reef conservation in the Philippines, to training to become the UK's first deaf watersports and mountaineering instructor.

Direct charitable expenditure in 1999/00 totalled £1.98 million, up 10% from the £1.8 million spent in the previous year.

Volunteers

More than 80 volunteer local representatives work with the full-time regional officers and family support workers referred to above. There is also a network of over 120 voluntary parent self-help groups. Most are independent registered charities affiliated to the NDCS; all of them fundraise and organise local social and other events for families with deaf children.

Funding, administration

The charity's income in 1999/00 was £3.9 million. By far the greatest part of this, or £3.6 million, came from voluntary contributions. This compares with a total income of £2.9 million in the previous year, when donations, gifts, etc. stood at £2.2 million. The sharp increase was largely because legacy income jumped from £606,000 to £1.6 million, as a result of the biggest single bequest in the charity's history.

About £250,000 extra was added to reserves at the year end, in order to meet anticipated expansion of the charity's activities – for example, it expects the need for its services to grow if the government introduces universal screening of neonatal hearing. Another £500,000 was set aside to fund future investment in what the charity refers to as 'new direct dialogue fundraising'.

At £993,000, the society's fundraising costs were 28p for each pound of voluntary income, or 28%, a reduction from the average of 31% over the previous three years.

The charity adds ...

Our investment in direct dialogue fundraising sees us ask individuals to support NDCS with regular standing orders. Since beginning the campaign, thousands of individuals have decided to support deaf children in this way.

12,000 people visit our website each month. A complete redesign is underway which will make updating far easier.

The information assessed

The annual review and annual report and accounts are good. The website is both good and interesting, but, when examined in autumn 2001, parts needed updating; for example, it invited volunteers to participate in the 2000 London Marathon, and carried financial results for the year to March 1998.

Contact

15 Dufferin Street
London
EC1Y 8UR
Tel 020 7490 8656
Website www.ndcs.org.uk
Chair Gareth Jones
Susan Daniels, Chief Executive

National Gallery

Income	£44,794,000 (1999/00)
Donated income	£4,500,000
Fundraising costs	£445,000
Statutory income	£19,478,000
Top salary	£111,000
Paid staff	
Full time	439
Part time	25

Aims, activities

The gallery is a non-departmental public body, whose trustees are appointed by the prime minister. It is also a fundraising charity, though one exempted from registration at the Charity Commission. It attracted 5 million visitors in 1999/00, an increase of almost 50% over 10 years. Half the visitors are from overseas. In recent years the gallery has been extended and refurbished and the pictures rehung. It has become, in this editor's view, one of the glories of London.

The gallery is funded primarily by government grant, entry being free, but in 1999/00 the gallery's accounts also noted voluntary income in the form of 'sponsorship and donations' worth over £4 million. This figure may have included corporate sponsorship payments (which are not necessarily philanthropic) as well as charitable donations, but there is no further breakdown in the accounts. The annual report refers to a new legacy campaign, and £102,000 of legacy income was reported in 1999/00.

Fundraising costs of £445,000 represented a low 10p in the pound, or 10% of the value of cash donations. However, there were further gifts of works of art to a value of £15 million. This book does not normally classify 'gifts in kind' as part of a charity's voluntary income, but if they are included, as seems appropriate in this case, the cost of fundraising falls to a mere 2% of the relevant income.

In autumn 2001, as this entry was written, the gallery was reported to be at risk of losing its highly successful director, Neil MacGregor, to the British Museum.

The charity adds ...

The National Gallery's aim is to care for, strengthen and study its collection of old master paintings, so as to offer the fullest access to its pictures for the education and enjoyment of the widest possible public now and in the future. The collection is open, free of charge, to all.

The information assessed

As is usual for public bodies, there is an excellent, comprehensive annual report and accounts, as well as other literature and a fine website (which includes a copy of the full report and accounts, among more exciting offerings).

Contact

Trafalgar Square
London
WC2N 5DN
Tel 020 7747 2885
Website www.nationalgallery.org.uk
Chair Peter Scott
Neil MacGregor, Director

National Kidney Research Fund

Income	£3,050,000 (2000/01)
Donated income	£2,608,000
Fundraising costs	£1,422,000
Statutory income	£0
Top salary	£70,000–£75,000
Paid staff	
Full time	87
Part time	49
Volunteers	
Operational	40
Fundraising	96

Aims, activities

The charity seeks to improve the health and well-being of people living with kidney disease. It has three areas of work. They are (with their 2000/01 expenditures):

- Funding research (£2.6 million). The largest new commitment was £375,000 towards a project at Aberdeen University jointly funded with the Medical Research Council. Another 17 grants were also made, the largest an award of £98,000 to a joint project at Cambridge University and Hammersmith Hospital, London. There were also 12 fellowship or sponsorship awards.

- Raising awareness (£1.1 million). This involves 'informing and updating patients, families and carers, the general public and health professionals about kidney disease and the needs of those affected'. A key specific need in this area is to increase the rate of kidney donations for transplant. There is a severe shortage of kidney donors; the rate of such donations is just half that in Spain, the European leader in this field.

- Caring for patients (£203,000). A National Kidney Helpline has been established (**0845 300 1499**). During the year 83 patient support grants were offered to individuals or their families.

Volunteers

Volunteers are actively involved in the charity's fundraising. In addition, in order 'to develop a greater patient voice', a new Patient Advisory Group has been set up. It is intended that this will, 'in collaboration with the National Kidney Federation, be developed into regional groups of patients and carers, who will give us the benefit of their wisdom'.

Funding, administration

The charity is funded almost entirely by donations and legacies. The year 2000/01 was unfortunate in financial terms, despite the upbeat tone of the financial sections of the annual review and the annual report – where it was called 'another successful year'. There may have been good reasons for the relatively weak performance, but that is something different to success.

Voluntary income was down by almost a third, mainly due to an exceptionally low year for legacy income. Such income is volatile and outside the charity's control in the short term. More striking was a 40% increase in fundraising costs. This did not lead to anything like a proportionate increase in donations, which were up by a very much smaller 20%. Overall, the ratio of fundraising costs to voluntary income increased from 27p in the pound, or 27%, to a very high 55%. In the three years to 1999 the average had been a low 13%.

These high figures are at least in part because the charity is investing in order to double its income over the coming years, though the expected costs of doing so are not discussed. The annual review for the year notes the exceptional costs of relocating and re-equipping the telephone fundraising operation.

The fundraising effort appears to be led by door-to-door fundraising, which contributed more than two thirds of the total.

The information assessed

The annual report and accounts and the annual review have good (often very good) coverage of the activities of the charity, but, as described above, the upbeat tone of some of the text seemed inappropriate. The website is unusually good, both about the organisation and its activities and about kidney disease.

Contact

King's Chambers
39–41 Priestgate
Peterborough
PE1 1FG
Tel 01733 704650
Website www.nkrf.org.uk
Chair Professor David Kerr
Bertie Pinchera, Chief Executive

National Meningitis Trust

Income	£2,958,000 (2000/01)
Donated income	£2,852,000
Fundraising costs	£495,000
Statutory income	£0
Top salary	£40,000–£45,000
Paid staff	42

Aims, activities

The charity has three main aims:

- to give care and support to people affected by meningitis;
- to educate the public and professionals about the disease;
- to fund medical research into meningitis.

The disease affects more than 3,000 people in the UK every year. One in ten will die and many others will be left with permanent disabilities. Teenagers, the under-5s and people aged over 55 are most at risk.

The trust offers a range of services to those affected by the disease:

- a 24-hour helpline – **0845 6000 800**;
- financial grants, to the value of almost £100,000 in 2000/01;
- counselling, through a network of more than 30 professional counsellors;
- home visiting, by health professionals;
- more than 50 local support groups.

The charity also has a medical education programme for professionals with seminars, lectures, conferences, campaigns, CD-ROMs and internet-based learning packages. For the public there is a wide range of information materials.

Finally, the charity funds a range of medical research projects, to the value of £713,000 in 2000/01.

Volunteers

There are over 50 local groups which offer support to people with meningitis and run the smaller fundraising events.

Funding, administration

The charity is funded almost wholly by gifts and donations and by the proceeds of fundraising events, which are listed separately. Perhaps because it was only founded in 1986, legacies are not as prominent as is usual for charities concerned with serious medical conditions.

Nearly half of the value of donations and gifts in 2000/01 came in the unusual form of gifts in kind under the heading 'Corporate and trusts'. There is no indication of what these were. Fundraising costs were 17p in the pound, or 17%, of voluntary income.

The information assessed

The brief annual report came with a useful note attached on the activities of the charity, which might well have formed a main part of its text. However, the description of the management of the charity was exemplary. The excellent website seems much the best general source of information.

Contact

Fern House
Bath Road
Stroud
Gloucestershire
GL5 3TJ
Tel 01453 768000
Website www.meningitis-trust.org.uk
Chair Geoffrey Shaw
Philip Kirby, Chief Executive

National Osteoporosis Society

Income	£2,754,000 (1999/00)
Donated income	£2,652,000
Fundraising costs	£376,000
Statutory income	£28,000
Top salary	£90,000–£100,000
Paid staff	
Full time	34
Part time	17
Volunteers	500

Aims, activities

Osteoporosis affects 3 million people in the UK, mostly but by no means exclusively older people. It affects one in three women and one in twelve men during their lifetimes. The condition is largely preventable and treatable, but its incidence is still increasing.

As the leading charity in this field, the society's charitable work falls into the following four fields (with 1999/00 expenditures in brackets):

- services to members and public (£780,000);
- medical education (£561,000);
- research (£383,000);
- public education (£278,000).

The work of the charity in supporting people with the condition, and their families and carers, is carried out at the headquarters just outside Bath, and also by the 130 local groups around the UK. These are voluntary self-help organisations, with many of the volunteers having osteoporosis themselves, and they all offer support and information. Some local groups provide further specific services such as exercise classes or hydrotherapy sessions.

Local groups can be contacted via headquarters. The charity operates an important telephone helpline (**01761 472721**), staffed by five specialist nurses, which received almost 18,000 calls in 1999/00.

There is a medical education programme, which in 2001 led to new and greatly improved standards for the management of osteoporosis that doctors must follow as part of the NHS National Service Framework for Older People. The charity was particularly fast and energetic in its response to the establishment of Primary Care Groups for GPs in the NHS, and the new guidelines are in part the result of this.

The research programme, for which there is a voluntary advisory committee, funded 13 new studies in 1999/00. The society also organises the big annual Bath Conference on Osteoporosis, which attracted over 500 health professionals in April 2000.

Volunteers

Volunteers, organised in the local groups on the basis of mutual self-help, are the main resource of the charity; much of its resources go on their training and support.

Funding, administration

The society is overwhelmingly funded by donations and legacies from the public, and this income has been rising steadily (though there was a dip in 1999/00 in the always volatile legacy income). Fundraising costs of £376,000 were low, at just 14p for every pound donated, a ratio similar to those achieved over a number of years.

The information assessed

There is a good annual report and accounts and annual review, though the lack of clear guidance from the Charity Commission has led to the 'Annual Report' and the 'Trustees' Report' being different documents. These are backed by a first-class website and excellent supporting materials that include both professional and members' newsletters.

Contact

Camerton
Bath
BA2 0PJ
Tel 01761 471771
Website www.nos.org.uk
Chair Professor Graham Russell
Linda Edwards, Chief Executive

National Pyramid Trust

Support for children with educational and other difficulties

Income	£298,000 (2000/01)
Donated income	£182,000
Fundraising costs	£27,000
Statutory income	£74,000
Top salary	not disclosed
Paid staff	
Full time	5
Part time	7
Volunteers	
Operational	525

Aims, activities

The trust has developed a programme for the early identification, in primary schools, of children at risk of subsequent difficulties. Each child who needs help is given it, at the age of seven or eight, often in the form of after-school Pyramid Clubs, run by trained volunteers. Independent evaluation reported by the charity suggests that this intervention has a striking effect on resilience, peer relationships and school performance.

The trust does not organise the work itself, but establishes local self-financing schemes around the UK. By 2001 there were Pyramid schemes in 24 local education authority areas (up from 3 in 1997). They include Birmingham, Bristol and much of the south-west, four London boroughs, and Blackburn and Darwen in Lancashire. There is also a rapidly developing Pyramid Trust Cymru branch based in Cardiff.

Though the charity is financially modest, the extent and intensity of its volunteers' contribution justify its place in this book. It was originally used as a model when planning the entries for this book, but was not expected to be included in the actual volume as it was then too small. However, its rapid recent growth has changed the situation.

Volunteers

The work of the charity is based on the work of volunteers to an exceptional extent. The present chair is herself a former voluntary Pyramid Club leader.

Volunteers work in teams of three or four, each team running one after-school club for up to ten children. The aim is to give the children an opportunity (often their first) to develop their self-confidence and self-esteem; the results, as shown by formal evaluations, are striking. The system was endorsed in 2000 by both the chancellor of the exchequer, Gordon Brown, and the then secretary of state for education and employment, David Blunkett.

Most volunteers are students, often from related disciplines such as education or social work. They are carefully trained and supported, but also take on considerable responsibilities.

Funding, administration

The trust, as a development agency, is funded largely by grants from trusts, the Lottery's Community Fund and government programmes. Local schemes usually have their core costs met by the relevant education or other authority, but fundraise locally for the modest running costs of the individual club programmes.

Fundraising and publicity costs were £27,000 in 2000/01, representing a low 15p in the pound of donations received.

The charity adds ...

Schemes receive ongoing support from the Trust. The key documents are: a comprehensive handbook that contains everything from timetables to proformas and disks containing all materials needing reproduction; a club leader training manual; a Quality Assurance pack. Induction, training and regular support meetings are provided for co-ordinators.

The information assessed

The annual report and accounts and annual review are very good. There are also strong supporting materials and an excellent website.

Contact

84 Uxbridge Road
London
W13 8RA
Tel 020 8579 5108
Website www.nptrust.org.uk
Chair Suzan Baker
Allan Watson, Chief Executive

National Trust

for places of beauty or interest in England, Wales and Northern Ireland

Income	£199,252,000 (2000/01)
Donated income	£111,516,000
Fundraising costs	£14,032,000
Statutory income	£15,892,000
Top salary	£130,000–£140,000
Paid staff	4,124
Volunteers	38,000

Aims, activities

The social reformer Octavia Hill and her friends set up the trust at the end of the nineteenth century to act as a guardian for the nation in the acquisition and protection of threatened coastline, countryside and buildings.

The trust now cares for more than 200 buildings and gardens of outstanding interest and importance, over 248,000 hectares (612,000 acres) of beautiful countryside in England, Wales and Northern Ireland, plus almost 600 miles of coastline. Most of these properties are held in perpetuity, so that their future protection is secure. The vast majority are open to visitors. The trust has the unique characteristic that its inalienable possession of its properties is enshrined in law.

The long-term vision of the trust, set out in its 'Strategic Plan 2001–2004', is 'to inspire present and future generations with understanding and enjoyment of the historic and natural environment through exemplary and innovative work in conservation, education and presentation'.

The 2000/01 annual report describes the trust's specific aims as:

- showing leadership in tackling the problems facing the countryside and, where the trust can, in the towns;

- making education and lifelong learning integral to everything the trust does;

- humanising and personalising the way the trust interprets and explains the heritage to its visitors and the wider public.

The striking omission from this strategy is the continued acquisition of threatened property. Perhaps the trust feels that it already has all that it is able to manage to its impeccable and well known standards. In any event it is having the effect of leaving the way open for other charities, such as the *Woodland Trust*, to take on at least some of this role.

There is a separate entry for the *National Trust for Scotland*.

Volunteers

'The National Trust ... is dependent on the help of volunteers. Even our Chairman and members of our Council are volunteers, along with 38,000 others who assist us at a more local level. It would not be possible to open our houses without our volunteers ... Involving local supporters in the running of our properties also makes an important contribution to engaging local communities in the work of the National Trust.'

There are many roles that volunteers can play in the work of the trust and there is a special website section (www.nationaltrust.org.uk/volunteers), which sets out all the possibilities. There is also a volunteers' office (tel: 01285 651818).

An interesting research study of the value of volunteers to charities in 2001, conducted by the Institute for Volunteering Research, included information on this charity. It found that the average National Trust volunteer worked 60 hours a year, did work for the charity worth £339 and cost the charity £57 to recruit and organise. As there are 38,000 volunteers, the implication is that they contributed activity worth more than £10 million during the year.

Funding, administration

The accounts of the trust, though in conformity with legal requirements, are set out differently from those of other charities described in this book. For example, a distinction is drawn between one-off receipts and what the trust regards as its day-to-day income. Secondly, in common with other heritage and conservation charities, the trust benefits from a provision in the Charities Acts which allows members of conservation and heritage charities to receive substantial personal benefits in return for their subscriptions – in this case, reduced cost admissions to the trust's properties. The payments are nevertheless treated as charitable donations and can attract the appropriate tax reliefs.

For this reason the figures set out above may not be wholly comparable to those elsewhere in this book.

The charity's voluntary income of £112 million in 2000/01, up 5% from the previous year, was made up as follows:

- membership subscriptions etc. £63 million;

- legacies £39 million;

- other gifts and donations £10 million.

This was achieved at a fundraising and membership support and recruitment cost of just over

£14 million, a cost ratio of a low 13p in the pound, or 13%.

The other principal sources of income were:

- earnings of the properties £38 million;

- earnings from the £725 million in investments £26 million.

The main headings of expenditure were routine maintenance and running costs (£97 million) and capital projects (£51 million). Despite their absence from the annual report, acquisitions accounted for another £3.6 million, most of it spent on coastal and countryside areas.

In March 2001 the trust announced a major reorganisation. Among other things this is expected to involve the closure or merger of several of its regional offices and the relocation of its main offices from London to Bath.

The information assessed

The excellent annual report and accounts are backed by an extensive range of high-quality materials and a comprehensive website (though not as easy for potential visitors to use as that of the National Trust for Scotland).

Contact

36 Queen Anne's Gate
London
SW1H 9AS
Tel 01285 651818
Website www.nationaltrust.org.uk
Chair Charles Nunneley
Fiona Reynolds, Director General

National Trust for Scotland

for places of beauty or interest in Scotland

Income	£30,332,000 (2000/01)
Donated income	£11,268,000
Fundraising costs	£400,000
Statutory income	£12,500,000
Top salary	£60,000–£70,000
Paid staff	
Full time	507
Part time	840
Volunteers	2,000

Aims, activities

This charity, the equivalent in Scotland of the *National Trust* in England, owns or manages 126 properties for the public good. These include great houses such as Culzean and Newhailes, as well as large areas of mountain and forest – such as the huge, newly acquired Mar Lodge estate in the Cairngorms which covers no less than 31,000 of the charity's total landholdings of 76,000 hectares (about 185,000 acres).

There are over 2 million visitors a year to those properties where numbers can be counted. It is estimated that as many people again visit the countryside and open areas.

A major project in recent years has been the restoration of the south side of Charlotte Square in Edinburgh, which now houses the head office of the trust. Given the intention to show how such buildings can be conserved through making them suitable for modern office space, it seems an expensive location for a charity.

The charity's corporate plan for the years 1999–2004 concentrates on the development of support for the improved care of its existing properties, rather than on increasing their numbers. This is in the light of a decline in tourism which, as was noted in the 1998/99 annual report, 'has had a major effect on our income at properties and on our trading opportunities'. This was part of 'an adverse trend in our operating performance – that is the comparison of routine income against routine expenditure'.

One aspect of the plans to deal with this was an intention to increase the membership of the trust from its then 236,000 members to 275,000. There have been no more recent figures to see how far progress is being made towards this target.

Volunteers

There was little information in the materials seen by this editor about the role played by volunteers. The unencouraging website leads through an employment page to one noting the existence of both conservation volunteer groups and 'Thistle Camps' in the summer, with an e-mail address for information about them and the suggestion that volunteers should contact the charity's personnel manager. These Thistle Camps turned out to be a beautifully presented programme of residential working holidays, for anyone aged 16 or over, in some of the finest and remotest places in Europe, typically costing £45 for a week.

There was no obvious reference to volunteers working as staff or guides for visitors at the trust's properties in the way that forms such a prominent part in the work of the sister charity in England. Perhaps things are done differently here.

Funding, administration

The charity has recently changed its financial year. The figures in this entry are based on the unaudited accounts for the 12 months to February 2001, rather than the audited figures for the 16 months to that date.

The main sources of income were:

- grants (mostly for major repairs and improvements) £9.7 million;
- donations, subscriptions and legacies £11.3 million;
- investment income £4.2 million;
- admissions to properties £1.8 million;
- income from sales £0.9 million
- rents £0.8 million.

The grants, chiefly from statutory bodies, are nearly all tied to particular purposes. So is much of the investment income, as it comes from endowments in favour of the maintenance of particular properties.

Expenditure is divided between two main heads of expenditure: the routine care of the charity's properties (£12.4 million), and major repairs and improvements (£15.8 million).

The figures for voluntary income were:

- legacies £4.9 million (£6.9 million);
- membership £4.6 million (£3.9 million);
- appeals and donations £1.8 million (£1.6 million).

A characteristic of charities such as this is that membership brings with it significant financial benefits in the form of free access to the trust's properties, which can otherwise be visited only at substantial charge. To this extent, membership income is not the same as wholly philanthropic donations or subscriptions to other kinds of charity.

This voluntary income of £11.3 million was achieved at a cost of £400,000 million, a very low ratio of 4p in the pound. Even this was higher than in 1999 – but that had been an exceptionally favourable year, with a record-making pair of big legacies.

There are also substantial marketing costs incurred in encouraging paying visitors to the properties – but their admission charges are not so much donations as payments for pleasures about to be received.

The charity adds ...

Visitor numbers have been declining for many years. Foot and Mouth in 2001 hit Scotland hard and visitors in 2001 will be 10% down on 2000. In spite of this total membership has grown for the past three years to 245,000. With the changes to Gift Aid subscription income will be up 17% this year. Steps are in hand to balance the operating budget within three years and to retain legacy income for endowments, acquisitions and big capital projects.

The information assessed

In August 2001 the most recent annual report available was for the year to October 1999. Following a change in the charity's financial year, however, accounts (without a report) were available for the 16 months to February 2001. They provided adequate information.

The website was fast to use and has a good guide to the charity's properties.

Contact
Wemyss House
Charlotte Square
Edinburgh
EH2 4ET
Tel 0131 243 9300
Website www.nts.org.uk
Chair Professor Roger Wheater
Dr Robin Pellew, Director

NCH
(formerly NCH Action for Children)

Income	£91,125,000 (1999/00)
Donated income	£16,547,000
Fundraising costs	£6,871,000
Statutory income	£66,000,000
Top salary	£80,000–£90,000
Paid staff	
Full time	2,037
Part time	3,009

Aims, activities

NCH is the children's charity of the Methodist church. It is an important and wide-ranging social work agency.

This is one of a group of charities that act to a considerable extent as government sub-agents for social work with children, supplying their services mainly to statutory bodies under contracts or 'service agreements'. NCH is, it says, the largest provider of childcare in the UK and it is growing fast.

Most of the activity is described as running 'projects'. This term seems to be used, in most cases, simply to mean services for children or their families, often ongoing, without necessarily having any of the short-term character that the word 'project' might normally imply.

'NCH supports children, young people and families disadvantaged by poverty, disability, neglect and abuse. By working in partnership with local government, statutory providers and other agencies, we offer them a range of services to meet their needs, and work with them to ensure they have every opportunity they need to reach their unique potential.'

In 1999/00 the number of such projects grew from 370 to 430. The number of people helped also grew, though not so fast. The annual review describes the following range of activities. Where possible these have (in brackets) the relevant expenditure in 1999/00, but the figures cannot always be included as the accounts use different headings to those in the annual review:

● Children at risk
– residential homes (£10.4 million)
– adoption and fostering (£4.4 million)
– specialist education services (£5.7 million)
– therapeutic support for sexually abused children
– children's rights services
– independent visitors for children in care
– fostering projects.
● Families in need of support
– family centres (£17.4 million)
– community centres
– short breaks projects (probably £6.7 million)
– young carers' projects
● Vulnerable young people
– leaving care and homelessness projects
– youth justice projects (£3.2 million)

The six services whose expenditure is noted above account for £48 million out of the total £66 million of direct charitable expenditure, so the remaining seven services are likely to operate on a smaller scale.

An example of the work of the charity, taken from the annual review, is its Independent Visitor projects:

'NCH opened the first independent visitor service in London in 1998 and now runs four schemes in different boroughs. It is an area of rapid growth for the charity. We have won contracts to run the service in another six London boroughs and are negotiating in another eight. An independent visitor is an ordinary person who ... [volunteers] ... to spend some of their free time regularly with a child, befriending them and encouraging them in their interests. It is a statutory requirement ... for local authorities to appoint an independent visitor for any child they are looking after and who has infrequent contact with their parents ... The people who volunteer come from all walks of life and range from barristers to builders.'

The charity also spent £4.1 million in 1999/00 on its information services, but provided no details on this activity.

As well as the main contact details below, information can be obtained from one of the following:
– NCH Cymru; tel: 029 2022 2127
– NCH Scotland; tel: 0141 332 4041

Volunteers
The annual report for 1999/00 notes that 'Although the principal area of involvement of volunteers was in fundraising, volunteers are also involved alongside professional staff in the provision of operational social work.' The 'Support us' section of the

website refers only to fundraising, but a further link to 'Volunteering' has the following:

'A very important way in which people support our work is by giving some of their time to NCH through a range of voluntary activities such as:

- Volunteering in one of our 430 projects

- Organising house to house and street collections

- Helping to put on fundraising and awareness raising events

- Volunteering in one of our shops.

For more information about NCH's activities in your area, please contact our Supporter Helpline on 0845 762 6579.'

Funding, administration

Although contracts with statutory agencies, accounting for about £66 million in 1999/00, lie at the core of the charity's finances, the annual report and annual review have little to say about the contracts involved. In particular, there is an issue facing all such charities about how to respond in situations when the amount on offer is insufficient to run the project concerned to the standards the charity thinks necessary. It can turn such sums down, and end the project, or it can subsidise the contract to a greater or lesser extent from its donated income. It is not clear which position is taken by this charity.

In 1999/00 the £16.5 million of voluntary income was made up of approximately £11.9 million in donations and £4.7 million in legacies (plus £2.5 million worth of goods donated for sale in the charity's shops). Fundraising costs of £6.9 million represented a very high 42p per pound of voluntary income

(donated goods excluded). This, however, was a substantial reduction on the even higher 48p in the pound of the previous year. The income had increased by 27% and the costs by 11%, so perhaps the investment in the previous year was beginning to pay off. The average cost ratio for the three years to 1999 had been 45p in the pound.

The charity points out that its proportion of voluntary income, though less than 20% of the total, is essential to maintaining its independence and supports new developments and capital investment. Also, and perhaps alarmingly, 'statutory income could not be secured without it'.

The page of financial data in the annual review on 'Where the money comes from', uses an unsatisfactory euphemism, 'Social work income', to refer to the £66.5 million that came from government contracts. Every other source in the table is more specifically named, such as 'Individual supporters', or 'Legacies', or 'Investment income'. In the full accounts this statutory money is called 'Contract income', but still without identifying the source. There is of course nothing wrong with a charity being funded by government, but audited accounts might be expected to help readers identify the source of the funds concerned.

The charity adds ...

NCH improves the lives of the UK's most vulnerable children and young people by offering them diverse, innovative and responsive services and by campaigning for change. Our projects are varied and fall into three broad categories: those that help children at risk, those that help vulnerable young people, and those that help families in need of support.

The information assessed

The adequate annual report and accounts and annual review are difficult to read together, as different headings are used in each for the various activities. The website is a good source of information about the charity.

Contact

85 Highbury Park
London
N5 1UD
Tel 020 7704 7000
Website www.nch.org.uk
Chair Gordon Edington
Deryk Mead, Chief Executive

Norwood Ravenswood

Welfare in the Jewish community

Income	£22,784,000 (1999/00)
Donated income	£7,321,000
Fundraising costs	£1,152,000
Statutory income	£13,495,000
Top salary	£70,000–£80,000
Paid staff	905
Volunteers	600

Aims, activities

Norwood Ravenswood is a Jewish charity created by a merger in 1997 between Norwood Child Care, active in the field of childcare and family support for over 200 years, and the Ravenswood Foundation, a leading provider since 1953 of numerous residential and day services for children and adults with learning disabilities.

'It provides wide-ranging educational, community and residential services to socially disadvantaged children, vulnerable young adults and people of all ages with learning disabilities. We offer residential support, comprehensive day services and family centres, respite care, vocational training schemes to prepare disabled young adults for life in the community, education for special needs children and recreational services for learning disabled children and adults', and 'wherever practical, our services are available to anyone, irrespective of faith'.

In May 2001 the charity unveiled an ambitious plan 'aimed at meeting the enormous growth in demand for its services for the following three years'. Six new residential homes will be built around the London area at a cost of about £2 million each, while Ravenswood Village in Berkshire will be adapted to meet the changing needs. Some 20 of the village's residents will be rehoused in state-of-the-art facilities in Greater London, offering easier access to families and facilities. 'Norwood Ravenswood's most expensive initiative to date will see the Annie Lawson School for children with severe and profound disabilities relocate to Greater London in a £10 million move, which includes the development of residential homes. Following the success of its services in Hackney, Hendon and Redbridge, Norwood Ravenswood will also be launching multi-disciplinarily portable family centres from January 2002, offering its full range of facilities to those who would otherwise miss out.'

The charity wants its service users to have a greater say and involvement in how services are delivered. 'There will be a substantial increase in advocacy support and user consultative groups will be established for each area of provision.'

In the summer of 2001 the government announced that the charity, which already runs Norwood's Jewish Adoption Society, had been selected by the Department of Health to run the new Adoption Register for England and Wales (wholly statutorily funded).

Volunteers

'Volunteers are an essential part of our service.' Roles suggested include working with children and their families at the family centres, visiting people in the residential homes, working in one of the eight charity shops and helping in the administrative offices.

Ravenswood Village in Berkshire always needs volunteers for befriending residents, driving them to and from work and supporting them in the workplace.

Funding, administration

Fees and charges paid by statutory sources are the largest source of income, at £13.5 million in 1999/00. The £7.3 million of voluntary income, including only a modest £1 million from legacies, was up by a remarkable 28% from the previous year and was achieved at a fundraising cost of 16p for each pound given. This was a reduction on the average of 22p in the pound for the three years to 1999.

The information assessed

The good annual report and accounts are accompanied by an annual review (for 2000/01) whose complex design stretched the capacities of this editor. There is a clear and full website.

Contact

Broadway House
80–82 The Broadway
Stanmore
Middlesex
HA7 4HB
Tel 020 8954 4555
Website www.nwrw.org
Chair John Libson
Norma Brier, Chief Executive

NSPCC

England, Wales and Northern Ireland

Income	£88,998,000 (2000/01)
Donated income	£73,240,000
Fundraising costs	£12,588,000
Statutory income	£8,768,000
Top salary	£80,000–£90,000
Paid staff	1,865

Aims, activities

The NSPCC – the National Society for the Prevention of Cruelty to Children – says ' ... child abuse is still the reality for many children today. Yet we know that most child cruelty can be prevented – providing the will exists to do so.'

Since the 1960s the direct responsibility for children at risk of abuse or neglect has lain with local authorities, rather than with any charity. The role of the NSPCC has therefore changed. It still acts as a first line of advice and support for those worried about the possibility of cruelty in a situation known to them, often through its free Child Protection Helpline (**0808 800 5000**). This deals with about 45,000 calls a year, but where immediate action seems to be called for this will most commonly be carried out by the statutory services. The charity also has 180 Child Protection Teams and projects, which handled nearly 9,000 requests for help in 2000/01. The work of the teams varies, but it includes:

- investigations into allegations of abuse;
- assessment, counselling and therapy;
- support for professionals, schools and the police in their work on child abuse.

The NSPCC has not become a general social work sub-agency for the statutory welfare services. Less than 10% of its income is from statutory sources and much of its work is about prevention, rather than direct child protection work. The charity:

- acts as an independent voice campaigning on behalf of children;
- researches into child abuse trends and issues;
- advises and trains other organisations working with 'at risk' children;
- works with schools and other youth organisations to give children their own voice;
- publishes a range of books and other materials to educate parents, children and the public about abuse.

The charity's FULL STOP campaign, launched with much publicity in 1999, aims to bring about fundamental changes in attitudes and behaviour towards children. It seeks to lift the level of the NSPCC's work in five fields:

- Child protection. A total of 49 new services have been started, including an Offender Management Service to protect children visiting

prison inmates with convictions for sexual abuse.

- The child in the family. As most child abuse happens in the family home, parenting advice is a priority. For example, 600,000 copies of a Get Ready publication have been distributed to new or expectant mothers and fathers.
- The child in school. The NSPCC believes that the potential role of schools in forestalling or protecting against abuse has been neglected. Its school teams have developed a range of befriender schemes for isolated pupils. On another tack, the charity is researching school child protection procedures.
- The child in the community. A rethink of the way communities respond to the needs of children 'is long overdue'. For example, the charity is fighting to ensure safe play facilities for all children, especially in parks and playgrounds.
- The child in society. The charity aims to put and keep child cruelty 'on the agenda at the highest possible level'.

A recent development has been the government's Sure Start programme for tackling child poverty and social exclusion. The NSPCC is already in the lead in 5 of the initial local programmes and is a partner in 15 more.

Direct charitable expenditures in 2000/01 were classified as follows:

- child protection and preventative services and projects £36 million;
- campaigning and public education £16 million;
- child protection training and consultancy £2 million;

- child protection helpline £2 million;
- child protection research £2 million.

In November 2000 a damaging, and in this editor's view misguided, attack was launched on the NSPCC and on the FULL STOP campaign by *Community Care* magazine, a journal for social workers. The editorial article called for more to be spent by the NSPCC on children's social services and less on campaigning against child cruelty . The article said 'Surely when people give money to the NSPCC they imagine that most of it is spent directly on protecting children or helping them recover from abuse or neglect'. There seems no reason to expect a charity specifically for the prevention of cruelty to spend most of its money on helping recovery after cruelty has taken place – a different activity. And there seems little to suggest that the 'direct protection' of children is a more effective way of reducing cruelty than working to make it socially and legally unacceptable.

The whole article had an unfortunate air of special pleading by a professional group in defence of its own interests. However, it created an excuse for an outbreak of criticism in the media, despite the NSPCC's vigorous efforts to make its case in response. The FULL STOP campaign calls for a change in attitudes and behaviour across society; it is therefore relevant that a survey of MPs in 2001 found that the charity was the most effective campaigning organisation in the UK.

In autumn 2001 the charity announced that it was closing some projects and expanding others. The process involved certain redundancies as well as a (greater) number of new posts. This led to some staff protest as well as further press comment. It does

seem as if the charity, as it changes and develops, may be struggling to carry with it all of its considerable professional staff.

An equivalent organisation in Scotland is Children 1st (the Royal Scottish Society for Prevention of Cruelty to Children); tel: 0131 337 8539; website: www.children1st.org.uk

Volunteers

Though volunteers are active in the society's fundraising throughout the country, there has been tension in the past about the proper role of volunteers in the work of the charity. The issue is currently being addressed by developing a series of volunteering projects to offer services that support parents. 'The focus will be on working beside and making friends with parents to support the care of their children.' An example is the charity's New Links project in Coventry.

This work is no doubt building on the experience of similar work developed over many years on a national scale by the charity *Home-Start*.

Funding, administration

The FULL STOP campaign, launched in 1999, involved both a massive financial target – £250 million over five years – and what was widely thought an implausible and even counter-productive aim, that of 'ending child cruelty'. In the event an additional £8 million was spent on fundraising for the appeal, which raised £25 million in the same year. However, as the aim of the appeal is to generate ongoing commitments to support the charity, the payback on this investment will not be fully apparent for some years.

Though it has been reported as being 'behind target', since the launch of the appeal the charity's fundraising costs as a proportion of its voluntary income have actually fallen to 17p in the pound, or 17%, in 2000/01, against an average of 21% for the three years to 1999. Meanwhile the value of donations has risen remarkably, from £37 million in 1995/96 to £73 million in 2000/01.

The charity adds ...

The NSPCC had set itself a demanding and extraordinary task when it launched the FULL STOP Campaign in March 1999. The progress we have made for children is remarkable. We are making an impact at each stage in children's lives.

The information assessed

The excellent annual report and accounts are backed by extensive printed materials and a fine, fiery website. Unusually, and creditably, this shows the full annual reports and accounts for the last two years.

Contact

42 Curtain Road
London
EC2A 3NH
Tel 020 7825 2500
Website www.nspcc.org.uk
Chair Sir Christopher Kelly
Mary Marsh, Director

Oxfam

Income	£131,845,000 (2000/01)
Donated income	£63,607,000
Fundraising costs	£14,995,000
Statutory income	£62,731,000
Top salary	£60,000 – £70,000
Paid staff	4,181
Volunteers	23,000

Aims, activities

Oxfam is Britain's largest overseas aid charity. It developed from the Oxford Committee for Famine Relief, a body founded in 1942 mainly by people with a Christian motivation and led by a Quaker, Cecil Jackson-Cole (also the founder of two other major charities, *ActionAid* and *Help the Aged*).

The charity believes 'that in a world rich in resources, poverty isn't a fact of life but an injustice which must be overcome'. Its work, mainly but not only in developing countries, covers both long-term development and emergency relief in the third world, as well as campaigning on behalf of the poor at all levels from the local to the global.

'Much of Oxfam's development programme is carried out through grants to local organisations that support long term sustainable benefits for a community. Grants are also made to fund immediate emergency relief in times of crisis, catastrophe or natural disaster.' The total value of grants in 2000/01 was £15 million. They are numerous and not generally large; during the year the top 50 accounted for less than 10% of the total expenditure and all the rest were for less than £50,000. Apart from a transfer of £506,000 to Oxfam Canada for work in the Americas, only two grants were for more than £300,000: those made to Uganda Participatory Poverty Assessment Project (£744,000), and to *Care International* for work in South Africa (£465,000).

Oxfam's grants list is a remarkable and moving record not just of the charity's work, but of the resilience and determination of the people with whom it works, often living in the most daunting of circumstances. Many of the grants to partner organisations are very small. The list of 10 grants in Ghana in 1999/00 shows that half were for less than £5,000, such as the £2,737 for an inter-faction youth association formed in response to fighting in the north of the country. The largest grant in that country was an award of £66,000 towards a five-year programme to improve health in the five villages of the 25,000 strong 'Overseas' population. A larger grant in Central Africa was the £376,000 given to sustain the Mwangi camp in northern Zambia, home to 12,000 refugees fleeing from the war in the Democratic Republic of Congo (former Zaire).

'Programme development and support' (£60 million) covers the work of Oxfam's own staff, including that concerned with emergency relief. There are almost 1,600 locally employed Oxfam personnel; their tasks include selecting, supporting and monitoring the grant-aided partner organisations, and the development of new programmes.

Expenditure (and income) for emergency and disaster relief varies from year to year – in a typical year the charity responds to about 40 emergencies. In 2000/01 Kosovo was still a major preoccupation. As this entry was being written in the autumn of 2001, a new area was in the headlines. To quote from the Oxfam website: 'Right now, 2.5 million people in Afghanistan are in desperate need of food. There is very little time left to help these people. They have already endured severe drought and 20 years of war. If vital aid does not arrive by mid-November, many families could die this winter. Fear of US bombs and the breakdown of law and order have made truck drivers reluctant to deliver aid inside

Afghanistan. With food stocks virtually exhausted, Oxfam is continuing to press for guarantees over the safe passage of aid.' Practical information on the disaster (more drought than war at that time) and the practical measures needed to cope with it were excellently set out, in more detail than was available at the time from the press, on the Oxfam website.

The charity is at pains, however, to point out that it works in many emergency situations that rarely receive any media attention – indeed drought-afflicted Afghanistan would no doubt have been one of them but for the attack on the World Trade Centre.

Oxfam is also well known for its forceful campaigning on behalf of the world's poor, and for its educational programmes to raise awareness in the rich world of the situation of those who are poor; £7.7 million was spent on such information and campaigning in 2000/01. In the same year an Oxfam report, 'Cut the Cost', on the cost of patented drugs for people in poor countries, opened up a continued and effective international debate. Another example, available on the website in October 2001, but doubtless to be regularly updated thereafter, was a strong and cogent briefing paper on the then upcoming World Trade Organisation negotiations.

As part of its programme of advocacy, education and information, Oxfam is also a major publisher on poverty and development issues.

The charity's work covers the world, and the areas of greatest expenditure can vary quickly from year to year. This is illustrated in the following list, showing the percentage of expenditure in 2000/01 (with that for 1999/00 in brackets):

- Eastern Europe/Middle East 12% (31%);
- East and Central Africa 26% (20%);
- South and East Asia 24% (18%);
- Central/Southern America/ Caribbean 15% (15%);
- Southern Africa 17% (10%);
- West Africa 6% (6%).

The main headings by activity in 2000/01 were:

- health and nutrition £34 million (including £18 million worth of donated food aid);
- water supply and sanitation £18 million;
- institutional development and social organisation £13 million;
- agriculture £9 million;
- information and lobbying £6 million;
- education and legal aid £5 million.

The charity has recently been greatly reorganised, with most spending decisions now being taken at eight regional offices rather than at the main office in Oxford.

A striking publication in 2000 was the charity's first stakeholder survey. This is part of a continuing effort to make the charity accountable to its stakeholders (a key part of this effort is the annual Oxfam Assembly, bringing together all parties, partner organisations, staff, funders, managers and trustees). The new survey covered four countries overseas as well as supporters and staff in the UK. The responses showed that there is a level of active and constructive self-criticism that could be a model for other charities, not least in Oxfam's full public reporting.

Separate Oxfam organisations have grown up in other countries, including the USA, to form the group known as Oxfam International. Together they raised about a further £250 million during the year.

Volunteers

There are about 80 voluntary Oxfam groups around the country, and the 800 shops 'are almost wholly run by volunteers'. The website lists all current opportunities for volunteers, both in the shops and in other activities, ranging at the time of writing from a library assistant to a business analyst.

The annual review and report give full acknowledgement to the role of volunteers. The money to fund the charity's work is raised 'with the support of thousands of volunteers who help to run Oxfam shops and assist in campaigning, fundraising and other activities'.

Funding, administration

The charity's two main sources of income are donations and legacies from the public (£64 million in 2000/ 01) and grants from government organisations, both in the UK and beyond (£54 million) .

The well-known shops contributed a further £5 million, after the costs of running them had been deducted, but they have been facing declining profit margins in recent years. Book sales are becoming more prominent: 'We are now the largest second hand booksellers in the UK.'

Donations, on the other hand, have been rising; the charity takes particular satisfaction in the continuing recent growth in the numbers of regular donors. 'In seven years they have increased sevenfold. Oxfam can now rely on half a million regular givers, and the number is steadily growing.' Given a continuing good response to its disaster appeals, the charity regards the notion of 'donor fatigue' as a myth.

This 'committed giving' accounted for £39 million in income, with emergency appeals, events and other donations bringing a further £14 million and legacies £9 million.

Fundraising costs of £15 million were 24p for each pound of voluntary income, as in the previous year.

The information assessed

The annual report and accounts are generally exemplary, and there is an excellent annual review. The presentation of the charity's accounts is particularly clear, as well as detailed. Overall, there is a refreshing and rare self-critical tone. However, the classification of a government grant of £5.6 million as part of 'Donations, legacies and similar' income is unusual.

There is also a grants list (of exceptional quality, but unfortunately costing £10 and not on the website), saying exactly what partner organisations are doing with Oxfam's money – information of a kind that has often been found hard to obtain when writing this book.

The excellent website is, among other things, a fine source of information on a number of the world's problems. The charity is also a substantial publisher of books and reports on development issues.

Contact

274 Banbury Road
Oxford
OX2 7DZ
Tel 01865 311311
Website www.oxfam.org.uk
Chair Rosemary Thorp
Barbara Stocking, Director

Oxford University

As with *Cambridge University*, this university as a whole is a fundraising charity, and so are each of its colleges. They are exempt from registration at the Charity Commission but their accounts are publicly available to the determined in two convenient volumes. Those for the year 1999/00 have been examined and this established that the university was, collectively, one of the largest recipients of public donations and legacies in the country (though not as large as Cambridge in that year).

These accounts are, by law, presented according to unusual rules, and individual colleges have their own choice of headings even within these rules. The figures below are a total of all the donations, bequests, gifts, legacies, benefactions, charitable grants, appeal receipts and even 'accretions' that could be found. Where it was not obvious whether the money was in fact a charitable gift, we have tried to check whether or not it should be included.

Much of the fundraising is done through periodic appeals, so the list below may be greatly influenced by whether or not a particular college had an appeal running in the year in question. However, the total should represent a reasonable annual average.

Oxford University	*£23,909,000*
Colleges of the university:	
Pembroke College	£2,442,969
Mansfield College	£2,132,903
St Antony's College	£1,839,567
St Hilda's College	£1,594,041
Magdalen College	£1,478,562
Oriel College	£1,304,266
Keble College	£895,500
Worcester College	£808,062
Hertford College	£657,751
St Anne's College	£641,622
Wadham College	£560,074
University College	£526,076
St Edmund Hall	£512,619
Brasenose College	£442,401
St Catherine's College	£394,841
Somerville College	£382,562
Lady Margaret Hall	£371,998
Templeton College	£356,114
St Peter's College	£338,337
The Queen's College	£319,201
Linacre College	£304,698
Lincoln College	£304,021
Balliol College	£289,330
Trinity College	£168,292
Christ Church	£117,187
Jesus College	£103,483
New College	£90,000
Merton College	£75,341
Wolfson College	£59,645
St John's College	£51,426
Exeter College	£38,940
Corpus Christi College	£38,627
Colleges total	*£19,640,456*
Grand total	**£43,549,456**

The accounts of the individual colleges at Oxford and Cambridge universities are not just difficult to understand; they also omit, as present law permits, details of their capital funds. It is not therefore possible to get the usual overall view of the finances of these organisations. In this they are different from other charities exempt from registration with the Charity Commission (for example, the *National Gallery*) which generally have full and excellent annual reports and accounts. In November 2001 it was reported that this anomalous position was being examined by the review of charity law then being undertaken by the Cabinet Office.

Parkinson's Disease Society

Income	£9,929,000 (2000)
Donated income	£7,668,000
Fundraising costs	£932,000
Statutory income	£0
Top salary	£50,000–£60,000
Paid staff	
Full time	92
Part time	66
Volunteers	600

Aims, activities

Parkinson's disease is a progressive, neurological disorder that occurs when the chemical messenger responsible for movement stops being produced in the brain. Medication and other treatments mean that many people with Parkinson's can continue to lead a normal life, but others can have their quality of life affected dramatically. 'Everything that we learn in our life from movement and balance to our communication skills can be lost to Parkinson's.' The condition can affect anyone at any age.

The society is a membership organisation with 27,000 members and over 270 local branches.

Apart from the mutual support offered through the branches the charity has the following main activities:

- Parkinson's disease nurse specialists. These NHS posts are developed and initially funded by the charity, with the NHS taking over the funding after one or two years. There are at present 100 of these nurses, and the intention is to raise the number to 240.

- Welfare and employment rights. Some 2,000 enquiries were recorded in the year 2000. In particular, many people need help with filling in the complex Disabled Living Allowance and Attendance Allowance forms.

- Support and care. The charity's helpline (**0808 800 0303**) assists over 10,000 people a year. There are welfare visitors, a respite holiday programme and a network of field staff who support the branches.

- Research. The charity support research projects, both medical and welfare. During the year £1.3 million was put into this area, and nine new projects were funded.

- Campaigning, education and training. One major project has been a campaign in favour of legalising stem cell research, work which was given the government go-ahead early in 2001. The society runs an extensive information programme.

Volunteers

The many branches are normally wholly voluntary.

Funding, administration

Legacies form the core of the charity's income, representing £6.1 million out of the total £7.7 million of voluntary income in 2000. This income was achieved at a fundraising cost of £0.9 million, giving a cost ratio of a low 12p in the pound.

Nearly 20% of the income is generated through the branches.

The charity adds ...

The PDS helps people with Parkinson's and their carers by providing support and information, and funds research into Parkinson's. It works with health and social care professionals, advising on models of good practice such as residential care and nursing. It also has a dedicated medical research group and a group for young people with Parkinson's.

The information assessed

There is an excellent, straightforward, annual report and accounts and annual review, and a simple website.

Contact

215 Vauxhall Bridge Road
London
SW1V 1EJ
Tel 020 7931 8080
Website www.parkinsons.org.uk
Chair Lucianne Sawyer
Linda Kelly, Chief executive

PDSA

People's Dispensary for Sick Animals; England, Wales and Scotland

Income	£53,663,000 (2000)
Donated income	£32,777,000
Fundraising costs	£6,169,000
Statutory income	£0
Top salary	over £60,0000
Paid staff	
Full time	1,047
Part time	478
Volunteers	
Operational	200
Fundraising	3,300

Aims, activities

The purpose of the charity is to provide a free veterinary service for companion animals whose owners (clients) are unable to afford the cost of such treatment. To be eligible, pet owners must be receiving either Housing Benefit or Council Tax Benefit (about one in ten of the population). People who do not qualify for charitable help are referred on to private veterinary services. PDSA is therefore as much a welfare service for people who are living on low incomes, and are very often older people, as it is a charity for the benefit of animals.

The charity operates a nationwide network of 45 PetAid hospitals in cities and larger towns, employing 220 veterinary surgeons and 300 veterinary nurses as well as a range of other support and care staff. Two of these hospitals were new in 2000 – in Huyton, Liverpool and Thamesmead, London. Under its new and developing PetAid service, those living elsewhere can obtain PDSA-funded help from

250 PetAid private veterinary practices. Those wanting to know the location of their nearest PDSA service should ring the veterinary enquiries line on freephone **0800 731 2502**.

There is also a National Special Request Scheme which will fund treatment in cases where there is no nearby hospital or PetAid practitioner. More than 5,000 grants were made under this scheme in 2000, costing over £400,000.

PDSA delivered about 1.3 million free animal treatments in 2000, about 4,500 every day, and is one of Britain's largest charities.

After a highly successful year's fundraising in 2000, the charity is making big investments in upgrading its hospitals and in further developing its PetAid service.

The charity is an exemplar of one kind of philanthropy: raising money throughout society to be spent on improving the quality of life of its poorer members, and transferring funds and services into the least well off parts of the country – all in a way that has no overlap with the statutory welfare services.

This charity's description of its work appears to overlap to some extent with that of the *Blue Cross*; it would be interesting to know if the two charities cooperate to avoid duplication.

Volunteers

The main roles of volunteers involve fundraising and helping in one of the charity's 152 shops, although a limited number of other volunteering opportunities also exist. Potential volunteers are asked to commit to a certain number of hours each month; in return they receive full training and support, organised through the charity's National Volunteering Centre (freephone 0800 854194).

Funding, administration

The year 2000 was remarkably successful for the charity in financial terms. The two main sources of income were as follows (with 1999 figures in brackets):

- legacies £23 million (£18.5 million);
- donations £9.5 million (£9.2 million).

This voluntary income was achieved at a fundraising cost of £6.2 million (down from £6.6 million), giving a cost of 19p for each pound received (down from 24p). Both figures were substantially lower than the average fundraising cost of 33p in the pound for the three years to 1998. Perhaps earlier investments are now paying off.

Particularly successful for PDSA is direct marketing by mail and telephone, and especially in 'committed giving'; that is, persuading donors to contribute regularly and making use of the Gift Aid tax concessions that will increase the value of their donations to the charity.

The charity ended 2000 with almost £50 million in free reserves, some of which has already been committed to the expansion plans referred to above.

During the year the shops sold £12.6 million of donated goods, and it cost £11.6 million to do so, in a result the charity called disappointing.

The charity adds ...

PDSA is a professional and compassionate charity concerned solely with the provision of free veterinary services to the sick and injured pets of those who cannot afford private veterinary fees. Our aim quite simply is to treat and care for the largest number of pets belonging to needy owners that we can.

The information assessed

The excellent annual report and accounts and annual review are backed by good supporting literature and a clear website.

Contact

Whitechapel Way
Priorslee
Telford
TF2 9PQ
Tel 01952 290999
Website www.pdsa.org.uk
Chair Roy Trustram Eve
Marilyn Rydström, Director General

Phab

Integrating people with and without physical disabilities

Income	£622,000 (1999/00)
Donated income	£507,000
Fundraising costs	£120,000
Statutory income	£30,000
Top salary	less than £40,000
Paid staff	35

Aims, activities

Phab, which has 250 local clubs throughout the UK (whose accounts are not included in the financial figures above), works for the integration of people with and without physical disabilities. Despite its modest income, the charity's place in this book is earned by its resources in the form of the time donated by its extensive network of volunteers.

The charity:

● creates opportunities for people with and without physical disabilities to come together on equal terms;

● works to give disabled people greater independence and freedom;

● helps raise awareness and break down barriers of embarrassment and prejudice.

Phab club activities include holidays, day trips, quizzes, sports, discos, meals out, conferences and training. There are also Phab clubs for young and for older people.

Phab clubs 'are run by volunteers with the help of the disabled and able-bodied people who created them and make them thrive'.

The national charity also runs a Disability Awareness Programme. This trains qualified people to visit companies and organisations to offer 'in-house' training courses on how better to understand the disabled point of view. In January 2001 it appointed a full-time schools officer to try to break down the barriers of fear and ignorance surrounding disability at an early age.

Information about local clubs can be had from the address below, from the website, or by telephoning:

– Phab Scotland 0131 475 2313

– Phab Wales 029 2022 3677

– Phab Northern Ireland 028 9050 4800

Volunteers

The charity and its local clubs are overwhelmingly voluntary, with the national organisation providing the necessary central support.

Funding, administration

The clubs are responsible for their own finances, but as they are wholly voluntary their expenses are generally modest. The national organisation is funded mainly by individual donations, with long-time supporter

Sir Cliff Richard a leading donor through his Cliff Richard Charitable Trust (providing £50,000 in 1999/00). Fundraising costs in the year were 24p for each pound of voluntary income. The charity was also supported by the National Lottery Charities Board – now the Community Fund (£100,000) – and by the former Department for Education and Employment (£30,000).

The information assessed

The adequate annual report and accounts are backed by a good newsletter and supporting literature, and by a straightforward website.

Contact

Summit House
Wandle Road
Croydon
CR0 1DF
Tel 020 8667 9443
Website http://web.ukonline.co.uk/phab
Chair John Corless
Philip Lockwood, Chief Executive

PLAN International UK

Overseas development, children

Income	£18,404,000 (1999/00)
Donated income	£15,255,000
Fundraising costs	£2,507,000
Statutory income	£1,957,000
Top salary	£60,000–£70,000
Paid staff	31
Volunteers	130

Aims, activities

PLAN, one of the major child sponsorship charities, was set up in 1937 by two Britons to rescue orphans during the Spanish civil war. It has become 'one of the largest development and aid agencies in the world, seeking to enable families and communities in 43 of the poorest countries to make lasting improvements to the lives of their children. We achieve this by working closely with communities in developing countries to plan and run over 5,000 projects designed to raise the quality of their healthcare, education, environment, living conditions and livelihoods.'

PLAN International UK is not an operating charity so much as a fundraising body. It contributes 9% of the income of the international organisation generally known just as PLAN International but formally called FPPI Inc, on whose board it has three places.

As is usual and indeed desirable for a child sponsorship charity, none of the money donated goes directly to the child concerned, or to its family, but is pooled for the benefit of the whole of the community concerned. As the director of the charity pointed out in a magazine article in July 2001, 'modern sponsorship agencies do not use donations for cash handouts to individuals. They learned in the 1960s that this would breed a dangerous dependency on agencies and donors. Such handouts are also of little use without clean water to drink ... etc. Instead sponsorship funds go to community projects ... designed to benefit every child in a village.'

Such clear explanations are unusual in the promotional literature of child sponsorship agencies. Sometimes (with this charity as with other sponsorship agencies) the headlines and photos can give a different impression to that gained from the more detailed text that follows. In one of this charity's leaflets, for example, we have the line:

'Sponsor a Child and See the Difference'. In the same leaflet's list of questions and answers, one obvious question that is absent is: 'Does my money go directly to help the child I am sponsoring, or to its family?' However, the overall tone of this charity's materials, once you get past the headlines, is indeed concentrated heavily on the benefits to the community rather than to the individual sponsored child.

How is the money spent on the ground? There are two possible approaches for child sponsorship charities (which can be combined in different proportions). Some charities, such as *ActionAid*, work mainly by giving grants under contract to the best local organisations they can find. Others, like *World Vision*, have their own local staff permanently based in many or all of the communities concerned.

In this case the annual report for the whole PLAN movement shows that it falls largely into the second camp. There is a section on 'How PLAN works' , which states: 'Staff work directly with children, their families and communities to identify their needs and to develop programmes to meet those needs'. The accounts then show that there are over 5,000 field operations staff to do this – one to every 240 sponsored children.

The work is classified under the five main headings of health, education, livelihood, building relationships and habitat – the last referring to providing decent living conditions and safe and healthy homes and environments.

In all, PLAN worldwide has over 1.2 million sponsored children, with perhaps 9 million children living and benefiting in the communities

concerned. The sponsored children come from 43 different countries (with most of them living in the following areas):

- West Africa (212,000);
- Eastern and Southern Africa (282,000);
- Caribbean and Central America (207,000);
- Asia (356,000).

Volunteers
In the UK, this charity is mainly professionally staffed, although during 1999/00 around 130 volunteers also gave their time to its activities, and there is active participation from approximately 60,000 volunteers at the receiving end. 'During consultations before starting a sponsorship programme, the community learns how the system works and village volunteers take responsibility for the enrolment of children, helping with letters and documenting progress. Volunteers are not paid but they do receive training.'

Funding, administration
The annual review says in rather large letters that for every £10 given, 90p is spent on 'encouraging a new sponsor to join PLAN', but also in very small print that this figure applies to PLAN worldwide, not to the UK charity whose annual review this is, and for which the relevant – and still low – figure is £1.38 out of £10.

In this book, we have related fundraising costs not to the total income of the charity but to the voluntarily donated income that results from that fundraising. On this basis, the fundraising costs of PLAN in the UK in 1999/00 were 16%, or 16p in the pound, down from the 18% of the previous year and from the 20%

average of the three years to 1999. At that time voluntary income averaged £10.1 million, but it had risen very sharply to £15.3 million by 1999/00.

This money (£14.9 million, or 81% of the £18.4 million total after deducting the fundraising and administration costs) is transferred to FPPI Inc for the worldwide PLAN programmes, programme support costs and central service costs.

FPPI Inc, though a US-registered charity, has its main office in Woking, Surrey, and its work is well set out on the movement's website and in its annual review.

The child sponsorship model incurs costs at the receiving as well as at the giving end. The need to maintain contact between the donor and the child, and vice versa, is expensive in terms of staff time, translating letters, travel and other costs. Unusually, and very creditably, PLAN as a whole identifies these costs in its annual review. At $20 million they represent just under 10% of the organisation's charitable expenditures (and they include a big programme championing child rights internationally). The personal contact with an individual child will often be valued by the recipient as well as by the donor, and has benefits in its own right as well as being an effective marketing technique, so this money is not simply an additional cost caused by this form of funding.

The director of the charity has put this well: 'If sponsorship donations are used for community projects, why are sponsors linked to a child? Because this link – with a child, a family, a community – gives a human face to the complex issues of development'.

This charity is most unusual in the UK in that it supports nationally set standards for fundraising expenditure. PLAN 'believes that clear national standards for fundraising expenditure help the growth of a healthy voluntary sector'.

The charity adds ...

PLAN builds relationships between people in the United Kingdom, and people in the developing world. This enables some of the poorest communities in the world to achieve real results for their children: clean water, better health and an education. It also means that children have a real chance to realise their true potential. This is a largely voluntary effort, and next year we will be looking for even more volunteers in the UK. If you would like to help, contact us on 020 7485 6612.

The information assessed

The annual review and the less easily obtained directors' report and accounts give a good view of the charity, as does the international website. However, as all the money for charitable use is transferred to another organisation, FPPI Inc, it was necessary to obtain that charity's report and accounts to see the use that is made of the funds. These were slow to materialise, but first-class.

Contact

5–6 Underhill Street
London
NW1 7HS
Tel 020 7485 6612
Website www.plan-international.org
Chair Baroness Gardner
Marie Staunton, Chief Executive

Prince's Trust
Support for young people

Income	£36,834,000 (2000/01)
Donated income	£13,923,000
Fundraising costs	£4,332,000
Statutory income	£18,435,000
Top salary	£90,000–£100,000
Paid staff	
Full time	600
Part time	101
Volunteers	10,000

Aims, activities

The charity, headed by the Prince of Wales, works with young people who face barriers to success and provides them with the support and encouragement they need to fulfil their potential.

It has five main programmes, as follows (with 1999/00 expenditure in brackets):

- Business self-employment programme (£6.4 million). Each year this offers low-interest loans of up to £5,000 and ongoing support to more than 4,000 18–30 year-olds who are unemployed or under-employed, enabling them to set up their own businesses under the guidance of a volunteer business mentor. Over 47,000 young people have been helped in this way since 1983; the top 150 success stories now turn over almost £150 million a year and employ more than 1,700 people.

- Volunteers' personal development programme (£5.5 million). About 10,000 young people a year join a team of up to 15 others and undertake a personal development programme, including community benefit activities. The programmes are delivered by a range of other organisations on a franchise basis.

- Developing programmes (£4.3 million). These smaller programmes include the 'xl' programme in schools, supporting children who are truanting or at risk of exclusion; and awards for young people to attain work or development goals, carry out community projects, or take part in international programmes.

- Community action in Wales (£1.4 million). This focuses on environmental projects.

- The care leavers initiative (£0.3 million). The programme matches young people leaving care with volunteer mentors who support them through the transition to adult life.

Future plans include new initiatives working with young offenders and on improving basic skills.

Volunteers

Many of those who support and mentor young people on Prince's Trust programmes are volunteers. Full information on this is available, either directly or through the website.

There is also a range of regional and country voluntary committees which manage the activities in their areas.

There are about 10,000 volunteers in all.

Funding, administration

Nearly half the income of £37 million in 2000/01 was from statutory sources (£18 million, unusually classed in the accounts as 'voluntary income'). No doubt the charity has been able to benefit from a number of recent government schemes whose objects overlap with its own.

According to the classification used in this book, voluntary income – meaning donations, grants from non-statutory bodies, and legacies – totalled £13.9 million, plus a further £2.7 million in the form of 'gifts in kind', mainly the salaries and expenses of staff seconded to the charity by other employers.

Fundraising costs were £4.3 million, giving an apparent cost ratio of 31p in the pound, or 26p if gifts in kind are included. However, these costs include those incurred in negotiating government funding, so the actual ratio will have been substantially lower (the Charity Commission requirements call for the inclusion only of expenditures involved in obtaining 'voluntary contributions' and it is not usual to regard government payments in such a philanthropic light).

It is not every day that a charity drops £43 million off its balance sheet, but this happened to the Prince's Trust in March 2000, when the Queen's Silver Jubilee Trust, which had up previously shared its trustees and consolidated its annual accounts with this charity, appointed new independent trustees and struck out again on its own – 'again', because the two organisations had originally been independent charities. No information appears to have been given on the reasons for this move, one effect of which will be to reduce the income of the Prince's Trust in future by nearly £2 million a year.

If one goes, can another be far behind? King George's Jubilee Trust is in a similar position, as it is what the annual report calls a 'quasi-subsidiary', with common trustees and no separate accounts. The group structure already shows one other sign of breaking up, with the Prince's Trust withdrawing from the Common Investment Pool of the three charities. However, there is an entry in the 1999/00 accounts of the Prince's Trust saying that 'King George's Jubilee Trust has approved grants to the Prince's Trust Company totalling £7.5 million for 2000/01'. As the two charities have the same trustees and accounts, this sounded rather like an organisation giving money to itself.

The charity adds ...

The Prince's Trust is currently finalising a three year strategy, that will place the focus firmly on young people who would not otherwise have the opportunity to succeed. Its new 'Route 14–25 initiative', supported by the Royal Bank of Scotland, will position The Trust as a 'one stop shop' and signposting service for 14–25 year olds.

The information assessed

The generally good annual report and accounts and annual review are backed by a website and good material for young people.

Contact

18 Park Square East
London
NW1 4LH
Tel 020 7543 1234
Website www.princes-trust.org.uk
Chair Sir William Castell
Tom Shebbeare, Chief Executive

Queen Elizabeth's Foundation for Disabled People

Mainly south-east England

Income	£10,345,000 (1999/00)
Donated income	£2,284,000
Fundraising costs	£549,000
Statutory income	£7,511,000
Top salary	£70,000–£80,000
Paid staff	
Full time	249
Part time	119
Volunteers	
Operational	50
Fundraising	450

Aims, activities

The charity seeks to promote equal opportunities for disabled people by providing:

● training, guidance, advice and information;

● paid and unpaid employment;

● grants for holiday and respite care.

The charity operates seven units, three of them residential, mainly in south-east England.

They are (with 1999/00 expenditures):

● The Training College (£2.9 million) in Leatherhead, Surrey, which aims to gain its students a qualification and a job.

● The Development Centre (£1.4 million) in Leatherhead, Surrey, which works with severely disabled young people to give them the skills they require to enable them to move on to a lifestyle of their choice in the community.

● The Brain Injury Centre (£1.3 million) in Banstead, Surrey,

providing rehabilitation services for young adults.

● The Business Services Centre (£855,000) in Leatherhead, Surrey, which provides jobs in packaging, mail and print services.

● The Resource Centre (£438,000), in Dartford, Kent, which offers advice and support, as well as a wheelchair repair service and a complementary therapy centre.

● The Mobility Centre (£357,000) in Carshalton, Surrey, where clients can try a wide range of wheelchairs and scooters, and have driving tuition.

● The Disability Information Services, or DISS (£185,000), offering a range of services, nationally through the www.diss.org.uk website and through its database of service providers, with more specific local services in Surrey and West Sussex.

There is also a 'Care and Respite Fund' to help people who had previously stayed at the charity's Lulworth Court respite and holiday centre in Essex, which has now been closed (it cost £515,000 in 1999/00).

Volunteers

'Many volunteers are needed to help with the various fundraising events we undertake, and we rely on hundreds of volunteers to make our annual summer event – The Classic Car & Country Show – run smoothly.

'Also thanks to a team of around 500 dedicated volunteers the Foundation raises awareness of our work and funds through 14 shops throughout the Southeast.

'The mail order side of the Retail Trading Company is again handled entirely by volunteers.'

Funding, administration

Most of the charity's income comes from local and central government. Its voluntary donations of £2.3 million in 1999/00 were achieved with fundraising costs of £549,000, a ratio of 24p in the pound.

Most of the centres have their own specific sources of income, and the accounts usefully show each as a cost centre, giving the amount of further subsidy they require from the central funds of the charity. The largest centre in financial terms, the Training College, received statutory income of £2.8 million towards its costs of £2.9 million. The much smaller main DISS information service needed the charity to provide £114,000 of its total costs of £185,000.

The charity adds ...

Queen Elizabeth's Foundation is a national charity working to promote equality for disabled people, supporting over 100,000 people annually. It operates eight Centres in the South East, each with its own area of expertise: Brain Injury Rehabilitation, Mobility, Information, Business Services, Life Skills Development, Training for Work, Resource Centre, Care and Respite Fund.

The information assessed

The 'Annual Report', including the 'Chairman's and Directors' Report', is not the 'Report of the Executive Committee' that is attached to the accounts, which is presumably the one intended to meet the legal requirements for an annual reporting document. Collectively, the reports are good, though uneven. Some of the cost information for the different activities is as useful as it is unusual, but other parts presuppose existing familiarity with the work of the charity. There is a good website.

Contact
Leatherhead Court
Woodlands Road
Leatherhead
Surrey
KT22 0BN
Tel 01372 841100
Website www.qefd.org
Chair Lord Hamilton of Dalzell
Cynthia Robinson, Chief Executive

Raleigh International

Expeditions to carry out community and environmental projects

Income	£5,388,000 (2000/01)
Donated income	£2,581,000
Fundraising costs	£255,000
Statutory income	£1,800,000
Top salary	£50,000–£60,000
Paid staff	
Full time	98
Part time	1
Volunteers	
Operational	950
Fundraising	650

Aims, activities

The charity sends young people on expeditions to distant countries, where they work on environmental and community projects as well as taking part in adventure projects. About half the young people are from particular 'excluded' groups in the UK, or from the host communities themselves. The remaining half are volunteers who, to qualify for their expedition, first raise individually about £3,000 for the charity.

Benefits are gained both by the young people concerned, who have an opportunity to develop their personal capacities in ways that might not happen in less demanding circumstances, and by the host communities where the projects are carried out.

In the most recent year about 1,400 people went on the charity's expeditions, including nearly 400 volunteer staff – adults of all ages. There were 11 separate expeditions, each lasting 10 weeks, to Namibia, Mongolia, Chile, Ghana and Belize. Every participant, after an initial week settling in, spends three weeks each on their group's environmental and community projects, and a further three weeks on a demanding adventure expedition.

About 250 of the volunteers are winners of the charity's 'Millennium Awards' Lottery-funded programmes. This involves combining the 10-week expedition with activity in local community projects in the UK. The programmes, due to end in 2003, cover:

- Leeds
- Merseyside
- Cardiff
- Devon and Cornwall
- Northern Ireland
- Scotland

In each case, the award winners are selected to represent a cross-section of the young people who live in that area.

The Youth Development Programme, for socially excluded young people, attracts about 400 young people a year, of whom 200 choose to take part in one of the expeditions.

The charity also runs, as a commercial venture, a service for individual employers, organising similar activities for people in that company.

Volunteers

Almost all staff on the expeditions are volunteers; there are also a number of supporters' groups internationally and a further 40 in the UK. Many of the young people preparing to go on an expedition are also acting as volunteer fundraisers for the charity, bringing in almost half its income each year, as well as being among its beneficiaries.

Funding, administration

Of the 99 staff, 19 are involved in running the expeditions, 74 in their support and organisation in the UK, and 5 on fundraising and publicity. Though the regular participants raise money for the charity's activities, Raleigh International also relies on grant support for the more expensive programmes that enable young people from excluded or host communities to take part. The main sources of this support are the European Social Fund and various Lottery-funded programmes.

The accounts note that the law partnership of the chairman supplies legal services to the charity. There is a discussion of the issue of payments to trustees in the Introduction to this book (page 22).

Fundraising costs, at 10p in the pound of donated income, are low, no doubt helped by the fact that the income includes money raised by the young people for their own expeditions.

The information assessed

The excellent annual report and accounts and annual review are backed by an extensive and well-organised website.

Contact
Raleigh House
Parsons Green
London
SW6 4HZ
Tel 020 7371 8585
Website www.raleigh.org.uk
Chair Philip Tolhurst
James Robertson-Macleod, Chief Executive

Ramblers Association

Environmental campaigning

Income	£3,440,000 (1999/00)
Donated income	£2,305,000
Fundraising costs	£141,000
Statutory income	£27,000
Top salary	£50,000
Paid staff	
Full time	40
Part time	9

Aims, activities

Walking is the UK's most popular outdoor pastime and the Ramblers Association, with more than 420 local voluntary groups, fights to protect the paths used and to extend access to the countryside. An old organisation, founded between the wars, it recognises that its image had become, in many people's eyes, 'outdated and irrelevant to their lives and concerns'. It was seen, perhaps, as somewhat obsessive in its dedication to preserving rights from the past, and as having less interest in opportunities for the future.

This appears to have changed. The association is now growing rapidly, from 79,000 members in 1990 to 130,000 in 2000, and has a big new programme for the formation of young people's groups throughout the country – 15 such groups are already in existence, with 5 more being formed at the time of writing. The charity's extensive campaigning has also moved far beyond the simple protection of existing rights of way; it is now a major force for the conservation of the rural environment as a whole.

The great recent success has been the passing of the Countryside and Rights of Way Act 2000. As soon as the necessary maps have been agreed (it is hoped this will be complete within three years), there will a right of public access to most mountain, heath, down, common and permanently uncultivated land – a right for which the charity has been fighting for over 60 years. The Act also gives much stronger powers to local authorities to enable them to remove obstructions to rights of way; a duty which they often lacked the means to carry out effectively. The need for such work was emphasised in 2001 with the almost insulting eagerness of some county councils to close all footpaths on the outbreak of foot and mouth disease, and to keep them closed, even when expert official opinion regarded this as unnecessary.

The well-known Ramblers Association holiday programme is managed by an associated non-profit company, which contributed £400,000 to the charity in 1999/00.

Volunteers

Many of the 130,000 members join just to show support or to get the excellent magazine and other services, but thousands are actively involved in the work of the charity. Local areas have volunteer footpath workers and voluntary countryside officers, both backed by support and training from the association's permanent staff.

Funding, administration

The association is overwhelmingly funded by the subscriptions and donations of its members and supporters. Fundraising costs, of £141,000 in 1999/00, were a very low 6p for each pound donated. Reserves are kept at a low level (representing 2.5 months' expenditure), as are salaries, if the modest pay of the chief executive is a guide.

The charity adds ...

The last year has seen the RA play an important role in the foot and mouth crisis. The Ramblers led first on the promotion of responsible walking at the height of the epidemic and then campaigned hard for the footpaths to be re-opened in unaffected areas. The RA has sought to point out the links between an open and accessible countryside and a thriving rural economy.

The information assessed

The excellent annual report and accounts are complete, but simply produced in an old-fashioned style. The *Rambler* magazine and the fine website are crisp and well presented in an altogether more modern approach.

Contact

Camelford House
87 Albert Embankment
London
SE1 7TW
Tel 020 7339 8500
Website www.ramblers.org.uk
Chair Cath MacKay
Nick Barrett, Chief Executive

REACH
Voluntary work placements for professional people

Income	£431,000 (2000)
Top salary	less than £40,000
Paid staff	7
Volunteers	900

Aims, activities

'REACH ... helps voluntary organisations benefit from the business, managerial, technical and professional expertise of people who want to offer their career skills, working as volunteers. We do this by recruiting and supporting experienced men and women and placing them in part-time, unpaid roles with nearby voluntary organisations throughout the UK – for free.' Though financially modest, the extent and intensity of the contribution made by volunteers justify the charity's place in this book.

About 900 jobs are matched with volunteers each year, out of about 2,000 vacancies on the register. The average age of the volunteers is a surprisingly low 57 years. About two thirds of them are men, one third women. There are also some 30 REACH volunteers operating as area managers around the UK from home and local offices, providing local advice to potential volunteers and voluntary organisations.

All placements are part-time and unpaid, with out-of-pocket expenses reimbursed. The main career disciplines of the volunteers are given as follows:

- management 23%
- finance/accountancy 15%
- education/training 11%
- marketing/sales/PR 9%

- information technology 7%
- administration 5%
- consultancy 5%
- human resources 5%
- law/company secretary 5%
- technical/engineering 5%

The charity estimates that its placement service is injecting 'at least £16 million of new expertise each year into the voluntary sector', which would make it, in economic terms, one of the larger charities described in this book. The modest salaried central operation, whose figures appear above, is funded largely by grants from charitable trusts and from companies.

Further contact telephone numbers are:

- Scotland 0131 336 1080
- Wales 029 2040 8439
- Northern Ireland 028 9086 4286

The information assessed

The excellent annual review and annual report and accounts are supported by a straightforward website.

Contact

Bear Wharf
27 Bankside
London
SE1 9ET
Tel 020 7582 6543
Website www.volwork.org.uk
Sue Evans, Director

Redwings Horse Sanctuary

Income	£5,479,000 (2000/01)
Donated income	£4,788,000
Fundraising costs	£1,387,000
Statutory income	£0
Top salary	£50,000–£60,000
Paid staff	160
Volunteers	105

Aims, activities

This charity consists physically of five farms in Norfolk, one of them housing the offices of the charity, another having a visitor centre and yet another equipped with a veterinary centre.

The charity aims to relieve the suffering of horses, ponies and donkeys (equines), both by providing them with a caring home for the rest of their days and through the guidance and education of the public. A curious fact is that some of the work of the charity is nationwide, though the Charity Commission gives the area of benefit as just Norfolk.

The website describes the activities: 'One of the most difficult challenges we face at Redwings is balancing the enormous demand with the physical limits of the number of equines we can take into the sanctuary. The welfare team took over 2,600 requests in the last year to "take my horse", some six requests each day. Each request is likely to be valid in its own right and the majority of owners do not make that call to us lightly. At the moment we are only able to help a fraction of these callers.

'Our Humane Horse Handling team works with horses with behavioural problems and seek to assist their owners or future owners. They have worked with more than 110 horses outside the sanctuary over the last year, many of whom were originally considered to be beyond help and facing an uncertain future.

'Our voluntary Equine Welfare Advisors investigated 365 reports of neglect or cruelty last year. These were reported by supporters, together with members of the public and by the sanctuary working with other animal welfare organisations. Each investigation is different. For some the provision of advice and guidance is all that is needed – neglect is often not intentional but due to a lack of proper equine knowledge. Others are more serious, with the horse being immediately admitted to the sanctuary and where necessary the owner being prosecuted by the RSPCA.' The annual report notes that the charity is working hard to set up a full nationwide network of these advisers.

The autumn 2001 newsletter noted that the charity had over 1,000 horses, ponies, donkeys and mules in its charge.

Volunteers

The equine welfare advisers are voluntary and there are over 100 of them.

Funding, administration

The accounts for 2000/01 show that the charity is funded mainly by donations and legacies, in roughly equal proportions. The voluntary income of £4.8 million was achieved at a fundraising cost of £1.4 million, a ratio of 29p in the pound, or 29%, somewhat higher than the 26% average for the three years to 1999.

The annual report notes the fundraising expenditure in a simple but satisfactory way. Fundraising is carried out mainly by regular mailings of newsletters and leaflets; 'we do not yet rely on legacies in the same way as more established organisations and consequently we have a higher fundraising spend in the shorter term'. In fact the level of legacy income seems already impressive.

There was substantial income of £460,000 from the charity's lottery.

The accounts note that fees of £15,000 (and £45,000 in the previous year) were paid to estate agents of which one trustee was a director, while £6,000 (£16,000 in the previous year) was paid in fees to a legal firm of which another trustee was a partner. There is a discussion of the issue of payments to trustees in the Introduction to this book (page 22).

The charity adds ...

Redwings is the UK's largest horse sanctuary, directly caring for over a thousand horses, ponies and donkeys. In addition to helping as many horses as our resources allow, Redwings Horse Sanctuary spends time and effort in educating the public in an attempt to improve equine welfare throughout the country.

The information assessed

It took a long time and some effort to get a copy of the annual report and accounts or any other information. The website did not fill in all the gaps. Nevertheless the simple report, once received, was found to be good in most respects and excellent in some.

Contact

Administration Centre
Hapton
Norwich
NR15 1SP
Tel 01508 481000
Website www.redwings.co.uk
Chair Steven Clark
John Archibald, Chief Executive

Refugee and asylum seeker charities

A broad spectrum of voluntary and community organisations work with asylum seekers and refugees in the UK. These range from the Refugee Council (tel: 020 7820 3057; website: www.refugeecouncil.org.uk), an umbrella organisation with over 500 paid staff and volunteers, to the hundreds of community-based groups relying largely on volunteers. The easiest way of identifying one of these local groups is to ring the Refugee Council's information line (020 7820 3085).

The Refugee Council itself provides a range of services, including advice for asylum seekers and refugees, community development, support for unaccompanied refugee children, training and employment advice, and information on asylum and refugee issues.

Other refugee-assisting organisations may be more specialised:

- Refugee Action (tel: 020 735 5361) provides advice to asylum seekers and refugees, supports the development of refugee communities and produces information on asylum and refugee issues.

- The Refugee Arrivals Project (tel: 020 8759 5740) and Migrant Helpline (tel: 01304 203977) assist newly arrived asylum seekers at ports of entry.

- The *Medical Foundation for the Care of Victims of Torture* offers support for torture survivors.

- The Refugee Legal Centre (tel: 020 7780 3200), the Immigration Advisory Service (tel: 020 7967 1330), the Joint Council for the Welfare of Immigrants (tel: 020 7251 8708) and Asylum Aid (tel: 020 7377 5123) all specialise in advice on asylum claims.

- The Refugee Education and Training Advisory Service (tel: 020 7426 5801) provides employment and careers advice for refugees.

- The Refugee Housing Association (tel: 020 8829 8000) provides accommodation for asylum seekers and refugees, while a number of organisations such as the Detention Advisory Service (tel: 020 8802 3422) support asylum seekers held in detention centres and prisons.

Many mainstream voluntary organisations such as *Amnesty International* and *Oxfam* advocate and campaign on behalf of asylum seekers and refugees. Other mainstream organisations provide services or support. These include the *British Red Cross Society*, *Save the Children*, *Age Concern*, *Barnardo's*, Racial Equality Councils, *Citizens Advice Bureaux*, Law Centres, the *Children's Society* and *Voluntary Service Councils*, among others. On an international level, RefAid (tel: 020 7932 1019) works to raise awareness of refugee issues.

In Scotland and Wales, the main voluntary organisations working with refugees are the Scottish Refugee Council (tel: 0141 248 9799) and the Welsh Refugee Council (tel: 029 2066 6250), respectively. The Northern Ireland Council for Ethnic Minorities (tel: 028 9023 8645) is the chief refugee-assisting organisation in Northern Ireland.

Regional voluntary organisations have long had a key role in supporting refugees in several English regions. The North of England Refugee Service (tel: 0191 222 0406), Northern Refugee Centre (tel: 0114 275 3114) and Midlands Refugee Council (tel: 0121 242 2200) provide advice and other services to asylum seekers and refugees, as well as delivering community development and other support to local groups in their regions. The new policy of accommodating asylum seekers outside London and the south-east has seen the formation of many new local support groups and refugee organisations serving new communities in the dispersal areas.

A striking feature of voluntary and community sector support for refugees in the UK is the large number of refugee community organisations (RCOs). These vary in size, from small organisations relying on volunteers and limited resources to well-resourced organisations with paid staff. In London alone there are an estimated 400 RCOs, with an additional 100–200 outside London. Again, the best source of information is the Refugee Council's information line (tel: 020 7820 3085).

RCOs carry out a wide range of activities on behalf of their members, including the provision of social, cultural and leisure activities, material support, housing, advice and advocacy on a range of services and entitlements, information, educational activities, mother tongue classes for children, interpreting and translation, support for victims of racial harassment, and peer learning that helps members adapt to life in the UK. RCOs also provide links between the host and refugee communities, including information about community needs that can influence policy and service provision. In addition, RCOs offer valuable work and management experience for community members employed as staff and volunteers.

Local authorities are an important source of funding for RCOs, and voluntary and community organisations of all sizes raise funds through donations, appeals, fundraising events and revenue-generating activities. However, smaller refugee organisations are largely reliant on trusts and foundations. The Community Fund (formerly the National Lotteries Charity Board) is a substantial funder of voluntary sector support for refugees, and there is a range of statutory schemes.

Riding for the Disabled

This is a federation of more than 600 independent local Riding for the Disabled charities, most of them wholly voluntary, whose aim is to provide disabled people with the opportunity to ride and/or to carriage-drive in order to benefit their health and well-being.

The movement collectively is very large. 'Each week well over 25,000 children and adults enjoy the experience of riding or carriage driving – with opportunities to join in social activities and competitions, or to take a holiday – which combine to bring a new dimension to necessarily restricted lives, encourage independence, and do much to improve a wide range of medical conditions.'

This is made possible by more than 14,000 volunteers who enable Riding for the Disabled Association member groups to provide more than 500,000 rides and drives each year. Over 4,000 horses, ponies and donkeys are involved. The most frequent activities for new volunteers involve physically helping and supervising disabled riders and carrying out basic stable work.

All riders and drivers receive professional tuition tailored to their personal ambitions and capabilities. Instructors work closely with physiotherapists and other health professionals to encourage every individual to aim for attainable goals – some modest, others far more ambitious. 'While competition plays a healthy role in RDA activities, our focus is to ensure that all our riders and drivers derive maximum benefit from a positive and enjoyable form of therapy.'

The national association can put potential volunteers or donors in touch with their local member group; it can be contacted on 024 7669 6510; website: www.riding-for-disabled.org.uk

RNIB

Royal National Institute for the Blind

Income	£75,139,000 (2000/01)
Donated income	£43,561,000
Fundraising costs	£11,076,000
Statutory income	£29,311,000
Top salary	£80,000–£90,000
Paid staff	
Full time	1,638
Part time	1,333
Volunteers	338,000

Aims, activities

The charity looks to a 'world where people who are blind or partially sighted enjoy the same rights, responsibilities, opportunities and quality of life as people who are sighted'. It sets out to empower such people, to remove the barriers they face and to help to prevent blindness.

In practice, the prevention of blindness plays only a minor part in the work of the charity.

Over one and a half million people in the UK have serious sight problems – about 1 in 50 of the population.

The work in 2000/01 was categorised as follows (with expenditures in brackets):

● Supporting adults of working age (£20 million). 'Only a quarter of blind and partially sighted people have a job, yet more than half say they would like to work. Our role is to provide training and job support, and to break down the barriers which prevent disabled people from competing on equal terms.' Among other activities, the charity runs well-known Braille and tape services, an education and employment support service, two training colleges and a housing service.

- Support and care for older people (£15 million). 'About 90% of people with impaired sight are over 60, and many have lost their sight later in life.' The talking book service is particularly important for this age group, lending over 2.5 million books a year. There is a range of other products too, such as talking clocks and weighing scales. RNIB also runs three residential homes for those who cannot live independently, and gives grants and pension supplements to those who are in exceptional financial need. The value of these grants is not separately identified, but it makes up less than 4% of the total expenditure.

- Helping the public and professionals (£11 million). This heading covers all the charity's campaigning and public awareness activities. A good example was the fight in 1999 to retain the 'Articles for the Blind' postal concession on which many blind and partially sighted people are heavily dependent. There is also ongoing work to make public services as accessible as possible – for example for gas and electricity bills to be available in accessible forms. A major recent achievement has been the successful campaign for the reinstatement of free eye tests for those aged over 60.

- Working with children and families (£11 million). Most of this money was spent on the charity's five schools, which educate over 250 children each year, and also support their families. There are two primary and three secondary schools. One of the latter, New College in Worcester for able youngsters, has won the much prized Beacon School status. The charity has an education and employment service, and a website specifically for blind and partially sighted students (www.rnib.org.uk/student). RNIB also has a range of educational materials, games and toys for children, and runs holiday schemes across the UK.

- The charity's website development also comes under this heading. IT developments are acknowledged to be both an opportunity and a threat: on the one hand, they create new forms of communication which depend on sight, but on the other they provide new ways of presenting information. RNIB has become a leader in the expertise involved.

A key service is the RNIB Helpline (**0845 766 9999**), which takes nearly 40,000 calls a year.

Research into the prevention of blindness accounted for a modest £327,000 in 2000/01, though it may get higher priority in coming years.

In 2000 the director general noted that in the previous six years the charity had doubled the number of people it helped each year.

Volunteers

The website has comprehensive information for potential volunteers. Apart from the fundraising activities (many of them common to most charities in this book), there is a whole list of other things that need to be done. Examples of voluntary input in 1999/00 include 100,000 hours, the equivalent of over 70 full time staff, spent by volunteers in Brailling or recording information on tape. The talking book service also depends on over 2,000 volunteers to help members in their homes.

Funding, administration

In 2000/01 the charity's voluntary income totalled £44 million from donations (£16 million) and legacies (£28 million). This was achieved at a fundraising cost of £11 million, giving a cost ratio of 25p in the pound, or 25%, up from 22% the previous year and from the average of 23% for the three years to 1998. Almost 40% of the total income comes from fees, grants and charges for services, mostly from statutory sources.

Most of RNIB's services are funded by a mixture of voluntary and statutory support, all set out with exceptional clarity in the accounts. At one extreme, the vocational training college is 80% statutorily funded; at the other, the advisory services are funded overwhelmingly from voluntary donations.

The charity is governed by an executive council with 96 members, representing a wide range of charities and other organisations with an interest in visual impairment, and two thirds of whom are themselves blind or partially sighted. The figure of 96 is formidably large in management terms, especially as the charity does not have a single, smaller, executive committee but rather four main sub-committees, covering:

● community services;

● education and employment;

● policy and resources;

● technical consumer services.

It was timely, therefore, to see that one of the themes for the period 2000–06 includes the improvement of governance and structure.

The information assessed

The annual report and accounts are exemplary, showing that full coverage is possible without excessive length. Oddly, although extracts from the full audited accounts were available when this entry was being written, the charity could not supply the full accounts themselves. As a result, apart from the income and expenditure totals above, other figures in this entry are from the 1999/00 report and accounts.

There is in addition an annual review and much supporting material, as well as a comprehensive website.

Contact

105 Judd Street
London
WC1H 9NE
Tel 020 7388 1266
Website www.rnib.org.uk
Chair Colin Low
Professor Ian Bruce, Director General

RNID
Royal National Institute for Deaf People

Income	£40,531,000 (2000/01)
Donated income	£14,513,000
Fundraising costs	£3,810,000
Statutory income	c. £10,000,000
Top salary	£90,000–£100,000
Paid staff	1,374
Volunteers	200

Aims, activities

The charity believes that 'in the last four years RNID has been reborn as a dynamic organisation making a real impact on people's lives through its services, research and campaigns'. Part of this has been a structural change from an 'umbrella' body whose membership comprised other organisations in its field, to one with a mainly individual membership.

The principal services, with their 2000/01 expenditures, were as follows:

- Typetalk £11.8 million. This is a 'national telephone relay service' for deaf people, enabling them to communicate with hearing people over a telephone/textphone combination. Over 26,000 people use the service regularly. The translation from one service to another is funded by BT, though users pay for the actual calls.

- Care services £8.7 million. These include the 20 or so residential and community projects. There is also increasing outreach and day care provision 'to enable some residents to move to independent accommodation, learn new skills or take part in social activities'.

- Campaigns and information services £4.4 million. The information services include an Information Line, sometimes called the helpline (**0808 808 0123**; textphone **0808 808 9000**), which gets about 73,000 calls a year; a Tinnitus Helpline (**0808 808 6666**; textphone **0808 808 0007**), with about 10,000 enquiries; and a staff of information officers at the headquarters and in the regional offices.

'Through campaigns and parliamentary lobbying, RNID are constantly working to raise the level of awareness of deaf issues.' This activity receives great prominence in the charity's reports. One of many examples of success that it quotes has been the fight to get more subtitling on digital television, when that is introduced.

- Communication services and training £3.3 million. 'Our Communication Services Units provide communication services to more than 10,000 people each year.' Communication services include sign language interpreters, palantypists, lipspeakers and Speed Text operators.

- RNID Sound Advantage £2.4 million. This is a mail order service offering communication, alerting, telephone and listening devices for deaf and hard of hearing users.

- Training and consultancy £1.7 million. This covers the provision of training in deaf awareness and on the Disability Discrimination Act (DDA) for employers, and sign language for interpreters.

- Policy and research £1.6 million. This provides fellowships for research development in areas affecting deaf and hard of hearing people, such as tinnitus.

- Employment services £1.3 million. There are 12 Employment, Learning and Skills Centres which work with deaf and hard of hearing people to secure employment and training places.

The charity emphasises its programme of targets for future developments, and its successes in meeting previous ones, rather than just in recording what the activities of the charity have been.

The 'Impact Report' for 2000/01 gives a large number of quantified achievements – for example, 20 more sign language interpreters were trained, 40 more people with additional disabilities were being supported in their own homes, 6 research fellowships were awarded –

and many of these are related to the previously stated aims for the year.

Admirable in intention, the lack of enough context makes it difficult to form a view in practice about whether such targets represented ambitious moves forward or were the regular development of ongoing activities. However, the effort to try to report systematically on what has been achieved as well as on how the money has been spent is unusual and welcome.

Volunteers

Volunteers are said to be involved in different aspects of the charity, including the residential homes, befriending, awareness raising and fundraising. This activity is probably organised locally, as there was no information for or about volunteer input, other than for fundraising, in the charity's materials or on its website.

Funding, administration

There is no description in the annual report or the annual review of how the charity is organised and managed, though there is a reference to an apparently recently launched membership scheme for individuals. There are also organisational members, but there is no system of branches of affiliated local groups. Most of the trustees are elected, others are coopted.

The annual report notes that RNID employed 94 people who are deaf or hard of hearing, and that this represented 22% of all employees other than those, such as telephone operators, for whom hearing ability is fundamental to doing the job.

There are 54 RNID locations throughout the UK, including offices in the devolved countries and regional offices in different parts of England. The main telephone contact details are:

- RNID Scotland 0141 554 0053; textphone 0141 550 5754
- RNID Cymru 029 2033 3034; textphone 020 2033 3036
- RNID Northern Ireland 028 9023 9619; textphone 028 9031 2033

At the end of 2001 the charity was in the process of setting up independent advisory committees in the three devolved countries.

Many of the services described above are wholly or partly funded by fees, which come from either individuals, local health authorities or other service providers. This fee income totalled £11 million in 2000/01. The Typetalk service is nearly 90% funded by BT (which is paid normally for the resulting calls). The Sound Advantage hearing aid business is nearly self-financing. An estimate of the total of statutory funding, though this could not be confirmed by the charity, is about £10 million, or 25% of the total.

The remaining voluntary income came from donations, legacies and grants (though the latter may have been from government rather than from charitable trusts and companies). This totalled £14.5 million, well up from the £12.2 million of the previous year. It was achieved at a fundraising cost of £3.8 million, giving a ratio of 26p in the pound, or 26%. This was a slight reduction from the 29% of the previous year, but up from the average of 22% for the three years to 1999.

The charity adds ...

RNID has a wealth of experience of fundraising from a range of sources. It continues to work successfully with large UK blue chip companies, major trusts, European bodies, key statutory and voluntary sector agencies, and the Community Fund. The organisation also has an innovative, ongoing fundraising programme targeting individual and major gift sources.

The information assessed
The annual report consists of a few pages attached to the financial statements and is largely concerned with explaining financial changes. The section on policies for employing deaf and hard of hearing staff is the most informative. The 'Impact Report' for 2000/01, which stands in for the former annual review, is hard to relate to the accounts, but is otherwise an unusual and interesting attempt to report on what was achieved rather than just on what was spent. The website, though good in other ways, has limited information about the charity itself.

Contact
19–23 Featherstone Street
London
EC1Y 8SL
Tel 0808 808 0123; textphone 0808 808 9000
Website www.rnid.org.uk
Chair David Livermore
James Strachan, Chief Executive

RNLI
Royal National Lifeboat Institution

Income	£99,700,000 (2000)
Donated income	£80,200,000
Fundraising costs	£13,700,000
Statutory income	£0
Top salary	£80,000–£90,000
Paid staff	
Full time	882
Part time	63
Volunteers	
Operational	4,500
Fundraising	55,500

Aims, activities
The RNLI's purpose is to save lives at sea. It has set itself, and has probably achieved, the task of being the world's best lifeboat service. It has done this wholly from voluntary donations and legacies, and its lifeboats have mostly volunteer crews. For many people, it is an exemplar of what a voluntary organisation should be.

The charity runs over 300 active lifeboats in the UK and Ireland at 224 stations, and has no fewer than 111 boats in its 'relief fleet'. The RNLI launches boats on active service more than 6,000 times a year, rescues over 1,000 lives and brings ashore about 4,000 people in danger from the sea. It does not make a charge for its services, either to those rescued or to the owners of the ships or boats concerned.

The RNLI has been enjoying remarkable financial growth in recent years, based largely on its huge income from legacies – over £50 million a year. As a result there is a massive investment programme in new boats and shore stations, and even in a £22 million residential training college at the headquarters in Poole, Dorset. At the same time, by the end of 2000 the charity had built up an enormous unrestricted reserve of £200 million, equivalent to almost two and a half years of the cost of the service, and had another £150 million in reserves already committed in advance to future expenditure.

Plans for the years up to 2005 will see this reserve mountain reduce, if present levels of income are maintained, but the charity still seeks to maintain a reserve of two to five years' cover for its expenditure. This seems far too high; other major charities seem to be comfortable with, say, six months' to a year's cover. Despite earlier downturns in revenues, the RNLI's income seems to be at least as soundly based as that of any other charity of similar size, and the institution should be able to sustain an excellent service from current income in any likely future. The charity is under an obligation to put its wealth to use, rather than to continue to accumulate it, and more of this retained wealth should now be put to work.

Recent investments, together with the increasing part in sea rescue played by helicopters (not operated by the RNLI), may mean that the service is near the limit of what can be reasonably provided for the UK, though some relatively modest new activities are being introduced, such as an enhanced Sea Safety public education programme, new Beach Rescue schemes, and an expansion into services on inland waters such as Lough Enniskillen and the tidal Thames. For the main service, the charity says that over the last 10 years 'calls on the lifeboat service have increased by 50%', but its figures show that the number of launches decreased from 4,971 in 1991 to 3,918 in 2000.

The most interesting possibility, only hinted at in the annual report for 2000, is to direct more resources towards areas and countries where people still drown without effective help being available. A small precedent was established with the sending of four boats and crews to help with flood rescue in Mozambique in March 2000. A rapid response unit has been set up to answer future requests of this kind.

Expansion internationally, probably more in the way of training and support rather than the direct provision of lifeboats, would be an appropriate way forward – for the RNLI to seek, in this new century, to save lives at sea wherever this needs to be done, rather than just in UK and Irish waters.

In December 2001, after this entry had been drafted, an organisation called Ethical Audit took matters into its own hands. It circulated a letter (duly reported in the national press) to all the fundraising committees of the charity, asking them to reduce their fundraising activities by at least 50%. The letter noted that over the previous eight years the institution had raised an average £25 million more annually than it had spent, but that fundraising expenditure had nevertheless doubled in the same period. 'Those who respond to your appeals ... believe that all this money is actually needed. Clearly it is not!'

The figures were indeed compelling, but the recommendation that fundraising should be reduced seems weak when many lives are still being lost at sea, and while the public is willing to contribute to reducing this toll.

Volunteers

There are about 4,500 voluntary lifeboat crew (including 250 women) and each station is run by a voluntary management committee with its key honorary secretary, who authorises each launch of the lifeboat. There is also a huge network of 1,500 local fundraising branches. The charity notes its determination to maintain the voluntary ethos for which it is so well known.

The website has a good section for potential volunteers, though it might be helpful to highlight a more accessible means of contact than the filling in of an online form.

Funding, administration

The accounts for 2000 are less specific about the sources of the charity's income than might be expected, with no breakdown of the main headings beyond the following:

- income from fundraising £28.2 million;
- legacies £52 million;
- investment income £10 million (net);
- merchandising and lotteries £2.2 million (net).

It would be interesting, for example, to know how much was raised, and at what cost, by the local branches and by the central fundraising unit respectively.

Fundraising costs, of 17p in the pound, had risen slightly from the previous year, the ratio having increased because of a small drop in legacy income. This figure is still just below the average for large fundraising charities, but is an increase on the institution's own average of 15p in the pound for the three years to 1998.

Expenditure was as follows:

- lifeboat maintenance (presumably including building and replacement) £40.9 million;
- crew and station costs £23.7 million;
- fundraising and publicity £13.7 million;
- management and administration £3.1 million;
- crew training £2.2 million;
- dependants' pensions £1.5 million;
- Sea Safety programme £1.3 million.

The RNLI covers both the UK and Ireland, having sailed impressively through the division of almost all other activities when the two countries separated, and it receives a grant from the Irish government towards part of the cost of the service in Ireland. This could not be identified in the annual accounts (and so is not recorded in the data above), but to some slight degree this must qualify the charity's claim that it is 'relying totally on voluntary contributions'.

The information assessed

The annual report and accounts and annual review are generally excellent, though, given the charity's size, more detail of income and expenditures would be welcome. There is an award-winning website, good supporting literature and an excellent magazine, *The Lifeboat*.

Contact

West Quay Road
Poole
Dorset
BH15 1HZ
Tel 01202 663000
Website www.rnli.org.uk
Chair Peter Nicholson
Andrew Freemantle, Director

Royal Academy

Income	£33,922,000 (1999/00)
Donated income	£15,600,000
Fundraising costs	£2,082,000
Statutory income	£0
Top salary	£90,000–£100,000

Aims, activities

The Royal Academy of Arts is the well-known gallery and art school charity in Piccadilly, London. It is privately funded and the academicians are elected by their peers. Much of the income comes from its famous exhibitions. It is supported by two

further charities, The Royal Academy
Trust and The Friends of the Royal
Academy, and the figures above are
our best estimate for the group as a
whole.

Perhaps surprisingly for such an
august institution, the academy
appears to have only the most modest
reserves. It has no general
endowment, its building is on lease
from the government, its enormously
valuable works of art are generally
inalienable and its funds in special
restricted trusts total less than
£3 million. Its net current assets in
August 1999 were £1.4 million, very
small in relation to expenditures of
more than £15 million in the year.

The structure of the charity allows for
three of the trustees and council
members who hold named offices to be
paid for doing so. In 1999/00 these
payments were substantially higher in
two cases than they had been for the
previous years (figures in brackets):

- President, Professor Phillip King
£46,366 (£33,000, £15,000);

- Keeper, Professor Brendan Neiland
£36,000 (£32,083, £21,000).

As is proper, council members are
reimbursed for their expenses, but
some of the amounts in this case were
higher than is usually seen in the
accounts of charities, two of them
being for more than £8,000 in the
year. No doubt there were good
reasons for this (such as repeated
foreign travel) arising from the nature
of the charity's business. It would be
helpful if such reasons were reported.

The information assessed
There is a good narrative annual report
covering the work of the academy, though it
presupposes some familiarity with the
complexities of the institution. However, it

was difficult to get a full view of the
finances of the group from the interrelated
accounts of the three charities involved.

Contact
Burlington House
Piccadilly
London
W1J 0BD
Tel 020 7300 8000
Website www.royalacademy.org.uk
David Gordon, Secretary

Royal Air Force Benevolent Fund

Income	£17,683,000 (2000)
Donated income	£10,124,000
Fundraising costs	£932,000
Statutory income	£0
Top salary	£80,000–£90,000
Paid staff	340
Volunteers	4,847

Aims, activities
The work of this charity is well
described on its website. 'The Royal
Air Force Benevolent Fund exists to
provide assistance to those of the
extended Royal Air Force Family who
need support as a consequence of
sickness, disability, accident,
infirmity, poverty or other adversity.
This extended family embraces all
ranks, male and female, who are
serving or have served in the Royal
Air Force or its associated Air Forces
and their dependants.' Help is given
'regardless of rank, job or length of
service', and eligibility lasts for life.

Founded in 1919, the fund's direct
charitable expenditure is now
£19 million a year and reaches over
30,000 beneficiaries. In addition to
general welfare assistance, the charity

provides housing, education and care services, including both its own and jointly owned nursing, residential and short-term care homes.

Welfare work carried out by the fund is extensive, but in general terms can be subdivided into four areas (with their expenditures in 2000):

- welfare grants to individuals £8.7 million;
- residential homes £4.2 million;
- grants to other institutions £3.1 million;
- educational grants to individuals £0.3 million.

A further £4.2 million was lent for house purchases, money which will revert to the charity in due course.

'One-off help is normally by grant, except where the help is property-related, when a loan is considered more appropriate. Help might be the provision of wheelchairs or specialist furniture. For pensioners in need, a small regular addition to income may be provided.

'For those requiring urgent assistance, help can be almost instantaneous. Independent committees, staffed by volunteers, sit weekly to consider upward of 120 applications for fund assistance at each meeting. Sympathetic and careful consideration is given to each case and committee sittings sometimes last for many hours.

'The RAFBF is determined to reach out to as many of the RAF Family in need or distress as it can – either directly or through other charities. There is no ceiling put on the amount we are willing to spend on welfare – even at a time when our income may be decreasing.

'As those who served during the Second World War and shortly afterwards either in the RAF or its associated forces – including National Service in the RAF – reach old age, they are more likely to need their Fund's help. Add to this an increasing need from those currently leaving the Service, many on medical discharge, and it becomes clear that welfare spending will continue to rise year on year.'

The fund's grants to other charities serving ex-air force personnel and their dependants totalled £3 million in 2000. The largest was a £1 million grant to Haig Homes for a new home in Morden, Surrey.

Volunteers

The work of volunteers in deciding on applications for assistance is described above. Otherwise most volunteer activity is in the fundraising field; the possibilities are well described on the website.

Funding, administration

The RAF Benevolent Fund is not a membership organisation. It relies on voluntary income. Most importantly, over 80% of serving personnel contribute one half day's pay annually; the majority do so under the Gift Aid scheme. Additional money comes from legacies and investment revenue.

The RAF assists the charity by donating money raised at air shows, open days and other fundraising events.

In the expensive field of residential care, this charity works closely with the *Royal Air Force Association*.

The voluntary income of £10 million in 2000 was achieved at a fundraising cost of £0.9 million, giving a low cost ratio of 9p in the pound.

Charitable expenditure in 2000 was very sharply up on the previous year, rising from £14 to £19 million, although income was little changed. This moved the charity from a surplus on the year of £1.3 million (before taking investment charges into account) to a deficit of £2.5 million. The increased spending may have been partly in response to the remarkable investment gains of £22 million in the previous year (likely to have gone into sharp reverse in 2001) and to the charity's high level of reserves.

At the end of 2000 the charity still had unrestricted free reserves of no less than £132 million, equal to about seven years' worth of charitable expenditure. The trustees believe this to be an appropriate level, but it is probably the highest for any charity described in this book.

The information assessed

The good annual report and accounts and annual review are backed by a particularly accessible and well laid out website.

Contact

67 Portland Place
London
W1N 4AR
Tel 020 7580 8343 (ext. 231)
Website www.raf-benfund.org.uk
Chair Sir Richard George
Air Chief Marshal Sir David Cousins, Controller

Royal Air Forces Association

Income	£10,165,000 (2000)
Donated income	£5,349,000
Fundraising costs	£1,371,000
Statutory income	£1,338,000
Top salary	less than £50,000
Paid staff	
Full time	177
Part time	128
Volunteers	
Operational	2,000
Fundraising	6,000

Aims, activities

This organisation provides friendship and welfare support for its 100,000 members and for other serving and ex-serving men and women, and their dependants.

The main activity of the charity, at least in financial terms, is the running of residential, respite and nursing homes and sheltered housing schemes. These have several hundred residents at any one time and the programme accounts for well over half of RAFA's charitable expenditure. There is also a welfare service operated through a network of 600 honorary welfare officers, based in the 600 branches of the charity nationwide. These are also an avenue to the financial support of people in need provided by the sister charity, the *RAF Benevolent Fund*.

Volunteers

There are 600 voluntary welfare officers, through whom much of the welfare work of the charity is carried on.

Funding, administration

Donations, legacies and membership subscriptions account for 50% of the income of the charity, with most of the rest coming in the form of fees from statutory bodies for the residents in the charity's accommodation.

Much of the capital expenditure on the homes comes from the RAF Benevolent Fund.

Voluntary income at £5.3 million in 2000 was up from the £4.9 million of the previous year, largely because of the success of the annual Wings appeal in the 60th anniversary year of the Battle of Britain. However, fundraising costs had risen faster still, up by no less than 63%, leading to a cost of 26p per pound donated compared with the 17p average of the previous four years.

The increase is noted in the honorary treasurer's report as being necessary to maintain and if possible increase the charity's profile. For once this charity does not blame the rising costs on the perennial 'increasing competition', but instead notes that more innovative ideas are needed if the charity is to obtain its share of 'this burgeoning market'.

The association is finding it a struggle to maintain its membership, perhaps unsurprisingly given the reduction in the size of the RAF and an ageing Second World War generation.

The charity adds ...
During the next ten years our welfare services will be vitally important to the second world war generation, as they reach their 80s and beyond. To help us meet this increasing demand we have opened our fourth welfare care home in Wales. If you are interested in finding out more call or write to us ...

The information assessed
The good and very detailed annual report and accounts would benefit from a general

introduction to the charity for those unfamiliar with its work. There is a range of newsletters and leaflets, and a workmanlike website.

Contact
43 Grove Park Road
London
W4 3RX
Tel 020 8994 8504
Website www.rafa.org.uk
Chair Air Vice-Marshal N S Howlett
Ian McNeil, Secretary General

Royal British Legion
Ex-service personnel and their dependants

Income	£51,911,000 (1999/00)
Donated income	£29,240,000
Fundraising costs	£5,243,000
Statutory income	£354,000
Top salary	£80,000–£90,000
Paid staff	779
Volunteers	135,000

Aims, activities
The Royal British Legion seeks to be Britain's leading ex-service charity, with a mission of safeguarding the welfare, interests and memory of those who have served in the armed forces, as well as their dependants.

There are three main aspects to the charity's work. First it is a membership organisation for self-help and mutual support, with 500,000 members, over 4,500 branches – including nearly 1,500 women's branches – and about 850 British Legion clubs, which are independent but licensed by the legion and attached to their local branch. This side of the legion's activity is funded mainly by affiliation fees.

Secondly, the legion is a big welfare organisation, with its work supported by fundraising (especially its well-known annual Poppy Appeal) and by fees paid by statutory agencies for its residential and nursing care homes.

Thirdly, the legion is accepted as the custodian of Britain's remembrance of those who served in its armed forces, many of them at the cost of their lives. The charity organises the annual Remembrance Sunday events across the country.

Charitable expenditures in 2000 were as follows:

- residential and nursing homes £9.3 million;
- welfare services £7 million;
- welfare grants to individuals £6.9 million;
- membership and branch support £6.5 million;
- grants to other ex-service charities £1.6 million;
- training and resettlement £1.9 million.

Ex-service people and their dependants still make up 25% of the population, but in the absence of another major war this proportion will drop by nearly half during the next ten years. However, as they age, those who remain will need greater levels of support. Actual demand is expected to peak in 2010, fall back to present levels by 2021 and probably diminish sharply after that.

At the same time the public will be becoming ever more distant from the events in which these veterans were involved. Many ex-service charities, some of them described elsewhere in this book, are already finding it hard

to sustain their level of donations without incurring awkwardly high fundraising costs. The legion has embarked on a comprehensive 'Ten-year Strategic Framework' to address this situation.

One of the charity's plans is highly ambitious: 'The legion is currently 23rd in the Charities Aid Foundation league of the top fundraising charities. We aim to be in the top 10 by 2010.' Given the stability of that 'league' over the last ten years, this would be a remarkable achievement.

In a different field, the charity is already having some difficulty in maintaining itself as a membership organisation. Membership fell by 3% in 1999/00 and, with it, the income of the General Fund which pays for branch and membership support. In addition, 'branches and counties are having difficulty in finding [voluntary] officers to manage their activities'.

The charity is therefore considering some important changes to its membership structure, including separate classes of membership for those active in the charity as a whole and those who join solely for social reasons; the extension of membership to all those interested in its activities, whether ex-service people or not; the replacement of the present affiliation fee system for one of voluntary donations; and the introduction of a central membership system.

Ex-service welfare charities form an untidy part of the voluntary sector, with many overlapping organisations. The legion is already cooperating so closely with *SSAFA Forces Help*, a charity with an overlapping remit, that 'in many parts of the country case workers for the two organisations are interchangeable'. Even closer amalgamation will hopefully follow, as in August 2000 the charity signed an agreement with SSAFA saying (in the latter's words) that they 'would work more closely together to achieve amalgamation in due course'. Already the charities are using a common application form for those seeking financial assistance. A year later, though, there was as yet no news on further steps towards a merger. In addition, the charity intends to welcome smaller ex-service organisations into the legion family 'as their membership numbers fall and they become non-viable'.

Finally, two snippets of news. First, in the year 2000 legion members joined lovers of the Book of Common Prayer in rejecting an overdose of 'plain English'. A redraft of the charity's royal charter, intended to facilitate some of the developments mentioned above, was rejected by the National Council, who felt that the rewrite had removed too much of the 'regal and legal language' of the original.

Secondly, in October 2001 the legion announced that it is to market its 'own label' beer and whisky: Poppy Pride ale and Royal British Legion scotch whisky are to go on sale in Safeway stores, with the Legion hoping thereby to raise £20.1 million for its funds.

Volunteers

The Royal British Legion is one of the largest voluntary and mutual self-help organisations in the country. All branches are run on a wholly voluntary basis.

Funding, administration

The charity's income has been rising fast, from £32 million in 1995 to £52 million in 2000, mainly through the revived success of the Poppy Day Appeal and because of an increased level of donations.

This income was achieved in 1999/00 at a fundraising cost of £5.2 million, or 18p for each pound donated. The legion itself absorbs the £3.4 million cost of the poppies and wreaths produced for Remembrance Day. These are made in the charity's own factory by disabled ex-service people and the expenditure, at least in part, can be seen as part of the charity's benevolent work rather than as a fundraising cost. If this amount is included as a cost of fundraising, the ratio of cost to income would rise to 29p in the donated pound.

The process of consolidating the branches' assets and revenues into the accounts of the charity as a whole, required under the 1993 Charities Act unless each branch becomes a separate and independent charity, is incomplete. Each branch pays an affiliation fee to the general funds of £7.50 for every member, but members also pay a variable branch membership fee, and it does not seem that this income yet appears in the consolidated accounts of the charity. To this extent, the legion's income is understated; nor does the balance sheet reflect all the capital assets held at branch level – mainly, no doubt, the many well-known British Legion buildings. The accounts do not reflect this situation clearly.

Ten years ago the charity was heavily criticised by the Charity Commission for having weak administrative structures and practices, so it is unusually important that its reports and accounts should be of the utmost clarity.

The accounts show an average of £4,884 of costs, principally for travel, for each member of the charity's council (all of them volunteers), a rise of 13% from the previous year. It might be sensible to spell out the constituent parts of the £127,000 total.

The information assessed

The annual report and accounts and annual review are good, except that the layout of the accounts is not fully to the usual Charity Commission specifications. There is an excellent ten-year strategic plan. There is also a modest website, with a useful 'message' area that, among other things, enables veterans to renew old contacts.

Contact

48 Pall Mall
London
SW1Y 5JY
Tel 020 7973 7200
Website www.britishlegion.org.uk
Chair J G Champ
Ian Townsend, Secretary General

Royal Hospital for Neuro-disability

Income	19,370,000 (1999/00)
Donated income	£3,337,000
Fundraising costs	£461,000
Statutory income	£11,442,000
Top salary	£80,000–£90,000
Paid staff	
Full time	339
Part time	115
Volunteers	160

Aims, activities

This a charitable hospital and home in London serving up to 240 adults with acquired brain damage and other neurological disorders. The hospital treats patients on the basis of need, regardless of their financial circumstances; most of the fees are paid by the NHS. While at the leading edge of clinical treatment, it also provides a long- or short-term home for around 180 people.

The hospital is an important research centre too, with this work again being funded by the NHS. One of its key initiatives is its SMART programme: 'It is vital to assess properly whether or not someone has potential to recover from the Vegetative State (VS). SMART is an assessment programme, which has been developed by Occupational Therapy staff at the Royal Hospital for Neuro-disability over a ten-year period. The result is that a patient's potential for recovery and interaction with their environment is now greatly enhanced.'

Volunteers

Volunteers help with the charity's fundraising events, and also in the hospital. 'Our volunteers provide us with vital support. They help us with social and recreational activities, working directly with patients. This is done either through organised group activities or by developing one-to-one friendships. Volunteers help in many other ways – driving ambulances, assisting with fundraising, escorting on outings and helping in the snack bar.'

Funding, administration

The regular costs of the hospital are met by statutory or other fees. The voluntary income, of £3.3 million in 1999/00, is used for capital improvements, put towards part of the research costs and used to provide additional services for patients over and above the minimum allowed for in the statutory support. This voluntary income was achieved at a fundraising cost of £461,000, representing a low 14p in the pound. This was a big reduction on the 20p in the pound of the previous year, chiefly because of exceptionally high income from legacies. The average for the three years to 1999 was 16p in the pound.

The charity adds ...

We believe that all disabled people should have the opportunity to enjoy an optimal quality of life. Through specialist services, research and social and recreational activities we enable people with brain damage resulting from trauma and degenerative disease to enjoy greater independence.

The information assessed

The excellent annual report and accounts and annual review were beautifully produced and a pleasure to read. The website is straightforward and attractive.

Contact

West Hill
Putney
London
SW15 3SW
Tel 020 8780 4500
Website www.neuro-disability.org.uk
Chair Sir Michael Bett
Peter Franklyn, Chief Executive

Royal London Society for the Blind

Income	£9,275,000 (1999/00)
Donated income	£2,664,000
Fundraising costs	£897,000
Statutory income	£4,902,000
Top salary	£70,000–£80,000
Paid staff	342
Volunteers	100

Aims, activities

Founded as the London Society for the Blind in 1838, this is probably the oldest established charity described in this book. It needs to be distinguished from the former London Association for the Blind (now *Action for Blind People*). The purpose of the charity is to enable people with visual impairments to lead independent lives through the provision of high-quality education, training and employment services.

This charity has four activities:

- Dorton House in Kent is a nursery, school and further education college for blind or visually impaired pupils.

- RLSB Family Services, also based at Dorton, provides practical help with the education and care of visually impaired children. There are close links with Great Ormond Street and Moorfields Eye hospitals in London.

- Dorton Training services and Workbridge, based on a site in north-west London, help adults with whatever is needed to get them into employment. The latter service is run jointly with Action for Blind People.

- RLSB Industrial Services provides employment as well as training in the charity's engineering factory, at the same London site.

The education and training activities probably account for well over half the RLSB's charitable expenditure.

Volunteers

References to voluntary input, other than the donation of money, include a note of the welcome fact that all the trustees take part in the work of at least one of the charity's various committees as well as in that of the main trustee body. There is also a reference to the existence of LOOK, an organisation for parents.

Funding, administration

Most of the charity's income, £6 million in 1999/00, came from the fees paid by statutory bodies for the children and adults in the society's school and other schemes, and from the earnings of the engineering factory.

There was £2.7 million in voluntary income, £1.1 million of it in the form of legacies. A total of £897,000 was spent on fundraising, giving a high cost ratio of 34%, or 34p in the pound. Though slightly up on the previous year, this represented a reduction from the average of 37% for the three years before that. The annual report simply notes that 'fundraising costs inevitably rise with increased competition from similar charities'.

The charity adds ...

The RLSB is dedicated to advancing the status of individuals who are visually impaired by promoting equality of opportunity and inclusive practice in education, training and employment.

The information assessed

The adequate annual report and accounts and annual review are marred by the assumption in the former of prior knowledge of the charity's work. There are good supporting leaflets and newsletters, and an equally informative website.

Contact

Dorton House
Wilderness Avenue
Seal, Sevenoaks
Kent
TN15 0ED
Tel 01732 592500
Website www.rlsb.org.uk
Chair Howard Hughes
Brian Cooney, Chief Executive

Royal Opera House Covent Garden

Income	£133,896,000 (1999/00)
Donated income	£22,457,000
Statutory income	£21,259,000
Top salary	£330,000–£340,000
Paid staff	612

Aims, activities

The figures above are not comparable with those of most other charities in this book. First, the income includes a massive £73 million of commercial income from the property development associated with the rebuilding of the opera house (achieved on time and on budget), as well as the charity's regular Arts Council grant. Secondly, the voluntary income includes £10 million from the separate Royal Opera House Trust rebuilding appeal, and £7 million in other donations towards the development.

However, the remaining £6 million, in donations for productions, touring, sponsored performances and other activities and projects, is itself enough to earn the charity its place in this book. Much of this came from charitable trusts and companies, but there were also a substantial number of individual donors.

Fundraising costs are not shown as such in the accounts, being borne by subsidiary charities.

The figure for the 'top salary', more than double any other in this book, is taken from the accounts. It is for an artistic rather than an executive post. No doubt opera lovers will be able to identify the likely beneficiary of this great sum. The highest paid executive salary is said by the charity to be in the £150,000–£160,000 range, still the highest recorded in this book.

In the summer of 2001 it was announced that the Royal Opera House Trust and the Friends of Covent Garden were to be merged into one charity bearing the name the Royal Opera House Foundation. This will make easier the reporting of the public support for the organisation.

The information assessed
The poor annual report, which is exceedingly brief, does not review the activities of the charity, as is expected by the Charity Commission (better is promised for future years). There is an excellent new website, after a slow but musical load of the initial images.

Contact
Covent Garden
London
WC2E 9DD
Tel 020 7212 9267/9268
Website www.royalopera.org
Chair Sir Colin Southgate
Tony Hall, Executive Director

Royal Star and Garter Home
For disabled sailors, soldiers and airforce personnel

Income	£11,287,000 (2000)
Donated income	£5,700,000
Fundraising costs	£1,125,000
Statutory income	£3,755,000
Top salary	£50,000–£60,000
Paid staff	360
Volunteers	300

Aims, activities
This 'home' is an actual building, the mighty Star and Garter nursing and residential home that dominates much of the skyline above the river Thames in Richmond, Middlesex. About 170 former servicemen and women live there, and a full range of nursing and other services is available to them.

The basic income in the form of residential fees from local authorities and others is supplemented by voluntary donations. These have risen to a level that enables the charity both to fund extensive improvements to the facilities to meet new standards and needs, and to consider extensions of its work. First, an EMI centre is being built (for older people with mental impairments). Secondly, the charity is developing a grants system for needy ex-service personnel. This last is surprising, as there are already many charities operating in this field and two of the largest, *SSAFA Forces Help* and the *Royal British Legion*, are considering amalgamation.

To be eligible for admission, rank, age and length of service are immaterial and no distinction is made between those injured on active service and those disabled by accident or illness in civilian life. Admission may be one of three types:

- permanent;
- rehabilitation (e.g. after a hip replacement or stroke);
- respite care.

'The home provides an exceptionally high standard of care and a wide range of facilities.' Charges (at the time of writing this entry) are £464 per week for nursing care and £382 per week for residential care. 'Depending upon the applicant's financial circumstances, we advise that their Local Authority Social Services Department be contacted for advice on assistance with paying the fees.'

Volunteers

Of the charity's 300 or so volunteers, more than 130 work in the home at Richmond. Most of the rest are involved in fundraising, often helped by the charity's network of paid regional coordinators. The charity's annual review is exceptional in the attention it pays to the input of its volunteers.

Funding, administration

About half the costs of the home are met by voluntary contributions, £5.7 million in 2000, nearly two thirds of it from legacies. The total was well up from the £5 million of the previous year, largely because that had been a relatively poor year for legacies, always a volatile source of income in the short term. The fundraising costs of £1.1 million gave a cost ratio of 20%, or 20p in the pound, one that has been little changed for a number of years.

The information assessed

The annual report and accounts and annual review are good. There is also a colourful fundraising magazine. Though not identifiable from any of these publications, an internet search engine revealed an excellent website, which is much the best source of information on the charity.

Contact

Richmond
Surrey
TW10 6RR
Tel 020 8940 3314
Website www.starandgarter.org
Chair Vice-Admiral Sir David Dobson
Ian Lashbrooke, Chief Executive

RSPB
Royal Society for the Protection of Birds

Income	£51,514,000 (2000/01)
Donated income	£44,074,000
Fundraising costs	£6,668,000
Statutory income	£5,343,000
Top salary	£80,000–£90,000
Paid staff	
Full time	916
Part time	273
Volunteers	8,500

Aims, activities

The mission of the RSPB is to strive to conserve, maintain and where practicable enhance:

- the populations and natural ranges of wild birds;
- the extent and quality of important habitat;
- the value of the wider countryside and the marine environment for birds and other wildlife.

This is one of the largest membership charities in Britain, and indeed in the world. It is a major force for the conservation of the environment, on which the future for any species of bird must largely rest, at all levels from the local to the global.

Expenditures are classified as follows in the accounts.

Species and habitat protection, including research
Expenditure was £18 million. The charity's UK-wide Land for Life campaign contributed to a major success of 2000, the passage of the Countryside and Rights of Way Act. Besides affording greater public access to the countryside (the aspect that got most of the publicity), the Act also brought in much stronger protection for many protected sites around the country. However, the charity still regards the present farming system under the Common Agricultural Policy as unsustainable and damaging in conservation terms.

International work under this heading accounted for £2.8 million of the expenditure. There was a big campaign to keep EU bird protection laws in place, against opposition mainly from rural shooting interests in France. A total of 521,000 UK signatures were collected for the largest conservation petition ever presented to Brussels and the proposed French laws were not enacted.

The RSPB also makes several hundred grants each year to mainly overseas organisations for activities that directly support the charity's work. These totalled £2.2 million in 2000/01, with almost half the total going in one grant to BirdLife International, a global partnership in which the RSPB plays a major part. Other beneficiaries were widely spread, including Sociedad Española de Ornitologia (£84,000), Bombay Natural History Society (£77,000) and the Romanian Ornithological Society (£38,000). The largest UK beneficiary was the Game Conservancy Trust (£45,000, mainly for research into and the provision of advice to farmers on black grouse).

Management of nature reserves
Expenditure was £9.4 million. Locally, the charity owns 150 reserves, covering 240,000 acres, in all parts of the UK. These are usually open to the public, either with free access via footpaths, or at a charge. The charity is steadily acquiring new reserves, or, more strikingly, creating them. In particular it is buying coastal farmland and breaching the sea defences so that new wetlands are created or old ones re-established. Similar work is being done to restore former heathlands. The locations of all the reserves are set out neatly on the website (under 'Wildlife and conservation').

The RSPB's local work was seriously disrupted by the foot and mouth outbreak in 2001, which closed public access to many of its reserves, with the knock-on effect of reducing the charity's ability to recruit new members from its visitors. However, so far as can be told from the charity's reports, the overall scene is one of continuing success; there are specific references to more sea eagles, kites, cirl buntings and black grouse (though the spectacular capercaillie population at Abernethy is only 'holding up well'), and, apparently, few setbacks to record.

Acquisition of nature reserves
Expenditure was £3.5 million. Extensions as much as new acquisitions dominated expenditure in

2000/01, with the exception of the purchase of Rainham marshes in Essex. Large areas were added to the flow country reserve in Caithness.

Membership support and enquiries
Expenditure was £4.4 million. The membership enquiry service handles about 5,000 enquiries a week. These are mainly received in the form of letters and telephone calls, but there are also personal enquirers (especially at reserves and local offices) and web enquiries. Support is also offered to members (and non-members) in other ways, including through membership magazines and publications, other conservation literature, and a range of primary conservation resources such as wild bird feeders and educational videos.

Education, publications and films
Expenditure was £3.8 million. The society has developed a groundbreaking new education resource, 'Elemental Suitcase', 'an innovative package of teaching material for use in after school clubs', aimed at 'encouraging children to develop an interest in the wise use of the environment'. In 2000/01 only £20,000 was generated from educational resources because it is the society's policy to provide resources free of charge wherever possible (but not unsolicited).

Volunteers

'More than 8,500 people regularly volunteer, contributing over 640,000 hours of work each year – equivalent to employing an additional 350 staff.' This compares with total paid staff of 1,189. In addition, many thousands of RSPB members and others take part in bird-counting schemes, such as Garden Bird Watch in 2000.

The full list of opportunities for volunteers listed in the 2000/01 annual review covered the following areas of work:

- ' in our offices
- in our tearooms
- on our nature reserves – meeting people, guiding visitors or carrying out essential practical management
- guarding nest sites
- surveying farmland birds
- recruiting new members
- as part of a corporate team building day
- as a week's break from city life
- as a means to keep active in retirement
- as a foot in the door towards a conservation career.'

The society is currently reviewing its medium-term programme, and is looking at, among other things, 'more opportunities for members wishing to participate in a wider range of our activities'.

Funding, administration

The RSPB has headquarters in all four UK countries, and nine regional offices in England and Scotland. 'These local offices are your first point of contact with the Society.'

- RSPB Scotland headquarters, 0131 311 6500
- RSPB Northern Ireland headquarters, 01232 491547
- RSPB south Wales office, 029 2035 3000

The society is almost wholly voluntarily funded, with membership subscriptions the largest single source of income (£18 million in 2000/01). The society has had a high response to sending out information about the new and simpler Gift Aid tax concession scheme; such mailings accounted for 31% of its new family memberships in the year.

Like other heritage and conservation charities, such as the *National Trust*, subscriptions are not wholly philanthropic, but bring specific benefits; in this case free entry to the society's reserves. However, entry charges are modest and subscription fees are substantial (£26 for an ordinary membership), so the financial benefits will usually be slight. Legacies in 2000/01, at £15 million, were almost unchanged from the previous year, while a further £6 million came in from other donations and appeals.

The total voluntary income of £44 million was achieved at a fundraising cost of £6.7 million, giving a cost ratio of a low 15%. This was similar to the previous year and a reduction from the 20% average of the three years to 1999.

The charity, one of the largest in the country, nevertheless operates on a modest level of financial reserves. Its £12 million represents cover for just three months' expenditure.

The accounts are striking for the exemplary detail and clarity with which they set out the charity's various sources of income and its heads of expenditure.

The charity adds ...

This entry offers a snapshot of some of the RSPB's main activities. The Society is always pleased to provide further specific information to enquirers. More details of the Society's work may be found on the RSPB website: www.rspb.org.uk

The information assessed

There are good annual reviews and annual reports and accounts. A new and comprehensive website was introduced in 2001.

Contact

The Lodge
Sandy
Bedfordshire
SG19 2DL
Tel 01767 680551
Website www.rspb.org.uk
Chair Professor John Croxall
Graham Wynne, Chief Executive

RSPCA

Royal Society for the Prevention of Cruelty to Animals

Income	£66,612,000 (2000)
Donated income	£56,900,000
Fundraising costs	£5,878,000
Statutory income	£0
Top salary	£80,00 –£90,000
Paid staff	
Full time	1,347
Part time	337
Volunteers	7,000

Aims, activities

The growth of this charity in recent years has been remarkable, its income, almost all from voluntary contributions and legacies, rising from £37 million in 1995 to £67 million in 2000.

The two largest areas of charitable expenditures in 2000 were as follows (with 1999 figures in brackets):

● Inspectorate and prosecutions £24 million (£20 million) – over 1.5 million calls were received on the charity's cruelty and advice line (**0870 55 55 999**) and its 328 inspectors conducted 127,000 investigations. There were 824 prosecutions and 180,000 animals (up from 157,000 and 144,000 in the two previous years) were collected or rescued, many of them by the society's new force of 146 animal collection officers. Costs rose sharply in the year, by 17%, due to both more staff and improved salary levels.

- Animal establishments £13 million (£12 million) – the society runs 25 animal hospitals, clinics and centres (another 87 are run by its independent local branches). Expenditure was up by 16%, the increase including the costs of big capital projects such as completing the rebuilding of the Southridge Animal Centre in Hertfordshire. This centre can now hold 108 dogs and 128 other animals.

Other major areas of work include:

- Education, especially in schools. In all, 50 part-time school liaison officers visited 10% of schools in England and Wales, seeing half a million pupils.

- 'Freedom Food', the society's labelling scheme to ensure that animal foods come from animals that have been treated throughout to the RSPCA's welfare standards. In a major recent success, eggs from battery hens will be labelled 'caged' from 2005.

- Branch support. The society contributed £2.4 million towards the work of its local branches.

The RSPCA is also a major campaigning institution. In 2000 the main areas concerned included:

- animal testing – though a declining practice recently, there are new threats from chemical safety testing proposals and from increased genetic engineering programmes;

- hunting with dogs – this campaign was helped by the wonderfully phrased conclusion of the Burns Enquiry Report that 'hunting with dogs seriously compromises the welfare' of the animals being pursued;

- exotics – calling for tighter controls on trade in exotic species;

- furs – the Fur Farming (Prohibition) Act was passed;

- whaling – the society is part of the international lobby against the resumption of whaling.

During the year, a potentially important new initiative concerning the causes of animal cruelty was launched when, with the support of the annual general meeting, the society commissioned a six-month study at Manchester University into why some young children abuse animals.

In another development of potentially great importance for other charities as well as for the RSPCA, the society has succeeded in getting legal approval for its blocking of membership applications from over 500 people whom it believed wished to join simply to overturn the policy of campaigning against the hunting of animals by dogs. This form of 'entryism' is a potential threat to many charities, and it is particularly welcome that the judge concerned specifically ruled that the charity's reaction was in accordance with the Human Rights Act.

The charity is also active internationally. Given its strong financial position and the level of its reserves (referred to below), it may be appropriate for this work to receive even greater emphasis in future.

Volunteers

The society has over 550,0000 active supporters on its mailing list. There are also 189 independent local branches, most of them wholly voluntary and subscribing to the society's rules and carrying out similar welfare activities at a local level.

Funding, administration

More than half the society's income in 2000 (£38 million, or 56%) was from legacies. A further £19 million, or 29%, came from donations and subscriptions, an area that saw a remarkable 27% increase over the previous year. The charity attributes this to a 14% increase in fundraising costs in 1999. These costs nevertheless remain low, at 10p in the pound in 2000.

The charity has large reserves, despite continuing high levels of investment in 2000 and an overall excess of expenditure over income of £4 million for the year. The RSPCA's policy is to hold free reserves at a level of £45 million. At the end of 2000 there were unrestricted funds of £81 million, excluding the value of the charity's tangible assets, though there were plans for putting much of this to use.

The charity adds ...

The RSPCA prevents cruelty and promotes kindness to all animals. It is concerned not only with the welfare of domestic pets but with farm, wild and research animals as well as cruelty overseas. The RSPCA receives no Government funding and relies solely on donations and legacy income.

The information assessed

The annual report and accounts and annual review are excellent. The charity also has one of this editor's favourite websites (which has a link to the full report and accounts).

Contact

Wilberforce Way
Southwater
Horsham
West Sussex
RH13 9RS
Tel 0870 0101181
Website www.rspca.org.uk
Chair Mike Tomlinson
Peter Davies, Director General

Rukba
Royal United Kingdom Beneficent Association, supporting older people in financial difficulty

Income	£11,409,000 (2000)
Donated income	£3,136,000
Fundraising costs	£823,000
Statutory income	£3,013,000
Top salary	£60,000–£70,000
Paid staff	
Full time	131
Part time	111
Volunteers	1,100

Aims, activities

'Rukba helps older people who, through circumstances largely outside their control, find themselves in financial difficulty. Our main aim is to enable them to live in their own homes ... For some, we may be able to contribute to nursing or residential home fees, enabling them to live either in the home of their choice or in one of our homes.' Rukba's support, though usually modest in scale, is for life.

'The misfortunes that cause people to need us vary considerably; our beneficiaries, on the other hand, have much in common. Typically they are people more used to giving than to taking – such as nurses, teachers, ministers, missionaries and carers; we can also help the husbands and wives of such people, including those that are divorced or separated.' Help is given without regard to religion or ethnic origin.

The charity seeks to help 'with the utmost discretion and sensitivity; restoring and maintaining the self-esteem of our beneficiaries is at the heart of our work'. Support and friendship are offered to the more than 5,000 beneficiaries by a team of over 1,000 volunteers, known as honorary secretaries.

Financial help is on a sufficiently modest scale to prevent the withdrawal of other (state) benefits, though the charity points out that 70% of pensioners do not have enough money to make possible a modest but comfortable life. Such help is given in a number of ways (with 2000 expenditure in brackets):

- A small regular payment – this is called an annuity and is currently paid to over 5,000 people, with 441 new annuitants in the year (costing £4.8 million).

- Grants to meet emergencies – for people with little or no savings, for items such as boiler repairs or travel costs to visit sick relatives (4,500 at a cost of £0.5 million).

- Interest-free loans – for house repairs (£67,000).

- Equipment to help with independent living – such as grab rails or scooters (90 beneficiaries at £60,000).

- Clothing – volunteers collect and send out over 3,000 parcels of new and good quality used clothing.

- Holidays and holiday grants and respite care provision (£63,000).

- Residential care – the charity has 3 nursing or residential homes and 30 bungalows or flats (£3.5 million).

There is a Grants and Applicants sub-committee which decides on applications for help. These can be submitted through local honorary secretaries or directly. Advice is available from the telephone number given below.

In addition, this charity also runs, as the managing trustee, the splendidly named Universal Beneficent Society (UBS), which also supports older people in severe financial difficulties.

Volunteers

There were 1,043 honorary secretaries at the end of 2000. Their presence and support probably constitute one of the most valued services of the charity for many of its beneficiaries.

Funding, administration

Apart from the residential care, which is largely funded by statutory fees, the charity relies on the income from its endowments (about £5 million arriving in 2000) and from donations and legacies (£3 million). This voluntary income benefited from an exceptional £2.2 million in legacies in 2000, up from the more typical £1 million of the previous year.

Fundraising costs were £823,000, giving a cost ratio of 26%. This was a big reduction on the 42% of the previous year and marked a return towards the average 25% of the three years to 1998.

The charity adds ...

*Rukba and UBS provide financial support for
life. So most of our funds are already
committed. We need to continue raising
more money if we are to help more elderly
people in need.*

The information assessed
The unpretentious but excellent annual
report and accounts, brief annual review and
admirable financial review with summary
accounts are backed by a clear and effective
website.

Contact
6 Avonmore Road
London
W14 8RL
Tel 020 7605 4200
Website www.rukba.org.uk
Chair William Underwood
Jonathan Powell, Director

St Dunstan's
Care for blind ex-service people

Income	£17,698,000 (2000/01)
Donated income	£11,128,000
Fundraising costs	£1,292,000
Statutory income	£349,000
Top salary	£60,000–£70,0000
Paid staff	
Full time	200
Part time	44
Volunteers	
Operational	55
Fundraising	20

Aims, activities
Originally a charity for those blinded
in war, St Dunstan's purposes have
been extended to cover all ex-service
people who are blind, even if this was
not the result of their military service.

This has greatly widened the number
of potential beneficiaries, as it has
brought in many people who have lost
or may lose their sight in old age –
effectively including, among others,
all men born before about 1940 who
were therefore liable for compulsory
military service. Though the charity
has reserved its existing funds
specifically to support the original
beneficiaries, it now fundraises
actively in order to help its widened
client group.

Once taken on, all beneficiaries are
beneficiaries for life, and the charity
suggests that, on average, this
represents a £110,000 commitment.

The work of the charity is of two
kinds: support at home, and services
provided at the charity's centre at
Ovingdean, near Brighton.

The accounts for 2000/01 break down
the expenditure as follows:

- welfare, including grants and
technical, medical and welfare
visiting services, £2.6 million
- St Dunstan's, £4.4 million
- repairs and maintenance of
beneficiaries homes, £1.7 million
- identification and follow-up of new
and potential beneficiaries,
£0.6 million.

The charity does not say how many St
Dunstaners there are, but states that
there are at present 100 new
admissions a year.

St Dunstan's is probably best known
for its Ovingdean training, nursing,
residential and holiday centre,
'purpose built in 1938, in the design
of an aeroplane, and atop the cliffs to
the east of Brighton overlooking the
English Channel. Facilities include a
swimming pool and gymnasium, sports
including indoor archery and bowling
alley, craft workshop, computer suite,

ballroom, chapel for worship, pub and training kitchen.'

Staff at Ovingdean include Rehabilitation Officers for the Visually Impaired (ROVI), who teach people who are newly blind skills that will enable them to return to their own communities and lead lives that are as independent and normal as possible. New St Dunstaners are helped to identify job and career opportunities and assisted in obtaining any necessary adapted equipment. 'Frequent visits to Ovingdean over the years make it a secure and familiar haven to St Dunstaners. The ability to move freely and unaided around the building and its grounds enables a greater degree of independence.'

The chairman's foreword to the annual report speaks of the charity's desire for the greatest possible independence for those it seeks to help, and gives a good example to show this in action: 'at the earliest opportunity each new St Dunstaner is presented with either a Braille watch or a talking watch ... The renewed ability to tell the time marks the first important step in rebuilding self-esteem and shows that new skills can be acquired in spite of blindness.'

Volunteers

The charity noted in 2001 that, although at present the contribution of volunteers to its work was limited, this was under review and it was hoped that it would shortly be expanded.

Funding, administration

The charity has an unusual financial history. In the early 1960s it was asked by the Charity Commission to stop fundraising because it already had enough assets to give lifetime care to its then limited number of beneficiaries. In the early 1990s it

became clear that there had been a miscalculation and that more money was needed. Fundraising restarted, so successfully that in a few years it was clear that the 1960s situation of overfunding was reappearing. This time the solution, implemented in March 2000, was to increase the number of potential beneficiaries by extending care not just to those blinded by war (and to their widows and dependants), but to all ex-servicemen or women who became blind for any reason and at any age. This category has been estimated by other ex-service charities to cover potentially a quarter of the UK's population.

The original beneficiary group, solely those who were blinded in war, were protected by reserving all the assets of the charity to that date (about £100 million) for their exclusive benefit. Only future income would be available to help the newly widened constituency.

In 2000/01, the income of £17.7 million, sharply up from the £15 million of the previous year, came from donations (£6 million), legacies (£5 million), investment income (£4.2 million), and rent and charges for the accommodation provided to the beneficiaries (£2.2 million). The voluntary income of £11.1 million was achieved at a fundraising cost of £1.3 million, giving a cost ratio of a low 12p in the pound.

These were excellent results, with the key level of individual donations rising by over 60% and far surpassing even the high levels of two years previously.

The charity adds ...

St Dunstan's is undertaking a wide-ranging appraisal of its strategic objectives and is committed to developing a continuous *improvement in the scale and calibre of its services.*

The information assessed

The adequate annual report and accounts are supported by a simple website, but this was due to be upgraded in December 2001.

Contact

12–14 Harcourt Street
London
W1A 4XB
Tel 020 7723 5021
Chair Captain Michael Gordon-Lennox
Robert Leader, Chief Executive

St John Ambulance

England, Channel Islands and Isle of Man

Income	£46,519,000	(1999/00, annual rate)
Donated income		£9,795,000
Fundraising costs		£2,578,000
Statutory income		£4,005,000
Top salary		£80,000–£90,000
Paid staff		1,037
Volunteers		47,000

Aims, activities

There is an excellent overall description of the charity on its website. St John Ambulance's mission is to provide first aid, medical support services and caring services in support of community needs; and education, training and personal development to young people. 'As the leading first aid training provider, St John Ambulance trains over half a million people each year, running a range of first aid courses for children, the general public and the workforce.

'St John Ambulance has over 47,000 volunteers who are committed to training, caring and saving lives. Every day, St John Ambulance volunteers give 10,000 hours of voluntary service to the public and travel 5,000 miles providing patient care. Every year 200,000 casualties are treated by our volunteers ... They are all fully trained and they give over half a million hours of care to their communities each year. The charity also runs courses for carers. With well over half of its volunteers under the age of 18, St John Ambulance is a major youth organisation. Through participation in a structured programme of first aid and care activities, young people can develop both their personal and social skills and prepare for citizenship.

'The first aid and caring services are carried out within a county-based structure, but the development and co-ordination of policies for the charity is undertaken at National Headquarters in London.'

The 1999/00 annual report notes that the charity has adopted ambitious targets for the next five years. These include raising the proportion of the population who are first-aid qualified from 1% to 5%, and increasing its own membership by 5% a year over the same period.

The services are listed as follows in the report, with their direct costs and their earned income :

- first aid training – direct costs £22 million, earnings £22 million;
- first aid services and transport – direct costs £17 million, earnings £6.7 million;
- first aid equipment – direct costs £2.3 million, earnings £2.6 million;
- community care – direct costs £3.5 million, earnings £2 million;

- youth groups – direct costs £0.5 million, earnings £35,000.

Volunteers

'Volunteering is what our charity is about ... At the minimum wage the time contributed by our volunteers can be valued at approximately £15 million and at the average wage approximately £40 million.' The website has an excellent listing of all the volunteering opportunities that are available. They include:

- first aider;
- helping the homeless;
- social care;
- fundraiser;
- administrative support;
- PR and marketing;
- make-up artist;
- charity shop worker;
- youth leader;
- library service.

There is a regular volunteers' magazine, *St John Life*.

Funding, administration

The charity's trustees are the 'Council of The Priory of England and the Islands of the most venerable Order of the Hospital of St John of Jerusalem'. The charity is part of an international healthcare organisation, descended from the monks of St John's Hospital in Jerusalem who took up arms to become the Knights Hospitaller in the savage wars for control of that area; they later conquered Rhodes; were expelled to and from Malta (by Napoleon in the latter case); retreated to their present headquarters in Rome; and have now returned from their military diversion of many centuries to their healthcare origins. The extraordinary story is briefly told on the website.

There seems to be no indication of whether the charity in England, or indeed the headquarters in Rome, retain any connection with the Roman Catholic or any other church.

Due to constitutional rearrangements in 1999, the accounts to December 2000 cover a period of a little over 14 months. The figures above have been reduced pro rata to annual rates.

The largest source of income in that period was from first aid and other chargeable services, which produced £34 million. Voluntary income over the 14-month period was £11.6 million, with £2.7 million of this from legacies, and was achieved at a fundraising cost of £3.1 million, a ratio of 26p in the pound.

The information assessed

The good annual report and accounts are backed by an informative website and supporting materials.

Contact

27 St John's Lane
London
EC1M 4BU
Tel 0870 235 5231
Website www.sja.org.uk
Chair Lord Slynn
L V Martin, Chief Executive

Salvation Army

Income	£141,925,000 (1999/00)
Donated income	£73,154,000
Fundraising costs	£3,470,000
Statutory income	£36,051,000
Top salary	£48,000, but see below
Paid staff	2,799
Volunteers	100,000

Aims, activities

'The Salvation Army is an integral part of the universal Christian church. Its message is based on the Bible, its motivation is the love of God as revealed in Jesus Christ. Its mission is to proclaim his gospel, to persuade men and women to become his disciples and to engage in a programme of practical concern for the needs of humanity. Its ministry is offered to all, regardless of race, creed, colour or sex.'

The army is itself a church and its officers are ministers of religion. It is also 'the biggest provider of social care after the government'; this entry concentrates on that role.

Salvation Army community services in the UK are both extensive and wide-ranging. For adults they include care homes for older people, community centres, detoxification centres, night shelters, centres for homeless people, rehabilitation units, day and domiciliary care, prisons and emergency relief units, and a marriage guidance service. The website gives some figures:

- 986 evangelical and community service centres;
- 28 goodwill centres giving a service to needy people in inner-city areas;
- 27 eventide homes for almost 1,000 older people;
- 50 hostels offering 3,355 beds;
- 7 centres offering accommodation for approximately 100 family units;
- 5 centres for the treatment and rehabilitation of alcoholics;
- 3 residential community homes for 84 children and adolescents in need of care and protection;
- a prison chaplaincy service to 111 penal establishments in the UK;
- 5,000 investigations for missing relatives undertaken annually.

For young people there are after-school clubs, breakfast clubs and around 400 mother and toddler groups. The army runs 89 senior youth clubs and 221 junior youth clubs. Its STOPGAP project enables young people to serve voluntarily overseas and, more recently, with Salvation Army centres in the UK.

The Salvation Army is an international movement and has over 100 people from the UK working overseas in some of the poorest parts of the world. One programme, Mustard Seeds, developed from the UK, involves a system of micro-credit for those at the very bottom of the economic ladder, whereby 'each participant recieves a small loan to start a business which, once repaid, can be made available for more projects'. This programme is now operating in Tanzania and the Philippines.

The army itself points out that the military format, adopted at a time when all things military enjoyed great esteem, may now be anachronistic. It asks the question of itself: 'As the quasi-military structure now has less appeal and attraction, why does the Army keep it?'

It answers: 'It still has some advantages. The distinctive uniform and structure identify Salvationists as people who are "available" in a way similar to how the distinctive clothing of clergy in other denominations identifies their purpose. The Army simply extends this identification through uniform to its members (called soldiers) as well as its clergy (known as officers). The ... disciplined structure enables decisions to be implemented effectively and, when necessary, rapidly. Its officers can be moved to areas where they are most needed with the maximum of ease and the minimum of delay.'

It seems to be effective in other ways as well. New public attitude research published in September 2001 showed that 87% of the British public say that if someone came to their door collecting for the Salvation Army they would trust them to make good use of their donation.

Contrary to some popular misconceptions, members are not required to wear the uniform (except to play in a uniformed band), and many don't; while the 'citadels' and so on are simply churches where everyone is welcome, whether or not they are members or supporters. The rule that officers, if they wish to remain in the ministry, can only marry fellow officers is currently under review.

A highlight of the year to March 2000 was the publication of a report, 'The Paradox of Prosperity', looking at the likely demand for the army's services and support over for the next ten years, which received widespread publicity. It makes saddening reading. One notable feature was the anticipated continuing rise in the number of human casualties from the more prosperous parts of society.

In October 2001 the army said that it was looking at the possibility of setting up Salvation Army schools in the UK, a possibility opened up by the Education White Paper of that month. It already runs over 1,000 schools in other countries. Indeed, 'a number of high-ranking members of African governments have been educated in Salvation Army schools'.

Volunteers

Members of the army, its 'soldiers', carry out many of the social and community activities wholly voluntarily. The officers are ministers of religion as well as often having extensive responsibilities for the army's social and community activities. They are not salaried, but receive a modest standard allowance (less than £7,000 a year), plus their accommodation and board.

Funding, administration

The army keeps separate accounts for its central funds and its social work funds. Both are supported by public donations and so for this entry they have been added together.

Though the army received over £40 million in statutory fees and grants for its welfare and housing activities in 1999/00, this was far outweighed by its £73 million in voluntary income. Of this, £30 million came in the form of legacies, £21 million in donations from the public, and £20 million in subscriptions and donations from the church's own members. Total fundraising costs represented a very low 5p in the pound of this, or £3.5 million, a ratio that has been maintained for some years even while the voluntary income has been steadily growing.

The charity's reserves of £39 million at the end of the year were mostly held in a fund designated for planned capital spending programmes, and even then represented less than four months' normal expenditure.

The information assessed

There is an excellent annual report and accounts and annual review. The website is quite exceptionally comprehensive and informative; it is worth a visit from other charities seeking to use this major means of communication.

Contact

101 Newington Causeway
London
SE1 6BN
Tel 020 7367 4500
Website www.salvationarmy.org.uk
Chair Commissioner Alex Hughes
Colonel Gordon Becker, Chief Executive

Samaritans

Telephone service for people in distress

Income	£6,054,000 (2000/01)
Donated income	£5,734,000
Fundraising costs	£1,578,000
Statutory income	£210,000
Top salary	£60,000–£70,000
Paid staff	
Full time	46
Volunteers	
Operational	18,700

Aims, activities

The Samaritans provides confidential emotional support to any person who is suicidal or despairing; and increases public awareness of issues around suicide and depression. They are available 24 hours a day (on **08457 909090**) to provide confidential emotional support for people who are experiencing feelings of distress or despair, including those which may lead to suicide.

The work is funded primarily by voluntary donations, and the service is delivered wholly by 18,700 Samaritan volunteers who gave 3 million hours of listening time in 2000. They are organised into 203 voluntary branches, each of which is an independent charity with its own management committee.

The figures for the service are remarkable:

- on average, each volunteer gave 183 hours of listening in 2000, the equivalent of 26 working days;
- the Samaritans cover 500 telephone helplines for 24 hours a day, 7 days a week, throughout the year;
- 96% of all contacts are by telephone;
- it cost the Samaritans £2.19 to answer each of the 4.8 million calls in 2000;
- if paid at the national minimum wage, the time dedicated by Samaritan volunteers to answering the phones would cost the country £11 million;
- since 1978, verbal contacts have doubled.

Volunteers

Within the Samaritans, the ratio of volunteers to centrally paid staff is 390:1 and it is not the few paid staff but the volunteers who take even the most difficult or distressing calls. The paid staff simply provide all the necessary administrative and fundraising support to enable the volunteers to operate the actual service.

In September 2001 the Samaritans launched a volunteer recruiting drive.

'The Samaritans is committed to being there 24-hours a day for anyone who needs us, but a lot of people don't realise that our service is provided entirely by volunteers. Without them, we couldn't offer this unique service. Volunteer numbers have been falling for some years now, and we are going to reverse that trend. The Samaritans is run by ordinary people doing something extraordinary. By volunteering for The Samaritans, you could be helping to save lives.

'Anyone who is over 18 and able to listen without prejudice can be a volunteer. Volunteers give up 3 or 4 hours a week and one overnight duty every month.' There is a National Volunteer Hotline on 08705 627282.

Funding, administration

Each Samaritan branch raises its own funding locally. They also make small contributions to the central costs of the organisation, which, in its turn, supports the local branches when they need it. The figures in this entry are just for the central organisation.

For 2000/01, 95% of the total income of £6.1 million was in the form of donations or legacies. This was achieved at a fundraising cost of £1.6 million, giving a cost ratio of 28p in the pound. However, this expenditure included a large element (£654,000) of donor development costs intended to secure the income streams that will be needed in the future. If successful, this should lead to lower cost ratios in the future.

The information assessed

There is an exemplary annual report and accounts and a fine website.

Contact
The Upper Mill
Kingston Road
Ewell
Surrey
KT17 2AF
Tel 020 8394 8300
Website www.samaritans.org.uk
Chair Bernard Finnemore
Simon Armson, Chief Executive

Sargent Cancer Care for Children

Income	£8,017,000 (2000/01)
Donated income	£7,770,000
Fundraising costs	£3,607,000
Statutory income	£0
Top salary	not disclosed
Paid staff	
Full time	50

Aims, activities

The charity's mission is 'to support all young people with cancer and their families through high quality counselling, financial help and practical care'.

Sargent Cancer Care teams are based at more than 30 major cancer treatment centres throughout the UK to support the nearly 2,000 children, and their families, who are diagnosed with cancer each year. Altogether there are over 100 Sargent care professionals. They are employed by local authorities but are funded by this charity, and they work as part of the hospital teams.

The charity also has two residential centres, one in London and one in Scotland, where children and their families can take short breaks either during or after treatment for cancer.

Financial assistance is given for a variety of needs, with the costs of travel to and from hospitals being the largest.

The expenditure for 2000/01 is classified under the following main headings:

- Sargent Care Teams £2.2 million;
- grants for the children £1.8 million;
- residential centres £0.8 million.

Following a systematic study in 2000 of the needs of children with cancer, a review of the services was underway in 2001 and some new pilot projects had begun, including two that specifically address the needs of adolescents.

The charity has been growing remarkably, with income trebling over the last five years. At a time when there is much comment about increasing government funding of charities, this is an interesting example of the opposite: a charity giving increasing support through the NHS.

Volunteers

There is a reference to local supporters' groups in the annual review.

Funding, administration

The charity is almost wholly funded by donations and legacies. These totalled £7.8 million in 2000/01, of which £1.3 million came from legacies, and were achieved at a fundraising cost of £3.6 million, giving a cost ratio for the year of a very high 46p in the pound, or 46% (compared with 44% in the previous year and the 33% average for the three years to 1999). However, the reasons for this level of expenditure are clearly set out.

The total is divided in the accounts between ordinary fundraising (£2.5 million) and 'New donor recruitment' (£1.2 million). The excellent treasurer's report notes that this latter amount was funded entirely from reserves as an investment in future revenues, so the benefit can be expected in years to come.

Without the £1.2 million of such investment the costs represented a still high 33p in the pound. The report notes that the year's income was well below the charity's targets, and that 'in the short term, we have had to take painful corrective action'.

The information assessed

There is a simply presented but excellent annual report, with a particularly detailed and impressive honorary treasurer's report, and a much more promotional annual review. The nice website is the work of one of the charity's volunteers.

Contact

Griffin House
161 Hammersmith Road
London
W6 8SG
Tel 020 8752 2800
Website www.sargent.org
Chair David Knowles

Save the Children

Income	£106,578,000 (2000/01)
Donated income	£53,300,000
Fundraising costs	£13,810,000
Statutory income	£28,982,000
Top salary	£82,000
Paid staff	3,614
Volunteers	14,000

Aims, activities

Save the Children sets out to be primarily a children's rights organisation, rather than mainly a deliverer of services, operating around the world but with substantial activity in both Europe, recently especially in Kosovo, and in the UK.

'Our mission is to strive for the basic human rights of children.' This concept is itself in large part the work of Eglantyne Jebb, the founder of the charity in 1919 and the drafter of the original Declaration of the Rights of the Child. Under her guidance, the charity was one of the first to make use of professional publicity and advertising: 'wide, systematic and persevering propaganda' was needed to get across the truth about the sufferings of children (at that time in post-First World War Europe).

The charity works mainly by encouraging and supporting others in tackling the issues it and they identify. It defines opportunities and problems, puts forward possible initiatives and remedies, creates and sustains limited and usually short-term projects, and publicises local, national and international needs. It seldom runs continuing 'service delivery' projects on its own.

In 2000/01 the charity identified the following eight main areas of work (expenditure is given in brackets):

- Food security and nutrition (£22 million) – 'We aim to prevent malnutrition and starvation by ensuring that families have access to enough food all of the time.'
- Emergency (£16 million) – This is one of Britain's largest responders to disasters and emergencies worldwide.
- Information, campaigning and awareness (£16 million) – One example given was 'helping major companies such as Littlewoods, Pentland and Sainsburys develop responsible approaches to child labour'. Another involved a 25,000 face 'photo petition' to the UN on protecting children forced from their homes by war.
- Children and work (£15 million) – 'Save the Children is working to end exploitative child labour. But we don't believe a ban is the answer. [We] support projects that raise family income.'
- Health (£13 million) – 'We work with governments and other agencies to develop and improve national health systems, and make them more accessible to children.'
- Social protection, welfare and inclusion (£10.5 million) – 'We believe that children have the right to basic care and protection and that children who are marginalised because of poverty, disability or gender should have the same opportunities as others.'
- Education – the way out of poverty (£7.7 million). 'Once I have an education, I can find a better job and look after myself.'
- HIV-AIDS (£1.7 million) – 'We believe that children have the right to information and services to help them avoid HIV ... and that children living with HIV or orphaned because of AIDS should be cared for in their communities rather than institutions.'

The work is categorised geographically as follows for 2000/01:

- East and Central Africa £29 million
- UK, Central and East Europe £12 million

- Southern and West Africa
  £15 million

- Asia £14 million

- Latin America/Caribbean/Middle
  East £6 million

In 1999 the charity launched a big public campaign, Save the Children from Violence, which led to international agreement on the wording of a new, optional, protocol to the UN Convention on the Rights of the Child that would raise the minimum age for those fighting in wars from 15 to 18.

Save the Children at present is working hard towards achieving a greater voice for children themselves in its and the world's affairs. An example is its promotion of 'children's parliaments' and the 'children's select committee' in Britain, organised by the charity and the Foreign and Commonwealth Office.

The charity made its name by providing emergency aid in response to major crises. This is now much less of a priority, with Save the Children concentrating on prevention and on early warning systems in areas where the danger of such crises can already be identified. However, this has not stopped it playing a major role, for instance, in the work to rebuild the institutions in Kosovo on which children's welfare depends.

The charity has a large overseas staff and much of the work is undertaken by its own field offices working through local community groups and other organisations. Only a small part of the expenditure is classified as grants to other bodies (£7 million in 2000/01).

The activities reported in 2000/01 are varied, ranging from getting 22,000 Venezuelan children registered for healthcare and education, to helping the Chinese government develop a national model for foster care. One example shows two aspects of the work in a single setting. The first involved spending £496,000 in Mongolia on services for street children and working children – working with the Mongolian government to implement its National Poverty Alleviation Programme, improving the quality of the national pre-school programme, working with the government to develop social welfare and social policy initiatives, and increasing access to education for poor children. However, in early 2001 the country was struck by an appallingly harsh winter, with great loss of the livestock on which many families depend for a living, and Save the Children launched a second, different kind of programme – a big emergency relief operation.

Examples of work being undertaken in the UK include providing support to self-help groups of young people (England); challenging political parties on levels of youth participation (Northern Ireland); supporting an information line for prisoners' families (Scotland); and awareness raising in schools about refugee children (Wales).

Save the Children organisations have developed in 28 other countries. With the UK organisation they form the International Save the Children Alliance, which enables them to put forward a common response to major issues, such as the recent and continuing Balkan emergencies and the overall level of implementation of the UN Convention on the Rights of the Child. The alliance has its own chief executive and office in London (020 8748 2554) and fundraises on an international basis, especially from large international companies.

Volunteers

'The main volunteer activity is fundraising; over 13,000 volunteers throughout the UK raise money for Save the Children, chiefly through 600 fundraising branches or groups and through over 140 shops', each wholly staffed by volunteers and selling goods also voluntarily donated. The branches contributed over £5 million of the charity's income in 2000/01.

Within the branches there are specific roles for people to take on jobs such as:

- trading secretary (promoting sales through the charity's sales catalogue);
- press officer;
- school speaker, through the 'Speaking Out' programme (which is not primarily for fundraising).

The shops offer a wide range of roles, with training provided by the charity.

There are 30 area managers to support the volunteers. They can be contacted through the Volunteer Support Help Desk (020 7703 5400). The excellent information sheet notes that being a Save the Children volunteer, besides being tremendously rewarding, 'can also be great fun!'

Also, 'Save the Children always needs volunteers to help at our headquarters in London, mostly for administrative tasks.' There may be similar opportunities at the Cardiff and Belfast offices. Such volunteering is, among other things, 'a very useful way of gaining insights into how a large charity works'.

The charity also runs a Lottery-funded Millennium Award scheme which enables young people across the UK to manage a variety of projects in their local communities.

There are no opportunities for volunteers in the charity's projects and programmes overseas.

Funding, administration

Save the Children's income has been rising very fast, from £74 million in 1997/98 to £107 million in 2000/01, driven largely by increased donations and legacies, which now account for half the total income. A further quarter of income came from the UK and other governments and from the European Union, usually in the form of grants for specific programmes (for example, £43,000 from the Department for International Development to help Bhutanese refugee families in Nepal). A large amount, over £4 million in 2000/01, was in the form of gifts in kind, such as food and blankets.

The value of the goods donated for sale in the charity's shops was remarkable, at £4.5 million. After the costs of running these shops, £1.5 million remained for the charity: an excellent margin. Uniquely, the shops are all managed by volunteers, a policy abandoned by most of the other major charities.

The voluntary income was made up as follows (with the figures for the two previous years in brackets):

- donations £22.7 million (£25.9 million, £17.9 million);
- legacies £19.2 million (£13.3 million, £13.9 million);
- branch fundraising £5 million (£5.3 million, £4.8 million);
- companies £4.4 million (£4.6 million, £4.9 million);
- charitable trusts £2 million (£2.3 million, £1.5 million).

There was an additional net income of £6 million from catalogue and Christmas card sales.

The voluntary income was achieved at a fundraising cost of £13.8 million, giving a cost ratio of 26% (26p in the pound), the same as in the previous year, compared with an average of 23% for the three years to 1998/99.

The previous annual report had noted: 'It is important to invest in fundraising. During the year [1999/00] our expenditure in this area increased by 28% to £14 million. This has enabled us to secure future income streams in the form of committed giving, and look to new sources of income, such as global fundraising.' This is part of the first year of 'an exciting marketing strategy aimed at growing significantly our voluntary income over a five year period.' It may therefore have been disappointing that the value of donations fell in 2000/01, though in the short term this was counterbalanced by the greater value of legacies.

The charity adds ...

Our investment in recruiting committed givers is paying off: in two years we have increased the number from 70,000 to 170,000. This makes us more able to make long-term plans for our programme work and less dependent on one-off donations.

The information assessed

There is an excellent 'Report of the Trustees' with the accounts (which is the statutorily required annual report), as well as an 'Annual Report' (which is not), and a brief annual review. The accounts are particularly complete and clear. There are fine information sheets for potential volunteers and a helpful Public Enquiry Unit (020 7716 2268).

The website is comprehensive, with further detailed information for potential volunteers, though this editor was particularly taken with a linked 'unofficial' site run by a local branch in the north-west of England.

Contact

Mary Datchelor House
17 Grove Lane
London
SE5 8RD
Tel 020 7703 5400
Website www.savethechildren.org.uk
Chair Barry Clarke
Michael Aaronson, Director General

Schools and charitable donations

Collectively, schools probably receive about £250 million a year in charitable donations. They also benefit from very large but unquantified amounts of voluntarily donated time, by people acting as governors and in a wide range of other roles.

The amounts donated in a year were analysed as follows in a report published in 2000 by the Directory of Social Change (the publishers of this book):

- 3,567 state secondary schools £143 million;
- 18,312 state primary schools £77 million;

- 850 independent secondary schools £25 million;
- 1,129 special schools £11 million.

Education of almost any kind is a charitable activity and all schools can therefore make use of charitable funds, whether or not they are charitable institutions themselves. There is a 'public benefit' requirement that must be met, but it is at present a weak one (though there are moves to strengthen this, which might represent a challenge to the charitable status of some independent schools).

Fee-paying independent schools are usually charities (being, as the law stands, for public rather than private benefit). Most of their income, though, comes in the form of fees rather than donations. In 1999 Eton College, to take perhaps the most prominent example, received £20 million in fees but only £110,000 in donations. Typically, donations come in response to occasional appeals for new building projects and the like, rather than as a regular source of income.

Among state schools, voluntary schools (that is, schools with church affiliations), grant-maintained schools and city technology colleges are charities. The rest are classed rather as statutory bodies. Some Parent-Teacher Associations are independent charities; others are not.

The amounts donated, though large in themselves, make up less than 1% of the total income of the state school sector. There is a fundamental difficulty with charitable support for state schools, which are intended to be part of a fair national system – those in prosperous areas or with prosperous supporters may receive more than others where the needs are likely to be greater, thus reinforcing rather than reducing inequities.

Information is best sought from the individual school concerned.

Science Museum

Income	£61,008,000(1999/00)
Donated income	£12,468,000
Fundraising costs	£376,000
Statutory income	£23,756,000
Top salary	£110,000–£120,000

Aims, activities

This book covers all organisations receiving donations of over £5 million a year. The Science Museum comes into in this category, but almost all the donations are from institutions, many of them commercial companies, rather than from the philanthropy of individuals. Furthermore, a proportion of the receipts under the relevant heading are 'sponsorships', rather than gifts, in the sense that the museum 'extends sponsorship benefits at a level commensurate with the level of financial support received'. A donation is different, being a gift for which nothing is received in return – except, perhaps, a deserved glow of virtue. So this entry is brief.

The museum is a non-departmental public body and also a charity exempt from registration at the Charity Commission. It operates, in addition to the well-known museum in London, the National Railway Museum in York, the National Museum of

Photography, Film and Television in Bradford, and aeronautics exhibitions at Wroughton and Yeovilton.

Readers may have seen that free admission was reintroduced to the museum towards the end of 2001. This appears to apply only to the main location in London, and not to York or Bradford.

Volunteers

The annual report has an unusually full section covering the work of volunteers. There are 95 regular volunteer workers at the railway museum in York, and it has been decided that in future some operational activities there will be delivered entirely by volunteers. These include staffing the museum's information points and acting as drivers and guards on the miniature railway (perhaps on the model of the extensive narrow gauge railway above Budapest, where staff are not only volunteers but children).

The information assessed

There is an excellent annual report and accounts, and a suitably impressive website.

Contact

Exhibition Road
London
SW7 2DD
Tel 020 7942 4000
Website www.nmsi.ac.uk
Chair Sir Peter Williams
Dr Lindsay Sharp, Chief Executive

Scope
Support for people with cerebral palsy in England and Wales

Income	£66,814,000 (1999/00)
Donated income	£18,821,000
Fundraising costs	£5,626,000
Statutory income	£38,844,000
Top salary	£80,000–£90,000
Paid staff	3,362
Volunteers	6,746

Aims, activities

'One in every 400 babies born in this country has cerebral palsy: that's 1,500 people every year. As they grow up many will find that communication, getting around or simple things like opening cans are harder for them than for other people ... That sort of inconvenience is frustrating, but it's the attitudes of other people that can make it infuriating. Looking different, speaking through an enabler or using a wheelchair do not make you inferior, stupid or unfeeling ... We campaign to improve the way disabled people are treated and we provide housing, information and advice, education and all the other kinds of support that enable people with cerebral palsy to live the way they choose.'

Services in the past have been extensive, including the provision of local support for disabled people and their families, some of it through local groups affiliated to Scope; schools and a college; residential and small group homes, supported independent living schemes and day and respite services; and employment and training opportunities. In recent years the charity has been changing. Following the launch of an individual membership scheme in 1996, Scope has been transforming itself from an organisation for disabled people into one of disabled people.

For a long time the charity has struggled to raise sufficient voluntary income to support its extensive and often pioneering services. Following a widespread research and planning exercise, Scope finally bit the bullet and announced big changes in November 2000. These involved:

- adjusting its former structure of local 'partnership teams': 'We are simply unable to sustain these teams with their current wide-ranging role';
- replacing the charity's scheme for individual grants in time of need by a member of staff who will help families in need to find other sources of such help;
- ending the national advisory and assessment service;
- ending the charity's subsidy to its schools and college.

In addition £1 million was to be cut from the budget for corporate costs such as public relations and the annual conference.

In future the charity would concentrate on four priority areas:

- support for children newly diagnosed with cerebral palsy (and their families) and ensuring pre-school opportunities;
- education support for children with cerebral palsy and support for their families;
- support for disabled people in obtaining and keeping work;
- support for disabled adults in daily living.

The announcement of these changes provoked a strong reaction from Scope's members which led, perhaps belatedly, to a full consultation exercise. In July 2001 there was a partial reinstatement of the 'partnership teams' function, especially in supporting adults living in the community. The money to finance this was transferred from that allocated to work with children. The ending of the school and college subsidies is also proving slow to implement. Action has started elsewhere. There was no annual conference in 2001, head office staff have been reduced, and savings have been made in fundraising, as reported below.

However painful in the short term, the charity is surely right to accept that it must cut its coat according to its means and re-establish itself on a basis from which it can again move forward.

Volunteers

At a local level there are numerous Scope groups that provide mutual support and self-help. There is extensive voluntary involvement in the charity's fundraising, including 6,000 volunteers in the charity's shops.

Funding, administration

The main sources of income in 2000/01 were (with 1999/00 figures in brackets):

- statutory fees and grants £38.8 million (£40.5 million);
- donations £11 million (£10.6 million);
- legacies £6.2 million (£8 million);
- net income from shops £1 million (£1.5 million).

The voluntary income totalled £19 million and was achieved at a reduced fundraising cost of £5.6 million, giving a cost ratio of 30p in the pound, or 30%, a substantial reduction from the 34% and 44% of the previous two years and from the 46% average of the three years to 1999. A specific cost reduction has come from the closing of the collection box department, 'as this ... is no longer a cost-effective fundraising activity'.

Bravely, the annual report published in November 2001 says that 'a new income generation strategy has been developed to boost Scope's non-statutory income by 60% over the next five years'.

The charity adds ...

Scope's 50th anniversary year, 2002, sees the charity working towards its very specific goals within a carefully developed financial strategy. At the end of September 2001 Scope reported a surplus of around £1.5 million. Although still at an early stage in our strategy we believe that this figure

gives grounds for cautious optimism that the hard decisions have been worthwhile, and is a good position from which to work towards our goal of equality for disabled people.

The information assessed
The annual report is adequate but very brief. The accounts, on the other hand, are unusually full. There is a good website which includes the charity's full report and accounts.

Contact
6 Market Road
London
N7 9PW
Tel 020 7619 7100
Website www.scope.org.uk
Chair Gerald McCarthy
Richard Brewster, Chief Executive

The Scouting movement

The scouting movement is not a single organisation, but a gathering of independent charities under the umbrella of a national association. There are Scout Councils of Scotland, Wales and Northern Ireland (see below for contact details), with further Scout Counties, Areas, Districts and Groups, all of which are independent charities.

This is a uniformed organisation that runs activities for young people (boys and girls). There are approximately 24,400 local groups of Beavers, Cub Scouts, Scouts, Explorer Scouts and Scout Network, including about 401,000 young people aged between 6 and 25 and led by around 82,400 adult volunteers. Total membership of the association is almost half a million people of all ages.

The central Scout Association had an income of £15.2 million in 2000/01, including membership income of £5.2 million (the annual membership fee is £12.50). It employs over 400 staff, although the lion's share of its activities is carried out by its legions of volunteer leaders. It has been very successful in attracting sponsorship for its 'curriculum' of badge work. There are now over 250 badges that young people can work towards. English Heritage is the most recent sponsor, contributing £10,000 over two years to support the Scout Heritage Badge. Other sponsors include Agfa, the Bank of Scotland, British Energy, British Gas, BNFL, British Telecom, Esso, the Met Office,

Ordnance Survey, Savlon and Weetabix. Proctor & Gamble currently sponsors the Scout Job Week.

All the local groups are charities, many of them big enough to have registered with the Charity Commission. All have a standard charitable object, which is to develop the physical, intellectual, social and spiritual potential of young people. A large number of local groups have been successful in attracting support from the National Lottery distribution boards, often to fund camping equipment, expeditions or adventure holidays.

Nationally, the Scout Association works to promote scouting and its benefits for young people. Its successful trading activities include a scout insurance scheme, scout shops, a campsite, a conference facility and adventure centres. The national headquarters decides scouting policy, resources leaders and groups, and offers training, advice and support.

Scouting is an international movement for young people and links are made with scout associations and groups in other countries.

Locally, groups can be contacted through scout shops or the district headquarters (listed in the phone book), or through Councils for Voluntary Service, see page 385 or nationally through the Information Centre (tel: 0845 300 1818).

The central contact in England is the Scout Association (tel: 020 8433 7100; website: www.scouts.org.uk). For the other councils, contact:

- Scotland; tel: 01383 419073; website: www.scouts-scotland.org.uk
- Wales; tel: 01446 795277; website: www.scoutbase.org.uk/wales
- Northern Ireland; tel: 028 9049 2829; website: www.scouting-ni.org.uk

Sense

The National Deafblind and Rubella Association

Income	£35,837,000 (2000/01)
Donated income	£5,085,000
Fundraising costs	£1,643,000
Statutory income	£27,401,000
Top salary	more than £60,000
Paid staff	
Full time	1,229
Part time	892
Volunteers	750

Aims, activities

There are about 23,000 deafblind people in the UK, some of whom were born deafblind and others who have lost one or both of these senses at a later stage. 'Deafblindness – a combination of sight and hearing loss – is one of the most challenging disabilities someone can face. Yet given the right services and support, deafblind people can develop their talents and choose how they wish to live their lives.'

When Rodney Clark started work with this charity in 1981, he was the only paid member of staff. When he retired in 2001 it was reported to be the largest deafblind organisation in the world.

The charity has a range of services and activities. They are described in two lists, approaching the work from different directions. The following, taken from the website, is probably addressed primarily to individuals interested in help for particular people.

- Regional advice. Sense's regional advisory service is the first point of contact for information about local services. 'A vital part of the service is assessing the needs of individual deafblind people, in order to help identify appropriate services and support. Regional advisory workers help people find the services and benefits they need – housing, vocational opportunities, education, medical information and respite care are just some of the issues this service covers.'
- Family support
- The Sense Family Network, a national network of families run by families, friends and Sense staff.
- Sense branches, a network of national and local support groups. They are run by families for families, and offer support, campaigning, raising awareness and fundraising.
- Usher UK, a national branch of Sense run by people with Usher, a particular genetic condition leading to the development of deafblindness.
- Membership. 'Joining Sense brings people together and keeps members up to date. A strong membership also gives us a greater campaigning voice.'
- Campaigns

Current campaigns include 'Yes to Access Health', a campaign highlighting the discrimination faced by deafblind people using the health service, and 'See the Deafblind Person', campaigning for full civil rights to protect deafblind people from discrimination in employment, education, access to goods and services, and transport.

The annual review, and the part of the website titled 'Information for social services', has further details of services which may only be available in areas where the appropriate contracts have been agreed with the social services department concerned, but there is no information on the scale or distribution of these varied activities. They include:

- 4 family centres offering early assessments for the youngest children.
- 25 specialist outreach workers and advisers.
- A respite care programme, on offer to social services departments.
- Trained 'intervenors' offering intensive one-to-one attention to help children learn to communicate.
- Supported work settings in Sense workshops where service users work with qualified instructors to develop pre-vocational and vocational skills at workshops across the country.
- A wide range of day opportunities, through social services departments.
- Communicator-guides who can enable people who are deafblind to enjoy greater independence and a better quality of life by acting as the eyes and ears of a deafblind person. This might include visiting the deafblind person at home to help them deal with correspondence and bills; acting as an escort when someone goes shopping, visits friends, or takes part in leisure activities; or accompanying the user

on an appointment to facilitate communication.

- Vocational and employment opportunities. Sense can help service users with accessing appropriate vocational and job-specific training.
- Housing and accommodation: certainly the charity's largest programme in financial terms. Sense provides a range of options, such as staffed family-style homes with no more than six people in each; independent supported living – flats for more able service users; specialist facilities for those with profound and multiple needs.

Sense International was created in 1994 to enable Sense to respond appropriately to the many international requests for support, and is registered as an independent charity. 'In most developing countries there is little understanding about deafblindness and services do not exist. There are hundreds of thousands of deafblind people throughout the world who receive no support at all. In many countries deafblind children are put in institutions, kept in isolation at home or literally left on the streets to fend for themselves.'

Sense International works with partner organisations to set up specialist education units and community outreach programmes for deafblind children and their families, also providing training and expertise for teachers, resources, and support in advocacy, fundraising and management.

There are offices in the UK, India and Romania 'and we are taking exciting steps in Latin America and East Africa.'

Volunteers

'Volunteers are valued by Sense not only for their time and energy but for the unique atmosphere they create.' Two specific suggestions are made on the website: volunteering to help on a Sense holiday and volunteering to work in a Sense shop.

Funding, administration

In financial terms, this is largely a trading charity, charging local authorities for most of its services, and its income is growing.

The accounts give little information about the charity's expenditures. The main heading of 'Residential and community services' accounted for £23 million out of the total £32 million in 2000/01, but is not easy to differentiate from 'Individual and family services' (another £3 million). Neither of these headings is explained or broken down in more detail.

The chief source of income is 'Fees and allowances', at £26.3 million out of the total £35.8 million. Though their source is not stated, this is likely to be mainly or wholly statutory payments for services given, and there is a further £1 million in 'Grants receivable', which are those from government departments. Grants from charitable trusts and companies are included in the 'Fundraising income' of £4.3 million.

Together with legacies of £0.8 million, the total voluntary income of £5.1 million was achieved at a fundraising cost of £1.6 million, a ratio of a high 32p in the pound, or 32%. This was, though, a sharp reduction from the average of the three years to 1999, when it had been 46%. The average expenditure on fundraising has remained relatively constant but there has been increased income, no doubt as the result of this earlier investment. The annual report notes a very good year for fundraising generally, singling out the direct mail Christmas appeal. A weak spot (as for some other charities in this book) was the overseas events programme, where income was 'very disappointing'.

The charity adds ...

Sense is the leading national voluntary organisation that works with and campaigns for the needs of people who are both deaf and blind; providing advice, support, information and services for them, their families, carers and the professionals who work with them. In addition we work with many of the thousands of people who have a combination of sight and hearing problems plus other disabilities.

The information assessed

The good annual report and powerful annual review are backed by accounts which lack detail, and by first-class supporting literature. The website is a good source of information.

Contact

11–13 Clifton Terrace
London
N4 3SR
Tel 020 7272 7774
Website www.sense.org.uk
Chair Jessica Hills
Tony Best, Chief Executive

Shelter
Homelessness in England, Scotland and Wales

Income	£26,030,000 (1999/00)
Donated income	£14,678,000
Fundraising costs	£4,322,000
Statutory income	£3,293,000
Top salary	£60,000–£70,000
Paid staff	659
Volunteers	950

Aims, activities

Shelter is an advice, information and campaigning organisation. It does not provide housing itself but rather seeks to:

- prevent and alleviate homelessness by providing information, advice and advocacy for people with housing problems;

- pilot innovative schemes which will provide new solutions for homelessness and housing problems;

- campaign for lasting changes to housing policy and practice.

Founded following Ken Loach's *Cathy Come Home* television programme broadcast in 1966, Shelter is perhaps best known for its campaigning and advocacy work at a national level. This involves working with a range of government departments in London, and in 1999/00 very extensively with the new Scottish Executive. Key messages for 2000/01 included the need to strengthen the homelessness laws, to improve the partnership working of different agencies at a local level and to create a greater emphasis on action to prevent homelessness. 'The Homelessness Bill, due to be enacted in late 2001 and the new Housing Act in Scotland are testament to Shelter's campaigning ability.'

In 1999/00 Shelter spent £10.4 million on its housing aid services and £2.4 million on campaigning and education. The annual report identifies four key services areas:

- Housing Aid Centres. There are 59 of these centres. They do more than offer advice. Where necessary they act as advocates for their clients in court, at homelessness reviews and appeals, and at housing benefit review boards. They are also sources of information and expertise for the relevant local authorities. This programme probably accounts for most of the money spent on housing advice.

- National Housing Advisory Service (NHAS). Also referred to as the National Homelessness Advice Service, this is a joint government-funded venture with the National Association of *Citizens Advice Bureaux* (NACAB) in which Shelter staff give specialist support to the local bureaux.

- Shelterline. Set up at the end of 1998, this is a 24-hour free telephone helpline (**0808 800 444**). In the first year there were over 80,000 calls. The annual review notes that the pattern of calls revealed three key issues: housing and homelessness in London; financial problems; and domestic violence.

- Homeless to Home projects. These five projects, funded with £165,000 of Lottery money from the Community Fund in 1999/00, aim to work with parents and children to help them turn their new house into a home.

In the summer of 2001 the charity reported that it was discussing a merger with *Crisis*. Though it was hoped to reach a decision by October that year, in the event it looked as if the process of coming to an agreement might take longer than expected.

Volunteers

Some 800 volunteers help to run Shelter's shops. Volunteers also work in other areas; for example, up to 10% of Shelterline calls are taken by volunteers. However, during 1999/00 funding was gained from the National Lottery Charities Board (now the Community Fund) for a national 'volunteer involvement programme' aimed specifically at people who would normally be excluded from volunteering, so expansion is expected in the overall volunteer role.

Funding, administration

Shelter is funded mainly by donations and to a lesser extent by legacies from the public. Both streams of income grew sharply in 1999/00, yielding an increase of 26% and a total of £14.7 million. This was achieved at a fundraising cost of £4,322,000, a ratio of 29p for every pound raised. There has been a substantial reduction in fundraising costs, relative to donated income, over recent years. However, the figures for 1999/00 were greatly helped by a single legacy of over £1.5 million, a windfall that almost doubled legacy income over the previous year and is unlikely to be repeated soon.

The former Department of Transport, Local Government and the Regions provided £1.7 million towards the National Housing Advisory Service, while many local authorities contributed amounts, generally modest, towards Shelter's local Housing Aid Centres.

The Shelter shops, which had sales of £5.7 million in 1999/00, cost £5.6 million to run. The annual report notes that management changes are underway.

The charity adds ...

Shelter's primary aims are to prevent and alleviate homelessness and bad housing and to campaign for long-term change. In 2001, it launched Homework, a project aimed at educating young people about homelessness and bad housing. It is due to launch Shelternet, an online information system, in early 2002.

The information assessed

There is a choice between the 'Annual Report' and the 'Report and Accounts', which have different texts. Together, though, they give an excellent view of the charity's work. The website is comprehensive.

Contact

88 Old Street
London
EC1V 9HU
Tel 020 7505 2000
Website www.shelter.org.uk
Chair Peter Robson
Chris Holmes, Director

Sight Savers International

Ophthalmic care overseas

Income	£13,588,000 (2000)
Donated income	£13,096,000
Fundraising costs	£3,568,000
Statutory income	£306,000
Top salary	£70,000–£80,000, but see below
Paid staff	
Full time	190
Part time	14
Volunteers	
Fundraising	120

Aims, activities

Also known as the Royal Commonwealth Society for the Blind, the charity works across the world, though primarily in Commonwealth countries, to prevent blindness, restore sight and support irreversibly blinded people.

The charity's mission is to focus on communities with the greatest need, where eye care is poorly developed. Much of its present work is tied in to VISION 2020: The Right to Sight, an international partnership of dozens of eye care agencies and the World Health Organisation. Sight Savers notes that some of VISION 2020's priorities, including the prevention of childhood blindness, do not have well-established models suitable for developing countries, and the charity is now working to change this situation.

The charity is also encouraging a shift away from provider-led to community-led service provision: services for the people provided by the people. The core delivery model is becoming one of 'comprehensive eye services where health education and promotion, prevention, treatment and rehabilitation are provided together rather than as separate services'.

The charity's leaflets describe its achievements in a way that could lead people to suppose that its own staff are doing the work around the world: for instance, 'Sight Savers has restored sight to four million people and treated 50 million for potentially blinding conditions.' In fact Sight Savers does not treat patients at all; it funds other organisations to do so, which seems to be a different activity, though not necessarily in any way less effective or desirable. The charity points out, correctly enough, that many other agencies make similar claims, and in this case there are also reasonably prominent references to 'working through partners'.

Even the largest recipients of Sight Saver funding are not identified in the accounts (such disclosure is called for by the Charity Commission standards for charity accounts, the SORP, as explained in the introduction to this book). However, the partners are classified into four types in the charity's 'Strategic Framework for 2001–03':

● medical non-government partners, such as hospitals;

● governments;

● community organisations;

● national non-governmental organisations and community organisations.

The main countries and regions in which such partner organisations were funded in 2000 were as follows (with the figures for 1999 in brackets):

– India £1,554,000 (£1,454,000)

– Africa (regional projects) £1,041,000 (£1,150,000)

– Pakistan £899,000 (£769,000)
– Bangladesh £647,000 (£694,000)
– Malawi £502,000

Volunteers
In an earlier survey, the charity reported that it had 120 active volunteers.

Funding, administration
The charity's income, which comes overwhelmingly from donations and legacies, has been growing fast, with the total increasing from £9.7 million in 1998 to £13.1 million in 2000. Legacies represented almost a quarter of this figure. Donations were particularly satisfactory, increasing by 15% over the previous year. The number of regular givers, all signing Gift Aid declarations to enable tax to be recovered by the charity, jumped from 22,000 to 41,000.

The associated fundraising costs in 2000 were £3.6 million, giving a ratio of 27%, or 27p for every pound donated. This was an increase from the average 23% of the three previous years. However, the charity points out (in its 'Strategic Framework', rather than in the annual report where it might be expected) that 'the policy of fundraising investment over the past three years has been strikingly successful. It is intended to continue this policy over the next three years as long as an acceptable rate of return on investment is being achieved.'

New income streams are being sought, with one enterprising approach being an emphasis on generating income overseas from English-speaking developed countries.

The 'top salary' noted above is not paid to any of the charity's management team but reflects the cost of a senior medical adviser. The charity has an unusually flexible and enterprising budgeting system.

The charity adds ...

We believe sight is a basic human right. Seven million people become blind each year, yet 80% could be prevented or cured. We will continue to support local organisations in seeking to prevent and cure blindness and improve the lives of blind and visually impaired people in developing countries.

The information assessed

The annual report and accounts (for 2000) and the annual review (for an unstated period in 2000/01) are no more than adequate. They are excellent on many aspects of the prevention and treatment of blindness, but are thin on how the charity does its work. There is a similar website and a well-produced *Sight Savers News*.

Much the best source of information about the charity's work is not its annual reports but another and impressive document, 'Strategic Framework 2001–2003'.

Contact

Grosvenor Hall
Bolnore Road
Haywards Heath
West Sussex
RH16 4BX
Tel 01444 446600
Website www.sightsavers.org
Chair Sir John Coles
Richard Porter, Executive Director

Sisters of Charity

Hospice, residential home and pastoral care

Income	£10,449,000 (2000/01)
Donated income	£5,566,000
Fundraising costs	£208,000
Statutory income	£3,185,000
Top salary	£60,000–£70,000
Paid staff	280
Volunteers	500

Aims, activities

The Sisters of Charity are a Roman Catholic order of nuns, founded in Ireland but long active in Britain too. There are three main charitable activities, in decreasing order of financial importance:

● St Joseph's Hospice, Hackney, London, described below.

● St Margaret's Home for 'elderly ladies' in Birkenhead.

● Various forms of social and pastoral work throughout the country, carried out by nuns of the order.

In financial terms the hospice is the dominant activity. Long-established, it has recently developed a Holistic Care Centre where patients can receive complementary therapies such as art therapy, aromatherapy, creative writing and reflexology.

The home for 'elderly ladies' in Birkenhead is run in collaboration with Riverside Housing Trust. The 2000/01 annual report noted a difficult year – both in the working arrangements with the housing association, and in the overall challenge for the home to survive at the level of funding available for the residents from statutory programmes.

Volunteers

The sisters, whose numbers do not appear in the annual report, are of course 'volunteers' in the widest sense. In this instance, when they are in salaried or pensionable positions, these incomes appear to be covenanted back to the charity, which then provides them with the necessities of life.

Funding, administration

Most of the charity's income relates to the hospice. It receives support from the district health authority, but this was less than the £5.6 million in voluntary income from donations and legacies in 2000/01. These are not identified separately in the accounts but it is likely, from the experience of other long-established hospice charities, that legacies are the dominant element.

The information assessed

There are good annual reports and accounts.

Contact

Caritas
55 Barrowgate
London
W4 4QT
Tel 020 8995 1963
Chair Sister Mary Benton
Sister Geraldine O'Connor, Chief Executive

Spurgeon's Child Care

England and Wales, with smaller programmes overseas

Income	£4,090,000 (2000/01)
Donated income	£774,000
Fundraising costs	£145,000
Statutory income	£1,663,000
Top salary	£50,000–£60,000
Paid staff	
Full time	87
Part time	158
Volunteers	
Operational	500

Aims, activities

The charity is 'the social work arm of the Baptist Church', a connection not noted in either the annual report, the annual review or the charity's leaflets, and not immediately apparent on the website. The charity points out that it works happily in partnership with other Christian denominations. Though financially smaller than most other charities described in this book, its number of active volunteers justifies its place here.

Originally founded as the Stockwell Orphanage, this energetic and fast-growing organisation now works through 60 or so local child welfare projects, all in England except for one in south Wales. In 2000 it was 'looking to God for guidance about expansion into Scotland'.

The projects themselves are varied and often enterprising. They include tackling youth homelessness by finding local people to open their own homes to the youngsters concerned, running playschemes at prisons during visiting hours, and organising young carers' groups. Others involve running out of school clubs, parental contact centres, bail support schemes, family centres and mentoring and other youth projects.

Projects are usually run in partnership with local churches and relevant public authorities, which may also provide some, though seldom all, of the funding. For instance, the first Welsh project (in Merthyr Tydfil) provides a bail support service to work alongside the local Youth Offending Team.

The overseas activity is extensive and diverse, though it accounted for expenditure of less than £200,000 in 1999/00. This was enough for:

- 11 centres in Romania and Moldova, employing 45 staff (all Romanian) and with 10 local volunteers;

- the support of 71 children in Uganda through a sponsorship scheme, and work at 4 other Ugandan locations;

- training and consultancy work in Latvia, Ukraine and Mexico.

This last activity continues to grow as 'individuals, small groups and teams work together with partner organisations, developing services caring for children and families'. In Latvia, for example, the charity trained trustees and staff for the local Hope for Children group working in safe houses for children in danger or distress.

Volunteers

There are over 500 active volunteers working in the local projects, many of them acting as 'independent visitors' for children in the care of local authorities. They are all trained in the same way as the paid staff and are probably recruited largely through Baptist churches with which the charity has connections.

Funding, administration

The charity raised £774,000 from donations and legacies in 1999/00. Fundraising costs were £145,000, giving a cost ratio of 19p in the pound, or 19%.

The charity adds ...

We continue to grow rapidly to serve the growing need for our services, both here and overseas. This has only been possible by working in partnership with churches, local authorities and other agencies, to maximise our income and work effectively.

The information assessed

The weak annual report is backed by a very limited annual review. The accounts are hard to relate to and need a more modern presentation. However, the website and various leaflets give good information about the individual projects.

Contact

74 Wellingborough Road
Rushden
Northants
NN10 9TY
Tel 01933 412412
Website www.spurgeonschildcare.org
Chair Richard Cottrell
David Culwick, Chief Executive

SSAFA Forces Help

The Soldiers, Sailors, Airmen and Families Association – Forces Help

Income	£31,060,000
Donated income	£3,987,000
Fundraising costs	£1,407,000
Statutory income	£13,050,000
Top salary	c. £70,000
Paid staff	
Full time	471
Part time	60
Volunteers	7,500

Aims, activities

The charity assists all serving and ex-service people, as well as their families and dependants, who are in need, suffering or distress. Formerly the Soldiers', Sailors' and Airmen's Family Association, the charity amalgamated with the Forces Help Society in 1997. The combined charity has two main activities, which are in some ways quite different though both are aimed at supporting serving and ex-service people and their families – there being about 220,000 of the former and 13 million of the latter. Though the armed forces are being cut back, the charity says that the emphasis of its work remains equally balanced between the serving and the ex-service communities.

First, the charity operates what is almost certainly the UK's most extensive volunteer-based community welfare service for serving and former personnel alike, although the latter naturally predominate. This work accounted for expenditure of £1.4 million of the charity's funds in the year 2000, while caseworkers distributed a further £12 million in support of individual or family need that was contributed by other service funds or charities – typically the charitable funds of the regiment or unit with which particular beneficiaries are connected.

Secondly, the charity provides, under contract and at a cost of £8.7 million from public funds, a professional primary healthcare service to the families of servicemen and women stationed overseas. It also provides a social work service for the RAF communities in the UK and, separately, for all service personnel and families based in Northern Ireland.

The SSAFA welfare service is remarkable. It has 7,500 trained volunteers, organised through an extensive branch system. Oddly, what are called community volunteers are drawn from serving men and women and their families and work at service establishments at home and overseas. Those working with ex-service people and their families are called branch volunteers.

At the core of the charity's work are the local branch caseworkers, to whom individuals in need are referred. These caseworkers have the great advantage of ready access to the multitude of smaller service charities. Almost every unit or former unit has its own charitable funds, or is represented by a larger charity. The SSAFA caseworkers can call on these funds, in addition to others, for help in any individual case, and indeed they did so to the extent of almost £12 million in the year 2000.

The recruitment and training of these branch volunteers, by no means all of them ex-service personnel themselves, forms one of the charity's major tasks, in which it has been helped by a big grant from the National Lottery

Charities Board (now the Community Fund).

The charity also runs one residential home (there are many such homes for ex-service people run by other charities), 36 bungalows for disabled but self-supporting ex-service people and their families, and three Stepping Stone Homes for estranged wives of servicemen who can stay for up to three months and are given assistance in finding permanent accommodation and employment.

In August 2000 the charity signed a joint 'vision statement' with the *Royal British Legion*, a charity with an overlapping remit, agreeing to 'work more closely together to achieve amalgamation in due course'. The charities already use a common application form for those seeking financial assistance. A trial in Buckinghamshire to improve coordination and cooperation between the caseworkers of both charities has been extended to a further six counties. 'The charity recognises that there is a need for rationalisation in the ex-service charity sector, but has no detailed prescription for this process.'

Volunteers

This must be one of the biggest voluntary welfare organisations in the country. Great efforts have been made by the charity to support the work of its volunteers, for example by giving them access to a computerised welfare benefits package and also a specially written branch management system.

There are also well-thought-out materials on what the charity can and cannot do for those in need, and a Volunteer Policy setting out what volunteers can expect from the charity, and vice versa. The role of the branch volunteer is described as follows:

'The majority of their work concerns casework with ex-service people and their families, which may involve getting financial grants or simply giving friendly support, advice and help on a wide variety of issues. But they also handle casework for those still serving, often with requests for compassionate leave, postings, discharge or with requests for news of relatives at home. All volunteers are given training to support their role.'

The charity notes that 'volunteers join us from all walks of life and are of all ages. Many do not have a specific service background, many do. The reason they join us is that they want to use their skills to help people in their local community.'

Funding, administration

The total income of the charity in 2000 included £12 million of transfer payments from regimental funds and other charities to be spent in full on the needs of individual welfare clients.

Apart from the £8.7 million government payment for its professional healthcare services services, the charity also receives a government grant (£4.2 million in 2000) for its social services programme for serving personnel.

Otherwise SSAFA is mainly reliant on its own income from donations and legacies, amounting to £2.8 million and £1.2 million, respectively, in 2000, and on block grants from other service charities (£521,000). This total of £4.5 million, plus the £12 million contribution of other charities to be passed on to individual clients in need, was achieved at a fundraising cost of £1.4 million, or a very low 8p in the pound. If the transfers and grants from other charities (which have already incurred their own fundraising costs) are omitted from the voluntary income, the cost of fundraising for donations and legacies direct to SSAFA rises to a high 35p in the pound.

Many ex-service charities seem to be struggling to raise the money they require at a reasonable cost; the needs of their clients are still increasing as the large group of ex-service people from the Second World War enters old age, and these needs are unlikely to peak for another decade. Meanwhile the attention of the charitably minded public is at risk of moving on to other, more recent, issues.

In this case, the proposed amalgamation with the Royal British Legion will be interesting. The Legion has a massively greater voluntary income (achieved at no more than an average cost), largely through its rejuvenated Poppy Day 'brand', and it has committed itself to a big further increase in this income.

The charity adds ...
SSAFA Forces Help is proud to be one of the five charities officially nominated to receive donations on the occasion of the Queen's Jubilee.

The information assessed
The good annual report and accounts are backed by a range of other publications, including a good leaflet for potential volunteers. There is a new and effective website.

Contact
19 Queen Elizabeth Street
London
SE1 2LP
Tel 020 7403 8783
Website www.ssafa.org.uk
Chair Lieutenant-General Sir Robin Ross
Major-General Peter Sheppard, Controller

Stroke Association
England and Wales

Income	£12,266,000 (2000/01)
Donated income	£8,462,000
Fundraising costs	£1,345,000
Statutory income	£3,052,000
Top salary	£50,000 £60,000
Paid staff	322
Volunteers	4,000

Aims, activities
A stroke happens when the blood supply to the brain is disrupted, most commonly when a blood clot blocks an artery carrying blood to the brain. Some strokes are fatal, while others cause permanent or temporary disabilities. Around a third of people who have a stroke die within a year, a third are left with serious disabilities and the remainder make a good recovery.

Each year over 100,000 people in England and Wales have their first stroke. It is the third most common cause of death, after heart disease and cancer, and is the largest single cause of severe disability in England and Wales, with over 300,000 people being affected at any one time.

This charity aims to reduce the effect of strokes on patients, their families and others. The amounts spent in 2000/01 to achieve this were categorised under the following headings.

- Community services contracts, £3.5 million – these included contracts with either the NHS or with social services departments for 106 dysphasia support groups (which each year help around 8,000 people with communications difficulties), and for 65 family support services. The notes to the accounts say that it has been the charity's practice to support the cost of these contracts from its own income (no doubt from funds under the next heading below), but that it is now negotiating to change these contracts so that these subsidies are ended. Unfortunately some of the authorities concerned may not play ball, so difficult decisions may have to be taken.

- Community services support, £3.2 million – apart from subsidising the contracts above, another identifiable activity under this heading is the Stroke Information Service. During the year there were nearly 100 calls each working day, 70% more than in the previous year. This heading also covers support for volunteers, whose activities are described below.

- Research and development, £2.1 million – research grants are assessed by a research and development committee. Recent awards have covered issues such as prevention, ethnic factors, psychology and service provision in primary care. The charity also supports a chair in stroke medicine, as well as bursaries and fellowships.

- Information and awareness, £1.5 million – work which has two

aspects. The first is the establishment of an education, training and information service organiser in each of 16 regions. These serve both members of the public seeking information and also professionals concerned with the care of those who have had strokes. Not under this heading in the annual review, but perhaps covered by this expenditure, are PR and campaigning activities, such as Stroke Awareness Week.

- Welfare and special grants, £160,000 – these are one-off payments for people with exceptional financial needs, such as those having difficulty in paying fuel bills, or in getting the aids needed to cope with the problems faced by stroke patients.

There are two further major headings in the annual review which do not appear in the expenditure breakdown in the accounts:

- Making a difference at home – there is a reference here to Family Support Organisers. These only exist where there is an appropriate NHS or social services contract. The charity points out, in this context, that 'if there is no contract, there is no service'. Expenditure in this category comes under 'Community services contracts' above.

- Education and training – this is as prominent in the annual review as the other headings above, but it does not have any separately identifiable expenditure in the accounts; the amount spent appears as part of 'Community services support'. The work included training over 42 of the charity's staff to teach other professional carers, as well as 15 training courses for nursing home professionals.

There are 400 affiliated but independent stroke clubs, wholly voluntary, which offer mutual support to sufferers and their families and carers. 'Different clubs have different activities – some offer therapy, others are just social, but all are friendly and helpful.'

In 2000/01 there was a restructuring of the charity's 'Community Services Management and Information Service', a term covering a number of the activities described above. This meant the loss of Stroke Association presence in some localities, and some difficult staff changes, but was necessary 'as we have to bring our expenditure more closely in line with our income'. The redundancy and reorganisation costs were £335,000.

Volunteers

'The association benefits from donated time by in excess of 4,000 volunteers, the majority of whom devote their time to helping those affected by stroke.' This is in addition to the local affiliated but independent stroke clubs described above.

The charity relies on volunteers for its dysphasia service, over 3,000 of them – 'ordinary people with basic training who have been chosen for their intelligence, sympathy, and desire to help'. Volunteers mostly work with patients in weekly group meetings where they will meet people with similar problems and work together on communication. They also go into stroke survivors' homes to work with them on a one-to-one basis towards better communications.

In a new development in 2000/01 volunteer-staffed information points were established in five hospital out-patient departments.

To find out more about helping out, call 0845 30 33 100 (local rate).

Funding, administration

The charity has been running deficits and is taking action to reduce them, as mentioned above. Its income in 2000/01 was £12.2 million, up by 8% over the previous year mainly because of increased legacy income.

Voluntary receipts totalled £8.5 million, made up of donations and appeals (£3.4 million) and legacies (£5 million). This was achieved at a fundraising cost of £1.3 million, giving a cost ratio of 16p in the pound, or 16%. This was lower than the 20% average of the three years to 1999.

The accounts have an unusual and admirable breakdown of the fundraising income, with the main headings as follows:

- regional fundraising £777,000;
- community services misc. income £577,000;
- trusts and companies £472,000;
- house to house collections £446,000;
- direct mail £307,000;
- in memoriam £242,000;
- general £206,000;
- events £148,000;
- national raffle £109,000.

The charity adds ...

Our work is very wide and varied and has to be as there is little other support for those affected by strokes. 2002 promises to be even busier with materials for ethnic groups on line and the development of support for children affected by strokes.

The information assessed

The annual report and accounts and the annual review are weak in that, compared with those of other similar charities, they do not clearly explain how the association is organised and how it allocates its money. The annual report is very short in its description of the activities, while the review does not use the same headings that are found in the accounts. The website is also weak in these respects, but admirably full on other aspects.

Contact

Stroke House
123 Whitecross Street
London
EC1Y 8JJ
Tel 020 7566 0300
Website www.stroke.org.uk
Chair Lord Skelmersdale
Margaret Goose, Chief Executive

Sue Ryder Care

Care for people with illnesses or disabilities

Income	£26,649,000 (2000)
Donated income	£9,095,000
Fundraising costs	£1,058,000
Statutory income	£13,802,000
Top salary	£50,000–£60,000
Paid staff	1,857

Aims, activities

This charity, now 're-branded' from the former the Sue Ryder Foundation, operates 20 care centres in the UK (previously known as nursing homes) for people with generally severe disabilities, as well as day centres and mobile clinics, and makes grants to support similar work conducted by independent Sue Ryder charities overseas.

The present care centres are mostly located in large former country houses in England and Scotland, some of them of great age and beauty. The homes deliver 'individual, holistic health and social care'. 'Our daily experience shows only too clearly that gaps exist in the health service and that there is an enormous need for the kind of care we provide. These shortfalls ... are what inspired Sue Ryder to found our charity in 1953.'

Lady Ryder (whose husband founded the *Leonard Cheshire Foundation*) died in 2000. Unfortunately, she apparently found it hard to hand on control of the charity towards the end of her life, and some estrangement was reported. However, her remarkable legacy can now be seen in the round.

The homes each have their own specialisms, with neurological care and palliative care for those with terminal illnesses being the most common. 'The people we care for include those with neurological conditions such as Parkinson's disease, Huntingdon's disease, Motor Neurone disease, Multiple Sclerosis and brain injuries as well as Cerebral Palsy, cancer and many other conditions.'

With its impressive re-branding, the charity also says it is undertaking substantial development and change, and the annual report notes that the trustees have made a number of key decisions. Two of these are described in the annual report for 2000 (called the 'Chairman's Statement'). First, 'we have decided to focus our activities in areas of particular need where we have most experience and expertise', for example, neurological and palliative care. Secondly, 'we have decided that we will not deliver care from historic buildings where they compromise care standards or cannot be economically converted for use'. As an example of this, a new purpose-built home is being constructed in Aberdeen.

Overseas, the charity supported, to the extent of £2.2 million in 2000, Sue Ryder charities in Poland, Macedonia, Albania, the Czech Republic, Italy, Malawi and Tanzania.

The charity has been having difficulty in obtaining adequate statutory support for its two homes in Scotland, and in 2001 announced that they were to be closed. However, in November 2001 a reprieve was announced for Marchmont (in the Borders), though not for Binny Lodge (in West Lothian). The charity had said that it had expected a £500,000 a year loss on Marchmont.

The impression was received of a charity that is rapidly changing and developing. After the departure of the former chief executive, one of the trustees became acting chief executive until Mr Iain Henderson took up his present post in autumn 2001.

Volunteers

There are many Sue Ryder Support Groups raising funds for the charity, and volunteers donate goods and work in the charity's shops, which have been undergoing an impressive makeover under the charity's new name. The charity also works 'with local people to provide in-patient care, day care, home care, respite care and other services in the community'.

Funding, administration

'All of our care centres receive some statutory funding from health authorities and social services. However, this is not enough to run a care centre and the shortfall (which can be as much as 60% of the total) is met by legacies, donations, fundraising and income from our shops.'

The accounts for 2000 do not identify the extent of this issue, as 'Receipts for patients' and 'Residential maintenance' come under a single heading, without separately identifying monies received from statutory sources. However, the £13.8 million total represented the largest source of income. The shops contributed an impressive £2.3 million, but the other main source of income comprised donations (£3.3 million) and legacies (£5.8 million).

This £9.1 million in voluntary income was achieved at a fundraising cost of £1.1 million, a ratio of a low 12p in the pound, or 12%. Despite being a low figure, this £1.1 million in costs represented a huge jump from the £0.3 million of the previous year. The annual report notes: 'we have commenced a long term plan to significantly increase our income'. Benefits from this investment were not yet apparent in the year, when donations actually showed a slight reduction, compensated for by a rise in legacy income (which cannot have been the result of any short-term measures).

The charity adds ...

We know from our experiences, both in the UK and abroad, that many people are in great need of the care we offer. With the help of our many committed supporters and loyal volunteers, we aim to expand our specialist palliative and neurological care services.

The information assessed

The adequate annual report and accounts (called the 'Financial Statements') are backed by impressive printed materials. The website, though simple, is also unusually stylish.

Contact

Sue Ryder Care Central Office
2nd Floor
114–118 Southampton Row
London
WC1B 5AA
Tel 020 7400 0440
Website www.suerydercare.org
Chair Mrs J R Nicholson
Iain Henderson, Chief Executive

Sustrans

Sustainable transport

Income	£21,010,000 (2000/01)
Donated income	£2,957,000
Fundraising costs	£413,000
Statutory income	£16,000,000
Top salary	less than £50,000
Paid staff	107
Volunteers	1,500

Aims, activities

'Sustrans – it stands for sustainable transport – is a charity working on practical projects to encourage people to walk and cycle more, so as to help reduce motor traffic and its adverse effects.'

Sustrans' flagship project, the National Cycle Network, was opened in June 2001 with 5,000 miles of continuous traffic-free routes and traffic-calmed and minor roads, running right through urban centres and reaching all parts of the UK. This is the first stage of a larger network. It is 'a Millennium Commission project supported by £43.5m of National Lottery funds. It involves over 400 local authorities, as well as businesses, landowners, environmental bodies and others.

'The Sustrans Safe Routes to Schools project enables and encourages children to cycle and walk to school by improving street design, calming traffic, creating traffic-free spaces and linking with the National Cycle Network.'

This remarkable charity has succeeded in tapping into massive public support and into large sources of public funding, especially various distributors of Lottery grants and the grants available through the new landfill tax.

Volunteers

'Sustrans welcomes help from volunteers – their assistance is crucial in promoting and maintaining the National Cycle Network. There are a variety of ways to get involved, including:

- Spreading the word! Passing out literature to family and friends about the work that Sustrans is doing, distributing supporter recruitment leaflets in your local shops and generally raising public awareness.

- Lending a helping hand in the office: if there is a Sustrans office near you.'

There are plenty of other volunteer opportunities, including the Volunteer Ranger programme, taking photographs, surveying bridges and doing traffic counts. The national volunteer programme coordinator can be contacted on 0117 929 0888.

Funding, administration

The charity's accounts have been dominated by massive income from the Millennium Commission for the National Cycle Network, but much of this has simply been passed on to the local authorities or whatever other bodies have been actually constructing the routes. There are similar sources of funding for the growing Safe Routes to Schools programme. The charity earns its own living largely by charging others for its expertise – it is, at heart, a transport engineering outfit – and this raised £3.9 million in 2000/01. This was supplemented by £3 million in voluntary income, achieved at a fundraising cost of £413,000, or a low 14p in the pound.

The information assessed

The short and simple, but good, annual report and accounts are supplemented by excellent information sheets and newsletters, and a fine website. This may, by the time this book is published, have a full mapping service for all of the National Cycle Network.

Contact

35 King Street
Bristol
BS1 4DZ
Tel 0117 926 8893
Website www.sustrans.org.uk
Chair R Farrant
John Grimshaw, Director

Tate
The Tate Galleries

Income	£71,681,000 (1999/00)
Donated income	£23,112,000
Fundraising costs	£1,634,000
Statutory income	£19,727,000
Top salary	£170,000–£180,000
Paid staff	665

Aims, activities

This is a charity, though one exempt from registration at the Charity Commission. It is also a non-departmental public body, most of whose trustees are appointed by the prime minister. Tate is now a group of four galleries: Tate Britain and Tate Modern in London, Tate Liverpool, and Tate St Ives in Cornwall.

The annual report notes that 2.5 million people visited the galleries during 1999/00.

Funded basically by a grant in aid from the government, Tate also enjoys considerable income from public donations. The voluntary income total of £23.1 million in 1999/00 included £7.6 million in the form of works of art, at their commercial valuation. If any of the income was in the form of legacies, this is not recorded. This voluntary income was achieved at a fundraising cost of £1.6 million, giving a very low cost ratio of 7p in the pound.

The information assessed

The 'Report' is not the annual report required by law, but a separate document. Once the full annual report had been obtained, however, and with a further volume of 'Facts', the various documents gave an excellent account of the work of the galleries. The website is splendid.

Contact

Millbank
London
SW1P 4RG
Tel 020 7887 8000
Chair David Verey
Nicholas Serota, Chief Executive

Tearfund
Overseas development

Income	£32,632,000 (2000/01)
Donated income	£28,464,000
Fundraising costs	£2,568,000
Statutory income	£1,758,000
Top salary	£50,000–£60,000
Paid staff	315
Volunteers	2,800

Aims, activities

This is a major disaster relief and development charity, supporting over 500 projects in nearly 100 countries and working in the following areas of development:

- healthcare;
- urban renewal;
- conflict and justice;
- environment and agriculture;
- education and training.

The full nature of the charity's work was not apparent at first. The purposes and activities described in its annual report and its leaflet 'Mission, Beliefs, Values, Strategy' appeared to be mainly those of a Christian missionary organisation.

Some of the Christian charities described in this book minimise the religious underpinnings of their work and instead stress the practical benefits they bring to those in need or distress. Tearfund is more robust. Its 'principal activity' is 'to serve Jesus Christ by enabling those who share evangelical Christian beliefs to bring good news to the poor'. It does this by 'proclaiming and demonstrating the gospel ... through the support of Christian relief and development'.

The bringing of relief and support is described as follows: 'The causes of poverty ... are complex, but we believe they stem from broken relationships. The goal of Christian development is restored relations with the Creator, with others in the community and with the environment.' The charity's 'basis of faith', that of the Evangelical Alliance which founded the charity, includes acceptance of 'the divine inspiration of the holy scripture and its consequent entire trustworthiness and supreme authority in all matters of faith and conduct', of 'the universal sinfulness and guilt of fallen man, making him subject to God's wrath and condemnation', and of 'the expectation of the personal, visible return of the Lord Jesus Christ, in power and glory'.

The charity enables churches in the UK and Ireland to respond to the needs of the poor around the world and it works through a worldwide network of evangelical Christian partners. It is committed to building the capacity of churches to work with the poor.

Tearfund is primarily a grant-making body, so it is unfortunate that the accounts do not disclose the organisations that are the main beneficiaries of its grants, in the way called for by the Charity Commission accounting standards (the SORP). However, on further request the charity provided a list of its 20 largest grants, covering a third of its grantmaking. The largest recipient was the Kale Heywet Church in Africa, three branches of which received a total of over £1 million, most of which went to the church's Ethiopian operation. The next two largest beneficiaries were both in India, the Evangelical Fellowship of India Commission on Relief and the Discipleship Centre in Delhi.

The main expenditure heads in 2000/01 were (with 1999/000 figures in brackets):

- grants for one to three years £18.1 million (£17 million);
- disaster response £2.3 million (£5.7 million);
- training and technical advice £1.9 million (£1.6 million);
- international staff to work with the partner £0.5 million (£0.5 million).

There is also substantial advocacy work, both in northern countries and in support of partner organisations overseas.

Tearfund has a long-standing relationship with the US-based charity Compassion, which runs a worldwide child sponsorship programme. In 1999 it was decided that Tearfund would not recruit any new supporters to the sponsorship programme and that this would be carried out by Compassion UK. About 20,000 children are sponsored through Tearfund and in 2000/01 £3.9 million was transferred to Compassion for the support of these children (Compassion UK is still too small a charity to be featured in this book in its own right).

Tearfund works with 410 partners in 91 countries. At a regional level, expenditure was as follows:

- Eastern and Southern Africa £5.1 million (£2.6 million);
- Asia £3.3 million (£2.9 million);

- Latin America/Caribbean £2.3 million (£2.6 million);
- West and Central Africa £1.8 million (£1.8 million);
- Mediterranean and Central Asia £1.7 million (£2.5 million).

Country by country, many of the funding levels were modest. The largest recipients were:

- India £1.8 million (£1.3 million);
- Ethiopia £1.2 million (£0.4 million);
- Mozambique £1 million (£0.3 million).

However, total expenditures in many countries were less than £50,000, such as:

- Georgia £40,000;
- Chile £34,000;
- Iraq £31,000;
- Vietnam £24,000;
- Somalia £10,000.

The Disaster Response Team provides operational emergency relief and rehabilitation. It has been involved in response to disasters in conflict-related situations such as Sierra Leone, Afghanistan and Burundi, in addition to work after earthquakes in India and El Salvador. Some of this work is funded by the Disasters Emergency Committee's appeals.

Tearcraft is the trading arm of Tearfund. Working with over 30 producer groups in 15 countries, Tearcraft markets a range of fairly traded craft goods in the UK and Ireland.

Volunteers

'Volunteers are at the heart of of Tearfund's work.' They are involved in representation, campaigning and selling fairly traded goods as well as in fundraising.

Funding, administration

Unlike many overseas aid charities, Tearfund is almost overwhelmingly reliant on voluntary contributions in the form of donations and, to very much smaller extent, legacies, with income from governments being relatively low, led by £854,000 from the Department for International Development.

In 2000/01, 72% of total income came from individuals and families and 12% from churches giving collectively. The donations include a high proportion of regular givers so the charity was able to reclaim £2.6 million in tax through covenants and the newer Gift Aid schemes, a level not usually achievable except from regular supporters.

The steady flow of voluntary income is inflated in some years by emergency appeals. In 2000/01 £4.9 million was received for appeals and emergencies, while in the previous year the corresponding figure was £9.7 million.

Fundraising costs of £2.6 million represented a very low 9p in the pound, or 9% of voluntary income, though in the previous year they had been an even more remarkable 7%. This cost ratio has been less than 10% for each of the last four years.

The information assessed

The website is a better source of information about how the charity works than the only adequate annual report and accounts and annual review.

Contact
100 Church Road
Teddington
Middlesex
TW11 8QE
Tel 020 8977 9144
Website www.tearfund.org
Chair David White
Doug Balfour, General Director

Tenovus

Cancer research and information, especially in Wales

Income	£4,367,042 (1999/00)
Donated income	£2,345,000
Fundraising costs	£540,000
Statutory income	£0
Top salary	less than £40,000
Paid staff	56
Volunteers	1,000

Aims, activities

Established in 1943 by 10 Cardiff businessmen (the original 'ten of us'), the charity concentrates on cancer research (especially into breast and prostate cancers, lymphomas and leukaemias) and the alleviation of the effects of the disease. The core of its work lies in grants given to specific research projects at Cardiff University, the University of Kent, Royal Bournemouth Hospital and the University of Southampton. Smaller grants are also given to other scientific and educational projects. It is one of the most important charities that is based in Wales.

The charity has pledged £5 million over a seven-year period (starting in 1999/00) to Tenovus Cancer Research Laboratories, based at Cardiff University. This centre has helped to develop a range of drugs, including

Tamoxifen, which is used in the treatment of breast cancer. At the University of Wales, Cardiff, Tenovus-funded researchers work in the field of genetics and cancer, which includes a project aimed at identifying genes involved in the development of bowel cancer.

Research teams in Southampton and Bournemouth are working on anti-cancer 'vaccines' and antibodies, particularly relating to lymphomas and leukaemias, while Tenovus researchers in Liverpool are examining ways of preventing bowel disease through dietary methods.

Regarding the charity's involvement in developing new drug and vaccine treatments, it would be interesting to know the commercial basis of their licensing and introduction.

Other activities include participation in the Pink Ribbon campaign, run worldwide each October by several charities to promote awareness of breast cancer. This was complemented in April 1999 by the introduction of the Purple Ribbon, designed to raise cancer awareness among men. *The Rough Guide to Cancer*, a series of videos aimed at teenagers, was launched in July 1999 with the help of a grant from the National Lottery Charities Fund (since renamed the Community Fund) and distributed free of charge to every secondary school and youth club in Wales.

A sister charity, the Tenovus Cancer Information Centre, employing 20 nurses, counsellors and social workers, provides a telephone helpline service, counselling and a range of information services for cancer sufferers and their families and friends.

Volunteers

The charity has a network of 40 voluntary fundraising groups known as the Friends of Tenovus. Most of these are based in Wales, although there are also groups in Bournemouth and Hampshire. In addition, over 1,000 volunteers work in Tenovus charity shops (whose number increased from 48 to 51 in 1999/00), which stretch from Anglesey to the south coast of England.

Funding, administration

In 1999/00 the charity's total income was £4.4 million (£5.3 million in 1998/99), of which £2.3 million (£3.6 million) was voluntary income, as follows:

- legacies £1.2 million (£2.4 million);
- 'Alpha Omega (Cancer League)' – which seems to be a voluntary arm – £340,000 (£360,000);
- National Lottery Charities Board £57,000 (£152,000);
- other donations and gifts £800,000 (£790,000).

The very high legacy income for 1998/99 included a single bequest of £1.3 million.

During the year another £316,000 net was contributed by the charity shops.

Fundraising costs of £540,000 represented 23p for every pound of voluntary income, or 23%, following an exceptionally low 13% in 1998/99. The average for the three years to 1999 was 17%.

The charity notes that during the year £8,000 was paid for legal services provided by a company where one of its trustees is a partner and another is a consultant. There is a discussion of the issue of payments to trustees in the Introduction to this book (page 22).

The information assessed

The annual report and financial statements are excellent; there is a separate 'Annual Report and Summarised Accounts'. The website is comprehensive.

Contact

43 The Parade
Cardiff
CF24 3AB
Tel 029 2048 2000
Website www.tenovus.com
Chair Guy Clarke
D Marc Phillips, Chief Executive

Terrence Higgins Trust

HIV/AIDS

Income	£11,129,000 (2000/01)
Donated income	£2,909,000
Fundraising costs	£1,049,000
Statutory income	£5,119,000
Top salary	£50,000–£60,000
Paid staff	217
Volunteers	
Operational	595
Fundraising	5

Aims, activities

This is Britain's largest HIV/AIDS charity. 'We aim to reduce the spread of HIV and promote good sexual health. We provide services to improve the health and quality of life of those affected by HIV, and campaign for greater understanding of the personal, social and medical impact of HIV and AIDS.'

The services are largely delivered under contract to health and local authorities (£2.5 million in 2000/01), or are funded by a grant from the Department of Health (£1.3 million). For example, the charity has a contract to supply benefits advice, legal advice, counselling and emotional support, and transport and services coordination for people with HIV/AIDS in south London.

In 2000 the charity merged with London Lighthouse and other HIV charities around the UK. This has made possible savings of over £1 million.

Volunteers

The 2000/01 annual report of the Terrence Higgins Trust notes that over 600 volunteers support its work in a number of ways. 'Volunteers continue to provide many valuable hours of service and are the backbone of many services which otherwise could not exist.

'All volunteers receive full training and ongoing support, starting with an orientation session to help you find out more about the organisation and the range of different volunteering opportunities open to you'.

Funding, administration

Apart from the statutory funding mentioned above, the charity received £2.9 million in donations in 2000/01. Of this, £1.9 million came as direct gifts from the public and from money raised at benefits and events; the rest came from charitable trusts and companies, and from legacies. This voluntary income was achieved at a fundraising cost of £1 million, giving a cost ratio of a high 36p in the pound. However, this was a substantial reduction from the 42p in the pound average of the previous three years, and was achieved by seeing the level of donations increase while the fundraising spend remained much the same.

The financial position of the charity will be eased by the recent mergers, which are expected to lead to considerable savings through shared overhead costs.

The charity adds ...

Fundraising is difficult – 86% of people recently surveyed said that they would not give to HIV – so we are delighted that voluntary income had risen by £779,000 (37%) without increasing costs. More people are living with HIV in the UK each year (50% increase expected in the next five years), so voluntary income is more important than ever.

The information assessed

The good annual report and accounts is backed by a no-holds-barred website.

Contact

52–54 Grays Inn Road
London
WC1X 8JU
Tel 020 7831 0330
Website www.tht.org.uk
Chair Professor Ian Weller
Nick Partridge, Chief Executive

Tools for Self Reliance (TFSR)

Overseas development

Income	£1,132,000 (1999/00)
Donated income	£423,000
Fundraising costs	£31,000
Statutory income	£0
Top salary	£25,000
Volunteers	700

Aims, activities

'Tools for Self Reliance works with local organisations in six African countries. We provide tools and skills training to help artisans and craftworkers.' The charity was inspired by the ideas of the late Julius Nyerere (former president of Tanzania), and the founding group included the Reverend Trevor Huddleston (former president of the Anti-Apartheid Movement). Though financially modest compared with other charities listed in this book, TFSR qualifies for an entry because it has many active volunteers, the value of whose time (though real) does not appear in the accounts.

The work of the charity is best described in text from its website:

'Have you ever wanted to bang a nail and didn't have a hammer? What did you do? Maybe you looked in the garden shed or popped down to the DIY. If you live in the countryside in Africa, you might have to think of something else. There's nothing in the garden shed except a bush knife and a hoe. The market might be a day's walk away and a hammer costs two weeks' wages.

'Tools for Self Reliance is doing something about this. Today, hundreds of TFSR volunteers in Britain collect, refurbish, and ship tools and sewing machines to six countries in Africa. Each kit contains the tools needed to do a job – carpentry, blacksmithing, building, or sewing. We work with honest, effective local organisations with roots in some of the poorest communities in Africa.

'Each kit of tools makes a real difference to the people using them. However, tools are needed in their millions, so TFSR also supports the maker of tools – Africa's blacksmiths. With a few thousand tools sent from Britain they have already made well over a million items, now in daily use in their communities.

'We have nine staff and four full time volunteers at the Netley Marsh Workshops near Southampton. About 700 volunteers in the UK collect, refurbish, and pack tools and sewing machines. There are nearly 70 groups refurbishing tools and 100 tool collection points, from the Orkneys to the Channel Islands.

'Tools most requested

- Woodworking
- Blacksmithing
- Building and plumbing
- Shoemaking and leather working
- Car and bicycle repairing
- Metal working and tinsmithing

'We need quality not quantity. We refurbish top quality second hand tools to a first class standard. There's no DIY store down the road for our partners to replace a broken tool. Shipping costs are the same for good tools or bad tools so we only send the best.

'"Aid must reach the people ... the easiest way to reach them is with tools. Tractors rust away but not the hammer in the hand of the person who uses it." Julius Nyerere.'

Volunteers

The whole organisation is based on voluntary activity, with the minimum number of paid staff to organise their efforts.

Funding, administration

Much of the income shown above is represented by gifts of refurbished tools. Cash income in 1999/00 was just £474,000, of which voluntary donations and grants constituted £423,000. Fundraising costs of £31,000 were a very low 7% of this, or just 2% if the value of donations in kind is included.

The charity adds ...

We work in partnership with experienced African organisations with strong grassroots links. TFSR responds to their requests to provide the tools they need for their poverty fighting projects. They provide the business and technical training that the artisans need to be better able to develop their communities.

The information assessed

The good annual report and accounts are backed by an excellent website, from which much of the information here is taken.

Contact

Netley Marsh
Southampton
SO40 7GY
Tel 023 8086 9697
Website www.tfsr.org.uk
Chair Dave Harries
Jan Kidd, Chief Executive

Traidcraft Exchange
Reducing poverty through trade

Income	£2,187,000 (2000/01)
Donated income	£945,000
Fundraising costs	£287,000
Statutory income	£1,002,000
Top salary	less than £40,000
Paid staff	39
Volunteers	4,300

Aims, activities

The Traidcraft movement has a commercial side, Traidcraft plc, and an associated charity, Traidcraft Exchange. Between them, they work to enable producers in the 'third world' to participate in world trade on a fair basis. Despite its modest income,

Traidcraft's place in this book is earned by its resources in the form of time given through its extensive network of volunteers.

Traidcraft plc imports and sells products, from food to footballs, to wholesalers, retailers and the public in the UK, to the value of over £8 million in 2000/01. It has done so at a modest profit for each of the last four years.

Traidcraft Exchange (the charity whose financial figures appear above) seeks to promote fair trade generally through three programmes:

- Trade facilitation – identifying and seeking to remove barriers to fair trade.

- 'Partner' programme – identifying and supporting organisations in developing countries that are working to develop fair trade locally.

- Ethical business promotion – for example, by persuading the pensions industry to adopt actively socially responsible investment practices.

Volunteers

Much of the active promotion of fair trade is carried out by the more than 4,000 'Fair Traders'. They sell Traidcraft goods to family and friends, raising awareness about fair trade. Many sell by giving out catalogues and collecting orders. Others sell from a stall at regular or special events or by having parties and coffee mornings.

They buy the goods at a small discount (10% to 15%), so in principle this could be an income-generating activity, but in practice it seems clear that this network puts a great deal more into the movement than could possibly be taken out, and the Fair Traders form the basic means for spreading the movement's message.

Funding, administration

The business turned over £8.4 million in 2000/01, and made a profit of £72,000, both figures being well up on the previous year.

The charity, which cannot use its funds to subsidise the business, had an income of £2.2 million, of which £945,000 was in the form of donations from individuals, trusts and companies. This was achieved at a fundraising cost of £287,000, giving a cost ratio of 30p in the pound.

The charity adds ...

Traidcraft has a single mission – to fight poverty through trade. Help us build on 21 years of achievement and success. To find out more go to www.traidcraft.co.uk

The information assessed

The good annual report and accounts and annual review are backed by an exemplary set of social accounts and a simple website.

Contact

Kingsway
Gateshead
NE11 0NE
Tel 0191 491 0591
Website www.traidcraft.co.uk
Chair David Nussbaum
Paul Chandler, Chief Executive

UNICEF UK
United Nations Children's Fund

Income	£27,789,000 (2000)
Donated income	£19,329,000
Fundraising costs	£4,564,000
Statutory income	£6,228,000
Top salary	£50,000–£60,000
Paid staff	92
Volunteers	100

Aims, activities

UNICEF UK (the United Nations Children's Fund) is a UK charity raising money for UNICEF programmes worldwide. UNICEF is not part of the United Nations funding system, which receives dues as of right from UN member countries. All support for this charity, whether from governments or individuals, is voluntary.

UNICEF UK both chooses particular UNICEF programmes to support and also contributes money for UNICEF to use at its own discretion. Most of the money comes from individual supporters, but there is a substantial contribution from the Department for International Development (which also gives direct support, on a far larger scale, to UNICEF internationally). The charity also raises awareness in the UK of UNICEF's work and promotes children's rights issues.

UNICEF programmes operate in 161 countries worldwide in fields such as health, emergency relief, HIV/AIDS prevention, education and child protection. The programmes cover almost every kind of development activity. At the top level, UNICEF works directly with governments on national programmes such as immunisation (where it might, for example, provide the vaccines for delivery by the country's health services), but it also funds very small-scale activities. For instance, in Cambodia UNICEF funds a village-based programme combining health, nutrition, sanitation, women's literacy and early childhood care, a project which 'had reduced malnutrition among women and children under five by 10% and more'.

There are also direct services provided by UNICEF staff on the ground, most commonly in emergency or disaster situations where there may no local institutions capable of doing the work.

Funds can be allocated from the UK in two main ways. First, money is given to UNICEF International for activities both large and small in scale within its core campaign-based programmes, such as immunisation or water and sanitation. In 2001 a major example was the millennium Growing up Alone campaign, focusing on the more than 100 million children worldwide who are without the care and protection of a family or even of the state in which they live. The kinds of issues addressed, in just one part of the programme, are described as follows:

'UNICEF UK is campaigning to protect children from conflict. Children are massively affected by conflict on several accounts. They are:

- killed or injured by small portable weapons
- fighting on the front line as child soldiers
- forced to flee their homes, either to another part of their country or to leave their homeland all together.'

Such general programmes, and the local projects within them, accounted for £4.9 million spent by the UK

charity in 2000, down from
£5.3 million in the previous year.

Secondly, UNICEF UK supports its
own choice of specific UNICEF
country programmes, or projects
within countries, to the tune of
£15 million in 2000. The charity sets
its own priorities, taking the
organisation's policies as a whole into
account, and then discusses with
UNICEF offices in the programme
countries what activities they would
like to put forward for support.

In the UK, UNICEF is also active in
raising awareness of issues of
children's rights, much helped by the
forthcoming introduction of citizenship
teaching into the national curriculum.
UNICEF's worldwide Baby Friendly
campaign to promote breastfeeding
was also advanced in Britain.
Expenditures on such programmes in
the UK totalled £1.4 million in 2000.

Like many of the development
charities described in this book,
UNICEF is keen to emphasise that it
integrates its local projects with its
country and worldwide campaigns.
'Project-based advocacy' is a good
term used to describe this. In
UNICEF's case, it is particularly well
placed to influence governments
because it is already working with
many of them on a day-to-day basis
through its larger area-based health
and child protection programmes.

Volunteers

There are active voluntary fundraising
groups in the UK and a range of other
voluntary opportunities, all very well
set out on the website. They include
active campaigning, and promoting the
UNICEF message in schools and to
other organisations, as well as
fundraising.

Funding, administration

The main sources of voluntary income
in 2000 were as follows (with 1999
figures in brackets):

- direct mail £9.3 million (£9 million);
- other donations £5.4 million (£4 million);
- specific appeals £3 million (£2.4 million);
- legacies £1.2 million (£1.5 million).

This was achieved at a recorded
fundraising cost of £4.6 million
(£3.6 million), representing a ratio of
24p for every pound given. An
additional £638,000 in fundraising
development money was provided by
UNICEF headquarters in New York,
but as it is not a cost to the charity it
does not appear in the total. It can be
seen as a subsidy to UK donors, but it
does also show how much needs to be
spent to raise the large amounts
concerned.

The charity adds ...

UNICEF's priorities over the next five years
are girls' education, immunisation, early
childhood development, HIV/Aids and
prevention of children at risk from
exploitation and abuse. UNICEF is supported
by a number of blue-chip companies such as
British Airways, Kodak, Manchester United
and Sheraton Hotels. It is well known for its
committed celebrity supporters such as Roger
Moore, Robbie Williams and Jemima Khan,
and is reliant entirely on voluntary donations
to fund its work world-wide.

The information assessed

There is an excellent annual report and
accounts and annual review. There is also a
good annual report for UNICEF as a whole,
which receives most of the money raised by
this charity.

Contact

Africa House
74 Kingsway
WC2B 6NB
Tel 020 7405 5592
Website www.unicef.org.uk
Chair Sir John Waite
David Bull, Executive Director

United Jewish Israel Appeal

UK and overseas

Income	£13,965,000 (2000)
Donated income	£12,207,000
Fundraising costs	£1,832,000
Statutory income	£0
Top salary	£110,000–£120,000
Paid staff	108
Volunteers	2,000

Aims, activities

The charity was established to act as a focal point for charities concerned with Jewish education in the UK, and to work in saving Jewish life in Israel and the Near and Middle East by providing assistance and support for refugees and new immigrants. It is primarily a fundraising and grant-making organisation.

Apparently UJIA was successfully formed in 1996 from two ailing parent groups, the Joint Israel Appeal and Jewish Continuity. A new chief executive was appointed (whose name is not disclosed in the materials available from the charity), and this is now said to be the largest Jewish voluntary organisation in the UK, with over 2,000 volunteers and 'dynamic educational training programmes'.

In 1999/00 'the UJIA helped support 80,000 people in Israel, fund programmes for 20,000 young people in the UK, and provide Jewish educational activities for over 100,000 people in the former Soviet Union'.

Though the accounts presuppose some understanding of the fields of work involved, it looks as if most of the main charitable expenditures in 2000 can be classified as follows:

Rescue programmes, helping Jewish people resettle in Israel, totalling £6.7 million, including:

- absorption (presumably in Israel) £5.4 million;

- Jewish education (perhaps in the former Soviet Union) £0.8 million.

Renewal programmes, for the Jewish community in the UK, totalling £3.9 million, including:

- informal education £1.5 million;

- educational leadership £1 million.

Volunteers

The annual review suggests that much if not most of the fundraising is volunteer-based.

Funding, administration

The voluntary income of £12.2 million in 2000 was achieved at a fundraising cost of £1,832,000, a ratio of a low 15p in the pound. It was made up of £10.3 million in donations and £1.9 million in legacies.

In 2001 the charity was reported to have increased its voluntary income and raised the number of major gifts it makes by 60% (over an unstated period). The accounts show that between 1999 and 2000 both voluntary and total income dropped, though only slightly.

The information assessed

The annual report being ridiculously short but the accounts informative, the total effect was at best adequate. The annual review, apparently for a different period covering part of the previous year, was good. There is a website for UJIA Israel, but it was not clear whether this was a connected organisation.

Much of the information in this entry comes not from the charity but from the report of an awards scheme in 2001, where it was a winner in a category for 'Bringing community involvement together'.

Contact

Balfour House
741 High Road
Finchley
London
N12 0BQ
Tel 020 8446 1477
Website www.ujia.org
Chair David M Cohen

Variety Club
Children's charity

Income	£8,094,000 (2000)
Donated income	£4,078,000
Fundraising costs	£942,000
Statutory income	£0
Top salary	less than £40,000
Paid staff	
Full time	27
Volunteers	550

Aims, activities

This organisation calls itself 'The Greatest Children's Charity in the World' and is the UK part of an international children's charity established in the USA in the 1920s. It raises money which it then passes on to other charities through grants, in particular for the well-known 'Sunshine Coaches'.

The fundraising is carried out with the help of 1,700 members of the Variety Club of Great Britain, many of them celebrities from the world of entertainment, sport or business, and usually through the medium of fundraising events such as film premieres, golf-days, or lunches and dinners.

In 2000 'the funds raised enabled us to supply 155 Sunshine Coaches to schools, homes and other institutions. We gave 28 electric wheelchairs, buggies and trikes, and with them the gift of mobility, to children previously reliant on others. 8,600 children enjoyed days out with our Variety at Work committees at exciting locations.'

The club also made grants, mostly of amounts between £15,000 and £30,000, to 225 institutions, and, for lesser amounts, for the benefit of 28 children. A typical organisation grant might be the £23,000 given to the Cedars Special School in Doncaster.

Volunteers

The fundraising is based on the time of Variety Club members, freely given, with regional groups around the country. An unusually large part of the organisational work appears to be undertaken voluntarily. The annual report names almost 100 chairs or co-chairs of the charity's various committees, such as those of the Golfing Society Liaison and the Events Liaison Committees.

Funding, administration

Of the £8.1 million income in 2000, £1 million was spent on making grants or on the club's own charitable expenditure. Another £497,000 was spent on the accompanying administration and £942,000 on fundraising. This last represented 23p for every pound of income voluntarily donated (23%), down from 27% in the previous year.

The annual accounts note that small amounts were paid for agency and printing costs to companies owned by trustees, and a rather larger £19,000 to a video production company owned by the wife of a trustee. There is a discussion of the issue of payments to trustees in the Introduction to this book (page 22).

The information assessed

The annual report and accounts are adequate, though thin, but there is an extensive website.

Contact

Variety Club House
93 Bayham Street
London
NW1 0AG
Tel 020 7428 8100
Website www.varietyclub.org.uk
Chair Richard Freeman, Chief Barker 2001
Martin Shaw, General Manager

Victim Support schemes

Victim Support is the network of volunteer-based charities that help people cope with crime. They are completely independent organisations, offering a free and confidential service, irrespective of whether or not a crime has been reported to the police.

Every year Victim Support offers help to over a million people who have been affected by crime. It operates through a network of local Victim Support schemes across England, Wales and Northern Ireland (there is a separate organisation covering Scotland – Victim Support Scotland; tel: 0131 668 4486).

Victim Support also runs the Witness Service, based in every crown court centre in England and Wales and in a growing number of magistrates' courts. Staff and volunteers are trained to provide support and information about the court process to witnesses, victims and their families, before, during and after the trial. The aim is that by April 2002 witnesses in all the criminal courts in England and Wales should be able to receive help.

People can also contact the Victim Supportline – a national low-call telephone number – on **0845 30 30 900**.

Trained volunteers provide free, confidential support and advice following all types of crimes. People react to crime in many ways. Although most victims don't suffer long-term harm, both adults and children can be seriously affected and often need help in order to recover. Typically, they seek:

● someone to talk to;

● information on police and court procedures;

● reassurance and emotional support;

● information and support when attending court;

- help with compensation and insurance;
- crime prevention advice;
- help with housing or benefit problems;
- contact with other local organisations.

Victim Support volunteers help individuals by:

- visiting victims of crime;
- helping victims in court;
- providing information and support to victims and witnesses attending trials.

Volunteers also help in many other ways, for example on management committees, with publicity and fundraising, with interpreting and training, or with legal advice. People with practical skills are sometimes needed to help with repairs after burglary.

'We look for volunteers who are understanding and good listeners and who can get on with people of all ages, cultures and backgrounds. Anyone can apply. No previous experience of this kind of work is necessary.

'All Victim Support volunteers are given training before they help victims. Further training is available for some volunteers who wish to work with people who have suffered serious crimes, like women victims of sexual violence and families of murder victims. We aim for the highest professional standards in our work and we attach great importance to the training our volunteers receive.

'Some volunteers work several hours a week, while others offer occasional help. Court volunteers need to be free to work during the day. Volunteers are not paid but they receive their travelling and some other expenses.'

Potential volunteers should contact their local scheme. Details are available from the local Council for Voluntary Service (see page 385) or police station, or from the Victim Support National Office, Cranmer House, 39 Brixton Road, London, SW9 6DZ (tel: 020 7735 9166; website: www.victimsupport.org).

As independent charities, Victim Support and its local schemes must raise money in every community in England and Wales. This is achieved by holding events, through corporate partnerships, trusts and foundations and the National Lottery, and through sales of Christmas cards and merchandise. The Home Office also provides support through an annual grant which helps cover some of the running costs of the national office, local schemes, the Witness Service and the Supportline.

Victoria and Albert Museum

Income	£54,509,000 (2000/01)
Donated income	£4,654,000
Fundraising costs	£1,941,000
Statutory income	£36,645,000
Top salary	£90,000–£100,000
Paid staff	806
Volunteers	250

Aims, activities

The V&A in London is the national museum of art, craft and design. It sets out to help people explore, enjoy and shape the designed world and to stimulate creativity. It is a charity, though one that is exempt from registration at the Charity Commission. In November 2001 its charges for admission, which raised £2.4 million in 2000/01, were dropped, in return for concessions in its VAT status and other forms of increased support from the government.

The main funding comes as an annual government grant, of £30 million in 2000/01, but its voluntary income also makes the V&A a significant fundraising charity.

Volunteers

Substantial numbers of volunteers work with the museum. Those interested should contact the personnel department.

Funding, administration

The voluntary income in 2000/01 came mainly from sponsorship and donations, and totalled £5 million. The audited accounts show this as having been achieved at a fundraising cost of £1.9 million, which would represent a high 42p in the pound.

However, the museum notes that this heading also covers other marketing costs not to do with fundraising (which it should not, according to the accounting standard being used), and that the actual fundraising costs were only £585,000. In this case they represented a low 13p in the pound. Perhaps the charity should have a word with its auditor, who is no less a figure than the Comptroller and Auditor General to the Houses of Parliament.

The charity adds ...

With the British Galleries successfully opening in 2001, the V & A is embarking on a major programme to redisplay the Museum's collections and to enhance the layout of the Museum for visitors. Plans are progressing for architect Daniel Libeskind's Spiral extension, which will be the contemporary face of the Museum. If you would like to support these initiatives, please contact the Development Department, on 020 7942 2152.

The information assessed

As a non-departmental public body, as well as a charity, the excellent annual report is far more comprehensive than those of most of the charities described in this book.

Contact

South Kensington
London
SW7 2RL
Tel 020 7942 2000
Website www.vam.ac.uk
Chair Paula Ridley
Mark Jones, Director

Volunteer Reading Help

Income	£1,118,000 (2000/01)
Donated income	£658,000
Fundraising costs	£167,000
Statutory income	£436,000
Top salary	less than £50,000
Paid staff	
Full time	10
Part time	104
Volunteers	
Operational	2,305
Fundraising	50

Aims, activities

Though comparatively modest in financial terms, the main economic resource of this charity is its volunteers, who are cumulatively and probably literally worth millions.

The charity recruits, trains and places volunteers from the local community to help children in primary schools who have poor literacy skills. The 2,350 volunteers provide one-to-one support for 8,000 children and are in turn supported by branch staff in 50 English locations. Volunteers go into schools which have asked for their help. The children concerned are chosen by their teachers.

Each volunteer gets six to eight hours of training and is expected to work with the same three children for a full academic year.

'The sessions are informal and vary with each child, responding to their individual interests and abilities. They are relaxed, happy times, leaving the children with a feeling of success'.

Volunteers

The whole charitable activity is voluntary. There are over 50 voluntary local committees which operate the scheme in their areas.

Funding, administration

The charity's main sources of income are the Department for Education and other government sources, charitable trusts, the Lottery (Community Fund) and the schools themselves.

In 2000/01 the charity invested in a nationally based fundraising team. This increased the fundraising cost ratio to 25p in the pound, but the effect should only be temporary as new funding streams arrive as a result of the investment.

The information assessed

There are two different documents headed 'Annual Report', one for '1999–2000' and the other for 'the year ended 31 March 2000'. Together they give a good account of the charity.

Contact

High Holborn House
52–54 High Holborn
London
WC1V 6RL
Tel 020 7404 6204
Chair Anna Weitzman
Heather Brandon, National Organiser

Volunteering opportunities and Volunteer Bureaux

Many of the charities described in this book are staffed in whole or part by volunteers, as the entries describe. But there are tens of thousands of smaller charities, often wholly local, which rely on volunteers to carry out their work. There are a number of sources of information about opportunities for such volunteering.

The Do-It website

Though it does not have 100% coverage, this website (www.do-it.org.uk) both offers details of specific opportunities around the UK (about 35,000 in summer 2001) and gives cross-references to the nearest Volunteer Bureau.

TimeBank

TimeBank was launched in 2000 to make the giving of time easier and more accessible. The vision was to inspire a new generation of volunteers, or TimeGivers, through the creation of a media-based campaign that would encourage people to give as much or as little time as they chose. Partly funded by the Home Office and backed by the BBC, TimeBank had held two national TimeBank days by autumn 2001 and had registered over 25,000 volunteers. An independent survey revealed that of the 18,000 individuals who registered in the first year, 80% had not given time before.

Using web and database technology, TimeBank matches people's interests and skills to volunteering opportunities in their area, via a network of over 400 TimePartner organisations, primarily local Volunteer Bureaux. They provide advice, support and follow up for volunteers.

For more information on TimeBank, telephone 0845 601 4008, or log on to www.timebank.org.uk

Volunteer Bureaux

These are local volunteer recruitment and advice centres. Also known as Volunteer Centres, Voluntary Action or Volunteer Development Agencies, they offer information and advice to help people choose the right type of voluntary work. There are more than 350 in England, plus networks in Wales, Scotland and Northern Ireland. In many cases they share premises with local Councils for Voluntary Service, or may even be a part of such a council. These are listed on pages 385–395 and may be the best way to make initial contact.

As well as giving a range of opportunities to choose from, the bureaux can help people decide what is best for them, acting as a recruitment agent between volunteers and and the organisations of their choice, making introductions and in some cases negotiating or developing the role to be undertaken.

Information about local Volunteer Bureaux can also be obtained from the following offices:

- England: National Association of Volunteer Bureaux; tel: 0121 633 4555
- Scotland: Volunteer Development Scotland; tel: 01786 479593
- Wales: Wales Council of Voluntary Action; tel: 029 2043 1700
- Northern Ireland: NI Development Agency; tel: 0128 9023 6100

VSO
Voluntary Service Overseas

Income	£29,83,000 (2000/01)
Donated income	£6,043,000
Fundraising costs	£1,366,000
Statutory income	£22,129,000
Top salary	£50,000–£60,000
Paid staff	550
Volunteers	2,500

Aims, activities

VSO is an international development charity that works through volunteers, enabling skilled people to share these skills with local communities in the developing world. 'VSO is open to professional people from many different occupations.' They can come from anywhere in the European Union, Canada or the USA, and there are pilot programmes for volunteers from Kenya and the Philippines.

The standard volunteer programme lasts for two years.

There is an overseas network of 40 programme offices supporting the work of more than 2,000 volunteers. VSO is trying to focus its work where it can benefit the most disadvantaged people. It is ending its work in much of East and Central Europe, and in Belize, while reopening in Guinea Bissau and expanding activities in Central Africa and Indonesia.

One of the examples given in the annual review for 2001 is that of Marie Lequin. She is a volunteer radio producer who formerly worked for the BBC and is now a VSO volunteer in Cameroon, where she has helped establish the *100% jeune on-air* radio show. This combines a soap opera, newspaper and poster campaign with the show, all concerned with safe sex in a country whose young people are at terrible risk from HIV/AIDS.

The charity also has four youth schemes which include programmes for recent graduates and for school leavers.

Volunteers

In 2000/01 VSO supplied 1,876 years of volunteer work and 927 volunteers went overseas during the year. There were 5,000 applications from 20,000 people to whom application forms were issued. Of the 5,000, 1,110 were selected as volunteers. Some 60% of the volunteers are women and the average age is 36.

In the UK there is a network of 71 local VSO groups which promote the charity's work. Around 230 people, themselves acting voluntarily, took part in the meetings to select the volunteers to go overseas.

Funding, administration

The charity is funded primarily by the government through a core grant, of £22 million in 2000/01, from the

Department for International Development (DfID).

In its accounts the charity noted, as 'Income from fundraising activities', further grants totalling £550,000 from the DfID and of £329,000 from the Millennium Commission. Grants from these bodies are not classified in this book as fundraised or voluntary income. Without them, voluntary donations totalled £6 million, achieved at a fundraising cost of £1.4 million. This gives a cost ratio of 23p in the pound.

The information assessed
An excellent annual report and accounts is backed by a comprehensive website.

Contact
317 Putney Bridge Road
London
SW15 2PN
Tel 020 8780 7200
Website www.vso.org.uk
Chair Baroness Warwick
Mark Goldring, Chief Executive

WaterAid
Providing clean water and sanitation overseas

Income	£9,928,000 (2000/01)
Donated income	£7,508,000
Fundraising costs	£1,285,000
Statutory income	£1,784,000
Top salary	£50,000–£60,000
Paid staff	72
Volunteers	225

Aims, activities
WaterAid works to provide clean water and sanitation to the world's poorest people. The work is carried forward locally by partner organisations with WaterAid's funding and advice.

The charity is 20 years old and grew out of the UK water industry (then publicly owned) as its response to the UN Water Decade (1981–90). It now works in 11 countries in Africa and in Pakistan, India, Nepal and Bangladesh. In each, it has its own country representative, usually a water engineer, who is normally responsible for allocating the funds to appropriate local partner organisations and for supervising their use.

In its projects WaterAid seeks to:

- use locally appropriate low-cost technologies;
- involve local communities in planning and construction;
- train villagers in repairs and maintenance;
- work in partnership with local organisations;
- integrate safe water with sanitation and hygiene education.

The charity's projects have helped over 6.5 million people to have access to clean water – but it notes that 1.4 billion people still do not have a safe supply close to home (WHO/UNICEF Global Water Supply and Sanitation Assessment 2000 Report).

WaterAid also 'uses its experience, research and documented good practice to influence other international organisations and feed into wider development policies. In this way it generates waves of change far beyond the physical boundaries of its work.'

Expenditure in 2000/01 was classified as follows:

- Asia £2.7 million
- East Africa £2.4 million

– West Africa £0.9 million

– Southern Africa £0.8 million

The charity spends £7 million a year on its charitable activities but has only 70 staff of its own worldwide, so it operates by making payments to partner organisations overseas. There is little information about these partners, other than that they are sometimes governments but are often local non-profit agencies. Because the transfers to them are regarded as 'contracts', which are not required by law to be disclosed (though they they could be), rather than grants, which must be disclosed, it is not possible to find out the number, the identity, or the size of the contracts concerned.

However, these editors were provided with information on a small sample of seven organisations which receive funding. They include a governmental partner, Niassa provincial government in Mozambique (which received £290,000), and NGOs ranging from ACDEP in Ghana (£11,000) to Nepal Water for Health, or NEWAH, in Nepal (£688,000).

With so few staff of its own, a core challenge for the charity must be the management of considerable expenditures at a distance and a fuller review of this activity would be welcome.

Volunteers

Now that the charity has full time expert staff in all the countries in which it works, the scope for volunteers on short term assignments is very limited and usually confined to people with very specific skills. In the UK, the charity has a panel of voluntary speakers to talk to community groups, schools and the like about its work.

Funding, administration

The total income of the charity has nearly doubled since 1995.

A main source of funding has been regular contributions from water industry staff. Though this continues, it has now been overtaken by other, wider, forms of support, which produced £5.4 million from the general public in 2000/01, as against £1.9 million from industry sources. The charity also received £1.3 million from the government's Department for International Development

Voluntary income in total showed an impressive rise in the year, from £6.3 million to £7.5 million. This was achieved at a fundraising cost of £1.3 million, a ratio of 17p, or 17%, for each pound raised, very slightly up on the 16% of immediately previous years.

An unusual feature of the accounts is that income from legacies is not separately identified; perhaps there wasn't any.

The charity adds ...

WaterAid is the UK's only major charity dedicated exclusively to the provision of safe domestic water, sanitation and hygiene promotion to the world's poorest people. WaterAid vision is of a world where all people have access to safe water and effective sanitation.

The information assessed

The generally good annual report and accounts are backed by a fine website, with a particularly good section of 'frequently asked questions' (FAQs), and a detailed though unquantified five-year plan to 2005. However, the charity does not identify the organisations which it funds to carry out the work overseas, so it is hard to see how its projects are organised or managed.

Contact
Prince Consort House
27–29 Albert Embankment
London
SE1 7UB
Tel 020 7793 4500
Website www.wateraid.org.uk
Chair John Isherwood
Ravi Narayan, Director

Whizz-Kidz

Mobility for children with disabilities

Income	£3,728,000 (2000)
Donated income	£3,684,000
Fundraising costs	£1,783,000
Statutory income	£0
Top salary	£60,000–£70,000
Paid staff	
Full time	42
Part time	3
Volunteers	
Operational	24
Fundraising	16

Aims, activities

Whizz-Kidz was founded in 1990 by Michael Dickson, its present chief executive, among others. Since then it has grown with impressive speed.

The charity provides customised mobility aids, mainly wheelchairs, for children with disabilities. Applicants are professionally assessed so that their individual needs can be appropriately met. An attractive feature is the 'Kidz Board', which brings a child's-eye viewpoint to the charity's work, and whose members often represent the charity publicly. (In 2000, they held one of their meetings in the Cabinet room at 10 Downing Street.)

The special wheelchairs, tricycles and other equipment are of a quality beyond what is normally available through the NHS and they enable children with disabilities to enjoy everyday things that able-bodied children often take for granted, such as going to mainstream schools, playing sport and being able to participate fully in family life.

In 2000, £704,000 was spent on wheelchairs and other equipment, £614,000 on the costs of running the services, and £314,000 on education and publicity about mobility issues. A further £284,000 was spent on the administration of the charity. The charity helped 448 children in 1999 and 229 in 2000.

The charity also campaigns for better provision generally for children whose disabilities restrict their ability to get around. In 2001 it received government funding to pilot a national standardised wheelchair training programme for children.

Volunteers

Volunteers play a significant part in the fundraising of the charity, but its work is mainly carried out by the paid staff. A regional network of volunteers was developed in 2000, to help with promoting the work of the charity and to organise fundraising events in their areas. In autumn 2001 there were 24 such volunteers in place, including in Northern Ireland.

Funding, administration

The charity spent £1.8 million on fundraising in 2000, raising £3.7 million in voluntary income, a cost ratio of a very high 48p in the pound, up from 37p in the previous year. In the three previous years this ratio had averaged 22p in the pound. Surprisingly, there is no review in the annual report of how this significant change came about, beyond an expectation that voluntary income will rise in the next two years.

Unusually, nearly two thirds of the money comes from fundraising events, especially sponsored marathons and other overseas initiatives. These brought in £2.4 million at a fundraising cost of £1.5 million, so they are an apparently expensive way of raising money. On the other hand, many of these events may be providing the participants with tangible and valuable benefits, such as an activity holiday in an interesting place, as well as allowing them to support the charity from philanthropic motives. The costs of organising such activities are usually higher than for many other forms of fundraising.

The charity is almost wholly dependent on voluntary income. Wherever possible it seeks joint funding from the NHS and other statutory services for the wheelchairs and aids that it provides. About one in three cases are joint-funded with the NHS voucher scheme, and on average the NHS meets between a quarter and a third of the costs involved.

The accounts note a number of connected party transactions. The wife of the chief executive and founder of the charity is a trustee; £12,636 was paid to a firm of solicitors one of whose partners is another trustee; and £10,400 was paid, on commercial terms, to the accountancy practice of the charity's chief financial officer. There is a discussion of the issue of payments to trustees in the Introduction to this book (page 22).

The information assessed
The annual report is adequate but very brief. The accounts are good, as are the bright promotional materials and website.

Contact
1 Warwick Row
London
SW1E 5ER
Tel 020 7233 6600
Fax 020 7233 6611
Website www.whizz-kidz.org.uk
Chair Gary Iceton
Michael Dickson, Chief Executive

Wildfowl & Wetlands Trust
Conservation

Income	£8,001,000 (2000)
Donated income	£4,620,000
Fundraising costs	£373,000
Statutory income	£274,000
Top salary	£50,000–£60,000
Paid staff	
Full time	177
Part time	115
Volunteers	750

Aims, activities
The charity's mission is to conserve wetlands and their bio-diversity. While its present work on the ground is almost entirely in the UK, the trust's experience and advice, and its specific conservation programmes for particular species, are influential worldwide.

The trust has nine wetland centres where it welcomed 687,000 visitors in 2000, up by 16% from the previous year, largely due to the opening of the much-acclaimed new Wetland Centre in Barnes, London. It also runs a research centre at its headquarters, and acts as a positive force for wildfowl conservation around the world.

Founded by the naturalist Sir Peter Scott at its well-known headquarters at Slimbridge, Gloucestershire, the charity now has centres in Scotland, Wales and Northern Ireland as well as around England.

In 2000 the charitable expenditure was classified as follows:

- grounds £2.3 million;
- education £988,000;
- research £567,000;
- conservation £470,000.

Besides the new centre in London, a major expansion of the Slimbridge facilities was opened in 2000, funded largely by Lottery money from the Millennium Commission.

For information on other wildlife trusts, see separate group entry, the *Wildlife Trusts*.

Volunteers

The trust appears, from its annual reports, to be primarily a professionally operated body, but the website notes that 'many [of the charity's] centres have Friends Groups and committed teams of volunteers, providing important local support and help at the centres'.

Funding, administration

The funding of the trust is varied. The main headings for 2000 were:

- subscriptions and donations £3.6 million;
- grants £1.4 million;
- admissions £1.3 million;
- legacies £1 million;

- sales and trading £0.6 million.

The fundraising cost of raising the £4.6 million in legacies and donations was £373,000, giving a very low cost ratio of just 8p in the pound. This was a great reduction on figures reported in the three years up to 1998, but this may be the result, in part, of separating fundraising costs from those for marketing and publicity, as is now Charity Commission recommended practice.

The grant income was dominated by support from Lottery money from both the Millennium Commission and the Heritage Lottery Fund. In the previous year, when visitor numbers had been 'a little disappointing', the accounts recorded large grants from Thames Water and from Berkeley Homes, whose funding of the new London centre so boosted admissions the following year.

The charity adds ...

If you are interested in wildfowl and wetland conservation, please help us save wetland birds and their habitats by becoming a member of WWT or making a donation to our conservation and education work. To enquire about volunteering, contact your nearest WWT centre.

The information assessed

The adequate annual report is backed by an excellent quarterly magazine, *Wildfowl and Wetlands*, and supporting leaflets. There is a website with nice bird pictures.

Contact

Slimbridge
Gloucestershire
GL2 7BT
Tel 01453 891900
Website www.wwt.org.uk
Chair Hugh Mellor
A E Richardson, Managing Director

Wildlife trusts

There is a network of 47 local wildlife trusts, working to protect wildlife in towns and the countryside.

The trusts care for more than 2,400 nature reserves, covering an area of 74,500 hectares, ranging from remote islands off the Scottish coast to restored industrial sites in the heart of London. 'From woods and meadows to mountains and moorlands, black bog ants and basking sharks to damselflies and dormice, The Wildlife Trusts protect a multitude of habitats and species' and 'campaign for better protection of our precious wildlife and habitats ... We have more than 355,000 members, and 22,200 regular volunteers.'

Each local trust is an independent charity. The partnership as a whole is represented nationally by the Royal Society for Nature Conservation, which is the central source of information about the network (tel: 01636 6777711; website: www.wildlifetrusts.org.uk).

The Royal Society, whose voluntary income is a little too low to gain its own entry in this book, was reported in 2001 to be in difficulties due to divisions among its members and trustees and to be undergoing a Charity Commission investigation into the possibility of poor internal financial controls.

The local wildlife trusts tend to be heavily dependent on their volunteers. 'Volunteers have been central to our growth, ever since we started in 1912 ... There are a huge range of activities to suit all interests, from "hands-on" conservation, building otter holts, to recording species, working in visitor centres and shops, with children through Wildlife Watch and fundraising.

'Wildlife Trusts also need help from those with skills in photography, illustration, accountancy, public relations, and administration – the list is endless.'

Local wildlife trusts on the lists below will have information about specific volunteering opportunities.

England

Avon Wildlife Trust; tel: 0117 9268018

Beds, Cambs, Northants & Peterborough Wildlife Trusts; tel: 01234 364213

Berks, Bucks & Oxon Wildlife Trust; tel: 01865 775476

Birmingham & Black Country Wildlife Trust; tel: 0121 454 1199

Cheshire Wildlife Trust; tel: 01270 610180

Cornwall Wildlife Trust; tel: 01872 273939

Cumbria Wildlife Trust; tel: 015394 48280

Derbyshire Wildlife Trust; tel: 01332 756610

Devon Wildlife Trust; tel: 01392 279244

Dorset Wildlife Trust; tel: 01305 264620

Durham Wildlife Trust; tel: 0191 584 3112

Essex Wildlife Trust; tel: 01621 862960

Gloucester Wildlife Trust; tel: 01452 383333

Hampshire & Isle of Wight Wildlife Trust; tel: 023 8061 3636

Herefordshire Wildlife Trust; tel: 01432 356872

Hertfordshire & Middlesex Wildlife Trust; tel: 01727 858901

Isles of Scilly Wildlife Trust; tel: 01720 422153

Kent Wildlife Trust; tel: 01622 662012

Lancashire, Manchester & N Merseyside Wildlife Trusts; tel: 01772 324129

Leicestershire & Rutland Wildlife Trust; tel: 0116 2702999

Lincolnshire Trust for Nature Conservation; tel: 01507 526667

London Wildlife Trust; tel: 020 7261 0447

Norfolk Wildlife Trust; tel: 01603 625540

Northumberland Wildlife Trust; tel: 0191 284 6884

Nottinghamshire Wildlife Trust; tel: 0115 958 8242

Sheffield Wildlife Trust; tel: 0114 263 4335

Shropshire Wildlife Trust; tel: 01743 241691

Somerset Wildlife Trust; tel: 01823 451587

Staffordshire Wildlife Trust; tel: 01889 508534

Suffolk Wildlife Trust; tel: 01473 890089

Surrey Wildlife Trust; tel: 01483 488055

Sussex Wildlife Trust; tel: 01273 492630

Tees Valley Wildlife Trust; tel: 01642 759900

Warwickshire Wildlife Trust; tel: 01203 302912

Wiltshire Wildlife Trust; tel: 01380 725670

Worcestershire Wildlife Trust; tel: 01905 754919

Yorkshire Wildlife Trust; tel: 01904 659570

Wales

Brecknock Wildlife Trust; tel: 01874 625708

Glamorgan Wildlife Trust; tel: 01656 724100

Gwent Wildlife Trust; tel: 01600 715501

Montgomeryshire Wildlife Trust; tel: 01938 555654

North Wales Wildlife Trust; tel: 01248 351541

Radnorshire Wildlife Trust; tel: 01597 823298

West Wales Wildlife Trust; tel: 01239 621212

Scotland

Scottish Wildlife Trust; tel: 0131 312 7765

Northern Ireland
Ulster Wildlife Trust; tel: 01396 830282

Isle of Man
Manx Nature Conservation Trust; tel: 01624 801985

Winged Fellowship Trust

Holidays for disabled people and breaks for their carers

Income	£6,724,000 (2000/01)
Donated income	£2,773,000
Fundraising costs	£594,000
Statutory income	£3,237,000
Top salary	£59,000
Paid staff	266
Volunteers	
Operational	5,300
Fundraising	1,200

Aims, activities

There are 8 million disabled people in the UK and 7 million who care for them – a million do so full time. The purpose of the Winged Fellowship Trust is:

● to enable carers to have planned breaks;

● to provide quality holidays, with personal care on full time call;

● to enlist the help of volunteers in providing both care and companionship.

The charity runs four major centres, in Southport, Lancashire; in Nottinghamshire; in south Essex; and, in partnership with the charity Refresh, in Netley, Hampshire. The New Discovery arm of the charity arranges overseas holidays. A fifth, uneconomic, centre has recently been closed, but in its place the charity has taken over the management of the overseas holiday programme of *Guide Dogs for the Blind* and is also discussing similar arrangements with other providers of holidays for the disabled.

A total of 6,700 holiday weeks were enjoyed in 2000/01, said in the annual report to be up sharply from the previous year; but on the figures given this was actually slightly down, from 7,200 (though average occupancy levels increased). The guests, most of whom are wheelchair users, are of any age from 16 upwards.

All holiday centres employ fully trained nursing and care staff, who are supported by 4,000 volunteers. The aim is to offer guests one-to-one support.

The charity emphasises the importance of its work to those who care for disabled people. A third of such carers simply never have a break at all from their responsibilities.

The charity was founded, with others, by Mrs Joan Brander who led its activities for many years. The departure of such a leader from a dominant role often creates a particularly difficult transition, so it is pleasant to see this charity moving ahead under energetic new leadership.

Volunteers

'Working with volunteers is an integral part of [the trust's] mission ... time is spent training, appraising and developing our volunteers. Involving volunteers adds a new dimension to the guests' stay with us. It also offers a unique (and sometimes life-changing) opportunity for the volunteer.' Two thirds of the volunteers are between the ages of 17 and 25.

Some volunteers come through the *Prince's Trust* and the *Duke of Edinburgh's Award* scheme. An increasing minority come from other parts of Europe, North America and Japan. Their costs are met by the charity.

Volunteers also work in the charity's offices, in London and at the centres, and in the 16 charity shops selling donated goods.

Funding, administration

The annual report to January 2000 referred to substantial financial difficulties. A year later it looked as if these were being successfully overcome. On the capital side this was achieved mainly though the closure of one uneconomic centre in Surrey, now handed over to another organisation to use as a nursing home.

Revenue also rose sharply. Fees paid by guests, and on their behalf by social services departments, rose slightly but donations were up by 28% to £2.3 million. Total voluntary income of £2.8 million was achieved at a fundraising cost of £552,000, giving a cost ratio of 21% (21p for each pound donated), a substantial reduction on the cost levels of previous years.

The shops and bars run by the charity raised almost £100,000 after a difficult previous year.

The information assessed

The annual report and accounts and annual review are good. There is a modest but effective website.

Contact

Angel House
20–32 Pentonville Road
London
N1 9XD
Tel 020 7833 2594
Website www.wft.org.uk
Chair R Hugh Kemsley
Mr Pat Wallace, Chief Executive

Women's Institutes

There are 8,000 Women's Institutes (WIs) in England and Wales, with 250,000 members and a total level of donations of about £4 million. Besides a range of what might be called 'personal interest' activities, such as those centring on the home, crafts and recreation, most WIs undertake or support a wide range of local charitable activities. Major categories include:

● the upkeep of local gardens, churchyards and the like;

● supporting local activities such as Neighbourhood Watch or the Red Cross;

● visiting sick or older people;

● fundraising for local causes.

Each branch is a separate charity, and they vary greatly in size. One with 1,000 members would be very large; one with just 10 would be unusually small. Each WI meets monthly, often affording a large range of social and educational activities.

At a national level, the National Federation of Women's Institutes is an active force, campaigning for the interests of its members. It hit the headlines in 2000 when its triennial general meeting was vociferous in disapproving a speech by the prime minister, Tony Blair, which was felt to be inappropriate and over party-political.

Campaigns by the movement in 2001 included those for the retention of rural post offices, for improvements in the assistance available for stroke sufferers, and in support of sustainable development. The small town and rural emphasis traditionally associated with WIs may be seen in its support for farming communities and the rural infrastructure, and for efforts to support local food producers.

To contact the national federation, telephone 020 7371 9300; website: www.nfwi.org.uk

Women's organisations

There are many large women's organisations, and several are already listed elsewhere in this book, such as the *Women's Royal Voluntary Service* (WRVS) and the *Women's Institutes*. Smaller or local women's organisations often focus on a particular issue, such as domestic violence, rape, abortion or equal opportunities; or alternatively represent women of a particular area, profession or faith. These organisations are often dependent both on donations and on the input of volunteers in all manner of capacities, from administration to mutual support to campaigning.

In England, a good source of general information about women's organisations is the Women's National Commission, or WNC (tel: 020 7276 2555), which is a government advisory body at the forefront of women's issues. It has a network of over 220 partners. Equivalent bodies are the Wales Assembly of Women (tel: 01267 267 428) and Women's Forum Northern Ireland (tel: 028 9047 1782). In Scotland, the Information Department of the Scottish Council of Voluntary Organisations should be able to help (tel: 0131 556 3882).

For more information concerning women's issues and local women's organisations, the Women's Resource Centre in London (tel: 020 7377 0088), which represents women in the voluntary sector, would be an alternative.

The Women's Aid Federation supports a large number of what are often called 'refuges' and which offer abused women and children an escape route from situations of domestic violence, along with emotional support and advice. The Women's Aid Federation is a national domestic violence charity, set up and run by women. They support over 250 local projects and over 400 'refuges, help lines, outreach services and advice centres'. The head office is run by full time staff, while the national helpline is a voluntary scheme, and each refuge is run autonomously, usually by volunteers.

Women's Aid Federations in the UK:

- England, tel: 0117 944 4411
- Wales, tel: 02920 390874
- Scotland, tel: 0131 475 2372
- Northern Ireland, tel: 028 9024 9041

National helplines:

- Women's Aid National Domestic Violence Helpline, tel: **08475 023 468**
- Northern Ireland 24-hour Helpline, tel: **028 9033 1818**
- Scottish Domestic Abuse Helpline, tel: **0800 027 1234**

The website offers extensive information and advice, including a regional listing of affiliated refuges – www.womensaid.org.uk

Contact telephone numbers (or e-mail) are given below for a wide range of WNC partner organisations, and for some other significant groups, but this list cannot be complete. Obviously, some of the organisations listed, such as those which support lone parents, are not run exclusively by and for women.

300 Group (political equality for women), 01403 733797

Asian Women's Counselling Service, 020 8570 6568

Associated Country Women of the World (improving women's living standards worldwide), 020 7233 0889

Association for Improvement in the Maternity Services, 01753 652781

Black Women's Mental Health Project, 020 8961 6324

British Pregnancy Advisory Service, 08457 304030

Business and Professional Women UK (BPW UK), 01332 862690

Connect Women's Network, 020 8971 6034

Co-operative Women's Guild (equal opportunities), 020 8804 5905

Empowering Widows in Development, widowsrights@hotmail.com

ENGENDER (Scottish women's organisation), 0131 558 9596

European Union of Women, 01386 710175

Fawcett Society (equality), 020 7628 4441

Federation of International Women's Associations in London, 020 7499 8159

Footprints UK (black women), 020 8523 4032

Foundation for Women's Health, Research and Development (FORWARD), 020 7725 2706

Full Time Mothers, 020 8879 7852

Gender Awareness in Education, 01344 422495

Genuine Empowerment for Mothers in Society, 020 766 3267

Girls Friendly Society – Platform for Young Women, 020 7589 9628

Gingerbread (lone parent advice), 020 7336 8183

Hindu Women's Network, 0121 777 3448

League of Jewish Women (voluntary welfare service organisation), 020 7387 7688

Married Women's Association, 020 7794 2884

Maternity Alliance, 020 75888583

Medical Women's Federation, 020 7387 7765

Menopausal Research and Information Service, 020 8444 5202

Methodist Women's Association, 028 9047 1782

Mothers' Union, 020 7222 5533

National Alliance of Women's Organisations (NAWO), 020 7266 5056

National Assembly of Women, 01422 846 302

National Association for Maternal and Child Welfare, 020 7383 4117

National Association of Ladies' Circles GB & Ireland, 01535 607617

National Association of Women's Clubs, 020 7837 1434

National Board of Catholic Women, 01676 522908

National Childbirth Trust, 020 8992 2616

National Childminding Association, 020 8464 6164

National Council for One Parent Families, 020 7428 5416

National Council of Women of Great Britain, 020 7354 2395

National Early Years Network, 020 7607 9573

National Endometriosis Society, 020 7222 2781

Northern Ireland Childminding Association, 028 9181 1015

Northern Ireland Women's European Platform, 028 9068 2296

Older Feminists Network, 020 8346 1900

Older Women's Network UK, 01369 830429

Overseas Women's Club, 01753 880452

Rape Crisis + Sexual Abuse Centre, 028 9024 9696

Rape Crisis Federation of Wales and England, 0115 934 8474

Scottish Joint Action Group (equality and empowerment), 01738 850607

Scottish Women's Rural Institutes, 0131 225 1724

Standing Conference of Women's Organisations, 01925 495278

Stonewall (lesbian and gay legal equality & social justice), 020 7336 8860

Suzy Lamplugh Trust (personal safety), 020 8392 1839

Townswomen's Guilds, 0121 456 3435

Training for Women Network, Northern Ireland, 028 907 77199

UK Asian Women's Conference, 0192 385 4947

Union of Catholic Mothers, 01924 270684

Wales Assembly of Women, 01267 267428

Wales Women National Coalition, 029 20381461

Womankind Worldwide, 020 7588 6096

Women in Faith, 028 4483 1772

Women in Management, 01536 204222

Women into Business, 01403 738107

Women Returners' Network, 01245 263796

Women's Corona Society (supporting overseas relocation), 020 7610 4407

Women's Design Service, 020 7490 5210

Women's Environmental Network, 020 7247 3327

Women's Farm and Garden Association, 01285 658339

Women's Food and Farming Union, 024 766 93171

Women's Forum Northern Ireland, 028 9047 1782

Women's Health, 020 7251 6333

Women's International League for Peace and Freedom (WILPF) UK, 020 8467 5367

Women's Nationwide Cancer Control Campaign (WNCC or CANCER AWARE), 020 7729 4688

Women's Resource Development Agency, 028 9023 0210

Women's Sport Foundation, 020 8697 5370

Young Women's Christian Association of Great Britain, 01865 304 200

Zonta International (equality and companionship), 0192 382 9938

Wood Green Animal Shelters

Animal rescue, mainly in south-east England

Income	£4,796,000 (1999/00)
Donated income	£4,468,000
Fundraising costs	£258,000
Statutory income	£0
Top salary	£40,000–£50,000
Paid staff	
Full time	127
Part time	60
Volunteers	
Operational	60
Fundraising	80

Aims, activities

The charity takes in animals needing rescue and, after their health and (if necessary) behaviour have been restored to normal, finds new homes for them. Founded in London in 1921, there are now three rescue centres: at Wood Green, London; Heydon in Hertfordshire; and Godmanchester in Cambridgeshire.

In 1999/00 about 7,000 animals were re-homed, with over 70,000 veterinary procedures being carried out. The animals involved go far beyond the cats and dogs to be expected – they include pigs, llamas, deer, sheep, horses, donkeys, rabbits, birds, goats and tortoises. The charity succeeds in finding new homes for over 80% of the animals it receives each year.

The organisation's impressive literature is in line with the chairman's comment that 'we do not aim to be the biggest charity ... but we do aim to be the best in in the re-homing and welfare of animals in need of care'.

Volunteers

Members and volunteers are actively involved in finding and providing new homes for the animals, as well as in animal care and fundraising.

Funding, administration

The organisation is wholly voluntarily funded, with most of its money coming in the form of legacies. There were over 180 such bequests in 1999/00.

Fundraising costs of £258,000 were just 6% of the value of donations, and had fallen by 21% since the previous year, while the donations had increased by a similar amount. The cost of fundraising has not risen above 9p in the pound for at least four years, which is impressive given the supposedly volatile income of charities that rely heavily on legacies.

The charity adds ...

We are in the process of building new, state of the art cattery and kennelling facilities at Godmanchester. These buildings, which are due to be open in Spring and Autumn 2002 respectively, will enhance greatly the well-being of the animals in our care. Any assistance, financial or otherwise, would be most gratefully received.

The information assessed

The annual report and accounts and annual review are of average quality, but the other literature, such as the *Animals Matter* magazine and the various leaflets, are both excellent and unpretentious.

Contact

Kings Bush Farm
London Road
Godmanchester
Cambridgeshire
PE18 8LJ
Tel 01480 830014
Website www.woodgreen.org.uk
Chair Peter Burton
Dennis Baker, Chief Executive

Woodland Trust

Conservation

Income	£17,251,000 (2000)
Donated income	£8,061,000
Fundraising costs	£2,049,000
Statutory income	£688,000
Top salary	£60,000–£70,000
Paid staff	165
Volunteers	3,600

Aims, activities

The trust, dedicated to protecting the UK's native woodland heritage, has acquired and now manages over 1,100 woods (many of them large), is planting new woods and has a membership of over 100,000 people, rising at a rate of over 25% a year. The charity's priority is ancient woodlands, described as those known to have been in existence since before the year 1600.

In recent years the trust has benefited from funding from the Lottery-funded Millennium Commission to pay for a massive 'Woods on your Doorstep' programme. This project is now winding down, so there will be a slowing in the headlong growth of the last few years.

The trust's woods are open to everyone, but are managed primarily to maintain and enhance their bio-diversity.

As part of its priority that there should be no further loss of ancient woodland, the charity not only seeks to acquire and protect threatened woods but also campaigns to influence policy, to build public awareness and to promote enjoyment of all woods, not just those it owns and manages.

Direct charitable expenditure in 2000 totalled £14 million. The main headings were as follows:

- tree planting £2.9 million;
- acquisition of woods and land £2.6 million;
- other woodland management £2.5 million;
- woodland access works £2 million;
- education and information £1.2 million.

The trust is an interesting example of a case where apparent duplication may achieve important public benefits. The older *National Trust* owns 62,000 acres of woodland, compared with the 45,000 of this charity, but the single focus of the newer charity has been a beneficial development, attracting new areas of support and activity.

Volunteers

Setting a standard for some other charities described in this book, the annual report for 2000 properly records the input of voluntary time as well as donations of money. The trust relies on about 3,600 volunteers 'to help with the following activities; fundraising, wardening and care of its woods, photography and promotion of the Woodland Trust's work'.

Funding, administration

The main source of income comprises donations and legacies from the public and, to a much smaller extent, grants from charitable trusts and companies, to a total value of £8.1 million in 2000. This was achieved at a fundraising cost of £2 million, representing 25p for each pound received.

In the last few years the accounts have been dominated by massive grants of Lottery money from the Millennium Commission for the Woods on your Doorstep programme. These totalled £3.4 million in 2000, with a final £1.6 million still to be received, and with £2.5 million and £1.6 million banked in the previous years. Other major grants in 2000 were received from the Forestry Commission (£1.2 million), the Heritage Lottery Fund (£0.5 million) and local authorities (£0.2 million).

The ownership and care of broad-leaved woodlands cost more than such areas can be expected to generate in income. A Woodland Management Fund has therefore been set up to provide a limited source of income, but the costs of maintenance and improvement must be generally met by fundraising. The continuing rise in membership is a good omen for the charity's future in this respect.

The charity adds ...

This country is one of the most deforested parts of Europe. Our remaining woodland is fragmented and isolated, making the woods and their wildlife especially vulnerable to the onslaught of climate change. The Woodland Trust has many active projects including plans to plant millions more trees. So please contact us now for news in your area.

The information assessed

The excellent annual report and accounts and annual review are backed by a fine directory of the charity's woods and by other supporting literature. The potentially good website was only partly working on the two occasions it was visited by this editor (in August 2001).

Contact

Autumn Park
Dysart Road
Grantham
Lincolnshire
NG31 6LL
Tel 01476 581111
Website www.woodland-trust.org.uk
Chair Peter J Oliver
Michael Townsend, Chief Executive

World Cancer Research Fund

Income	£5,655,000 (1999/00)
Donated income	£5,544,000
Fundraising costs	£1,024,000
Statutory income	£0
Top salary	not disclosed
Paid staff	33

Aims, activities

Confusingly, there are two charities using this name. The first is a charity described as its international affiliate by the American Institute for Cancer Research, on that institute's website (the institute itself is described as the third largest cancer charity in the USA). Called in full WCRF International, it is a non-profit making association, established by royal decree in Belgium, with headquarters in London and with operations in France, Germany and Holland as well as in the UK. Then there is WCRF, the British charity of that name and the main subject of this entry. The three separate organisations, WCRF, WCRF International and the

American Institute for Cancer Research, are closely connected in that they have the same chief executive, Marilyn Gentry.

These international connections were not apparent from the charity's reports. Only the unusual title, 'president', for the senior member of staff provoked this editor to look beyond them when a reference to the international connection was then found in three lines in note 10 of the full financial statements. There is of course nothing wrong with being part of an international charitable network, but the low visibility of the situation in the formal reports was surprising.

'World Cancer Research Fund (WCRF) in the UK has grown into the nation's leading charity in the field of diet, nutrition and cancer. WCRF supports research into the role of diet and nutrition in the prevention and treatment of cancer. It also offers a wide range of cancer prevention education programmes and publications for health professionals, schools and the public. Through these pioneering efforts, WCRF has helped focus attention on the link between cancer and the choices we make about food, drink, physical activity and body weight.

'By adopting WCRF's cancer prevention guidelines, people can reduce their risk of cancer by 30 to 40 percent. These changes, combined with not smoking, could reduce cancer risk by 60 to 70 percent according to recent expert estimates. The lifesaving potential of such changes is the core of WCRF's message.

'With a circulation of over 250,000, WCRF's Newsletter is the core publication of its education programmes and is, undoubtedly, the widest read publication dedicated exclusively to diet, lifestyle and cancer prevention in the UK.'

The charitable expenditure in 1999/00 was classified as:

- direct £3.1 million;
- grants £1.1 million.

The directors' report suggests that the 'Direct' heading probably refers to the educational activities of the charity, headed by its extensive range of publications, such as its healthy eating education packs for children.

The nine grant recipients were led by the universities of Leeds (£236,000) and North Carolina (£104,000). Awards are determined by an independent review panel.

Although the mission statement talks generally of lifestyle influences on cancer, the information available suggests that this is seen overwhelmingly in terms of diet. Smoking, another lifestyle choice that is prominent in the work of other charities in the field, gets little mention.

Volunteers

The members of the grant review panel probably act voluntarily.

Funding, administration

The only staff mentioned in the two annual reports are the president, Marilyn Gentry, and the chief financial officer.

The income in the UK is primarily from 'donations and gifts', and the charity says that its fundraising is based mainly on direct mail and legacies.

In 1999/00 the total voluntary income of £5.5 million was achieved at a fundraising cost of £1 million, giving a cost ratio of 18p in the pound, or 18%, up slightly from the 16% of the previous year but lower than the average of 21% for the three years to 1998.

The charity adds ...

The expert report, 'Food, Nutrition and the Prevention of Cancer: a global perspective', was published by WCRF in 1997. It is recognised throughout the world as the leading text on diet and cancer, and a catalyst for change. We will be working on updating the report during 2002.

The information assessed

The charity produces an 'Annual Report and Accounts', with the auditors' report saying that these are the 'financial statements' that give a true and fair view of the charity, but only four of the full six pages of the accounts appear. They are not identified as being 'summarised'.

There is a separate and different 'Directors' Report' attached to the full accounts, which are stated to be in accordance with the Charity Commission's SORP requirements for accounting by charities. However, they do not include details of the 'Emoluments of employees' required by that document.

Neither report explains the charity's position as part of an international network of organisations closely connected by having a single, common chief executive (the SORP calls, among other things, for the reporting of the names and addresses of other 'relevant organisations or persons'). Collectively, though, the total information gives a generally adequate, if patchy, view of the charity's work. The website is good.

Contact

19 Harley Street
London
W1G 9QJ
Tel 020 7343 4200
Website www.wrcf-uk.org
Chair not disclosed
Marilyn Gentry, President

World Society for the Protection of Animals

Income	£4,458,000 (2000)
Donated income	£4,422,000
Fundraising costs	£899,000
Statutory income	£0
Top salary	£70,000–£80,000
Paid staff	
Full time	44
Volunteers	
Operational	50
Fundraising	2,000

Aims, activities

WSPA is an international animal welfare charity registered in the UK, with its headquarters in London. WSPA (pronounced wis-pa) works with more than 500 member societies in around 100 countries to promote animal welfare. It aims to raise the standards of animal welfare throughout the world and it achieves this by taking action against cruelty, by rescuing animals and, through its legislative and educational work, by changing hearts and minds about animal welfare issues.

In 2000 WSPA (among other things) rescued and re-homed a family of chimpanzees kept in the back of a lorry in Spain; provided relief to animals following natural disasters in India, Peru, the Philippines and El Salvador; gave sanctuary to bears saved from the bear-dancing and bear-baiting industries in Pakistan; and implemented stray animal controls in Latvia and Dubai.

Volunteers

Volunteers help with fundraising: 'many supporters of the charity assist on a voluntary basis from time to time'. There are few opportunities for volunteers to work with animals overseas, but volunteers are usually needed to help with the administration in the London office.

Funding, administration

The charity is supported by public donations in response to appeals, and there is a smaller legacy income. The total voluntary income in 2000 of £4.4 million was achieved at a fundraising cost of £899,000, a ratio of 20p in the pound, up from the 17p of the previous year. This was due to a sharp drop in donations, from £4.1 to £3.4 million, which meant that the income of the charity as a whole also fell by 11%.

Though there may well have been specific reasons for this decline, they are not given in the trustees' annual report, which surprisingly just says: 'The society has had another excellent year with income in excess of £4.4 million.' The report also notes that the charity's modest mail order business has been turned over to a third-party catalogue fulfilment company. 'This new policy has proved successful', with the new company generating a profit of £8,000 for the year. However, in the previous year the profit had been £66,000, so the success is not apparent.

The charity adds ...

WSPA has regional offices in The United States, Denmark, Germany, Colombia, Costa Rica, Brazil, Canada, Australia, New Zealand and Scotland.

The information assessed

The annual report, called the 'Trustees' Report', and the annual report for the parent body are good, as is the website, though there is some criticism in this entry of differences between the tone of the report and some of the figures in the accounts.

There was considerable difficulty in getting to see the full accounts in the first place, with this editor being asked to justify his need to see them.

Contact

14th Floor, Camelford House
87–89 Albert Embankment
London
SE1 7TP
Tel 020 7793 0540
Website www.wspa.org.uk
Chair Peter Davies
Andrew Dickson, Chief Executive

World Vision UK
Overseas development

Income	£26,503,000 (1999/00)
Donated income	£19,681,000
Fundraising costs	£4,175,000
Statutory income	£5,408,000
Top salary	£60,00 –£70,000
Paid staff	82
Volunteers	40

Aims, activities

'World Vision is a Christian organisation and one of the world's leading aid and development agencies, working in almost 100 countries and helping over 85 million people in their struggle against poverty, hunger and injustice ... we work with people irrespective of their religious beliefs.' World Vision International, the federation or partnership of independent national units, has over 7,000 staff around the world and carries out more development work through its own staff than overseas aid charities that operate primarily by funding other local organisations.

Financially the group is dominated by the USA, which generated more than half the total income of $886 million in 2000. The annual review for World Vision as a whole, published in California, seems more strongly religious in tone than the information put out by World Vision UK. It talks of the group's work as its ministry and, apparently, of itself as a church – one of its ministry objectives is to undertake 'Strategic initiatives that serve the church in the fulfilment of its mission', which is 'to follow ... Jesus Christ in working with the poor and oppressed to promote human transformation, seek justice and bear witness to the good news of the Kingdom of God'.

The task in Britain of World Vision UK is primarily that of fundraising. The money is then passed on in response to proposals from other members of the federation working in developing countries, or in ones that have suffered from war or other disasters (though World Vision International also runs programmes in the USA, Canada, Australia and Western Europe).

The charity's long-term development work is mainly based on child sponsorship, where a supporter in Britain is put in contact with a specific child in the developing world, usually from a rural area, and contributes money to help with the development of the community in which that child lives. Income from this, and from other forms of committed regular giving, rose by 20% in 2000 – helped, among other things, by the more accessible Gift Aid tax-reclaim procedure recently introduced by the government which is particularly well suited to income from regular donors.

Sponsoring specific individual children in a village could be divisive. World Vision has addressed this issue by deciding that no money should pass to a particular sponsored child, or to its family. Instead the money is used to improve health and education in the village as a whole – work from which the sponsored child, like all others there, will benefit. The personal contact offers rather a mutual widening of horizons to the two people involved. Nor are anything other than token gifts sent to the sponsored children. World Vision, though, undertakes that letters will be translated and read to the child by its staff or volunteers (and vice versa).

The charity's website makes this situation clear in the response to one of the FAQs (frequently asked questions): 'How much of the money I give goes to my sponsored child?' Answer: 'None ... ' Nevertheless, not all donors may fully understand this. For example, a widely distributed leaflet in the summer of 2001 included the following: 'There's a child desperate for your help', and, in a quote from a donor, 'It is a privilege to be able to help someone – especially when you see them grow up and no longer need your support.'

The projects overseas that are supported include both work in disaster situations – which account for less than a fifth of the expenditure – and to a much greater extent long-term development projects. The 'sponsorship' model being less easy to maintain in urban areas with high levels of population movement, most of the sponsored children are from rural areas. Urban projects tend to be funded through means such as government grants and direct donations. The charity works equally to benefit people of all religions or none, but all of its senior staff (and more where this is practicable) throughout the world are Christians.

World Vision UK sent money to 89 countries in 1999/00, though not all of them have sponsored children. The main beneficiary areas were:

– Mozambique £3.5 million

– India £1.7 million

– Kosovo £1.6 million

– Ethiopia £1.3 million

– Bosnia £1.1 million

Volunteers

There is a supporters' telephone helpline: 01908 841010. The work overseas is normally carried out by locally recruited staff and volunteers. The 1999/00 annual report notes that 'the use of volunteers reduced this year and totalled 7,195 working hours (1998/99: 9,043 hours)'. This is the equivalent of perhaps 200 full time staff.

Funding, administration

In 1999/00 the main sources of income were as follows (with 1998/99 figures in brackets):

- child sponsorship for 64,000 children and other regular giving £14 million (£12 million);

- government grants £5.4 million (£5.4 million);

- donated goods and services (mostly from government in Kosovo and Ethiopia) £1.1 million.

Surprisingly, income from legacies is small, reaching only £120,000 in 1999/00 and just £22,000 the previous year. One attraction of the reliance on regular sponsorship giving is that the charity can get the agreement of most donors to arrange for tax relief on their donations. This

contributed no less than £3 million to the income of the charity.

The 20% rise in voluntary income was achieved at a fundraising cost of £4.2 million, giving a cost ratio of 21p in the pound, or 21%, down from 22% in the previous year and from an average 26% in the three years to 1998/99.

Child sponsorship programmes are unusual in that a large part of their cost lies in the time of staff or local volunteers in keeping the individual children in touch with their sponsors: arranging for letters to be written and translated; for school reports to be obtained; or in finding the reasons for a child having left the village concerned and so no longer being contactable. These expenditures, though, are not just a cost; the personal contact brings important benefits and rewards to both the child and the sponsor.

The charity adds ...

By working with other members of the World Vision partnership around the globe we can make sure that donations from our supporters in the UK are channelled directly to the areas of greatest need whether through long term development or emergency relief.

The information assessed

The adequate annual report and accounts are not as clear as they might be on the nature of the charity's child sponsorships and on the relationship with World Vision internationally, but the financial information is well presented. There is a website and a good-looking magazine.

Contact
World Vision House
599 Avebury Boulevard
Milton Keynes
MK9 3PG
Tel 01908 841000
Website www.worldvision.org.uk
Chair Anne Williams
Charles Clayton, Executive Director

WRVS
Women's Royal Voluntary Service; local community services in England, Scotland and Wales

Income	£61,594,000 (2000/01)
Donated income	£1,060,000
Fundraising costs	£1,813,000
Statutory income	£18,000,000
Top salary	£100,000–£110,000
Paid staff	
Full time	384
Part time	1,474
Volunteers	
Operational	98,000
Fundraising	100

Aims, activities
WRVS is one of the largest single providers of local community services in the UK (except Northern Ireland). It has 98,100 volunteers, of whom 12,000 are men.

The main activities are well set out on the WRVS website:

'WRVS works in hundreds of communities across England, Scotland and Wales. Because we focus on the needs of each local community you will find a huge variety and different combinations of work we do in each area, from Good Neighbours schemes, to Meals on Wheels and child contact centres ...

'Supporting staff, patients and visitors in hospitals, WRVS

- Is a leading provider of hospital services
- Runs WRVS trading projects in 450 hospitals, including cafes and shops
- Provides allied caring services such as guiding and information desks, trolley shops to the wards
- Donated £3.6 million to hospital trusts [in] 1999–2000, including four grants of over £100,000.

'For housebound and older people (£14 million), WRVS

- Serves around 10 million Meals on Wheels
- Runs 323 trolley shops in residential homes and over 1,000 lunch and social clubs
- Runs mobile services – 2,225 Books on Wheels rounds, 8 Good Neighbours and 11 social transport schemes.

'For families in crisis, WRVS runs

- 42 toy libraries
- 94 child contact centres for separated families
- five Connection projects for children needing emotional support
- 67 tea bars, five visitors' centres and six play areas and crèches in prisons
- Serves light refreshments in over 230 magistrates, county and sheriff courts.

'For people affected by disasters and emergencies

- WRVS' national network of emergency services volunteers and staff provides rapid response teams in times of emergency and is on call 24 hours a day, 7 days a week

● We gave assistance to victims and families of the Lockerbie air crash, the Hillsborough football tragedy, Selby, Paddington and Clapham train crashes, during the flood crisis, to the Kosovan refugees and events following the death of Princess Diana.'

Volunteers

The website says: 'WRVS can offer volunteering opportunities in retail, driving, customer service, communication, caring for older people, working with children, in a hospital environment, catering, event organising, fundraising, IT, plus we need people to support our teams in training, finance, health & safety and volunteer recruitment. Vacancies are available in England, Scotland and Wales.

'To find out more about vacancies near you, apply online or telephone 0845 601 4670 and your local volunteering manager will contact you.'

The annual review notes: 'A conservative estimate, based on the number of volunteer hours donated each year to communities at an hourly rate of £5.75 (the national average hourly earnings rate), duly weighted to reflect WRVS's membership, would equate to some £69 million a year'.

Funding, administration

The accounts are certified as giving a true and fair view of the affairs of the charity, but they do not show where most of its very large income comes from. By far the largest heading is £46 million recorded as coming from 'charitable projects' in the four fields of work set out above, but there is nothing about who pays for these activities.

However, much of the information that is not in the formal accounts is in fact to be found in the non-statutory annual review (though the figures are for 1999/00). It appears that about £33 million of income arises from sales to the public in the shops and cafés that are run in hospitals, courts and the like, and that up to £13 million comes from local authorities for Meals on Wheels and other food services (with a small fraction of recipients paying for an independent meals service).

These form the main income sources for the charity, but there is also a gradually decreasing grant from the Home Office, of £5 million in that year.

The 1999/00 annual report noted that, in view of the loss of the government grant, the charity is very reasonably seeking to 'increase our fundraising potential by strengthening our communications team and focusing our fundraising activities'. This refers to a jump of over 50% in fundraising expenditure, up to £1.5 million from the £1 million the year before. The fundraised income, however, had only risen very slightly to £1.1 million, meaning that the charity spent £1.41 for every £1 raised. The figure for the previous year had been £1.15 for each £1 donated.

According to the 2000/01 annual report the situation became even more extreme the following year, with £1.8 million spent to raise a slightly lower level of donations and legacies, giving a cost ratio of £1.71 to raise each pound, a ratio up from the £1.41 and £1.15 of the two previous years.

This most unusual position is ignored completely in the 'Report of the Board of Trustees', not warranting even the one-sentence mention of the previous year. It is still possible that the great fundraising investment may pay off satisfactorily in future years, but the fact that donations actually declined in the face of this spending must be seriously alarming. At the least, a full discussion of the issue, and of the expectations for the future, should appear in the annual report.

One mitigating factor, again not disclosed in the annual report, is that some of the expenditure may go on the recruitment of volunteers. This may have been a more successful project. Though it is reported that 7,000 new volunteers were recruited, it is not clear whether this is a higher figure than in previous years.

Five of the eight trustees were paid amounts of between £5,000 and £16,000 in the year for 'services beyond their duties as trustees', as is permitted under the constitution of the charity (and, it is reported, with the approval of the Charity Commission). There is no information in the annual report about the additional services that these trustees carry out, but the charity has noted that they were operational duties such as emergency services and training.

The charity adds ...

The 1999/2000 WRVS accounts were the first for which the Auditors gave an unqualified report. The charity has made significant improvements in its controls, procedures and efficiencies over the last few years.

The information assessed

The generally good annual report and accounts and annual review are let down by uninformative accounts. The website is fine, and has the first online sign-up for volunteers that this editor has seen.

Contact

Milton Hill House
Milton Hill
Steventon
Abingdon
Oxfordshire
OX13 6AD
Tel 01235 442900
Website www.wrvs.org.uk
Chair Tina Tietjen
Gerald Burton, Chief Executive

WWF-UK (Worldwide Fund for Nature)

Income	£26,729,000 1999/00
Donated income	£22,583,000
Fundraising costs	£5,484,000
Statutory income	£2,874,000
Top salary	£80,000–£90,000
Paid staff	256
Volunteers	5,000

Aims, activities

Still remembered by some as the World Wildlife Fund, this charity is the UK member of WW-International. It seeks to:

● conserve and protect endangered species;

● address global threats to nature.

The ultimate goal is to stop, and eventually to reverse, the accelerating degradation of the planet's natural environment.

The charity achieves its aims both through work in the UK – accounting for up to 15% of its charitable expenditures – and through supporting projects and activities overseas. These may be carried out by the charity itself, or by giving grants to other organisations in the area concerned. The titles of some of the major projects (with their costs in 1999/00) probably give a fair impression of the work as a whole:

- Mexico: people-centred conservation and development programme (£501,000);

- Global: forests and trade initiative (£307,000);

- UK: forest products trade fair (£232,000);

- Vietnam and Laos: transborder conservation and development project (£143,000);

- India: tiger conservation project (£113,000);

- UK: climate change scenario brochure (£89,000);

- Indonesia: conservation of the Indonesian rhinoceros (£69,000).

The charity is overwhelmingly dependent on voluntary donations, receiving less than 15% of its income from government grants and other aid agencies. It has more than 250,000 members, and individual donations totalled more than £12 million in 1999/00. A further £7 million was received in legacies.

A big and unusual project in Britain has been (with Essex Wildlife Trust) to buy Abbots Hall Farm and return it to natural salt marsh – the first time, the charity says, that such a 'retreat' has been undertaken solely in the interests of bio-diversity (though similar work is being reported by the *Royal Society for the Protection of Birds*).

An important part of the charity's work is its campaigning, accounting for about a fifth of its expenditure. Work in progress in 2000/01 included the Oceans Recovery Campaign

(ORCA) and the People and Planet Campaign.

The charity has been criticised for its willingness to take money from major corporations. The *Guardian* reported in September 2001 that the charity had been given $1 million for a conservation project in Papua New Guinea by the Chevron oil company – one of whose internal documents noted that 'WWF will act as a buffer against international environmental criticism'.

Volunteers

The charity is reliant on volunteers to help with its fundraising, but its work is mainly carried out by its paid staff or by other organisations whose projects it supports financially.

Funding, administration

The charity spent £5.5 million on fundraising in 1999/00, or 24p for every pound received in donations or legacies.

The annual report has unusually full and clear details of how this money is spent, and of the resulting income. The highest costs proportionately are for the quite modest regional fundraising programme, which scarcely covers the charity's expenditure – but which will generate further income down the line from new members and, ultimately, from legacies.

The charity adds ...

WWF-UK has just reached its 40th birthday and has greatly developed over the years so that we now fight environmental battles on many fronts. Our work continues to involve conserving endangered species, but also covers conservation of spaces, and tackling global threats by producing long term sustainable solutions. We continue to confront governments and businesses when necessary.

The information assessed

The excellent annual review and annual report and accounts are available in full on the charity's good website.

Contact
Panda House, Weyside Park
Godalming
Surrey
GU7 1XR
Tel 01483 426444
Website www.wwf.org.uk
Chair Mrs Sara Morrison
Robert Napier, Chief Executive

YMCA England

Established in 1844, the YMCA is now one of the world's largest groups of Christian youth and community charities. The movement in England has about 5,000 staff and nearly 4,500 volunteers. Each of the 151 local YMCAs is an independent charity and runs its own activities.

There are four main areas of work for the YMCA movement as a whole:

- Housing. The YMCA is the largest provider of safe, secure and affordable supported housing for young people. It offers 6,700 dwellings ranging from hostel rooms to self-contained flats. The YMCA is the UK's single largest provider of Foyer schemes, which are 'residential centres giving young people access to housing, training, job search and support'.

- Training. The charity provides training opportunities for disadvantaged and excluded groups. It offers training for national vocational qualifications (NVQs), basic numeracy and literacy, specific work on personal learning plans (such as life skills programmes for young people with high support needs), and preparation for training programmes where young people can explore their motivations and develop learning plans.

- Personal and social development. The YMCA's work with young people is based on the holistic personal development of individuals and is complementary to mainstream education. The wide range of opportunities offered provides an arena where young people can explore ideas and issues that affect their lives, and acquire skills to cope with a wide variety of situations.

- Sport, health, exercise and fitness. The YMCA is the largest voluntary sector provider of sport, health, exercise and fitness programmes across England. Most YMCAs provide programmes in partnership with other organisations, including community groups and schools, other charities, GPs and hospitals; often to groups of young people who have been otherwise excluded.

The role of YMCA England is to support and represent individual YMCA associations in England.

The movement as a whole operates in 123 countries worldwide, with more than 30 million members and staff. Y Care International, the development agency of the YMCA, works in developing countries by channelling financial support through grants to local YMCAs for projects developed in, and with, their local communities. In 2000/01, £2.3 million was spent on this overseas work through YMCA England. The largest single recipient was Action by Churches Together (ACT), which received £573,000 for its work in Africa and £288,000 for Eastern Europe.

(The Young Women's Christian Association, or YWCA, is a separate organisation, but not large enough to have its own entry in this book. It can be contacted on 01865 304200.)

Yorkshire Cancer Research

Income	£4,239,000 (1999/00)
Donated income	£3,761,000
Fundraising costs	£355,000
Statutory income	£0
Top salary	less than £40,000
Paid staff	
Full time	10
Part time	2
Volunteers	
Fundraising	600

Aims, activities

As the 'most successful regional cancer research charity in the UK', the charity primarily supports research into the cause and cure of cancer, carried out in universities, hospitals and research institutions in Yorkshire.The biggest projects are in the universities of Bradford, York, Leeds, Hull and Sheffield.

Formed over 75 years ago as the Yorkshire Council of the British Empire Cancer Campaign, it was the brainchild of 'a number of business professionals and prominent citizens of Yorkshire who decided that Yorkshire was big enough to raise enough money to support a cancer research centre of its own'.

Grant decisions are taken by a scientific advisory committee on the basis of independent peer review.

Volunteers

The charity has a network of over 50 voluntary committees working throughout Yorkshire, organising events and collections. In addition, there are three charity shops.

Funding, administration

Legacies of £2.8 million and donations of £1 million provided almost all the charity's income in 1999/00. This was achieved at a fundraising cost of £355,000, giving a cost ratio of a very low 9p in the pound, down from 13p in the pound the previous year. Donations in particular rose by 30% compared with 1998/99.

In March 2000 the charity had free reserves of over £12 million, equivalent to almost three years' expenditure. This is a level which the trustees thought appropriate, but which nevertheless seems high even in the light of the future commitments described.

In an enterprising initiative the charity has launched into television advertising.

The information assessed

The excellent annual reports and other information are normally backed by a website, but this was undergoing reconstruction when this entry was written.

Contact

39 East Parade
Harrogate
North Yorkshire
HG1 5LQ
Tel 01423 501269
Website www.ycr.org.uk
Chair Dr B P Jackson
Elaine King, Chief Executive and Secretary

Youth clubs and organisations

Work with young people is a big part of the charitable sector. Local authority services ('statutory' or 'maintained' youth work) cover 13 to 19 year-olds. 'Voluntary' youth organisations may also include activities for children of primary school age and young people aged up to 25.

Voluntary youth organisations can be independent, such as a youth club set up by local residents, or affiliated to a large association, such as the Guide Association (tel. 020 7834 6242). There may be a theme, activity, faith or culture that ties local groups into the main association, such as the Boys' and Girls' Brigades, the Association for Jewish Youth and *St John's Ambulance*. The separate entry for the major *Youth movements, uniformed* includes more information about some of these networks. There are also youth theatres, youth orchestras and youth branches of sports clubs.

Most voluntary youth organisations are registered as charities and their charitable object tends to be something along the lines of: 'to promote the development of young people in achieving their full physical, intellectual, social and spiritual potential'. Unlike the maintained youth service, voluntary groups often rely on subscriptions and membership fees and fundraising events, and are funded from a range of sources that may include public fundraising, charitable trusts and companies.

Local authorities are allocated funds by central government for work with young people. They are not usually keen on providing new buildings for youth work, but can provide support in the form of equipment, activity programmes and sessional youth workers. There are particular forms of statutory support available for individual activities from a variety of health, regeneration, urban, rural, environment, sport and arts funds.

Voluntary youth organisations almost all rely heavily on volunteers for all elements of their work, helping to run clubs and activities, fundraising, and administration. They also often need enthusiastic and effective members for their management committees to ensure the club or organisation is well run.

The national organisation with responsibility for youth work in England is the National Youth Agency,17–23 Albion Street, Leicester LE1 6GD (tel: 0116

285 3792; website: www.nya.org.uk). Elsewhere in the UK, telephone numbers and website addresses are as follows:

– Youth Scotland 0131 554 2561; www.youthscotland.org.uk

– Wales Youth Agency 029 2085 5700; www.wya.org.uk

– Northern Ireland Youth Council 028 9064 3882; www.youthcouncil-ni.org.uk

The British Youth Council is a membership body that represents organisations working with young people (tel: 020 7422 8640; website: www.byc.org.uk).

UK Youth, formerly known as Youth Clubs UK and the National Association of Youth Clubs, is the largest national non-uniformed youth organisation, with lots of affiliated clubs throughout the country which rely on local volunteer input (tel: 020 7242 4045; website: www.ukyouth.org.uk).

The Woodcraft Folk is a charitable, educational movement with about 500 groups in England, Scotland and Wales, mainly in urban areas. Many of its activities focus on environmental issues and the pursuit of peace and social justice. Adult volunteers coordinate the group activities, but about half the members of the charity's General Council are under the age of 21. The movement is keen to distinguish itself from the military overtones of some other youth organisations (tel: 020 8672 6031; website: www.poptel.org.uk/woodcraft).

At a local level, youth organisations can be found in the Yellow Pages (under 'Youth and community groups') or through local Councils for Voluntary Service (see page 385). Those that are keen to involve volunteers may have registered their needs at the local volunteer bureau (as above). For those with internet access, www.do-it.org.uk is a website developed by Youthnet, but covering volunteering opportunities for all age groups.

Youth movements, uniformed

'Uniformed' youth movements play a significant role in the voluntary youth culture of the UK. The following organisations are largely run by volunteers, and coordinated by small bodies of salaried staff who mainly work at a national level.

Air Training Corps (ATC)

The ATC is an important youth organisation, with approximately 50,000 members. It is supported by the RAF in terms of expertise, but the cadets are organised by about 10,000 volunteer staff, and 5,000 civilian committee members. Each ATC squadron is an exempted charity, organised by the charitable umbrella movement of the Air Cadets Organisation (ACO), which also coordinates the Combined Cadet Force (CCF).

For more information, the website provides regional contact details (www.cranwell.raf.mod.uk), or the ACO can be contacted on 01400 261201.

The Army Cadets Force Association (ACF)

This is a major organisation for young people in the UK, with over 50,000 members, including 10,000 girls. There are 1,700 Cadet Units, based in both urban and rural areas, organised by 8,000 voluntary leaders. The ACF is sponsored by the army and the Ministry of Defence, as well as charitable donations, which means that members' costs are kept to a minimum. Most of the training and activities are supplied for free. Besides developing the youth members, the ACF is also keen to challenge adults to train as voluntary youth leaders.

To find out more, contact 020 7730 9733; website: www.armycadets.com

The Boys' Brigade

This is an international charitable Christian youth movement, with a significant British contingent. The staff who manage the local 'Companies' are primarily trained volunteers, supported by a chaplain who can offer spiritual direction, along with general volunteers who aim to enhance the boys' community spirit with an interdenominational Christian emphasis. At a national level, there is a small team of full time professional staff who support and organise the 'Companies' and their voluntary leaders.

To find out more about volunteering, contact 01442 231681; website: www.boys-brigade.org.uk

The Girls' Brigade England and Wales

The volunteer base of each interdenominational Girls' Brigade Company includes trained Christian women as leaders, a chaplain and general helpers. They both support the girls' social and spiritual development, and develop their contribution to church and community life, on a local, national and global level.

For more information about volunteering, contact 01235 510425; website: www.girlsbrigadeew.org.uk

Girl Guides

The Guide Association is an international charity which caters for girls between the ages of 5 and 14. The organisation is divided into Guides, Brownies and Rainbows – subdivided into patrols, packs and units, respectively. These groups are then 'guided' by volunteers who support the girls in their personal development, and in the pursuit of reward badges.

Potential volunteers can contact 020 7834 6242; website: www.guides.org.uk

St John Ambulance Cadets

The *St John Ambulance* youth members (aged 6–16) are Badgers and Cadets, and make up more than half of the organisation's volunteers, who currently number about 50,000. Youth members are encouraged to help their community, and have opportunities to learn far more than basic first aid skills from their trained voluntary leaders.

See the main entry in this book, or, for those interested in volunteering, the contact number is 020 7253 6644; website: www.sja.org.uk

The scouting movement – see separate entry

Sea Cadets

This corps is sponsored by the Royal Navy, but is also supported by its own national charity, the Sea Cadet Association, which fundraises and maintains the sea cadet fleet. It claims the 'longest continuous history of any British youth movement' and currently operates some 400 units nationwide, with 16,000 cadets in total. Open to all young people between the ages of 10 and 18, it aims to encourage personal development based on the customs and traditions of the Royal Navy, and offers a range of opportunities to learn new skills and to travel to other parts of the country.

For more information contact 020 7928 8978; website: www.sea-cadets.org

The 500 largest fundraising charities

The information here is derived from the comprehensive listings published by the Charities Aid Foundation (tel: 01732 520000, www.charitynet.org) in its 2001 update to *Dimensions 2000 – CAF's Top 500 Fundraising Charities* – and is given with its kind permission.

The charities in italics have their own detailed entries in this book. Note that the figures given here may not be as recent as those used in the main text, and are not always compiled on a comparable basis. For example, the figures for donated income include legacies but not donated goods for sale in shops. There are some charities, mostly those 'exempt' from registration, that are described in the main text but do not appear in this list.

*Indicates that the figures were not confirmed to CAF by the charity.

	Donated income £000s	Total income £000s	Telephone number	Website	Final year end
1 National Trust*	£99,587	£220,778	020 7222 9251	www.nationaltrust.org.uk	Feb-99
2 Royal National Lifeboat Instn	£79,371	£93,746	01202 663000	www.rnli.org.uk	Dec-98
3 Imperial Cancer Research Fund	£71,816	£117,775	020 7242 0200	www.imperialcancer.co.uk	Sep-98
4 Salvation Army*	£66,417	£86,419	020 7367 4500	www.salvationarmy.org.uk	Mar-99
5 Oxfam	£61,917	£169,716	01865 311311	www.oxfam.org.uk	Apr-99
6 Cancer Research Campaign	£60,489	£88,820	020 7224 1333	www.crc.org.uk	Mar-99
7 Diana Princess of Wales Memorial Fund	£59,450	£97,399	020 7902 5500	www.theworkcontinues.org.uk	Dec-98
8 Macmillan Cancer Relief*	£53,579	£59,984	020 7840 7840	www.macmillan.org.uk	Dec-98
9 NSPCC	£48,541	£59,858	020 7825 2500	www.nspcc.org.uk	Mar-99
10 Save the Children Fund	£47,429	£95,585	020 7703 5400	www.savethechildren.org.uk	Mar-99
11 British Heart Foundation	£43,373	£87,864	020 7935 0185	www.bhf.org.uk	Mar-99
12 Marie Curie Cancer Care*	£42,718	£65,406	020 7599 7777	www.mariecurie.org.uk	Mar-99
13 Royal National Inst for the Blind	£40,475	£70,876	0845 766 9999	www.rnib.org.uk	Mar-99
14 RSPCA	£40,417	£50,777	0870 0101181	www.rspca.org.uk	Dec-98
15 British Red Cross	£40,122	£108,081	020 7235 5454	www.redcross.org.uk	Dec-98
16 Barnardo's	£39,690	£109,965	020 8550 8822	www.barnardos.org.uk	Mar-99
17 Guide Dogs for the Blind	£36,160	£43,190	0118 983 5555	www.guidedogs.org.uk	Dec-98
18 RSPB	£35,575	£41,131	01767 680551	www.rspb.org.uk	Mar-99
19 Christian Aid*	£34,804	£48,602	020 7620 4444	www.christian-aid.org	Mar-99
20 ActionAid	£33,817	£44,948	020 7561 7561	www.actionaid.org	Dec-98
21 Help the Aged	£32,941	£66,776	020 7253 0253	www.helptheaged.org.uk	Apr-99
22 Royal British Legion*	£31,518	£49,088	020 7973 7200	www.britishlegion.org.uk	Sep-98
23 Tearfund*	£30,729	£33,711	020 7554 5200	www.tearfund.org	Mar-99
24 Royal Opera House Covent Garden	£27,221	£53,679	020 7212 9267	www.royalopera.org	Mar-99
25 People's Dispensary for Sick Animals	£27,192	£43,982	01952 290999	www.pdsa.org.uk	Dec-98
26 WWF-UK	£21,283	£26,520	01483 426444	www.wwf.org.uk	Jun-99
27 Arthritis Research Campaign	£19,744	£22,852	01246 558033	www.arc.org.uk	Sep-98
28 Rathbone Community Industry*	£19,310	£26,246	0161 236 5358	www.rathbone-ci.co.uk	Mar-99
29 United Jewish Israel Appeal	£18,907	£19,132	020 8446 1477	www.ujia.org	Dec-97

	Donated income £000s	Total income £000s	Telephone number	Website	Final year end
30 Prince's Trust*	£18,643	£25,678	020 7543 1234	www.princes-trust.org.uk	Mar-99
31 BBC Children in Need Appeal	£17,712	£20,095	020 8576 7788	www.bbc.co.uk/cin	Sep-99
32 English National Opera	£17,403	£27,583	020 7836 0111	www.eno.org.uk	Mar-99
33 Scope*	£17,286	£89,725	020 7619 7100	www.scope.org.uk	Mar-99
34 Children's Society*	£16,704	£26,532	020 7841 4400	www.the-childrens-society.org.uk	Mar-99
35 World Vision UK	£16,611	£22,223	01908 841000	www.worldvision.org.uk	Sep-99
36 Multiple Sclerosis Society	£15,837	£24,303	020 7610 7171	www.mssociety.org.uk	Dec-98
37 SSAFA Forces Help*	£13,925	£27,898	020 7403 8783	www.ssafa.org.uk	Dec-98
38 CAFOD	£13,530	£21,127	020 7733 7900	www.cafod.org.uk	Sep-98
39 NCH (Action for Children)	£12,960	£88,298	020 7704 7058	www.nch.org.uk	Mar-99
40 Leonard Cheshire Foundation	£12,838	£86,716	020 7802 8200	www.leonard-cheshire.org	Mar-99
41 PLAN International UK	£12,765	£15,562	020 7485 6612	www.plan-international.org	Jun-99
42 Jewish Care	£12,259	£33,048	020 8922 2000	www.jewishcare.org	Dec-98
43 Shelter	£11,845	£17,612	020 7505 2000	www.shelter.org.uk	Mar-99
44 Cats Protection League*	£11,642	£12,816	01403 211900	www.cats.org.uk	Dec-98
45 UNICEF UK	£11,571	£13,806	020 7405 5592	www.unicef.org.uk	Mar-99
46 Freemasons Grand Charity*	£11,475	£13,662	020 7395 9293	www.plan-international.org	Nov-98
47 Blue Cross	£11,409	£12,127	01993 822651	www.bluecross.org.uk	Dec-98
48 Diabetes UK	£11,206	£14,423	020 7323 1531	www.diabetes.org.uk	Dec-98
49 Royal Society for Nature Conservation	£10,741	£12,415	01636 679291	www.rsnc.org	Mar-99
50 Great Ormond St Hospital Children's	£10,629	£23,981	020 7916 5678	www.gosh.org	Mar-99
51 St John Ambulance	£10,411	£45,362	020 7324 4000	www.sja.org.uk	Dec-98
52 Woodland Trust	£9,745	£14,657	01476 581111	www.woodland-trust.org.uk	Dec-98
53 Sight Savers	£9,699	£10,751	01444 446600	www.sightsavers.org	Dec-98
54 Alzheimer's Society*	£9,299	£16,114	020 7306 0606	www.alzheimers.org.uk	Mar-99
55 St Dunstan's	£9,286	£15,146	020 7723 5021	www.st-dunstans.org.uk	Mar-99
56 Donkey Sanctuary	£9,204	£9,921	01395 578222	www.thedonkeysanctuary.org.uk	Sep-98
57 Age Concern England *	£9,131	£26,866	020 8765 7200	www.ace.org.uk	Mar-99
58 Royal National Inst for Deaf People *	£9,039	£35,369	020 7296 8000	www.rnid.org.uk	Mar-99

		Donated income £000s	Total income £000s	Telephone number	Website	Final year end
59	National Canine Defence League	£8,796	£10,461	020 7837 0006	www.ncdl.org.uk	Dec-98
60	National Trust for Scotland	£8,618	£19,062	0131 243 9300	www.nts.org.uk	Oct-98
61	Leprosy Mission International	£8,505	£8,963	01733 370505	www.leprosymission.org	Dec-98
62	Leukaemia Research Fund	£8,249	£16,926	020 7405 0101	www.lrf.org.uk	Mar-99
63	Mencap *	£8,154	£98,362	020 7454 0454	www.mencap.org.uk	Mar-99
64	Sue Ryder Care *	£8,051	£37,789	020 7400 0440	www.suerydercare.org	Dec-97
65	Royal Air Force Benevolent Fund *	£7,873	£21,069	020 7580 8343	www.raf-benfund.org.uk	Dec-98
66	British Tennis Foundation	£7,850	£9,092	020 7381 7140	www.lta.org.uk	Sep-98
67	Parkinson's Disease Society	£7,836	£8,808	020 7931 8080	www.parkinsons.org.uk	Dec-98
68	Care International UK	£7,777	£29,756	020 7934 9334	www.careinternational.org.uk	Jun-99
69	Assn for Intl Cancer Research	£7,387	£7,865	01334 477910	www.aicr.org.uk	Sep-98
70	Royal Masonic Benevolent Institution	£7,337	£28,975	020 7405 8341	www.rmbi.org.uk	Dec-98
71	Christian Vision *	£7,151	£9,054	0121 522 6087	www.christian-vision.org	Dec-98
72	Bible Society *	£6,994	£10,208	01793 418100	www.biblesociety.org.uk	Dec-98
73	WaterAid	£6,671	£9,731	020 7793 4500	www.wateraid.org.uk	Mar-99
74	National Asthma Campaign	£6,561	£7,151	020 7226 2260	www.asthma.org.uk	Sep-98
75	Methodist Church Fund	£6,543	£20,385	020 7486 5502	www.methodist.org.uk	Aug-98
76	Princess Louise Scottish Hospital (Erskine) *	£6,417	£12,137	0141 812 1100	www.erskine.org.uk	Sep-98
77	Stroke Association	£6,397	£9,717	020 7566 0300	www.stroke.org.uk	Mar-99
78	Tidy Britain Group	£6,343	£8,709	01942 824620	www.tidybritain.org.uk	Mar-99
79	Church Mission Society	£6,292	£7,574	020 7928 8681	www.cms-uk.org	Jan-99
80	Irish Sisters of Charity *	£6,264	£10,831	020 8995 1963	not available	Mar-99
81	Civil Service Benevolent Fund *	£6,143	£10,527	020 8240 2401	www.csbf.org.uk	Dec-98
82	Royal Star & Garter Home *	£6,096	£10,487	020 8940 3314	www.starandgarter.org	Dec-98
83	Sustrans *	£5,919	£6,018	0117 926 8893	www.sustrans.org.uk	Mar-99
84	Arthritis Care *	£5,914	£8,121	020 7380 6500	www.arthritiscare.org.uk	Dec-98
85	National Council of YMCAs	£5,889	£25,917	020 8520 5599	www.ymca.org.uk	Mar-99
86	Norwood Ravenswood *	£5,718	£21,258	020 8954 4555	www.nwrw.org	Mar-99
87	Methodist Homes for the Aged *	£5,657	£26,051	01332 296200	www.mha.org.uk	Mar-99

		Donated income £000s	Total income £000s	Telephone number	Website	Final year end
88	Royal Air Forces Association*	£5,656	£7,676	020 8994 8504	www.rafa.org.uk	Dec-98
89	Friends of Hebrew Univ of Jerusalem*	£5,474	£6,062	020 7691 1500	not available	Sep-98
90	Voluntary Service Overseas	£5,461	£27,235	020 8780 7200	www.vso.org.uk	Mar-99
91	World Cancer Research Fund*	£5,389	£5,462	020 7343 4200	www.woodland-trust.org.uk	Sep-98
92	Institute of Cancer Research	£5,372	£37,563	020 7352 8133	www.icr.ac.uk/everyman	Jul-99
93	Project HOPE United Kingdom	£5,296	£5,353	020 8990 2246	www.projecthopeuk.org.	Jun-99
94	CBF World Jewish Relief	£5,228	£5,300	020 7387 3925	www.wjr.org.uk	Dec-98
95	Sense	£5,193	£31,848	020 7272 7774	www.sense.org.uk	Mar-99
96	Sargent Cancer Care for Children	£5,149	£5,483	020 8752 2800	www.sargent.org	Mar-99
97	Action for Blind People	£5,114	£10,524	020 7732 8771	www.afbp.org	Mar-99
98	ChildLine	£5,101	£5,884	020 7239 1000	www.childline.org.uk	Mar-99
99	JNF Charitable Trust*	£4,874	£4,915	020 8421 7600	www.jnf.co.uk	Dec-98
100	Crisis	£4,842	£5,851	020 7655 8300	www.crisis.org.uk	Jun-99
101	Redwings Horse Sanctuary	£4,721	£4,894	01603 737432	www.redwings.co.uk	Mar-99
102	Muscular Dystrophy Campaign*	£4,598	£4,840	020 7720 8055	www.muscular-dystrophy.org	Dec-98
103	BEN-Motor and Allied Trades Benevolent Fund	£4,516	£8,685	01344 620191	www.ben.org.uk	Mar-99
104	Cottage Homes	£4,515	£8,129	020 8201 0112	www.retailcharity.co.uk	Apr-99
105	St Christopher's Hospice	£4,439	£8,497	020 8778 9252	not available	Mar-99
106	Camphill Village Trust*	£4,426	£14,944	01384 372122	www.camphill.org.uk	Mar-99
107	Baptist Missionary Society	£4,249	£5,348	01235 517700	www.bms.org.uk	Oct-98
108	Samaritans	£4,248	£5,246	01753 216500	www.samaritans.org	Mar-99
109	OMF International (UK)	£4,238	£4,847	01732 887299	www.omf.org.uk	Dec-98
110	Animal Health Trust	£4,230	£7,342	01638 751000	www.aht.org.uk	Dec-98
111	Children with Leukaemia	£4,223	£4,287	020 7404 0808	www.leukaemia.org	Jun-98
112	Christian Children's Fund of GB*	£4,207	£4,275	020 7729 8339	www.ccfgb.org.uk	Sep-98
113	Variety Club	£4,142	£8,642	020 7428 8100	www.varietyclub.org.uk	Sep-98
114	Jubilee Sailing Trust	£4,133	£4,792	023 8044 9108	www.jst.org.uk	Mar-99
115	Mind	£4,090	£6,877	020 8519 2122	www.mind.org.uk	Mar-99
116	Motor Neurone Disease Assn	£4,078	£5,037	01604 250505	www.mndassociation.org	Jan-99

		Donated income £000s	Total income £000s	Telephone number	Website	Final year end
117	Cystic Fibrosis Trust	£3,977	£4,464	020 8464 7211	www.cftrust.org.uk	Mar-99
118	London Yearly Meeting, Society of Friends *	£3,930	£6,028	020 7663 1000	www.quaker.org/BYM	Dec-98
119	Dogs Home Battersea	£3,915	£6,197	020 7622 3626	www.dogshome.org	Dec-98
120	SSPCA	£3,839	£5,359	0131 339 0222	www.scottishspca.org	Dec-98
121	British Horse Society *	£3,838	£4,228	01926 707700	www.bhs.org.uk	Dec-99
122	Wildfowl & Wetlands Trust	£3,684	£9,189	01453 891900	www.wwt.org.uk	Dec-98
123	Wood Green Animal Shelters	£3,610	£3,915	01480 830014	www.woodgreen.org.uk	Mar-99
124	Baptist Union of GB	£3,591	£4,899	01235 517700	www.baptist.org.uk	Dec-98
125	World Soc for Protection of Animals	£3,590	£3,615	020 7793 0540	www.wspa.org.uk	Dec-98
126	Children's Aid Direct *	£3,581	£8,790	0118 958 4000	www.cad.org.uk	Sep-98
127	Book Aid International *	£3,572	£4,287	020 7733 3577	www.bookaid.org	Dec-98
128	Action Research *	£3,531	£4,487	01403 210406	www.actionresearch.co.uk	Oct-98
129	Congregation of the Daughters of the Cross	£3,524	£38,300	020 7556 1200	not available	Mar-99
130	Duke of Edinburgh's Award	£3,509	£5,971	01753 727400	www.theaward.org	Mar-99
131	Echoes of Service	£3,483	£3,827	01225 310893	www.echoes.org.uk	Dec-98
132	Amnesty Intl UK Charitable Trust *	£3,447	£3,511	020 7814 6200	www.amnesty.org.uk	Dec-98
133	Children 1st	£3,440	£3,955	0131 337 8539	www.children1st.org.uk	Dec-98
134	Northern Ireland Hospice *	£3,429	£4,649	028 9078 1836	www.nihospice.com	Mar-99
135	Elizabeth Finn Trust	£3,411	£13,534	020 7396 6700	www.elizabethfinntrust.org.uk	Dec-98
136	Pontifical Mission Societies	£3,404	£3,750	020 7821 9755	www.missionsocieties.org.uk	Dec-98
137	Intermediate Technology Dev Group *	£3,400	£11,873	01788 661100	www.itdg.org	Mar-99
138	Centrepoint Soho *	£3,381	£9,701	020 7629 2229	www.centrepoint.org.uk	Mar-99
139	Marie Stopes International	£3,351	£24,602	020 7574 7400	www.mariestopes.org.uk	Dec-98
140	John Grooms	£3,319	£9,744	020 7452 2100	www.johngrooms.org.uk	Mar-99
141	Yorkshire Cancer Research	£3,293	£3,582	01423 501269	www.ycr.org.uk	Mar-99
142	St Ann's Hospice	£3,288	£6,099	0161 437 8136	www.st-anns-hospice.org.uk	Mar-99
143	Lord's Taverners	£3,273	£3,511	020 7821 2828	www.lordstaverners.org	Dec-98
144	Breakthrough Breast Cancer *	£3,242	£4,198	020 7405 5111	www.breakthrough.org.uk	Jul-99
145	National Art Collections Fund	£3,141	£4,274	020 7225 4800	www.artfund.org	Dec-98

		Donated income £000s	Total income £000s	Telephone number	Website	Final year end
146	Tenovus	£3,139	£5,323	029 2048 2000	www.tenovus.com	Mar-99
147	Int'l League for Protection of Horses	£3,114	£3,770	01953 498682	www.ilph.org	Dec-98
148	Scripture Union	£3,090	£7,316	01908 856000	www.scripture.org.uk/	Mar-99
149	Wycliffe Bible Translators	£3,044	£3,178	01494 482521	www.wycliffe.org.uk	Sep-98
150	HCPT The Pilgrimage Trust	£3,044	£3,125	01737 353311	www.hcpt.org.uk	Oct-99
151	Whizz-Kidz	£3,042	£3,091	020 7233 6600	www.whizz-kidz.org.uk	Dec-98
152	Army Benevolent Fund	£3,013	£5,798	020 7591 2000	www.armybenevolentfund.com	Mar-99
153	United Soc for Propagation of the Gospel	£2,910	£5,046	020 7928 8681	www.uspg.org.uk	Dec-98
154	Anthony Nolan Bone Marrow Trust	£2,906	£7,543	020 7284 1234	www.anthonynolan.org.uk	Sep-98
155	Dulwich Picture Gallery	£2,893	£3,879	020 8693 5254	www.dulwichpicturegallery.org.uk	Mar-99
156	European Children's Trust	£2,889	£3,174	020 7248 2424	www.everychild.org.uk	Mar-99
157	Crusaid	£2,875	£3,159	020 7833 3939	www.crusaid.org.uk	Mar-99
158	Scottish Catholic International Aid Fund	£2,865	£3,284	0141 354 5555	www.sciaf.org.uk	Dec-98
159	Fairbridge	£2,844	£4,871	020 7928 1704	www.fairbridge.org.uk	Mar-99
160	Church Army	£2,835	£6,862	020 8318 1226	www.churcharmy.org.uk	Mar-99
161	Mental Health Foundation	£2,791	£3,016	020 7535 7400	www.mentalhealth.org.uk	Mar-99
162	Royal London Society for the Blind	£2,769	£9,123	01732 592500	www.rlsb.org.uk	Jun-99
163	Queen Elizabeth's Fdn Disabled People*	£2,752	£9,354	01372 841100	www.qefd.org	Mar-99
164	National Kidney Research Fund	£2,742	£3,362	01733 704650	www.nkrf.org.uk	Apr-99
165	Pilgrims Hospices in E. Kent	£2,742	£4,649	01227 812612	www.pilgrimshospice.org	Mar-99
166	Royal School for the Blind	£2,721	£8,106	01372 755000	www.seeability.org	Mar-98
167	Little Way Association	£2,678	£2,787	020 7622 0466	not available	Apr-97
168	Far East Broadcasting Association	£2,650	£2,740	not available	www.feba.org.uk	Sep-98
169	Fire Services National Benevolent Fund	£2,642	£3,436	01903 736063	www.fsnbf.org.uk	Dec-98
170	Gideons International in British Isles	£2,578	£2,657	01455 554241	www.gideons.org.uk	Dec-98
171	St Oswald's Hospice	£2,574	£3,699	0191 285 0063	www.northhse.demon.co.uk/St.Oswalds/	Mar-99
172	Friends of the Royal Academy	£2,573	£3,452	020 7300 5950	www.royalacademy.org.uk	Sep-98
173	Nightingale House	£2,543	£10,205	020 8673 3495	www.nightingalehouse.org.uk	Sep-98
174	Royal Hospital for Neuro-Disability	£2,528	£18,179	020 8780 4500	www.neuro-disability.org.uk	Sep-98

		Donated income £000s	Total income £000s	Telephone number	Website	Final year end
175	Winged Fellowship Trust	£2,526	£5,679	020 7833 2594	www.wft.org.uk	Jan-99
176	BTCV	£2,514	£9,902	01491 839766	www.btcv.org.uk/	Mar-99
177	Medical Fdn, Care of Victims of Torture	£2,488	£2,917	020 7813 7777	www.torturecare.org.uk	Dec-98
178	British Lung Foundation *	£2,443	£3,023	020 7831 5831	www.lunguk.org/	Jun-98
179	LEPRA	£2,436	£3,211	01206 562286	www.lepra.org.uk	Dec-98
180	Ayrshire Hospice	£2,398	£4,022	01292 269200	www.ayrshirehospice.org	Mar-99
181	Gurkha Welfare Trust	£2,393	£4,141	020 7251 5234	www.gwt.org.uk	Jun-99
182	Bible Lands Society*	£2,361	£2,745	01494 897950	www.biblelands.co.uk	Apr-99
183	National Meningitis Trust	£2,340	£2,663	01453 768000	www.meningitis-trust.org.uk	Apr-99
184	St Mary's Hospice	£2,321	£3,664	0121 472 1191	www.st-marys-hospice.org.uk	Mar-99
185	St Columba's Hospice *	£2,307	£4,378	0131 551 1381	www.stcolumbashospice.org.uk	Mar-99
186	National Autistic Society	£2,251	£31,367	020 7833 2299	www.oneworld.org/autism_uk/	Mar-99
187	Raleigh International	£2,238	£4,108	020 7371 8585	www.raleigh.org.uk	Mar-99
188	Henshaw's Society for the Blind	£2,223	£9,000	0161 872 1234	www.hsbp.co.uk	Mar-99
189	London City Mission	£2,214	£3,320	020 7407 7585	www.lcm.org.uk	Dec-98
190	Help the Hospices	£2,200	£2,264	020 7520 8200	www.helpthehospices.org.uk	Mar-99
191	British Council of Shaare Zedek	£2,153	£2,233	020 8201 8933	www.szmc.org.il	Dec-98
192	SIM International – UK Section	£2,137	£3,032	01449 766464	www.sim.org	Sep-98
193	National Deaf Children's Society	£2,135	£2,914	020 7490 8656	www.ndcs.org.uk	Mar-99
194	Terrence Higgins Trust*	£2,128	£5,050	020 7831 0330	www.tht.org.uk	Mar-99
195	Trinity Hospice	£2,106	£4,779	020 7787 1000	www.trinityhospice.co.uk	Mar-99
196	Universities & Colleges Christian Fellowship	£2,105	£3,819	0116 2551700	www.uccf.org.uk	Apr-99
197	Rukba	£2,094	£9,634	020 7605 4200	www.rukba.org.uk	Dec-98
198	Princess Alice Hospice Trust *	£2,092	£4,504	01372 468811	not available	Mar-99
199	Acorns Children's Hospice Trust	£2,063	£2,826	0121 248 4823	www.acorns.org.uk	Mar-99
200	Glyndebourne Productions Limited	£2,060	£13,652	01273 812321	www.glyndebourne.com	Dec-98
201	Dove House Hospice	£2,050	£3,271	01482 784343	www.dovehouse.org.uk	Mar-99
202	National Osteoporosis Society	£2,042	£2,161	01761 471771	www.nos.org.uk	Jun-97
203	Comic Relief	£2,021	£5,079	020 7820 5555	www.comicrelief.com	Jun-98

		Donated income £000s	Total income £000s	Telephone number	Website	Final year end
204	Ramblers Association	£2,014	£2,512	020 7339 8500	www.ramblers.org.uk	Sep-98
205	Mission to Seafarers	£1,992	£3,403	020 7248 5202	www.missiontoseafarers.org	Dec-98
206	Outward Bound Trust *	£1,982	£4,410	020 7928 1991	www.outwardbound-uk.org	Mar-99
207	Aid to the Church in Need UK	£1,972	£2,115	020 8642 8668	www.kirche-in-not.org	Dec-98
208	Church of England Pensions Board	£1,950	£16,739	020 7898 1800	not available	Dec-98
209	Scripture Gift Mission	£1,942	£2,717	020 7730 2155	www.asgm.org	Dec-98
210	Princess Royal Trust for Carers	£1,922	£2,053	0141 221 5066	www.carers.org	Mar-99
211	Interserve	£1,921	£2,089	028 9040 2211	www.isire.org	Dec-98
212	British Deaf Association *	£1,921	£2,327	020 7588 3520	www.bda.org.uk	Mar-99
213	Roy Castle Lung Cancer Foundation	£1,899	£2,215	0151 794 8800	www.roycastle.org	Dec-97
214	Brooke Hospital for Animals	£1,878	£2,671	020 7930 0210	www.brooke-hospital.org.uk	Mar-99
215	LOROS *	£1,846	£3,766	0116 2318431	www.fsmr.org.uk/loros.html	Mar-99
216	Shaftesbury Society	£1,837	£18,492	020 8239 5555	www.shaftesburysoc.org.uk	Mar-99
217	CLIC	£1,833	£3,075	0117 311 2600	www.clic.uk.com	Dec-98
218	Ex-Services Mental Welfare Society	£1,827	£4,807	020 8543 6333	www.combatstress.org.uk	Sep-98
219	St Luke's Hospice – Plymouth	£1,823	£2,696	01752 401172	www.stlukes-hospice.org.uk	Mar-99
220	Church Pastoral Aid Society	£1,820	£3,544	01926 458458	www.cpas.org.uk	Apr-99
221	SPARKS	£1,804	£1,952	020 7931 8899	www.sparks.org.uk	Jan-99
222	Catholic Institute for Intl Relations *	£1,802	£4,301	020 7354 0883	www.ciir.org	Mar-99
223	British Epilepsy Association	£1,785	£1,965	0113 210 8800	www.epilepsy.org.uk	Dec-98
224	Breast Cancer Care	£1,779	£2,146	020 7384 2984	www.breastcancercare.org.uk	Dec-98
225	National Museums of Scotland *	£1,778	£13,624	0131 225 7534	www.nms.ac.uk	Mar-99
226	St Catherine's Hospice	£1,760	£2,627	01293 447333	www.stch.org.uk	Mar-99
227	Medecins Sans Frontières (UK)	£1,722	£3,353	020 7713 5600	www.msf.org	Dec-97
228	Cleveland Community Foundation	£1,713	£2,017	01642 314200	not available	Mar-99
229	Capability Scotland	£1,712	£20,967	0131 337 9876	www.capability-scotland.org.uk	Mar-99
230	Alzheimer Scotland	£1,711	£5,598	0131 243 1453	www.alzscot.org	Mar-99
231	St Luke's Hospice – Sheffield *	£1,709	£3,690	0114 236 9911	www.stlukeshospice.org.uk	Mar-99
232	National Childbirth Trust	£1,704	£3,434	020 8992 2616	www.nct-online.org	Sep-98

		Donated income £000s	Total income £000s	Telephone number	Website	Final year end
233	Children's Trust Tadworth	£1,696	£8,960	01737 357171	c-trust@netcomuk.co.uk	Mar-99
234	Children's Hospice Association Scotland	£1,689	£2,644	0131 226 4933	www.chas.org.uk	Mar-99
235	Latin Link *	£1,688	£1,709	020 7939 9000	www.latinlink.org	Mar-99
236	Musicians Benevolent Fund	£1,685	£2,827	020 7636 4481	www.mbf.org.uk	Dec-98
237	Quarrier's 20	£1,675	£14,554	01505 612224	www.quarriers.org.uk/quarriers	Mar-99
238	Brain Research Trust	£1,673	£2,587	020 7636 3440	not available	Jul-99
239	Council for the Protection of Rural England *	£1,650	£2,152	020 7976 6433	www.cpre.org.uk	Dec-98
240	Hearing Dogs for Deaf People	£1,649	£1,805	01844 353898	www.hearing-dogs.co.uk	Mar-99
241	Wooden Spoon Society	£1,645	£1,692	01227 772295	www.woodenspoonsoc.org.uk	Mar-98
242	Royal Natl Mission to Deep Sea Fisherman	£1,635	£2,284	020 7487 5101	www.fishing-news.co.uk/rnmdsf	Oct-98
243	Crime Concern Trust *	£1,634	£5,145	01793 863500	www.crimeconcern.org.uk	Mar-99
244	Electrical/Electronics Industries Ben. Assn	£1,630	£2,035	020 8673 0131	not available	Dec-98
245	International Care and Relief	£1,617	£1,816	01892 519619	www.icrcharity.com	Jun-99
246	Weizmann Institute Foundation *	£1,613	£2,392	020 7424 6860	www.weizmann.org.uk	Sep-98
247	Home Farm Trust	£1,593	£18,883	0117 927 3746	www.hft.org.uk	Mar-99
248	St Peter's Hospice Ltd	£1,575	£3,961	0117 968 1864	not available	Mar-99
249	Edinburgh Festival Society	£1,572	£5,797	0131 473 2001	www.eif.co.uk	Nov-98
250	NCVO	£1,563	£3,709	020 7713 6161	www.ncvo-vol.org.uk	Mar-99
251	Young Enterprise	£1,557	£2,896	01865 311180	www.young-enterprise.org.uk	Jul-99
252	Hospice in the Weald	£1,557	£1,947	01892 820500	www.hospiceweald.co.uk	Mar-99
253	Ironbridge Gorge Museum Dev Trust *	£1,547	£4,340	01952 433522	www.vtbl.co.uk/igmt	Dec-97
254	Scottish Wildlife Trust *	£1,533	£3,623	0131 312 7765	www.swt.org.uk	Mar-99
255	North London Hospice Group	£1,533	£2,943	020 8343 8841	www.northlondonhospice.co.uk	Mar-99
256	Brian Wyers Memorial Fund *	£1,531	£3,287	01253 358881	www.trinitythehospice.inthefylde.org.uk	Mar-99
257	NABS *	£1,523	£2,197	020 7299 2888	www.nabs.org.uk	Apr-99
258	King Edward VII's Hospital for Officers	£1,508	£9,600	020 7486 4411	www.kingedwardvii.co.uk	Sep-98
259	Scottish National Inst for the War Blinded	£1,501	£3,459	0131 229 1456	not available	Mar-99
260	King George's Fund for Sailors	£1,501	£3,246	020 7932 0000	www.kgfs.org.uk	Dec-98
261	Africa Inland Mission International *	£1,497	£1,556	020 7281 1184	www.aim-evr.org	Dec-98

		Donated income £000s	Total income £000s	Telephone number	Website	Final year end
262	St Wilfrid's Hospice (South Coast)	£1,491	£2,306	01243 775302	not available	Mar-99
263	Prince & Princess of Wales Hospice *	£1,488	£2,294	0141 429 5599	www.ppwh.org.uk	Mar-99
264	Greater London Fund for the Blind	£1,482	£1,535	020 7620 2066	www.glfb.org.uk	Mar-99
265	Children Nationwide Medical Research Fund	£1,479	£1,571	020 7724 5727	www.children.org.uk	Apr-99
266	National Playing Fields Association	£1,464	£2,326	020 7581 2402	www.npfa.co.uk	Dec-98
267	Children's Hospice South West	£1,460	£1,590	01271 325270	www.chsw.co.uk	Jun-99
268	Carers National Association	£1,453	£2,658	020 7490 8818	www.carersuk.demon.co.uk	Mar-99
269	CancerBACUP	£1,431	£2,229	020 7696 9003	www.cancerbacup.org.uk	Mar-99
270	Youth Clubs UK *	£1,429	£2,398	020 7242 4045	www.youthclubs.org.uk	Mar-99
271	Gaia Foundation	£1,429	£1,444	020 7435 5000	www.thegaiafoundation.org	Jun-99
272	Hospital of St John & St Elizabeth	£1,428	£12,145	020 7286 5126	www.john-and-lizzies.org.uk	Dec-98
273	Demelza House Child Hospice *	£1,413	£1,691	01795 842111	www.demon.co.uk/charities/demelza	Sep-98
274	British & International Sailors' Society	£1,405	£3,598	023 8033 7333	www.biss.org.uk	Dec-98
275	St Helena Hospice	£1,404	£2,419	01206 845566	www.sthelenahospice.org.uk	Apr-99
276	London Lighthouse	£1,402	£3,377	020 7792 1200	www.london-lighthouse.org.uk	Mar-99
277	The Passage	£1,398	£2,286	020 7828 4183	www.passage.org.uk	Mar-99
278	Hope House – Children's Hospice	£1,392	£1,580	01691 671671	www.hopehouse.org.uk	Dec-98
279	Crosslinks	£1,382	£1,591	020 8691 6111	www.crosslinks.org/	Dec-98
280	Fight for Sight	£1,380	£1,912	020 7608 4000	www.fightforsight.org	Apr-99
281	Christ's Hospital	£1,379	£13,548	01403 211293	www.christs-hospital.org.uk	Jul-98
282	St Leonard's Hospice – York	£1,356	£2,272	01904 708553	www.stleonardshospice.org.uk	Mar-99
283	South American Mission Society *	£1,353	£1,421	01892 538647	www.ourworld.compuserve.com/homepages/samsgb	Dec-98
284	Earl Haig Fund (Scotland)	£1,351	£2,020	0131 557 2782	not available	Aug-98
285	National Aids Trust	£1,335	£1,799	020 7814 6767	www.nat.org.uk	Mar-99
286	St Catherine's Hospice (Lancashire)	£1,332	£1,798	01772 629171	www.stcatherines.co.uk	Dec-98
287	Oxford Centre for Hebrew and Jewish Studies	£1,330	£1,596	01865 377946	www.associnst.ox.ac.uk/ ochjs	Jul-98
288	St Francis Hospice	£1,323	£2,654	01708 753319	www.stfrancishospice.co.uk	Mar-99
289	BLISS	£1,317	£1,372	020 7820 9471	www.bliss.org.uk	Mar-99
290	Friends of the Earth Trust *	£1,316	£1,763	020 7490 1555	www.foe.co.uk	May-99

	Donated income £000s	Total income £000s	Telephone number	Website	Final year end
291 St Giles Hospice Whittington *	£1,315	£3,349	01543 432 031	www.st-giles-hospice.org.uk	Mar-99
292 Royal Blind Asylum & School Edinburgh *	£1,309	£2,636	0131 229 1456	www.schoolsite.edex.net.uk/ 220/ index.htm	Mar-99
293 Rainbow Family Trust Ltd	£1,307	£1,460	0161 434 4118	www.francishousechildshospice.co.uk	Mar-99
294 Hospice of Our Lady and St John	£1,306	£2,056	01908 663780	www.willen-hospice.org.uk	Mar-99
295 St John's Hospice in Wirral	£1,305	£1,801	0151 334 2778	not available	Mar-99
296 Jerusalem Foundation *	£1,295	£1,345	020 7482 6072	not available	Dec-97
297 Raystede Centre for Animal Welfare	£1,292	£1,909	01825 840 252	not available	Mar-99
298 Population Concern	£1,292	£3,167	020 7241 8500	www.populationconcern.org.uk	Mar-99
299 King's Medical Research Trust	£1,292	£1,787	020 7848 5866	not available	Mar-99
300 International Spinal Research Trust	£1,278	£1,559	01483 898786	www.spinal-research.org	Mar-99
301 National Catholic Fund *	£1,275	£1,509	020 7901 4810	www.catholic-ew.org.uk	Dec-98
302 St Luke's Hospital for the Clergy	£1,266	£1,426	020 7388 4954	www.stlukeshospital.org.uk	Dec-98
303 Housing Associations Charitable Trust *	£1,264	£1,433	020 7247 7800	www.hact.org.uk	Dec-98
304 MERLIN	£1,262	£7,515	020 7378 4888	www.merlin.org.uk	Dec-98
305 DEBRA	£1,247	£1,442	01344 771961	www.debra.org.uk	Dec-98
306 British Kidney Patient Association	£1,245	£2,425	01420 472021/2	not available	Dec-98
307 Ronald McDonald Children's Charities	£1,239	£1,364	020 8700 7331	not available	Dec-97
308 Earthwatch Europe	£1,238	£2,117	01865 311600	www.earthwatch.org	Sep-98
309 Friends of the Elderly & Gentlefolk's Help *	£1,235	£8,062	020 7730 8263	www.fote.org.uk	Sep-98
310 Meningitis Research Foundation *	£1,230	£1,820	01454 281811	www.meningitis.org	Mar-99
311 Crimestoppers Trust	£1,230	£1,270	020 8254 3200	www.crimestoppers-uk.org	Dec-98
312 Scottish Ballet	£1,229	£3,678	0141 331 2931	www.scottishballet.co.uk	Mar-98
313 Scottish Bible Society	£1,229	£1,929	0131 337 9701	www.scottishbiblesociety.org	Dec-98
314 BLESMA	£1,229	£2,862	020 8590 1124	www.blesma.org	Dec-98
315 Royal Naval Benevolent Trust	£1,217	£2,310	023 9269 0112	www.rnbt.org.uk	Mar-99
316 British Technion Society	£1,210	£1,253	020 7495 6824	not available	Dec-98
317 Officers' Association	£1,206	£2,194	020 7930 0125	www.oaed.org.uKoaed	Sep-98
318 East Cheshire Hospice	£1,202	£1,588	01625 610364	not available	Mar-99
319 Research Into Ageing	£1,200	£1,361	020 7843 1550	www.aging.org	Mar-99

		Donated income £000s	Total income £000s	Telephone number	Website	Final year end
320	Welsh National Opera Ltd.	£1,191	£11,902	029 2046 4666	www.wno.org.uk	Mar-99
321	Northern Ireland Chest, Heart & Stroke Assn	£1,187	£1,474	028 9032 0184	www.nichsa.com	Mar-99
322	Myton Hamlet Hospice Trust	£1,187	£2,320	01926 492518	www.mytonhospice.org	Mar-99
323	Landmark Trust	£1,174	£6,719	01628 825920	www.landmarktrust.co.uk	Mar-99
324	Motability Trust	£1,171	£15,816	01488 686335	www.motability.co.uk	Mar-99
325	Metropolitan Police Combined Benevolent Fund	£1,161	£1,164	020 7230 8924	not available	Dec-98
326	St Joseph's Hospice Assn – Jospice Int'l	£1,153	£1,613	0151 924 3812	www.jospice.org.uk	Dec-98
327	Boys' Brigade *	£1,146	£2,186	01442 231681	www.boys-brigade.org.uk	Mar-99
328	Ulster Cancer Foundation *	£1,144	£1,410	028 9066 3281	www.ulstercancer.co.uk	Jul-99
329	St Gemma's Hospice	£1,128	£2,748	0113 218 5500	www.st-gemma.co.uk	Dec-98
330	St David's Foundation *	£1,124	£1,896	01633 271364	www.stdavidsfoundation.co.uk	Mar-99
331	Navigators Great Britain	£1,124	£1,167	023 8022 3743	info@navigators.co.uk	Aug-98
332	Home of Rest for Horses	£1,116	£1,750	01494 488464	www.homeofrestforhorses.co.uk	Dec-98
333	Wellbeing *	£1,115	£1,295	020 7262 5337	www.wellbeing.org.uk	Sep-97
334	Society for the Protection of Animals Abroad	£1,101	£1,455	020 7828 0997	www.spana.org	Dec-98
335	Tommy's Campaign	£1,100	£2,546	020 7620 0188	www.tommys-campaign.org	Mar-99
336	Cruse – Bereavement Care *	£1,094	£2,439	020 8939 9530	www.crusebereavementcare.org.uk	Mar-99
337	Mission Aviation Fellowship (Europe)	£1,093	£2,208	01233 895521	www.maf-europe.org	Sep-98
338	Assn for Spina Bifida/Hydrocephalus	£1,092	£2,402	020 8954 5759	www.asbah.org	Mar-99
339	Rowcroft House Foundation	£1,086	£2,509	01803 210800	not available	Mar-99
340	North West Cancer Research Fund	£1,086	£1,332	0151 709 2919	www.merseyworld.com/ nwcrf	Oct-98
341	Foundation for the Study of Infant Deaths	£1,086	£1,223	020 7222 8001	www.sids.org.uk/fsid/	Jun-99
342	Nordoff-Robbins Music Therapy Ltd *	£1,085	£1,654	020 7371 8404	www.nordoff-robbins.org.uk	Dec-98
343	Greater Bristol Foundation	£1,082	£1,240	0117 989 7700	www.gbf.org.uk	Apr-99
344	Wessex Medical Trust	£1,081	£1,224	023 8033 3366	www.healthsearch2000@sutol.ac.uk	Dec-98
345	Action Cancer	£1,079	£1,382	028 9080 3344	www.actioncancer.org	Mar-99
346	Pattaya Orphanage Trust	£1,062	£1,162	020 7602 6203	www.pattayaorphanage.org.uk	Apr-99
347	Thames Valley Hospice	£1,061	£1,656	01753 842121	www.thamesvalleyhospice.windsor-gb.co.uk	May-99
348	East Anglia's Children's Hospices	£1,059	£1,392	01953 888604	www.each.org.uk	Mar-99

		Donated income £000s	Total income £000s	Telephone number	Website	Final year end
349	Highland Hospice	£1,056	£1,908	01463 243132	www.highlandhospice.org.uk	Mar-99
350	Down's Syndrome Association	£1,036	£1,242	020 8682 4001	www.downs-syndrome.org.uk	Mar-99
351	National Schizophrenia Fellowship	£1,033	£23,295	020 8547 3862	www.nsf.org.uk	Mar-99
352	SOS Children's Villages UK	£1,026	£1,101	01223 365589	www.sos-uk.org.uk	Dec-98
353	Child Health Research Appeal Trust	£1,026	£1,339	020 7905 2681	www.ich.ucl.ac.uk	Mar-99
354	Assn of Crossroads Care Attendant Schemes	£1,026	£2,386	01788 573653	www.crossroads.org.uk	Mar-99
355	Teachers' Benevolent Fund	£1,023	£3,258	020 7554 5202	www.teachersupport.org.uk	Dec-98
356	British Wireless for the Blind Fund *	£1,014	£1,187	01634 832501	www.blind.org.uk	Oct-98
357	Mount Edgcumbe Hospice *	£1,008	£1,619	01726 65711	not available	Mar-99
358	Methodist Relief & Development Fund	£1,003	£1,046	020 7467 5158	www.methodistchurch.org.uk	Aug-98
359	Greenpeace Environmental Trust	£998	£1,011	020 7865 8100	www.greenpeace.org.uk	Dec-97
360	Phyllis Tuckwell Memorial Hospice *	£990	£1,849	01252 729400	www.phyllistuckwellhospice.org.uk	Mar-99
361	Oasis Charitable Trust	£984	£1,763	020 7450 9000	www.u-net.com/ oasis	Aug-98
362	Make a Wish Foundation UK *	£983	£1,029	01276 24127	www.make-a-wish.org.uk	Mar-99
363	DePaul Trust	£981	£2,045	020 7935 0011	www.depaultrust.org	Mar-99
364	British Youth for Christ *	£971	£1,170	0121 550 8055	www.yfc.co.uk	Aug-98
365	World University Service (UK)	£960	£2,583	020 7426 5800	www.wusuk.org	Mar-99
366	Strathcarron Hospice	£957	£2,129	01324 826222	not available	Mar-99
367	Grace and Compassion Benedictines	£945	£2,955	01273 680720	www.dabnet.org/gcb.htm	Sep-98
368	Martin House	£941	£1,424	01937 845045	www.martinhouse.org.uk	Apr-99
369	National Grocers' Benevolent Fund	£936	£1,347	01252 515946	not available	Mar-99
370	British Home & Hospital for Incurables	£934	£4,646	020 8670 8261	not available	Dec-98
371	St Michael's Hospice	£933	£1,179	01432 851000	www.st-michaels-hospice.org.uk	Mar-99
372	Thrombosis Research Institute	£931	£2,957	020 7351 8311	www.tri-london.ac.uk	Jul-98
373	Royal Soc for the Prevention of Accidents	£930	£6,383	0121 248 2000	www.rospa.com	Mar-99
374	Barristers Benevolent Association	£930	£1,075	020 7242 4764	not available	Dec-98
375	Riding for the Disabled Assn	£924	£1,192	024 7669 6510	www.riding-for-disabled.org.uk	Mar-99
376	Oxford Group	£923	£3,561	020 7798 6000	www.mra.org.uk	Dec-98
377	Iris Fund for the Prevention of Blindness *	£916	£1,061	020 7928 7743	www.irisfund.org.uk	Dec-97

		Donated income £000s	Total income £000s	Telephone number	Website	Final year end
378	Solicitors' Benevolent Association	£908	£1,369	020 8675 6440	www.sba.org.uk	Dec-98
379	Action on Addiction	£901	£988	020 7793 1011	www.aona.co.uk	Mar-99
380	National Society for Epilepsy*	£893	£11,776	01494 601300	www.erg.ion.ucl.ac.uk/nsehome	Mar-99
381	North Lancs and Lakeland Continuing Care Trust	£890	£1,780	01524 382538	not available	Mar-99
382	National Library for the Blind	£890	£1,580	0161 355 2000	www.nlbuk.org	Mar-99
383	ORBIS Charitable Trust	£888	£1,160	020 7278 5528	www.orbis.org	Feb-99
384	UFM Worldwide*	£885	£918	01793 610515	www.ufm.org.uk	Oct-98
385	Family Welfare Association	£885	£5,424	020 7254 6251	not available	Mar-99
386	Derian House Children's Hospice	£882	£1,023	01257 233300	www.derianhouse.org.uk	Dec-98
387	FRAME *	£881	£1,042	0115 958 4740	www.frame.uk.demon.co.uk	Mar-99
388	Enham Trust *	£880	£6,692	01264 345800	www.enham.co.uk	Mar-99
389	Mildmay Mission Hospital	£877	£5,107	020 7613 6300	www.mildmay.org.uk	Mar-99
390	Coram Family	£873	£3,271	020 7520 0300	www.coram.org.uk	Mar-99
391	Treloar Trust	£872	£11,361	01420 526526	www.treloar.org.uk	Jul-99
392	Youth at Risk	£870	£1,077	01628 481814	www.youthatrisk.org.uk	Jun-99
393	St Elizabeth Hospice (Suffolk) *	£865	£1,800	01473 727776	www.stelizabethhospice.org.uk	Mar-99
394	Church Urban Fund	£860	£2,585	020 7898 1729	www.cuf.org.uk	Dec-98
395	National Eczema Society	£859	£1,365	020 7388 4097	www.eczema.org	Dec-98
396	London Connection	£858	£1,779	020 7766 5544	www.london-connection.org.uk	Mar-99
397	Assn of Commonwealth Universities	£856	£6,654	020 7380 6715	www.acu.ac.uk	Jul-99
398	Historic Churches Preservation Trust *	£851	£1,220	020 7736 3054	not available	Sep-99
399	Impact Foundation	£834	£1,006	01444 457080	www.impact.org.uk	Mar-99
400	War on Want *	£825	£999	020 7620 1111	www.waronwant.org	Mar-99
401	Royal Agricultural Benevolent Institution	£825	£2,492	01865 724931	www.rabi.org.uk	Dec-98
402	North Devon Hospice Care Trust	£824	£951	01271 44248	www.northdevonhospice.org.uk	Mar-99
403	Children in Crisis *	£823	£1,081	020 7978 5001	www.childrenincrisis.org.uk	Apr-99
404	English-Speaking Union of the Commonwealth	£822	£1,541	020 7529 1550	www.esu.org	Apr-99
405	Weston Spirit *	£820	£925	0151 258 1066	www.westonspirit.org.uk	Mar-99
406	Abbeyfield Society *	£817	£2,809	01727 857536	www.abbeyfield.com	Sep-98

		Donated income £000s	Total income £000s	Telephone number	Website	Final year end
407	ROKPA Trust	£815	£1,549	01387 373232	www.samye.org	Dec-98
408	Queen Alexandra Hospital Home	£815	£2,257	01903 213458	www.qahh.org.uk	Dec-98
409	CARE Fund	£815	£913	0116 279 3225	www.care-ltd.co.uk	Apr-99
410	Voluntary Service Aberdeen	£808	£8,354	01224 212021	www.vsa.org.uk	Mar-99
411	Jewish Blind & Disabled	£806	£1,378	020 7262 2003	www.jbd.org	Dec-98
412	Clatterbridge Cancer Research Trust	£801	£1,294	0151 343 4304/5	www.ccrt.org.uk	Apr-99
413	Hospice of St Francis (Berkhamstead)	£791	£1,260	01442 862960	www.dspace.dial.pipex.com/st.francis	Dec-98
414	Helen House (Society of All Saints)	£784	£1,282	01865 728251	www.helen-house.org.uk	Apr-99
415	Chartered Accountants' Benevolent Assn	£782	£1,348	020 7588 2662	not available	Dec-98
416	Council for World Mission *	£781	£5,796	020 7222 4214	www.cwmission.org.uk	Dec-98
417	Prospect Foundation	£777	£1,512	01793 813355	www.prospect-hospice.org.uk	Mar-98
418	Christian Witness to Israel *	£769	£1,026	01959 565955	www.cwi.org.uk	Mar-99
419	Addaction	£768	£3,502	020 7727 3366	www.addaction.org.uk	Mar-99
420	Tools for Self Reliance *	£763	£804	023 8086 9697	www.tfsr.org.uk	Aug-98
421	Sail Training Association *	£760	£4,017	01705 832055/6	www.sta.org.uk/ sta/	Feb-99
422	National Heart Research Fund	£757	£873	0113 234 7474	www.heartresearch.org.uk	Dec-98
423	Children and Youth Aliyah Committee	£757	£884	020 8446 4321	not available	Mar-99
424	Mid-Africa Ministry	£754	£797	020 7261 1370	www.midafricaministry.org	Jan-99
425	Catholic Children's Society	£750	£3,613	020 8668 2181	www.catholicchildrenssoc:ety.org.uk	Mar-99
426	King Edward VII Hospital	£749	£22,725	01730 812341	www.kingedwardhospital.co.uk	Mar-99
427	Institute for Public Policy Research	£749	£971	020 7470 6100	www.ippr.org	Dec-98
428	Royal Alexandra & Albert School	£748	£3,558	01737 642576	www.gatton-park.org.uk	Mar-99
429	Counsel & Care for the Elderly	£748	£868	020 7485 1550	www.counselandcare.org.uk	Dec-98
430	Injured Jockeys' Fund *	£745	£1,294	01638 662246	www.ijf.org.uk	Apr-99
431	Gardeners' Royal Benevolent Society	£745	£2,455	01372 373962	www.gardeners-grbs.org.uk	Dec-98
432	Ellenor Foundation	£745	£1,367	01322 221315	www.ellenorfoundation.org/	Dec-98
433	Co-operation Ireland	£741	£743	028 9032 1462	www.co-operation-ireland.ie/shtml/about.shtml	Dec-00
434	Child Resettlement Trust Fund	£740	£799	020 8203 6066	www.britishemunah.org	Dec-98
435	St Wilfrid's Hospice (Eastbourne) Ltd *	£739	£1,180	01323 644500	not available	Dec-98

		Donated income £000s	Total income £000s	Telephone number	Website	Final year end
436	Spinal Injuries Association *	£729	£1,134	020 8444 2121	www.spinal.co.uk	Apr-99
437	Elizabeth Fitzroy Homes	£729	£8,180	01428 656766	www.efitzroy.org.uk	Mar-99
438	Dorothy House Foundation	£725	£2,187	01225 722988	www.dorothyhouse.co.uk	Mar-99
439	Soil Association*	£722	£1,369	0117 929 0661	www.soilassociation.org	Mar-99
440	St Luke's Hospice – Harrow & Brent *	£720	£1,306	020 8382 8000	www.stlukes-hospice.org/	Dec-98
441	Defeating Deafness	£715	£754	020 7833 1733	www.defeatingdeafness.org	Jul-99
442	St Barnabas Hospice Trust	£712	£2,629	01522 511566	www.stbarnabashospicelincolnshire.co.uk	Mar-99
443	Universities Federation for Animal Welfare	£710	£882	01582 831818	www.ufaw.org.uk	Mar-99
444	National Newpin *	£709	£1,720	020 7703 6326	www.newpin.org.uk	Mar-99
445	Action Partners Ministries	£707	£756	01302 710750	www.actionpartners.org.uk	Dec-98
446	Trinitarian Bible Society	£705	£2,345	020 8543 7857	www.trinitarianbiblesociety.org	Dec-98
447	Catholic Children's Society (Westminster)	£705	£1,375	020 8969 5305	www.cathchild.org.uk	Dec-98
448	Karuna Trust	£700	£738	020 7700 3434	www.karuna.org	Dec-98
449	Friends of Magen David Adom	£695	£765	020 8381 4849	www.ukmda.org/	Dec-98
450	Toc H *	£694	£1,141	01296 623911	www.toch.org.uk	Mar-99
451	Health Unlimited	£694	£2,444	020 7840 3477	www.healthunlimited.org	Mar-99
452	Dorothy Kerin Trust	£694	£1,495	01892 863637	www.burrswood.org.uk	Dec-98
453	SANE	£693	£1,384	020 7375 1002	www.mkn.co.uk/help/charity/sane/index	Mar-99
454	National Assn for Colitis & Crohn's Disease	£690	£964	01727 830038	www.nacc.org.uk	Dec-98
455	Contact a Family	£690	£1,305	020 7383 3555	www.cafamily.org.uk	Mar-99
456	Leicester Charity Organisation Society	£685	£1,015	0116 222 2200	not available	Mar-99
457	White Lodge Centre	£672	£1,436	01932 567131	not available	Mar-99
458	National Spiritual Assembly of the Baha'is (UK) *	£666	£838	020 7584 2566	www.bahai.org.uk	Jan-99
459	Music for Youth	£661	£717	020 8870 9624	www.mfy.org.uk	Jan-99
460	British Polio Fellowship	£660	£1,300	020 8842 1898	www.britishpolio.org	Dec-98
461	Wessex Cancer Trust	£655	£708	02380 672200	www.wessexcancer.org/	Apr-99
462	DeafBlind UK	£651	£959	01733 35810	www.deafblind.org.uk	Sep-98
463	Pilgrim Homes	£648	£4,699	020 7407 5466	www.pilgrimhomes.org.uk	Dec-98
464	SOS Sahel International	£640	£2,376	020 7837 9129	not available	Mar-99

		Donated income £000s	Total income £000s	Telephone number	Website	Final year end
465	Entertainment Artistes' Benevolent Fund *	£634	£1,183	020 8898 8164	www.eabf.org.uk	Dec-98
466	Ulster SPCA	£632	£1,062	0801 2326 60479	not available	Mar-99
467	Prince of Wales Hospice	£616	£1,002	01977 708868	not available	Mar-99
468	Disabled Living Foundation	£615	£965	020 7289 6111	www.dlf.org.uk	Mar-99
469	QUIT – National Society of Non-Smokers *	£610	£1,705	020 7388 5775	www.quit.org.uk	Mar-99
470	Royal National College for the Blind	£609	£4,347	01432 265725	www.rncb.ac.uk	Mar-99
471	Catholic Housing Aid Society Dev. Fund	£605	£708	020 7723 7273	www.chasnational.org.uk	Sep-98
472	Katharine House Hospice Trust	£598	£1,145	01295 811866	www.katharinehouse.co.uk	Mar-99
473	Confectioners' Benevolent Fund	£598	£811	020 7404 5222	www.sweetcharity.net	Aug-98
474	Church's Ministry Among Jewish People	£589	£1,119	01727 833114	www.cmj.org.uk	Dec-97
475	Bristol Cancer Help Centre	£585	£1,044	0117 980 9500	www.bristolcancerhelp.org	May-99
476	Born Free Foundation *	£577	£593	01403 240170	www.bornfree.org.uk	Mar-97
477	Soldier's & Airmen's Scripture Readers Assn *	£575	£651	01252 310033	www.sasra.org.uk	Dec-98
478	Listening Books *	£569	£665	020 7407 9417	www.listening-books.org.uk	Mar-99
479	The Thistle Foundation *	£567	£2,122	0131 661 3366	www.thistle.org.uk	Sep-98
480	Heart of Kent Hospice	£562	£1,230	01622 792200	not available	Mar-99
481	Friends of the Bristol Horses Society *	£562	£754	01275 832425	www.bristolhorses.org.uk	Dec-98
482	NABC Clubs for Young People	£560	£976	020 7793 0787	www.nacyp.org.uk	Mar-99
483	Wiltshire Community Foundation	£559	£626	01380 729284	www.moneyshop.co.uk/charity/wiltshire.htm	Mar-99
484	Claire House	£559	£617	0151 343 0883	www.claire-house.org.uk	Dec-98
485	ASPIRE	£557	£693	020 8954 5759	www.aspire.org.uk	Mar-99
486	Inc Liverpool School of Tropical Medicine *	£555	£7,394	0151 708 9393	www.liv.ac.uk/lstm/lstm.htm	Jul-99
487	BIBIC (British Institute for Brain Injured Children) *	£553	£754	01278 684060	www.bibic.org.uk	Dec-98
488	St Andrew's Hospice	£542	£948	01236 766951	www.st-andrews-hospice.com	Mar-99
489	International Glaucoma Association *	£536	£634	020 7737 3265	www.iga.org.uk	Jul-98
490	St Basil's Centre *	£533	£2,904	0121 772 2483	www.stbasils.org.uk	Mar-99
491	Pestalozzi Children's Village Trust	£533	£560	01424 870444	www3.mistral.co.uk/dec/pestaloz.htm	Aug-98
492	Cardinal Hume Centre	£532	£892	020 7222 1602	www.cardinalhumecentre	Dec-98
493	Drive for Youth *	£530	£712	01654 710454	not available	Mar-98

	Donated income £000s	Total income £000s	Telephone number	Website	Final year end
494 Royal Association in Aid of Deaf People *	£521	£1,271	01206 509509	www.royaldeaf.org.uk	Mar-99
495 Motivation Charitable Trust	£516	£521	01275 464012	www.motivation.org.uk	Dec-98
496 The Sick Children's Trust	£515	£561	020 7404 3329	www.sickchildrenstrust	Mar-99
497 Springhill Hospice	£438	£1,217	01706 649920	www.springhill.u-net.com	Mar-99
498 Break	£259	£2,405	01263 822161	www.break-charity.org	Mar-99
499 Teesside Hospice Care Foundation	£143	£1,570	01642 816777	www.neglobal.co.uk/teessidehospice	Mar-99

Sources of local information and advice

Councils for Voluntary Service (CVS) are found throughout the UK, though sometimes under other names such as 'voluntary service council' or 'voluntary sector forum'. They aim to encourage, support and develop the effectiveness of local voluntary and community action by providing a range of services, including information and training support. They are often particularly important as an interface between local government and the voluntary sector in their area.

Many of them have associated volunteer bureaux and can suggest a range of local volunteering opportunities. Those without such a formal bureau will often be able to offer the same service in practice.

The national organisations are:

- England: the National Association of Councils for Voluntary Service, or NACVS (tel. 0114 278 6636; www.nacvs.org.uk);
- Wales: the Wales Council for Voluntary Action, or WCVO (tel. 029 2043 1700; www.wcva.org.uk);
- Scotland: CVS Scotland (tel. 01888 511254; www.cvsscotland.org.uk);
- In Northern Ireland, the Northern Ireland Council for Voluntary Action (NICVA) often plays a comparable role (tel. 028 9087 7777; www.nicva.org).

Rural Community Councils (RCCs) have been listed separately (see page **395**). They provide support for organisations in rural communities throughout England. They are coordinated and supported by ACRE (Action with Communities in Rural England), the national association of RCCs (tel. 01285 653477; www.acre.org.uk).

An example of a CVS: Lancaster District Council For Voluntary Service

'In an area such as Lancaster District, which has two main centres of population, a large rural hinterland, and a population of about 130,000, there are several hundred very local charitable organisations – even more, if you count every cub pack and play group individually. These organisations are usually run by a committee of half a dozen people, who often then double up as part of the volunteer team which delivers whatever service that group is about.

'It could be that its purpose is to run a village transport scheme or a handy person service; it could be a neighbourhood toddler group or a regular social gathering for people with a specific medical condition. The group could be campaigning for a local pedestrian crossing or transforming a piece of wasteland into a park; it may be offering a counselling service or information and advice for a particular social group. There are groups that provide sports and arts opportunities for young people. There are groups that look after stray animals. There are groups that provide housing for older people or day centres for people experiencing mental health difficulties. The list is endless.

'These groups are local – they exist alongside the branches of better known national organisations in their area – the two complementing each other and not necessarily being easily distinguished. Local groups are usually, but not exclusively, staffed by volunteers – there can be sizeable paid staff teams, for example, where an organisation runs a domiciliary care service for people with disabilities and employs careworkers.

'As the example of the domiciliary care service illustrates, some of these organisations can be quite large, with corresponding budgets and contracts. However, even the volunteer-only organisations can be significant. For example, some years ago CVS mapped all the luncheon clubs for older people it knew of in the district. There were over 20 of these, some of them meeting weekly, with memberships of 50–100 people. Suddenly, there was a picture of over a thousand people a week being provided with a meal and social contact, made possible usually by small teams of volunteers, often older people themselves.

'In the case of luncheon clubs, the group may receive some financial assistance from the local authority. However, this will not cover all the expenditure and, in plenty of other cases, such assistance isn't looked for or forthcoming. Many groups survive financially on members' fees, donations, small-scale fundraising events – raffles and coffee mornings etc. – and it can be salutary to see how far such money can stretch. CVS services a couple of local charitable trusts, and often receives requests where £100 can make a significant contribution to the work of a small local group.

'Before the rose-tinted specs take over completely, one of the downsides of this world is that groups are often dependent on one or two strong personalities who both have the vision and do the work. This can be fine while these key people are healthy, inspired, without other excess demands, and still in touch. However, local groups can grow old – both literally and metaphorically. The key people may have had enough, but be unable to spot a successor, and so either struggle on or risk the organisation's future by standing down. Groups that have failed to bring new people in at regular intervals can suddenly find that they have become too small to continue or that the gap between them and the people they wish to attract is too wide to bridge.

'In this local context, small contributions of time and money can be very cost-effective. To offer to take responsibility for a specific task in the organisation can ease the load on the key people. A small financial donation can sustain such a group for quite a while or make a special event happen.'

Lancaster CVS is just one of hundreds covering most of the country. A full listing follows. To know more about local organisations, like these, that you might be able to help, give them a ring.

(We would like to thank Fiona Gordon, of Lancaster District Council for Voluntary Service, for providing this information.)

Councils for Voluntary Service, and other similar organisations
England
East

Basildon, Billericay & Wickford CVS; tel: 01268 288870
Mid Bedfordshire CVS; tel: 01525 841160
North Bedfordshire CVS; tel: 01234 354366
South Bedfordshire Council of Voluntary Organisations; tel: 01582 662487
Braintree District Voluntary Support Agency; tel: 01376 550507
Brentwood CVS; tel: 01277 222299
Broxbourne Voluntary Sector Development Agency; tel: 01992 638633
Cambridge CVS; tel: 01223 464696
Castle Point Association of Voluntary Services; tel: 01268 512550
Chelmsford CVS; tel: 01245 351888
Colchester Community Voluntary Services; tel: 01206 505250
Dacorum CVS; tel: 01442 253935
Epping Forest CVS; tel: 01992 564178
Forest Heath (The Voluntary Network); tel: 01638 608047
Great Yarmouth Association of Voluntary Organisations; tel: 01493 445922
Harlow CVS; tel: 01279 308308
East Hertfordshire Voluntary Sector Development Agency; tel: 01920 487518
North Hertfordshire CVS; tel: 01462 450022
Hertsmere Community Voluntary Support; tel: 020 8207 4504
Hunts Forum of Voluntary Organisations; tel: 01480 415178
Ipswich & District CVS; tel: 01473 251834
Voluntary Action Luton; tel: 01582 733418
Maldon & District CVS; tel: 01621 851891
West Norfolk Association of Voluntary Organisations; tel: 01553 760568
Norwich & Norfolk Voluntary Services; tel: 01603 614474
Peterborough CVS; tel: 01733 342683
St Albans District CVSs; tel: 01727 852657
Southend Association of Voluntary Service; tel: 01702 356000
Stevenage CVS; tel: 01438 353951
Suffolk Association of Voluntary Organisations (SAVO); tel: 01473 230976
Tendring Community Voluntary Service; tel: 01255 425692
Three Rivers CVS; tel: 01923 711174
Thurrock CVS; tel: 01375 374093
Uttlesford CVS; tel: 01371 878400
Watford CVS; tel: 01923 254400
Welwyn Hatfield CVS; tel: 01707 274861

East Midlands

Amber Valley CVS; tel: 01773 512076
Ashfield Links Forum; tel: 01623 555551
Bassetlaw Community & Voluntary Service; tel: 01909 476118
Blaby District CVS; tel: 0116 275 1918

Bolsover & District CVS; tel; 01246 241730
Boston District CVS; tel:01205 365580
Charnwood CVS; tel: 01509 230131
Chesterfield & NE Derbyshire CVS & Action; tel: 01246 274844
Derby CVS; tel: 01332 346266
Derbyshire Dales CVS; tel: 01629 812154
South Derbyshire CVS; tel: 01283 550163
Erewash CVS; tel: 0115 849 0400
Gedling CVS; tel: 0115 926 6750
Hinckley & Bosworth Area CVS; tel: 01455 633002
Leicester CVS; tel: 0116 234 1577
Leicester Voluntary Action; tel: 0116 251 3999
North West Leicestershire CVS; tel: 01530 510515
South Leicestershire CVS; tel: 01858 433232
Mansfield CVS; tel: 01623 651177
Melton Borough CVS; tel: 01664 410007
Newark & Sherwood CVS; tel: 01636 679539
Northampton & County CVS; tel: 01604 624121
Nottingham CVS; tel: 0115 934 8400
Oadby & Wigston Voluntary Action; tel: 0116 281 0026
Rushcliffe CVS; tel: 0115 981 6988
Rutland Voluntary Action; tel: 01572 722622

London

Barking & Dagenham CVS; tel; 020 8591 5275
Barnet Voluntary Service Council; tel: 020 8446 6624
Bexley Voluntary Service Council; tel: 020 8304 0911
Bromley Community Links; tel: 020 8315 1900
Voluntary Action Camden; tel: 020 7284 6550
Chelsea Social Council; tel: 020 7351 3210
Croydon Voluntary Action; tel: 020 8684 3862
Ealing Voluntary Service Council; tel: 020 8579 6273
Enfield Voluntary Action; tel: 020 8373 6268
Voluntary Sector Resource Agency Hammersmith & Fulham; tel: 020 8762 0862
Harrow Association of Voluntary Service; tel: 020 8863 6707
Havering Association of Voluntary & Community Organisations; tel: 01708 742881
Hillingdon Association of Voluntary Services; tel: 01895 442722
Hounslow Voluntary Sector Forum; tel: 020 8572 5929
Islington Voluntary Action Council; tel; 020 7226 4862
Kingston Voluntary Action; tel: 020 8255 3335
Lambeth Voluntary Action Council; tel: 020 7737 1419
Voluntary Action Lewisham; tel: 020 8314 9411
London Voluntary Service Council; tel: 020 7700 8107
Merton Voluntary Service Council; tel: 020 8685 1771

Notting Hill Social Council; tel: 020 8969 9897
Redbridge CVS; tel: 020 8554 5049
Richmond-upon-Thames CVS; tel: 020 8255 8500
Southwark Action for Voluntary Organisations; tel: 020 7703 8733
Sutton Centre for Voluntary Service; tel: 020 8643 3277
Tower Hamlets Community Organisations Forum; tel: 020 7426 9970
Voluntary Action Waltham Forest; tel: 020 8521 0377
Wandsworth Volunteer Bureau; tel: 020 8870 4319
Voluntary Action Westminster; tel: 020 7723 1216

North-east

Blyth Valley CVS; tel: 01670 353623
Chester-le-Street & District CVS; tel: 0191 389 1960
Darlington CVS; tel: 01325 266 888
Derwentside CVS; tel: 01207 218855
Durham City District CVS; tel: 0191 383 1944
Durham Standing Conference of Voluntary Organisations; tel: 0191 384 9266
Easington District CVS; tel: 0191 586 5427
Gateshead Voluntary Organisations Council; tel: 0191 478 4103
Hartlepool Voluntary Development Agency; tel: 01429 262641
Newcastle-upon-Tyne CVS; tel: 0191 232 7445
Redcar & Cleveland Voluntary Development Agency; tel: 01642 440571
Community & Voluntary Organisations in Sedgefield; tel: 01740 652000
Stockton Borough Voluntary Development Agency; tel: 01642 355292
Sunderland CVS; tel: 0191 565 1566
One Voice Tees Valley; tel: 01642 240651
Teesdale & Wear Valley CVS (2D); tel: 01388 762220
Tynedale Voluntary Action; tel: 01434 601201
North Tyneside Voluntary Organisations Development Agency; tel: 0191 200 5790
South Tyneside CVS; tel: 0191 456 9551
Wansbeck CVS; tel: 01670 858688

North-west

Barrow & District CVS; tel: 01229 823144
Bebington CVS; tel: 0151 643 7275
Blackburn with Darwen CVS; tel: 01254 583957
Blackpool, Wyre & Fylde CVS; tel: 01253 624505
Bolton District CVS; tel: 01204 396011
Burnley, Pendle & Rossendale CVS; tel: 01282 433740
Bury CVS; tel: 0161 764 2161
Carlisle CVS; tel: 01228 512513
Chester CVS; tel: 01244 323527
Chorley & South Ribble CVS; tel: 01257 263254
Congleton District CVS; tel: 01270 763100
Crewe & Nantwich CVS & Volunteer Bureau; tel: 01270 211545
West Cumbria CVS; tel: 01946 852955

Eden CVS; tel: 01768 242138
Ellesmere Port & Neston CVS & Volunteer Bureau; tel: 0151 357 2931
Halton Voluntary Action; tel: 01928 592405
Heswall & District CVS; tel: 0151 342 6115
Knowsley CVS; tel: 0151 489 1222
South Lakeland Council for Voluntary Action; tel: 01539 729168
West Lancashire CVS; tel: 01695 733737
Lancaster District CVS; tel: 01524 63760
Liverpool CVS; tel: 0151 236 7728
Macclesfield District CVS; tel: 01625 428301
Voluntary Action Manchester; tel: 0161 236 3206
Greater Manchester Centre for Voluntary Organisation; tel: 0161 273 7451
Local Solutions (formerly Merseyside CVS); tel: 0151 709 0990
Oldham Development Agency for Community Action; tel: 0161 633 6222
Preston CVS; tel: 01772 251108
Rochdale & Volunteer Development Agency, CVS; tel: 01706 631291
St Helens District CVS; tel: 01744 21755
Salford CVS; tel: 0161 787 7795
Sefton CVS; tel: 0151 920 0726
Stockport CVS; tel: 0161 477 0246
Trafford CVS; tel: 0161 976 2448
Vale Royal CVS; tel: 01606 46485
Warrington CVS; tel: 01925 630239
Wigan & Leigh CVS; tel: 01942 514234
Wirral CVS; tel: 0151 647 5432

South-east
Adur CVS; tel: 01273 441662
Arun CVS; tel: 01903 726228
Banbury & District CVS; tel: 01295 279515
Basingstoke Voluntary Services; tel: 01256 321611
West Berkshire CVS; tel: 01635 523861
Bexhill Community Partnership; tel: 01424 220944
Bognor Regis & District CVS; tel: 01243 840305
Bracknell CVS; tel: 01344 304404
Brighton & Hove Voluntary Sector Forum; tel: 01273 234044
South Bucks Volunteer Bureau; tel: 01753 893793
Chichester & District CVS; tel: 01243 528615
Chiltern Voluntary Services; tel: 01494 793470
Crawley CVS; tel: 01293 526248
Voluntary Action for East Hampshire; tel: 01730 301334
Eastbourne Association of Voluntary Service; tel: 01323 639373
Eastleigh Community Services; tel: 023 8090 2400
Elmbridge CVS Steering Committee; tel: 01932 222759
Fareham Community Action; tel: 01329 231899
Farnham Voluntary Service Council; tel: 01252 725961

Gosport Voluntary Action; tel: 023 9258 3836
East Grinstead CVS; tel: 01342 328080
Guildford Association of Voluntary Service; tel: 01483 504626
Hart Voluntary Action; tel: 01252 815652
Hastings Voluntary Action; tel: 01424 444010
Havant Council of Community Service; tel: 023 9264 5777
High Wycombe CVS (The Priory Centre); tel: 01494 523440
Horsham Area CVS; tel: 01403 255277
East Kent CVS; tel: 01227 373293
North West Kent CVS; tel: 01322 291060
West Kent CVS; tel: 01892 530539
Medway CVS; tel: 01634 812850
Mid & South East Kent CVS; tel: 01233 610171
Mid Sussex (South) CVS; tel: 01444 258102
Milton Keynes Council of Voluntary Organisations; tel: 01908 661623
New Forest Voluntary Service Council; tel: 01425 482773
Oxfordshire Council for Voluntary Action; tel: 01865 251946
Portsmouth Council of Community Service; tel: 023 9282 7110
Reading Voluntary Action; tel: 0118 957 4123
Reigate & Banstead CVS; tel: 01737 763156
Runnymede Association of Voluntary Services; tel: 01932 571122
Rushmoor Voluntary Services; tel: 01252 540162
Rye & District CVS; tel: 01797 225466
Slough CVS; tel: 01753 524176
South Downs CVS; tel: 01273 483832
Southampton Voluntary Services; tel: 023 8022 8291
Voluntary Action in Spelthorne; tel: 01784 446358
Surrey Heath – Voluntary Service; tel: 01276 707565
Surrey Voluntary Service Council; tel: 01483 566072
Central Surrey CVS; tel: 01372 722911
Swale Volunteering & Community Development Centre; tel: 01795 473828
Test Valley Community Services; tel: 01794 519998
Wealden Federation of Voluntary Organisations; tel: 01892 669044
Winchester Area Community Action; tel: 01962 842293
Windsor & Maidenhead Voluntary Action; tel: 01753 856606
Woking Association of Voluntary Service; tel: 01483 751456
Wokingham District Voluntary Sector Forum; tel: 0118 977 0749
Worthing CVS; tel: 01903 528620

South-west

Voluntary First (Bath); tel: 01225 464015
Bournemouth CVS; tel: 01202 466130
Progress (Bristol); tel: 0117 989 7711
VOSCUR (Bristol); tel: 0117 909 9949
Cheltenham CVS; tel: 01242 227737
Cornwall Voluntary Sector Forum; tel: 01209 614952

Cotswold CVS; tel: 01285 658802
Devon Local Development Agencies Forum; tel: 01392 202057
East Devon CVS; tel: 01404 549045
North Dorset Volunteer Action; tel: 01258 454678
Exeter CVS; tel: 01392 202055
Forest Voluntary Action Forum; tel: 01594 822073
Gloucester Centre for Voluntary Services; tel: 01452 332424
Voluntary Action Kennet; tel: 01672 564140
Kingswood Centre for Voluntary Service; tel: 0117 947 6406
Voluntary Action Mendip; tel: 01749 344403
Okehampton & District CVS; tel: 01837 55047
Penwith Community Development Trust; tel: 01736 330045
Plymouth Guild of Voluntary Service; tel: 01752 201766
Poole CVS; tel: 01202 682046
Salisbury & District CVS; tel: 01722 421747
Sedgemoor Volunteer Bureau; tel: 01278 457685
North Somerset Local Development Working Group; tel: 01934 835991
West Somerset CVS; tel: 01643 707484
South Hams CVS; tel: 01803 862266
Stroud & District CVS; tel: 01452 530184
Voluntary Action Swindon; tel: 01793 538398
Taunton Deane CVS; tel: 01823 284470
Tavistock & District CVS; tel: 01822 618224
Teignbridge CVS; tel: 01626 203050
Torbay Voluntary Service; tel: 01803 212638
Torridge Voluntary Services; tel: 01237 425554
North Wiltshire CVS; tel: 01249 654089
Voluntary Action West Wiltshire; tel: 01225 767993
Yeovil & District CVS; tel: 01935 475914

West Midlands

Birmingham Voluntary Service Council; tel: 0121 643 4343
Bridgnorth Voluntary Action; tel: 01746 766477
Chase CVS (Cannock); tel: 01543 500404
Coventry Voluntary Service Council; tel: 024 7622 0381
Droitwich Spa & Rural CVS; tel: 01905 779115
Dudley CVS; tel: 01384 78166
Community First in Herefordshire & Worcestershire; tel: 01684 573334
Voluntary Action North Herefordshire; tel: 01568 611098/099
South Herefordshire Voluntary Action Ltd; tel: 01989 567653
Ledbury & District CVS; tel: 01531 636006
Lichfield & District CVS; tel: 01543 303030
Community Action Malvern District; tel: 01684 563872
Newcastle-under-Lyme CVS; tel: 01782 629269
Nuneaton & Bedworth CVS; tel: 024 7638 5765
Oswestry & District Helpmates; tel: 01691 656882

Redditch CVS; tel: 01527 68403
Rugby CVS; tel: 01788 574258
Sandwell Council of Voluntary Organisations; tel: 0121 558 7434
Shrewsbury Volunteer Bureau; tel: 01743 341700
South Shropshire Voluntary Action; tel: 01584 877756
Solihull CVS; tel: 0121 704 1619
Stafford District Voluntary Services; tel: 01785 606670
Staffordshire Moorlands CVS; tel: 01538 371544
Community Action & Support – East Staffordshire; tel: 01283 543414
South Staffordshire CVSs; tel: 01902 851675
Voluntary Action Stoke-on-Trent; tel: 01782 683030
Stratford-on-Avon District CVS; tel: 01789 298115
Tamworth Community Service Council; tel: 01827 709657
Telford & Wrekin CVS; tel: 01952 291350
Walsall CVS; tel: 01922 654700
Warwick District – CVS; tel: 01926 881151
North Warwickshire CVS; tel: 01827 718080
Regional Action West Midlands; tel: 0121 616 4720
Wolverhampton Voluntary Sector Council; tel: 01902 773761
Worcester City Volunteer Bureau; tel: 01905 723688
Community Action Wyre Forest; tel: 01562 67008

Yorkshire & the Humber

Voluntary Action Barnsley; tel: 01226 242726
Bingley Voluntary Action; tel: 01274 781222
Boothferry CVS; tel: 01405 837123
Bradford CVS; tel: 01274 722772
Calderdale Voluntary Action; tel: 01422 348777
Craven Voluntary Action; tel: 01756 701056
Doncaster CVS; tel: 01302 813333
Harrogate & Area CVS; tel: 01423 504074
Hull CVS; tel: 01482 324474
Ilkley & District CVS; tel: 01943 603348
Keighley Voluntary Services; tel: 01535 665258
Voluntary Action Kirklees; tel: 01484 518457
Voluntary Action Leeds; tel: 0113 297 7920
Voluntary Action North East Lincolnshire; tel: 01472 231123
Voluntary Action North Lincolnshire; tel: 01724 845155
Northallerton & District Voluntary Service Association; tel: 01609 780458
Richmondshire Volunteer Centre; tel: 01748 822537
East Riding (Central) CVS; tel: 01482 871077
Ripon CVS; tel: 01765 603631
Voluntary Action Rotherham; tel: 01709 829821
Ryedale Council for Voluntary Action; tel: 01653 600120
Scarborough District CVS; tel: 01723 362205
Selby District Association of Voluntary Service; tel: 01757 291111

Voluntary Action Sheffield; tel: 0114 249 3360
Thirsk, Sowerby & District Community Care Association; tel: 01845 523115
Voluntary Action Wakefield District; tel: 01924 367418
York CVS; tel: 01904 621133
East Yorkshire CVS; tel: 01262 677555
North Yorkshire Forum for Voluntary Organisations; tel: 01845 525997

Scotland

Central Scotland

East Ayrshire Council for Voluntary Organisations; tel: 01290 420262
Cambuslang and Rutherglen Community Forum; tel: 0141 647 8275
Falkirk Voluntary Action Resource Centre; tel: 01324 636571
Hamilton District CVS; tel: 01698 300 390
East Kilbride Voluntary Organisations Council; tel: 01355 237302/237171
North Lanarkshire North; tel: 01236 874238
Monklands Association for Voluntary Service; tel: 01236 764866
Motherwell District Community and Voluntary Organisations Council; tel: 01698 275 469

Glasgow

Glasgow Council for the Voluntary Sector; tel: 0141 332 2444

Highlands and Islands

Argyll CVS; tel: 01546 606808
Badenoch and Strathspey, Voluntary Action; tel: 01479 810004
Barra and Vatersay, Voluntary Action; tel: 01871 810401
Bute Community Links; tel: 01700 504438
Caithness Voluntary Group; tel: 01955 603453
Harris CVS; tel: 01859 502171
Voluntary Action Inverness; tel: 01463 220922
Islay and Jura CVS; tel: 01496 810743
Lewis, Voluntary Action; tel: 01851 702632
Lochaber, Voluntary Action; tel: 01397 706055
Moray Voluntary Service Organisation; tel: 01343 541713
Nairn Groups' Voluntary Association; tel: 01667 455234
North West Council for Community Action; tel: 01641 561214
Orkney, Voluntary Action; tel: 01856 872897
Ross-shire Voluntary Action; tel: 01349 862431
Shetland Council for Voluntary Service; tel: 01595 693816
Skye and Lochalsh Council for Voluntary Organisations; tel: 01478 612921
East Sutherland, Voluntary Groups; tel: 01408 633001
Uist Council for Voluntary Organisations; tel: 01870 602617

Lothians

Edinburgh Voluntary Organisations Council; tel: 0131 555 9100
West Lothian Voluntary Action; tel: 01506 634115
Midlothian Voluntary Action; tel: 0131 663 9471

Mid Scotland and Fife

Fife CVS; tel: 01592 414588
North East Fife Voluntary Organisations; tel: 01334 654080
Perth and Kinross Association for Voluntary Action; tel: 01738 639477
Stirling Voluntary Association; tel: 01786 639477

North-east Scotland

Aberdeen Council of Voluntary Organisations; tel: 01224 212021
Angus Association of Voluntary Organisations; tel: 01241 430349
Bridge CVS; tel: 01771 624787
Dundee Voluntary Action; tel: 01382 305732
Gordon Rural Action; tel: 01466 793676
K & D VOICE; tel: 01330 825027

South of Scotland

Annandale and Eskdale CVS; tel: 01387 810974
Berwickshire Association of Voluntary Service; tel: 01361 883137
Central Borders Association of Voluntary Service; tel: 01896 755370
Clydesdale Association of Local Voluntary Organisations; tel: 01555 661233
Council for Voluntary Organisations in Kyle and Carrick; tel: 01292 282897
East Lothian Voluntary Organisations Network; tel: 01875 615423
Nithsdale CVS; tel: 01387 269161
Roxburgh Association of Voluntary Service; tel: 01835 863554
Stewartry CVS; tel: 01557 331346
Tweeddale Association of Voluntary Organisations; tel: 01721 723123
Wigtown CVS; tel: 01776 705645

West of Scotland

Arran CVS; tel: 01770 600611
North Ayrshire CVS; tel: 01294 473137
East Dunbartonshire CVS; tel: 0141 931 5678
West Dunbartonshire CVS; tel: 0141 941 0886
Inverclyde Voluntary Sector Forum; tel: 01475 710207
Renfrewshire CVS; tel: 0141 587 2487

Wales

Blaenau Gwent

Gwent Association of Voluntary Organisations; tel: 01495 306602

Bridgend

Bridgend Assciation of Voluntary Organisations; tel: 01656 647255

Caerphilly

Gwent Association of Voluntary Organisations; tel: 01495 225200

Cardiff

Voluntary Action Cardif; tel: 029 2048 5722

Carmarthenshire

Carmarthenshire Association of Voluntary Services; tel: 01267 236367

Ceredigion
Ceredigion Association of Voluntary Organisations; tel: 01570 423232
Conwy
Conwy Voluntary Services Council; tel: 01492 534091
Denbighshire
Denbighshire Voluntary Services Council; tel: 01824 702441
Flintshire
Flintshire Local Voluntary Council; tel: 01352 755008
Gwynedd
Mantell Gwynedd; tel: 01286 672626
Isle of Anglesey
Medwrn Mon; tel: 01248 752550
Merthyr Tydfil
Voluntary Action Merthyr Tydfil; tel: 01685 350116
Monmouthshire
Gwent Association of Voluntary Organisations; tel: 01291 672352
Neath Port Talbot
Neath Port Talbot Council for Voluntary Service; tel: 01639 631246
Newport
Gwent Association of Voluntary Organisations; tel: 01633 213229
Pembrokeshire
Pembrokeshire Association of Voluntary Services; tel: 01437 769422
Powys
Powys Association of Voluntary Organisations; tel: 01686 621696/626220
Rhondda Cynon Taff
Interlink; tel: 01443 485337
Swansea
Swansea Council for Voluntary Service; tel: 01792 544000
Torfaen
Torfaen Voluntary Service; tel: 01495 766204
Vale of Glamorgan
Vale Council of Voluntary Services; tel: 01446 741706
Wrexham
Association of Voluntary Organisations in Wrexham; tel: 01978 312556

Rural Community Councils

Community Action (**Avon**); tel: 01275 393837
Bedfordshire Rural Communities Charity; tel: 01234 838771
Community Council for **Berkshire**; tel: 0118 961 2000
Buckinghamshire Community Action; tel: 01296 421036
Cambridgeshire ACRE; tel: 01353 860850
Cheshire Community Council; tel: 01244 323602
Cornwall RCC; tel: 01872 273952
Voluntary Action **Cumbria**; tel: 01768 242130
Derbyshire RCC; tel: 01629 824797
Community Council of **Devon**; tel: 01392 382533
Dorset Community Action; tel: 01305 250921
Durham RCC; tel: 01207 529621
Essex RCC; tel: 01245 352046
Gloucestershire RCC; tel: 01452 528491
Community Action **Hampshire**; tel: 01962 854971
Community Council of **Herefordshire and Worcestershire**; tel: 01684 573334
Community Development Agency for **Hertfordshire**; tel: 01727 852298
Humber & Wolds RCC; tel: 01430 430904
Isle of Wight RCC; tel: 01983 524058
Kent RCC; tel: 01303 850816
Community Council of **Lancashire** (Community Futures); tel: 01772 717461
Leicestershire and Rutland RCC; tel: 0116 266 2905
Community Council of **Lincolnshire**; tel: 01529 302466
Norfolk RCC; tel: 01953 851408
Northamptonshire ACRE; tel: 01604 765888
Community Council of **Northumberland**; tel: 01670 517178
Nottinghamshire RCC; tel: 01623 727600
Oxfordshire RCC; tel: 01865 883488
Community Council of **Shropshire**; tel: 01743 360641
Community Council for **Somerset**; tel: 01823 331222
Staffordshire Community Council; tel: 01785 242525
Suffolk ACRE; tel: 01473 242500
Surrey Voluntary Service Council; tel: 01483 566072
Sussex RCC; tel: 01273 473422
Tees Valley RCC; tel: 01642 213852
Warwickshire RCC; tel: 01926 499596
Yorkshire RCC; tel: 01904 645271

Subject index

Alphabetical index

Charities which appear in **bold** in this index have a full entry in the book. The others appear in group entries or in the table of the top 500 fundraising charities. Where two numbers are given after the name of an organisation, the second number (in parentheses) refers to its ranking in the top 500 table while the first is the page number.

Further information

About the Directory of Social Change

The Directory of Social Change (DSC) is an independent voice for positive social change, set up in 1975 to help voluntary organisations become more effective. It does this by providing practical, challenging and affordable information and training to meet the current, emerging and future needs of the sector.

DSC's main activities include:

- researching and publishing reference guides and handbooks;
- providing practical training courses;
- running conferences and briefing sessions;
- organising Charityfair, the biggest annual forum for the sector;
- encouraging voluntary groups to network and share information;
- campaigning to promote the interests of the voluntary sector as a whole.

Contact addresses and telephone numbers for all departments can be found at the start of this book, opposite the Contents page.

Books available from DSC

The following is a selection of titles available by mail order from the Publications department. Telephone 020 7209 5151 or e-mail info@dsc.org.uk for a complete catalogue, which can also be viewed at the DSC website: www.dsc.org.uk

Editions and prices were correct at the the time of going to press but may be subject to change.

Directories

The *Guides to the Major Trusts* provide full details and independent analysis of the top 1,500 grant-making trusts which make grants to organisations. (Volumes 1 and 2, 2001/2002 editions, £19.95 each; Volume 3, 2002/2003 edition, £17.95.)

Also available are *Guides to Local Trusts* in Greater London, the Midlands, the south of England, and the north of England, (2002/2003 editions, £17.95 each), and *A Guide to Scottish Trusts* (2002/2003 edition, £16.95).

The Directory of Grant Making Trusts (2001/2002 edition, £75), published in association with the Charities Aid Foundation, covers some 2,500 grant-making trusts, with entries based on information supplied by the trusts themselves.

All of these titles are renewed every two years.

Alternatively, the content of all the books listed above is contained on a single *Grant-Making Trusts CD-ROM*, which is published annually. (£110 +

VAT, existing users £80 + VAT). In the course of 2002, the data will also be made available to subscribers via the DSC website.

The following two directories contain details of trusts which offer financial support to individuals: *A Guide to Grants for Individuals in Need* and *The Educational Grants Directory* (2000 editions, £19.95 each).

Handbooks and practical guides

The Complete Fundraising Handbook (4th edition 2001, £16.95) provides a comprehensive introduction to fundraising in general, while a series of *How to* guides covers more specialist areas (various titles £10.95–£12.95).

The Campaigning Handbook (2nd edition 2000, £15.95) is essential reading for pressure groups, charities and social activists.

The *Starter guide* series includes accessible introductory titles for charity trustees, treasurers and minute takers (various titles £7.95–£9.95).

Training available from DSC

For a copy of the latest training guide, contact the training department on 020 7209 4949. e-mail training@dsc.org.uk or visit the DSC website: www.dsc.org.uk